Technical Support Essentials

Advice You Can Use to Succeed in
Technical Support

Andres R. Sanchez

CA
PRESS

Apress®

Technical Support Essentials: Advice you can use to Succeed in Technical Support

ISBN-13 (pbk): 978-1-4302-2547-8
ISBN-13 (electronic): 978-1-4302-2548-5
Printed and bound in the United States of America 9 8 7 6 5 4 3 2 1

President and Publisher: Paul Manning
Lead Editor: Jeffrey Pepper
Technical Reviewer: Nancy Machen
Editorial Board: Clay Andres, Steve Anglin, Mark Beckner, Ewan Buckingham, Gary Cornell, Jonathan Gennick, Jonathan Hassell, Michelle Lowman, Matthew Moodie, Duncan Parkes, Jeffrey Pepper, Frank Pohlmann, Douglas Pundick, Ben Renow-Clarke, Dominic Shakeshaft, Matt Wade, Tom Welsh
Coordinating Editor: Jim Markham
Copy Editor: Katie Stence
Compositor: bytheway Compositors
Indexer: Brenda Miller
Artist: April Milne
Cover Designer: Anna Ishchenko

Distributed to the book trade worldwide by Springer-Verlag New York, Inc., 233 Spring Street, 6th Floor, New York, NY 10013. Phone 1-800-SPRINGER, fax 201-348-4505, e-mail orders-ny@springer-sbm.com, or visit http://www.springeronline.com.

For information on translations, please contact Apress by e-mail info@apress.com, or visit http://www.apress.com.

Apress and friends of ED books may be purchased in bulk for academic, corporate, or promotional use. eBook versions and licenses are also available for most titles. For more information, reference our Special Bulk Sales–eBook Licensing web page at http://www.apress.com/info/bulksales.

To Victoria, Julio and Diana
The reasons and rewards behind all my endeavors.

Contents at a Glance

■ Contents at a Glance iv

■ Contents v

■ About the Author xi

■ Acknowledgments xii

■ Preface xiv

■ Introduction xvi

PART 1 ■ ■ ■ Advice for Dealing with Yourself and Your Work 1

■ Chapter 1: Your Work Ethic 3

■ Chapter 2: Intricacies of the Field 25

■ Chapter 3: Your Work Practices 43

PART 2 ■ ■ ■ Working with Others 65

■ Chapter 4: The Technical Support Group 67

■ Chapter 5: The Technical Support Colleague 95

■ Chapter 6: Leadership in Support 119

PART 3 ■ ■ ■ The Support Organization 139

■ Chapter 7: Support Roles and Behaviors 141

■ Chapter 8: Structures and Tiers 161

■ Chapter 9: Process and Practice 181

PART 4 ■ ■ ■ Working with Customers 199

■ Chapter 10: Customer Service 201

■ Chapter 11: Communications 225

■ Chapter 12: Perspectives 243

■ Index 261

Contents

Contents at a Glance iv

Contents v

About the Author xi

Acknowledgments xii

Preface xiv

Introduction xvi

PART 1 ■ ■ ■ Advice for Dealing with Yourself and Your Work 1

Chapter 1: Your Work Ethic 3

The Value of Technical Support Work 4

A Dynamic Career: Moving Up Laterally, and Even Down When Necessary 5

Keep Your Job 7

Yeah, It's a Job, But Make It More 9

Look Out for Your Company 10

Tell It Like It Is 12

You Either Have It or You Don't—Troubleshooting 14

Leave the Work Where It Belongs 15

Make a Difference in Every Call 17

Success is Up to You 18

Take the Initiative 20

Specialize in Something 21

Chapter 2: Intricacies of the Field 25

The Status of the Profession 26

The Curse of the One-Eyed Man 27

The Paradox of the Solo-Solver 29

Technical/Mechanical Support Style Theory 30

The Avit Phenomenon 32

Support Demand Function 33

The Multidisciplinary Field 35

The Vernacular of the Profession 37

The Expert Proletariat 38

One Last Note About Science 40

■ Chapter 3: Your Work Practices 43

Write Down Anything New Immediately After You Learn It 44

The Above-Average Performer 45

The Resource Collector 47

Work Smarter, Not Harder 49

Following the Watson Way 51

Don't Be Afraid of the Tough Issues 52

Find Your Zebra 54

The Knowledge Seeker 55

Reinventing the Wheel 57

The Technology Contributor 59

Recognizing Opportunities 60

The Approachable Expert 62

PART 2 ■   ■   ■ Working with Others 65

■ Chapter 4: The Technical Support Group 67

Group or Team: Which Is It? 68

Informal Groups 69

What's So Good About Groups Anyway? 71

Groups: What's In It for the Individual? 73

The Vision of a Group 75

Group Communication 77

The Involved Group 79

The Open Group 81

The Group Crisis 83

The Constructive Group 85

Support Group Development Cycle 87

The Successful Group: An Inventory 89

Cohesiveness 89

Collaboration 90

Sympathy 91

Total Value = 3 — The Dysfunctional Group 92

Total Value = 4–5 — The Struggling Group 92

Total Value = 6 — The Idiosyncratic Group 92

Total Value = 7–8 — The Healthy Group 92
Total Value = 9 — The Communal Group 92

■ **Chapter 5: The Technical Support Colleague** 95

Work on Trust 96

Respect Among Colleagues 97

Coworker Solidarity 99

Teach Them How to Fish 101

Personal Conflict 103

The Power of Criticism 105

Comforting the Demoralized Colleague 107

Understanding Your Colleagues' Behaviors 108

The Customer Within 110

The High Performer Vs. the High Producer 112

The Self-Sustaining Colleagues 114

Dealing with the Impossible Coworker 115

■ **Chapter 6: Leadership in Support** 119

What Is a Leader? 120

The Leader: Made or Born? 121

The Major Leadership Models 123

The Pragmatic Leader 125

The Linda Effect 126

Characteristics of a Support Leader 128

Leadership Development 130

The Situational Support Leader 132

Leading by Involving Others 134

Cultivating Leaders Within the Support Group 136

PART 3 ■   ■   ■ The Support Organization 139

■ **Chapter 7: Support Roles and Behaviors** 141

Your Excess Value 141

The Contributor Role in Regard to Management 143

The Role of the Support Manager 145

The Nature of Management 147

Systems Theory in Support 149

Managing Behaviors 151

The Davila Cycle 152

The Price of Recognition 154

The Management Support Structure... 155

The Fallible Manager 157

■ Chapter 8: Structures and Tiers.. 161

The Structure Dilemma.. 162

The Tiered Approach 163

Technology vs. Skill... 165

The Service-Oriented Structure 167

The Meaningful Support Structure... 168

The Reactive/Proactive Tiered Approach 170

The Performance-Driven Structure.. 172

Common Mistakes from the Upper Tiers 174

Wiping Off the Tiers: The Flat Structure 176

The Hybrid Support Structure 177

■ Chapter 9: Process and Practice 181

What's a Process? 182

Discretionary Process Principle... 184

The Reasons Behind Process Changes... 185

The Support Practice: A Definition... 187

Group Process Evolution 189

Process and Maturity 191

Practice and Incompetence 193

The Process Map: Friend or Foe?... 195

Problem Solving: A Waste of Time.. 197

PART 4 ■ ■ ■ Working with Customers 199

■ Chapter 10: Customer Service 201

Customer Service: A Dimensional Explanation 202

Customer Reality 204

The Customer's Iceberg 206

Find the Affliction... 207

Real Wants 208

Real Needs 208

All About the Behaviors 208

The Open Mind Approach 211

Problematic Interactions and Coping Strategies 213

Rational-Emotive Therapy.. 215

Systematic Desensitization Therapy 215
Cognitive Character Replacement 216
Mindful Agreement Technique 216
Customer Service: The Hierarchical Approach 216
Meet the Customer's Needs 217
Address the Customer's Requirements 217
Accommodate the Customer's Requests 218
Respect the Customer's Wishes 218
Consider the Customer's Suggestions 218
Reshape the Customer's Unrealistic Demands 219
The People Business 220
Talk Is Not Cheap 221
Inexperience 222
Buying Time 222
Inefficient Processes 223
■ Chapter 11: Communications 225
At the Core of Our Work 226
Colleague Communication: It's All About Us 228
Talk in Terms of "Us" 229
Be Genuine in Small Talk 229
Speak a Common Language 229
Communication Challenges with Language Accent 230
Get to the Point: Cutting the Useless Chatter 232
Situational Communication 234
Email 235
Online Chat 235
Online Forums 236
Phone Support 236
When All Else Fails 237
Spinning the No 239
■ Chapter 12: Perspectives 243
What the Future Holds 244
The Renaissance Professional 245
The Preventive Support Model 247
No More Training Down the Drain 248
The Support Contractor 250
Opportunities in Global Labor Dynamics 251

The Need for Uniformity **253**

Going Customerless **255**

The Extra Mile **256**

Where to Now? **258**

■ **Index** **261**

About the Author

■**Andres R. Sanchez** currently works at CA, Inc. as a Support Delivery Manager for the Clarity Project and Portfolio Management solution in Plano, Texas. He has been in Technical Support, in one form or another, for his entire IT career since 1991. He started out in a small entrepreneurial company selling computer systems and solutions to the printing industry and doing everything from selling to technical support where he learned all the stages in a small technology company. He has been in Enterprise Software support since 1998 when he joined Abirnet Inc. Early in is career in the 1990's, he worked in consumer product support, in medical office management software support and in an internal helpdesk for a large communications company. This experience allowed seeing the technical support field from different angles and with different customer mindsets.

Andres received a Bachelor of Business Administration in Economics from the School of Business at The University of Texas at Arlington, a Masters in Business Administration in Information Technology from the Graduate School of Management at the University of Dallas and is currently pursuing a PhD in Leadership Studies in Business from the Gary Cook Graduate School of Leadership at Dallas Baptist University.

He lives in Arlington, Texas with his wife and kids and spends his weekends running a cattle ranch in Navarro County, Texas.

Acknowledgments

First and foremost I thank the Almighty for His wisdom and grace. Writing a book takes the efforts of multiple people; writing one in an emerging field takes an even greater effort. This work could not have been possible without the efforts of my wife, Diana, and kids, Julio and Victoria, who not only provided moral support and patience with my hectic writing schedule but also ran from library to library chasing after my literary sources. I want to thank Ms. Nancy Machen, an experienced support professional, ex-English teacher and superb colleague and friend who took the time to do the technical review of this book and had to endure reading it several times. Also, to Karen Sleeth who handled the book proposal and ensured that this project became a reality and to Jim Markham and Jeff Pepper for their expertise in editing, publishing and handling of the manuscript... A very special thanks to Aurora Gaimon, a long time colleague and friend and a terrific role model, who read some of the early material and gave me great feedback and suggestions.

The insight and inspiration for the practical material in this book came from the experiences and influence from great support colleagues and managers. Those closest to me and who directly provided me with ideas include Naghma Qureshi, Jose Mugica and Paulino España, three of the greatest colleagues whom I never even met face to face. Karthic "Mike" Muthukrishnan, possibly the most inspiring colleague I worked with. Marek Slugocki, a man with ideas far ahead of our time. Diane Craddock, a long time respected manager, dear friend and great mentor. Ken Verrastro, my best model of the technical support professional whom I can only aspire to mimic. Of great inspiration and appreciation: Ross Decent, Mike Haering, the gifted David Daniel, Barbara Cevieux, German Kovacevic, the simply brilliant Avishay Dinar, Shawn Moore, Kelly Limberg for keeping quiet when I stole his Hawaiian shirt, my dear friend Cesar Garcia, the great Joe Lutz, Joe Sekura, Sabina Muhammed Ali, Yacoob (Raymond) Ateekurahman, Mona Matta, Anthony Iannarelli, Gustavo Azolas, Christian Ramos all embody the best that technical support has to offer and are model colleagues with great wisdom, maturity and expertise. I could not write a book and not acknowledge the huge impact on my career of Julian 'Richard' Ridgdill with whom I shared and learned a great deal from the early days in a small start-up company and through four separate acquisitions. Together Richard and I, and later with the company of Oscar Cruz, worked through it all; new products, new colleagues, departures, deaths, acquisitions, layoffs, successes, failures, disappointments, solidarity, arguments, laughs and sadness. To Richard and Oscar, I owe a world of gratitude.

My heart and love go out to my loving family who put up with the rigorous demands of writing a book: my loving kids Julio and Victoria, my greatest accomplishments, the reason behind all my endeavors and my greatest love and hope; the love of my life, my loving and beautiful wife Diana whom I managed to seduce during a lapse in her judgment and who stood by me during the long nights and weekends of research and typing. My father, Ruben, the wisest and most honest man I have ever known, inspired in me the pursuit of knowledge. And to my mother, Angelina, who gave me life and from whom I inherited my pragmatism. To my beautiful sisters, Jovita and Daniela, who inherited all the looks, talents, smarts, and left me only the ability to roll my tongue. To my nieces Andrea and Sarah who bring joy and tender love to my heart and to my family, I say thank you.

To all my fellow students in Cohort IV at the Gary Cook School of Leadership at Dallas Baptist University PhD Program with whom I shared the evolution of this book. To all my friends and colleagues in CA Support who work with passion and professionalism to bring the best that CA has to offer to every customer interaction.

Preface

Thank you for taking the time to pick up this book. I invite you to read the chapter introductions to get a sense of the themes discussed in the topics. Being a support person myself, I know how short we are on time and how much our days are interrupted by cases, issues and technical problems. For this reason, I wrote self-contained and concise topics of typically no more than 1,300 words each. You can read them in sequential or random order and still get the same value. Each topic does not assume that you have read the prior ones in the chapter so you can pick and choose.

Do not let the name Technical Support Essentials fool you; this is not a beginner's guide to technical support. The "essentials" refers to the core of our profession including the challenges, opportunities, and peculiarities. I wrote this book with the experienced professional technical support person in mind. In these pages, I will not tell you what support is; I assume you already know and I assume that support is what you do for a living. What I will do is expand your view of technical support and present the essentials, the fundamentals that make this a great profession.

I also do not assume that I am preaching to the choir. I want you to analyze what you are reading and make up your own mind. It is possible, and likely, that you come up with some new ideas out of reading the next twelve chapters. The text is deliberately written in a style that leaves it open to criticism and to entice you to think more about the topics as they apply to your own work and the products and technologies you support.

The book is intended for the general support profession. Some of the examples pertain to the software support field but that is only because that's where my experience lies but the topics are intended to provide value regardless of your line of technical support and its subject matter.

The tone and depth of the book change depending on the section. The first section is more personal and you will see a very internal style of writing of delivering the information. My intention is to make a personal connection with you and your work. The application of the advice and ideas are up to you individually and the material's intention is to give you some perspective on the preferred and most efficient approaches. The first three chapters are a must if you want to get a good glimpse of how the work applies to the individual. Chapter 2 is all about the field itself and how it has progressed and shaped individuals and the practitioners view it. It also includes some models on support styles. In chapter 2 I make the case that our field should come to the limelight and establish itself, through us, as a formal profession with all the benefits and opportunities of a discipline.

In the second section, comprised of chapters 3, 4 and 5, the material is all about working with others within the support group and the greater support organization. Chapter 4 deals exclusively with the support group and the dynamics of the collective. It is a must read for getting an insight into a theoretical and practical view into the grouping of individuals for support work. The last topic contains a group inventory which will help you determine the qualities of your group and the dynamics that affect it. Chapter 5 presents the topics dealing with colleagues and the interaction with you and the people with whom you share the work. It also presents some topics that are rarely mentioned but of uppermost importance such as solidarity and criticism. Section 2 ends with a chapter on leadership and presents it in a way that will probably be new to you. It challenges the popular belief that managers are leaders and that leadership only comes from those in power or authority. Leadership is presented as something within the reach of anyone. The chapter is based on the formal leadership body of knowledge and includes the Pragmatic leadership model that has never before seen the light of day. Leadership is fast becoming one of the most studied social sciences in masters and doctoral departments in universities everywhere and with Pragmatic leadership technical support is making its mark in this highly respected formal discipline.

In Section 3, the chapters revolve around the aspects of the technical support organization and include topics on everything from organizational behavior to the role of management. Chapter 7 deals with the roles and behaviors and goes in-depth into the causes and consequences of behaviors as well as its formations. Chapter 8 on structures and tiers is a must read for anyone wanting some perspectives on the formal structure of the technical support organization. It discusses different structural models and helps you make a comparison with the more typical structured model. Chapter 9 on process and practice digs a bit deeper into processes and the different variances of their origins and applications. It also discusses the concept of 'practice' and where it fits in to our line of work.

The last section is anything that did not fit into any the other sections and that which deals primarily with customers such as customer service and value added actions to the normal support. Chapter 10 deals with the often enigmatic topic of customer service. In the topics included in the chapter you will see a different angle to the classic view of customer service as the act of being nice and tolerant of customers' complaints and idiosyncrasies. The chapter makes the case that customer service must come down to value as a guiding principle to the determinant of its use. Chapter 11 is about the communication that takes place specifically within the support group and with the group's constituency. I did not get too much into technology and trends in communications because it is an area that changes quite frequently and the fad today becomes obsolete tomorrow. I addressed some of the communication behaviors that add detriment to the work and the causes and solutions to them. The chapter closes with a very valuable technique to change and impact customers' perception of the value we add to their cases. 'Spinning the No' is a technique that only the most experienced and effective support professionals develop over years of dealing with customers. However, having the right mentor, group support and now this documentation of the technique will assist you in mastering this technique. The book closes with Chapter 12 which is my formed perceptions on the potential of the profession as well as my message and to you. I have only the best professional intentions for you and for the advancement of the work itself. Predictions are not my forte not do I intend to do such thing in the last chapter. I just want to present possibilities as I see them with basis on market and industry conditions as well as the foreseeable revolution in the technology and the demands such changes will have on technical support.

Take this book as a short introduction into the vast array of possibilities that await our field and its participants. This book is for you and I, the people who actually do the work and toil in the trenches armed with knowledge, skills and techniques as our primary tools. There is a lot more left that needs thinking and writing in this field. This book is by no means exhaustive but merely to make the support expert, you, think and experience the vastness of the support discipline.

Introduction

A few months ago, I was entrusted with a project for the technical support organization at the company where I work. I needed some theoretical foundation for technical support as well as some insights into techniques, foundations and processes to go about doing the support work; something that did not originate with my support organization itself. I went to bookstores, libraries and search engines and found nothing of consequence. The few sources I found were on explaining what technical support consists of or how to setup a technical support operation. The rest of the sources were on how to take a lot of calls and the ways to run a helpdesk. All very practical topics but not profoundly developed ideas. I found a few books on technical jobs and they all said that technical support was growing at a huge pace and set to be one of the biggest fields in the future. That is when I realized that the reason we didn't have any foundational theories in technical support is because no one has yet sat down to write them.

Support is what I have always done as my professional career. I studied economics in school but upon graduation, I couldn't find a job that paid nearly as much as I was already making in technical support; therefore, like many of you, I came into and remained in technical support by necessity. Over the years and with the accumulation of experience I grew to love the profession and the work.

A good friend once told me that a man should do three things before leaving this world. He said every man, or woman for that matter, should have a son, plant a tree and write a book. I don't plan on dying anytime soon but I figure I might as well get ready; just in case. Seriously, I wrote this book with the intention and desire to give something back to the field that has given so much to me. This discipline has allowed me to grow, mature, and sustain a home, family and life. It is my attempt to add something to the technical support body of knowledge which is still quite young but growing.

Technical support has only been around for a three decades at most; at least with that name. Yet, the work is truly a very humanistic approach to that very fundamental need; provide answers and assistance to those who seek them. The need and demand for the work has grown exponentially with the information revolution that hit us in the late 1980's. However, it has its roots in the mainframe computing world of the 1970's. The technology industry is not the only one that uses technical support to provide customers with the information they need. Technical support exists in any industry whose products, services or projects are complex enough to warrant an expert professional to provide resolutions and advice to users' and customers' problems.

The next chapters you will read about my thoughts and experiences in and about this exciting field. You may agree or may think ridiculous the ideas and concepts I present to you. My intention is to induce you to think, reason, wonder, critique, concur, disagree and hopefully desire to add your own ideas and contributions to this young discipline. Only with contributions can we make it easier and more interesting to the ones that come after us.

Please don't think of me as any different than you and your colleagues. I have answered thousands of calls, closed thousands of issues, handled many upset customers, satisfied many customers, ticked off a few more, learned dozens of technologies, mentored a few colleagues, learned from many others, had my failures and successes, and still longed for more. I love my profession and cannot imagine doing anything else.

My biggest challenge in writing this book was my inexperience in book writing followed by the lack of sources on the subject. Writing extensively and deeply in a topic requires the author to have a foundation literature on the subject. Because such foundation is small in technical support, I was forced to go outside of the discipline and synthesize other works in fields like organizational theory, management, psychology, leadership and economics to name a few.

The other challenge was the time writing a book requires. With a full time job and the current pursuit of a PhD, my time was limited so I had to write this book from 10pm to 2am over a nine-month period. The writing and research takes a lot of time as does the thinking through the topics and the organizing of the concepts. I did my very best and hope you find this book useful.

PART 1

Advice for Dealing with Yourself and Your Work

In this part, you will look at the way you deal with the work itself. I will discuss the mindset of the ideal technical support person in regard to the work and the experiences gained from it. Often, it is the way the support person views the work that makes the difference. Besides the support level, technical expertise, and support experience, the technical support person with a positive and open attitude will produce the best work and act in the best interest of the customer and the company, and make a name for him- or herself in the process.

CHAPTER 1

■ ■ ■

Your Work Ethic

This chapter will explore the different aspects of the support person's work ethic that are conducive to a successful career in technical support. It will also give advice on the ideal principles and behaviors that make the support person's interactions with colleagues, management, and customers productive and as free of friction as possible. The advice will be limited to professional topics within the technical support realm. Specifically, this first chapter includes material on creating a dynamic career in technical support, the concept of troubleshooting, initiative, specializing and what it takes to keep your job and much more,

Look around you for the ideal support person: the guy or gal who produces the best work and, despite all the inherent work pressures in technical support, still manages to walk around with a smile and a positive outlook. When we study ideal support people, we find the follow common characteristics:

- A true and deep commitment to the customer. This is not just lip service. Admirable support people often take a true interest in the situation and problems of the customer. This empathy goes beyond just providing the necessary help and arises from having a genuine concern for the customer on the other end of the line.

- A deep belief in the company. Great support people believe in what they do and who they work for. When technical support people believe in their company and in their roles, it shows in their interaction with the customer.

- A real sense of collaboration. Support people who excel in their work rarely do it alone. Success in technical support requires working with others, from the support colleagues to the development and sales team.

- A talent for solving problems. Technical support is about solving customer problems in the most efficient and fastest way possible. A natural or acquired skill for problem solving is absolutely required for success in technical support. Some people appear to have it naturally, others have to learn it, but all must possess this essential skill.

■ **Tip** After all is said and done and you've proven yourself right or wrong, the only thing you have to show is how well you adhered to your principles.

The Value of Technical Support Work

Do you ever wonder what it would be like if your job did not exist? What if the buyers and users of your product or technology were left alone after their purchase to fend for themselves? How far do you think they would get? No one knows who the first technical support person was or where the idea for technical support originated. Our field is obscure enough as it is so no one has documented the history of the technical support field and its pioneers in a decisive manner. The truth is that our field is not the most glamorous. After all, did you ever wish you would grow up to be a technical support person? I know that was not my dream as a kid for I really wanted to be truck driver… right after I wanted to be an astronaut, but before I wanted to be an attorney. Anyway, you get the idea.

Let's face it. Most of us ended up in technical support by accident or by necessity. However, technical support is a very rewarding and important aspect of many industries. Technical support people are the ones who take care of customers and users after they purchase the product. As support people, we are often responsible for the success and adoption of products and technologies. If not for support people, the customer would be lost without a way to implement and solve the problems that arise during use.

Therefore, the first thing I want to address is how we look at our work and the value that we provide to our customers for the benefit of our company. Never think that support people are somehow less important than sales, development, or services personnel.

When you look at your job in technical support, think of it as the opportunity to act as a liaison between the customer and your company. The technical support position is very demanding and we often don't fully appreciate the skills that we must master:

- Customer service

- Technical knowledge

- Troubleshooting skills

- Time and task management

- Quality Assurance (QA)

- Technical services

- Pre- and post-sales support

- Training development and delivery

Can you imagine the type of work you are capable of doing by having all those skills? If you really think about it, technical support people have it great. We are exposed to a lot of challenges, customers, and even cultures, and all of those things keep the work from being boring. The variety in this line of work is what makes support so interesting and rarely dull. Because of the nature of our work, technical support people are very flexible and adaptable, even under pressure from multiple issues and customers. We are capable of handling complex technical issues while dealing with customer service at the same time.

What can you do with your technical support skills if you decide to leave your technical support position? You can do just about anything. You can develop, test, sell, install, plan, and do many other things that require a good perspective on dealing with customers, technology, technical people and technology users in general. While you may remain in technical support for a long-term career, know that you have the skills necessary to make it in many other positions. If, like many of us, you want to stick to support know that there will be technical support work for decades to come, with position availability all over the world. So the next time you think about your prospects and future in technical support, remember that as long as technical products are being developed and sold, there will be a need for someone to support them.

In my current job, I have colleagues who have worked in technical support for almost three decades. One such colleague has been in the industry for 29 years and when he started, he had to write down issues on paper because the company did not even have an issue-tracking system. I asked him why he chose to remain in technical support for so many years. His reasons for sticking to technical work were simply that he was good at it and he enjoyed it. During his career he had the chance to move briefly into management and development, but he chose to go back to support. He said that is where he felt most at home and where the company would get the most benefit from his work. He eventually made a move to QA and the skills he learned in technical support help him succeed to this day. For many, technical support may seem like a temporary position, but it can also be a lifelong career.

Another colleague started working in our group a few years ago. He was fresh out of college and needed a job. He started work in technical support for our security software. He was not particularly knowledgeable about security or well-versed in software troubleshooting, but he was ambitious and learned quickly. He became very productive and an expert in our technologies as well as familiar with our competitors' product offerings. After two years in technical support, he was offered a position in product management. The skills he learned in technical support allowed him to rapidly succeed in the product management arena. A little over a year after he took the position in product management, he took another job with a large news organization in the area of online offerings product development.

I have also seen many individuals who succeeded in other areas of technology fail miserably in technical support. The reason many of them could not make it in technical support is usually because they had one or two of the skills necessary but did not have them all or could not develop them all. The main reason that some cannot develop all of the skills necessary to succeed in technical support is because those individuals come from a strong paradigm that deals strictly with technology or people, but not both. An example is developers who work strictly with technology, but not with people. Another example is customer service people who are great with customers, but not with technology. Technical support is not for everyone, but a good technical support person can make it anywhere. So next time you think about your work, remember this: you are extraordinary and not just anyone can do your job. Learn it, do it well, and you can succeed in any area of technology.

■ **Note** Technical support is probably the most complete job you can get in technology in regard to skills requirements. Mastering technical support will enable you to do just about any other technical position and much more.

A Dynamic Career: Moving Up Laterally, and Even Down When Necessary

Technical support can be a very rewarding and exciting career if you make it dynamic. The typical technical support person starts out as a rookie, becomes proficient, and after a few years, rises up the technical ladder as an expert. Then what? The expert has two choices: keep doing the same thing day in and day out or make a move into some other area of technical support. The move does not necessarily mean going into development, sales, services or any other line of work altogether. A move can simply mean moving to another product, to another aspect of the product, or to another aspect of support. In a company with multiple products, this is a simple proposition. In a one-product company, this becomes a little harder, but not impossible. Why does the expert need to move? The support person who reaches the pinnacle of the product's support expertise runs the high risk of becoming comfortable in the position. There is nothing wrong with being comfortable in a position, if you are close to retirement and just need to coast for the last few years of your career. After all, you have already proven yourself by becoming an expert and putting in your time.

But what if you still have many years of service until retirement? Are you really planning to spend the next 5, 10, or 20 years supporting the exact same product and answering the same questions over and over again? Trust me, I've been there and know all about it. I have also seen colleagues who spend 20-plus years in the same product or in the same position with probably very little variety in their career other than the occasional merger or acquisition every few years. Yes, I know, I have been acquired four times. I once supported the same product for 10 years and got very tired of answering the same questions, year after year. How did I keep my sanity during those 10 years? I picked up additional products and got into different support roles to add variety to my career. It was not easy, but it also was a way to keep work less boring or monotonous.

Thinking about your technical support career as dynamic may be a foreign idea to you. Let us start by looking at what you do. If you are not yet an expert in your work, then you may want to become very proficient in your area before trying to make a change. The easiest thing to do is to acquire new skills not related to technical support. The second easiest is to move to another product or to management. Let's begin with the easiest option.

If you've already reached the guru level and you have been with the current product for a relatively short time, then look around you and find someone whose job you think is interesting and enviable. Is it the services person who gets to travel and visit customer sites? Is it the instructor who teaches a class to customers and seems to have a great time at it? It could even be the technical writer. Whoever it is, find someone whose work you like and then find a way to get involved. Making your technical support career dynamic simply means making it interesting by adding variety to your workday and by adding to the arsenal of skills you already possess. It also means adding value to the company and allowing your employer to benefit from your new skills. I am not suggesting that you leave technical support. What I am suggesting is that you explore and acquire skills to make it possible to leave technical support if you so desire.

The next step after finding someone whose job you find interesting is asking for an opportunity to help that person and to learn. Most people are eager to talk about themselves and what they do so all you have to do is ask. Start by helping out with small things that do not take away from your job. This will allow you to learn the basics and familiarize yourself with that new skill.

After you are acquainted with that new interest, implement it into your current role. Why implement something new, such as technical writing, onsite services, teaching, and so on into your current role? Simply because you are the expert in your field and no one is going to question you. After all, this is a book about succeeding in technical support, not leaving it. Using new skills, other than troubleshooting and product knowledge, will make your career more interesting and will increase your value to your employer.

The next thing you can do is make a lateral move and support a different product. This is a strong recommendation for people who have been doing the same thing for more than five years. There is nothing wrong with doing the same thing for many years, but it is probably not a dynamic career move either. At first it is very hard to make the adjustment but you will learn that change is healthy and keeps you learning new skills and eventually makes for a rewarding career. Also, remember that if you have in interest in management, there is always the possibility of a technical support management job.

I have a colleague doing technical support for the same product for more than 20 years. He asked me for advice about getting his career to be more interesting and rewarding. We work for a company with more than 400 products. The first thing I advised him was to move to another product with more future, people, and opportunities for growth. He responded that such a thing was out of the question. When I asked why he thought this was the case, he could not respond. After a few minutes, he told me that he has grown so used to his product that he fears doing anything else. Don't let this happen to you.

■ **Tip** Do everything you can to keep your career dynamic before you grow so comfortable that it is scary thinking about anything else.

Keep Your Job

This section's heading may seem like a very logical statement. No one takes a job and then tries to get fired, but it happens all the time. We have all seen the new colleague who seems like a great fit for the job and somehow manages to get fired in a few months or weeks. I have seen it many times. It is hardly ever due to lack of expertise or lack of work for everyone. So why does this happen? Is there logic to it? Let's first examine what it takes to keep a job and what the decision makers, typically management or team leaders, look for in an individual.

There are four specific characteristics that generally allow the individual to keep their job. The lack of any one of these makes the employee a good candidate for termination:

- Interest

- Capacity

- A team player's attitude

- Productivity

By *interest*, I am referring to the technical support person being engaged in his or her duties. Specifically, it means showing interest by being responsible and carrying his own weight in the group and complying with policies and work responsibilities. The disinterested individual usually shows specific behavior such as being late regularly, chronic absenteeism, not caring for the customer, leaving before the shift ends, and disregarding company policy. It is also possible for a seasoned technical support person to sometimes show a disinterest in the work or policies, and this is when good people lose their jobs. These are just a few of all the possible reasons why such a lack of interest may happen to an employee but the symptoms are usually the same.

How do we maintain our interest in the job? The first thing is to keep focused on the work itself. We all have personal problems from time to time. We may even have problems with colleagues or management. However, we must always remember that our duty is to the company and the customer. As hard as it may seem, the technical support person must leave personal problems at home. The type of work we do is extremely sensitive to anemic or depressive moods. Sometimes a vacation or a few days off will help. Seek help where it can be found. Take some training or find some new way to keep the job interesting. In the many years I have been in this field, I had my share of hard times where I wanted to do something else entirely and forget about customers and their problems. To my good fortune, there was always something that came up to make it a bit more interesting and keep me in technical support.

If you notice that you may be losing interest, assess your situation and have a talk with your manager, a counselor, your spouse, or someone else who can help. Keeping quiet is probably the worse thing you can do. Talking about the situation that is causing the loss of interest will make you feel better and reinvigorate your interest and passion for the work.

Another characteristic that can get you fired pretty quickly is lacking the capacity to do the job. Capacity refers to the potential and the ability to learn the technical or customer service skills to do the job. It takes a clever individual to get past a job interview by sounding intelligent and talking his way out of a question, but it takes a real genius to fake technical knowledge in front of colleagues and customers. In other words, it can't be done! Technical support is absolutely not a field for charlatans. If you got the job by lying about your skills, you better learn fast or leave on your own, because you will be discovered sooner than later.

An individual who lacks the capacity to do the job is different from someone who has the capacity but just lacks the experience or specific skills. The person with the capacity but no skills will generally be lost at first, but will pick up the skills necessary. I've found myself and have seen others in that situation many times. However, if the person also lacks the capacity, he or she will never learn or do it very slowly. These are the individuals who always ask the same questions, and who never seem to learn the concepts despite training and mentoring; they are usually the ones who never seem to progress technically or do it extremely slowly. People who lack the capacity for technical support are always in danger of losing their jobs because they use up the same resources, and sometimes more, than a person who has the capacity for the job. Therefore, if you think you lack the capacity for technical support, try to develop it with training and education. If you still find that technical support is too much for you, try another less demanding area.

The third aspect that may get you fired is not being a team player. What exactly does this mean? We hear it all the time. So and so is "a team player," or he "took one for the team," and many other references to team playing that typically get it wrong.

Being a team player means having the ability and willingness to collaborate to get the work done and the issues solved. Have you ever seen the expert who knows all about the product but never wants to answer your question and gives you a bad answer when you ask? Or the colleague who turns down the after-hours pager week after week and does not want to pull her own weight? Being a team player is looking out for each other without trying to compete or hide answers from the rest of support people in the group. Resources, such as time and energy, are scarce. A member of the team who becomes a destructive force is the ideal candidate for the next round of layoffs.

Even if you have the previous three aspects nailed down, if you don't produce enough to merit your salary you will probably lose your job sooner or later. This is the most important determinant for holding on to your support job. A good way to make sure you are in good standing is to find out the average of issue closures and issue handling per person. The idea is to strive to beat the average.

I have seen colleagues get fired when the company needs to cut employee numbers. Some of them I admired for their technical skills and others were good friends, but with all of them, I understood. I even tried to work with some, but they did not improve and the inevitable happened. I am also a firm believer that everyone has it in them to be a good employee, they just need to be in the right environment. Sometimes, they just need to go somewhere else to succeed.

A few years ago, I had a colleague that I admired for his immense knowledge of Microsoft Windows. This guy did not just know some intricacies; he knew Windows inside and out. I could ask him anything about any Windows version and he would know it. His work was great and customers were happy with him. Nevertheless, he liked to bad-mouth the company and management. He had no interest in the company and had a terrible attitude toward it. It was not only criticism but verged on defamation. Others around him were beginning to follow his example, and behave the same way. One day, I called but he was gone, walked out that morning. I reached him a few weeks later. He was working at another company and seemed very happy. This time he was very positive about his employer.

■ **Tip** It takes some effort to get a job and a little more to keep it. But it doesn't take a lot to get fired. In fact, put no effort into your job and that's probably what will happen.

Yeah, It's a Job, But Make It More

Back in the mid-1990s, I found myself working in an internal helpdesk at a large communications equipment company. It was a very tough physical environment. The work was not at all bad, but the conditions were. There were six helpdesk people working in a small room, along with a supervisor. We helpdesk workers had barely enough room to turn our chairs and we had to tiptoe our way out since it was that cramped.

The room we were in was next to a server room where the temperature was always around 45 degrees. In order for the network and server administrators to go into the server room, they had to squeeze through us. Every time they went in and out of the server room, the cold air would come out and freeze whoever was closest to the door. The oldest of the group was a man in his late forties named Don who, after a career in the military, had found his way in the civilian work force and somehow ended up working in this help desk. He had been there for a few years before I arrived.

It was apparent that Don did not like to work there and he made every effort to let everyone else know. He was usually grumpy with the rest of the group and his attitude was usually negative. I once asked him why he chose to stay if he disliked the job so much. I reasoned that after all, it was just a job. He answered me in a very annoyed tone with a face to go with it, "To me it's not just a job, it is my livelihood!" In a few words, he explained that he had to work there for financial reasons. I was in my early twenties, and when I heard him say that, I immediately pictured myself at his age saying the same words to another rookie like me. It was a scary proposition.

We all have to make a living somehow. Technical support is no exception. However, it does not have to be *just* a job. We can make it fulfilling. We can take the opportunity to achieve personal goals, develop skills, and simply find a way to make it interesting. It truly is all in our heads.

In Maslow's hierarchy of needs, human needs start from the most basic, physiological, to the highest need of self-actualization. The needs are the following:

- Physiological

- Safety

- Love/belonging

- Esteem

- Self-actualization

There is no reason why our job should only fulfill the physiological and safety needs. Yes, we all need a paycheck to keep a roof over our heads and food on the table. However, we spend a great deal of time and effort in our job. We might as well make it more fulfilling and, at least partly, allow it to fulfill the rest of our needs.

Just how can our technical support jobs fulfill these needs? If you analyze the typical technical support environment, you'll see that most of us spend at least eight hours a day sitting in a cubicle surrounded by people doing similar work. The most obvious thing to do is to socialize so that personal bonds form and there is a genuine sense of belonging. American culture is more individualistic than other cultures, but we still like to socialize. I always enjoy listening to the stories from my colleagues in India. It is not uncommon for them to go on picnics or weekend getaways with coworkers. I usually just get to see the pictures and wonder what it would be like to do the same. We probably would not do that type of thing in our office, but we still have picnics and the occasional dinner or holiday party. If you think that your job is not fulfilling and you feel like socially you don't belong, then you may be in the wrong place. Think about this: we spend half of our waking hours in our job, so we better find a way to make it fulfill as many of our needs as possible.

Humans also need esteem and respect. Technical support is a great field for gaining at least some level of respect. Working in a technical group, there is always an opportunity to specialize or stand out by way of skills or performance. Also, skills are not always technical. There are support people who are excellent mentors, instructors, team players, social supporters, researchers, and writers. There are numerous ways in which a technical support person can stand out and gain the respect of his peers. However, this will never happen if you view the work as just a job to pay the bills.

What I am referring to is commitment. It takes a lot more than just being there because they pay you. There has to be a level of motivation and feeling of responsibility to the work. The sense of responsibility that goes beyond what the job description requires and beyond financial expectations is dedication.

Dedication leads to self-actualization. The feeling of success is a mental state of satisfaction with your own achievements. It all starts and ends within us. Of course, it also needs a dose of reality and some harmony with external factors, but as long as you feel fulfilled with your job in technical support and as long as you are not getting bad reviews for lack of performance, then you have made it. At the end of the day, success is doing an outstanding job, and enjoying it at the same time.

A few months ago, I started a project to find out what made our top performers in technical support so good. I am referring to the handful of individuals who close the most issues and who receive the best customer feedback. I found two individuals who closed more issues than anyone by far out of close to eighty. I looked at and analyzed their issues carefully to see if there was a pattern of possibly closing issues prematurely or by using some trick or technique. I found nothing. I spoke with these two individuals, Naghma from our India office and Jose from our Barcelona office. I interviewed them trying to find out if they had some technique or system to attain such high numbers and excellent customer satisfaction. What I found instead was a genuine commitment to the work, their teams, the company, and the customers. Naghma summed it up by saying, "When a customer hangs up the phone after speaking with me, I want him to smile about the great service he just received." Jose, on the other hand, told me, "I take as many issues as possible and in each one I make the customer feel like he is the only issue and customer I have." How is that for a fulfilling job?

■ **Tip** On their deathbed, people never wish they worked more, only that they enjoyed it more.

Look Out for Your Company

"The company is number one!" Have you ever heard anyone say this before? I certainly never have. No company would gain new customers saying that they are the priority and not the customer. This is one of those complex principles that require some explanation.

I am not suggesting that the customer is not important. Customers are the reason a company is in business, but in the end, the priority of the company is to make money. We as technical support people should never lose sight of that important fact. Technical support also plays a vital role in the company staying in business. There are ways to take care of both constituencies at the same time.

All other things being equal, a company needs three things to stay in business. These are the following:

- Revenue from sales or licensing that exceeds expenses

- Control of expenses

- The continual development of revenue

Where does technical support come in? Support people may view themselves as just a cost center or expense to the company. Yes, technical support is a cost of doing business, but it can also be instrumental in controlling expenses and helping generate revenue. But, just how can we as technical support people help generate revenue? We can do this in four ways:

- Assessing gaps in the customer's environment that our products can meet

- Identifying educational or training needs

- Suggesting trials of new software to the customer

- Making sure the customer's product or technology is in compliance with licensing and maintenance

The information gleaned from these four activities should then go to someone who handles sales leads or to sales people directly. The generation of leads is not commonly the realm of technical support. Nevertheless, when you consider that technical support people speak with so many customers and typically become very familiar with the customers' level of knowledge and their technology needs, it only makes sense to have technical support people generating leads.

As customer-facing professionals, we are in a very unique situation because we know the customer's needs and wants. When customers speak with us, they don't have the same attitude as they have with sales people and are typically more open to suggestions and feedback. This is our strength and a great opportunity to add value to our jobs. This value does not have to be a formalized addition to our job description. It can merely be an ingrained desire to recognize the potential of adding value to our companies while in the process of servicing our customers. In a way, we are helping ourselves by helping our company in the process of helping our customers. It is a win-win situation for everyone involved, and it starts with technical support.

Have you ever had a call where the customer knows nothing about the product and calls in expecting a product tutorial? Referring that customer to the education department or training sales would be the ideal outcome of such a call. I often hear colleagues complain about customers who insist on being "trained" during tech support calls. I am sure we have all gone through that process in the early stages of a product or customer life cycle. We really cannot blame the customer for wanting to learn from the experts. We did it also when we came into the job. The junior support colleagues learn from the senior ones. It's only natural and the normal process of knowledge transfer. However, when it happens with customers, our companies can benefit by selling that inexperienced customer the training they need.

The same thing goes for product deployments, services, and customized solutions. I argue that technical support is an untapped resource for generating new revenue. I've rarely been in a situation where technical support people offered me new ways to spend money with them, even when it would benefit me in getting my needs met. Companies that use this vast resource to their advantage will inevitably save money in lead generation and maximize the revenue generation per customer, all while meeting the customer needs.

I have spoken with clients who even offered to provide me with a credit card number if I only could sell them one of our other solutions. They did not want to have to speak with a member of the sales force; they just wanted the solution on the spot. The same thing goes for maintenance contracts and renewals or even new licenses. Having support people selling is probably too aggressive an idea to pitch to our management and might seem like piling too much on the backs of support professionals. Nevertheless, companies must increase revenue wherever possible and technical support should be a revenue-generating entity, not merely a cost center. We can start by generating leads to help our companies make money. When our company enjoys financial stability and revenue growth, everyone benefits.

Controlling expenses is another aspect of technical support work which is not openly discussed, but one where it's very easy to lose money. I am not referring to cutting costs in technical support itself. Although it may seem appealing, cutting resources from technical support professionals may hinder their ability to effectively do their jobs and serve customers. I am specifically referring to cutting expenses in what we provide to our customers and in the time spent chasing answers that should be readily available. What is needed is a way to make support so efficient that there are no wastes and all efforts go into the real nature of the work, which is solving customers' problems and not in mundane tasks that sidetrack the support professional.

Suppose a customer calls in for support and does not know whether or not he has maintenance? The technical support person may or may not know and unless there is a good system of contract verification, it may be hard for the technical support person to deny the customer help. This is a very business critical area where support people can help keep costs down for the company. Then there is the mundane task of shipping replacements out to customers or the even more mundane tasks of having to create such replacements. Regardless of whether it involves duplicating a CD or packaging and shipping a replacement part, do we really want a support professional whose job it is to solve problems wasting time for tasks that can be done by a good system or an administrative assistant? Task ergonomics presents an opportunity where support can save costs and help add to the bottom line.

Next time you think about your work and company, know that it's in all of us to look out for our respective companies. In a way, when we put our company first we are putting our well-being on the forefront also.

■ **Tip** Think of your company like a treasure that can easily be wasted and do everything possible to protect it and help it grow. After all, you are part of it.

Tell It Like It Is

Should a customer be told the truth, even if it's not what he or she wants to hear? Should the supporter sugarcoat the message so as not to upset the supported? If the demands of the customer are ridiculous or impossible, should he be told so? Where exactly does customer service end and technical support ethics take over? These are questions that every support person faces, but are not defined in most support guidelines and policy. How then do we decide how far we can go in our sincerity?

Sincerity in technical support can carry good and bad consequences. If we are very sincere and let the customer know of our shortcomings, we risk sending the customer to the competition. If we are not sincere to the customer and just say what the customer wants to hear, sooner or later the truth will come out and we will lose our credibility. In our line of work, credibility is our greatest asset and we cannot risk losing it ever. When we lose the customer's trust, it will be very hard to get it back. Without it, nothing we can do will satisfy the customer.

Credibility is the only true advantage we have from the first moment we pick up the phone with a new issue. The customer looking for technical help calls the support department because there is an inherent trust that the person providing the help knows what he or she is talking about. There is an implied competence and sincerity that weighs on the support person by definition. No customer would call a helpdesk expecting to be lied to or to have someone sugarcoat the truth. The caller expects an expert and also expects to believe every word that expert says. By the same token, the support person must go into every issue with the intent to live up to that expectation. But how far we do we take it and what are the benefits to our company?

A few months ago, I needed to have internet access from my laptop regardless of where I was. Specifically, I needed a wireless broadband solution that would work in remote areas of Texas, especially on Galveston Island. I visited a large telecommunications company's storefront and inquired about their wireless broadband offerings. The sales person tried to talk me into buying the top-of-the-line product with the top-of-the-line service agreement. I told her I wanted to use it in Galveston, as I travel there quite often and like to write and do Internet research when I'm there.

My main concern was that my cellular phone from the same company does not always get good reception, and I wanted to make sure that it would not be the same situation with the wireless USB modem I was being offered. The sales person did not think twice about it and assured me it would work everywhere in Texas. She even pulled out a map and showed me all the areas and towers in and around Houston and Galveston.

I also explained that since I spend a lot of time on the island, I wanted to make sure that I could get fast connection speeds in case I had to VPN to the office and transfer large files. She told me her boyfriend visits that area quite often and never has any problems. Being a gullible consumer, I believed her and walked out with the product and the contract feeling proud of the decision I made. After all, a salesperson's boyfriend used the same service successfully.

It actually worked well in North Texas and all around the Dallas area, but as soon as I went to Galveston, the signal went dead. It did not even get one bar and when it finally connected, it did so at the incredibly slow speed of 3 Kbps and not the 1.5 Mbps I was getting back in the Dallas area. So either I had a bad modem or the sales woman's boyfriend was accustomed to molasses speed web surfing. Once in Galveston and with a homepage that took nearly ten minutes to load, I dialed the telecom's company technical support line. I was greeted by a very amiable technician who walked me through some fairly systematic troubleshooting to find out why the connection was so slow. After all the tests were done, he looked up similar issues from the same zip code and found many that had the same problem I was having. I told him that I had seen the map and all the circles around Galveston Island. He did some more searching and found that there are no broadband towers servicing my area, and that no one gets any better reception that the one I was getting. He said the maps I was shown were for cellular service, not broadband service. He even read me the description of one such case in which someone else was also getting turtle-pace connection speeds with the same model card.

He apologized for my inconvenience and gave me two choices: keep the card and service and look for a signal amplification antenna but with no guarantees of better speeds or terminate the service contract and he would waive the cancellation fee since it was no fault of my own. I let him know I appreciated his sincerity and he replied that he would rather tell me the truth, even if that resulted in me going to a competitor, rather than have me waste more time looking for a connection speed that he knew I would never get.

I opted for the contract cancellation but will keep doing more cellular phone business with that company because they have a technical support department where the people tell it like it is and value the customer's time. I had been doing business with that company for almost ten years and never had any strong feeling toward it. Now I have a very positive one. Not because of the quality of the products or the superiority of its signal strengths but because of the great experience I had with their broadband helpdesk.

Did the support person act against his company's best interest? I think not. Did he uphold his personal work ethic? Very much so. Did he harm his company's business? Not at all. In fact, I decided to keep the cell phones with them, mainly because of this experience. By being sincere, he reversed the damage caused by the smooth-talking saleswoman with the imaginary boyfriend, greatly improved my perception of his company, and even showed me how to check to see if they ever build a broadband tower in Galveston, Texas. Once they do, guess whose wireless broadband service I'll get?

■ **Tip** Customers expect sincerity as well as technical expertise from us. Telling it like it is with the customer's best interest in mind is an irreproachable work ethic.

You Either Have It or You Don't—Troubleshooting

There is one skill that you absolutely cannot do without in technical support. This is a skill that is foreign to many people outside of our field, yet our mastery level of it determines how successful we are in supporting complex products and technologies. This skill is troubleshooting. Sounds easy enough, doesn't it? But what is the ability to troubleshoot and why is it important in our line of work?

There are several reasons why a customer will want to call us for technical support. For smaller companies calling in a support issue, it may include not having the people to devote to addressing the problem or lacking knowledge on the product. However, the number one reason customers call into technical support for help with their complex problems is because it would take them much longer to troubleshoot the problem than it would the support person[1]. Think about it: Addressing complex problems effectively is not a skill that grows on trees. It is rare to find someone with good troubleshooting skills. For some, that skill is natural and people with this natural talent seem to find the answers to the most difficult problems that make the rest of us scratch our heads. For others, troubleshooting skills have to be learned, acquired by observation, or by trial and error.

Troubleshooting may be portrayed as a methodical set of steps to follow, but in reality it's much more than that. Successful troubleshooting in technical support needs several variables to be present:

- Confidence
- Analytic reasoning
- Experience

Notice that I am not attempting to define the skill of troubleshooting as a one-dimensional ability that can be easily summarized into a simple definition. Troubleshooting is a lot more than just an ability to find answers. It is a way of thinking, a different approach to the complexities of the work and the challenges afforded to us by our customers.

It would be very simple if we could just read a book and immediately become super-duper troubleshooters. To attain the level of problem-solving skills required in technical support, we need the right combination of internal intuition and external perception.

I have never seen a good troubleshooter who lacked confidence. I have worked with many support people over the years, some good and some great. I have also met a few that really were not meant for this line of work. However, all the good and great support people had a good degree of confidence in their abilities. This confidence is what allows the troubleshooter to view problems from different angles, despite what the apparent situation may suggest. Many times, I have seen excellent support people take approaches which I thought were unusual and even risky, only to see their hypothesis proven correct. The troubleshooter who lacks confidence will not be able to make risky decisions and will probably be limited to the conformist approach. How many times have you seen a support person rely solely on past similar issues? That approach will work with known problems, but it takes a confident troubleshooter to tackle the unknown causes and the odd issues that we seem to get so often. Additionally, the support

---

[1] Bill Huber, "Identifying the Value of Vendor Support," *Rock Products*, November 2006, 12.

person who has confidence does so because he has a way to get to the root of the problem. Confidence comes from the certainty of the approach. Without confidence, the troubleshooter is limited to the known solutions.

How does one gain confidence in technical support? The answer consists of three imperative factors which result in confidence for the most effective support person. First of all, the support person needs a team support system. This is why there are very few lone rangers in our field (that is, individuals with no peers or without a group of colleagues supporting the same product or technology from whom to learn). The initial stage of confidence building consists of having internal people who can lend a helping hand when the complex support issue gets to be too much for the new support person. Senior support engineers make great mentors and are very helpful in growing confident junior members of the support team.

The second factor is training. How can we expect for someone to help a customer solve a problem with a complex product if the support person has not had appropriate training? Training is a huge topic in itself and has always been a sticking point in almost every support organization I worked at. However, support work is not something that can develop in a few hours or by just watching; it requires training. Otherwise, the new support person will have a hard time learning, will simply fail, or will lose the little self-confidence he acquired from his mentors.

The third stage consists of having the right resources. Would it be possible for a support person to be confident if there isn't an internal lab to test in or if there are no manuals or knowledge systems to lookup answers? The resources are the tools and are an absolute necessity for support as well as for confidence building.

Analytic reasoning is the rare natural instinct present in some of the best troubleshooters. Those who don't have it must develop it. Without it, it's possible to troubleshoot, but it's a lot easier to troubleshoot when there is the ability to reason and form conclusions on the fly. Analytic reasoning allows the individual to looks at symptoms and come up with valid possibilities of the cause. It allows for the flow of logic and critical thinking in problem solving. In a way, it is an art, a creative approach to problem solving. Troubleshooting problems in a technical support environment requires the ability to reason creatively and swiftly.

The last ingredient for successful troubleshooting is experience. The previous exposure to similar problems, technologies, situations, and customers allows the support person to find patterns in the technical issues that make it much easier to troubleshoot. This also increases confidence over time. Experience makes the difference between spending time troubleshooting an issue in the wrong direction and knowing the answer from the top of your head. Experience is the best troubleshooting tool, but also the one that takes the longest to acquire. If you are going to stick around and make a lifelong career of technical support, you will inevitably need this skill.

■ **Tip** Troubleshooting ability is a multidimensional skill that comes easier to some than others.

Leave the Work Where It Belongs

In our profession, stress comes with the territory. Unlike technical people that work in operations, we usually deal with a high number of problems and situations on a daily basis. We are not merely maintaining one system, but maintaining many systems. With all the variety of problems and customers, it's normal for us to get stressed now and then. The pressure put on us by management, colleagues, the work, and even our own work practices are enough to keep us on edge at the office. However, such pressure does not have to follow us home or even get us emotionally involved.

The work has to be kept separate from our lives outside of the office in order for us to remain sane and make a long-term career out of support. This is meant to be intellectual work. When we go home, the work stops as soon as we walk in the door. I know it's not easy plus sometimes we have to be on call after hours. Somehow or another, we find ourselves taking a call every now and then and helping a customer from home. Yet, our work ethic should be that our work should not and must not interfere with our personal lives. This is not the easiest concept to explain so let me tell you about a couple of stories from past jobs in technical support.

Back in the early 1990s, I worked for a medium-sized reseller of medical office software. The support team was separated by time zones and appeared to work harmoniously when the people interviewing me for the job showed me around. However, when I started working for this reseller, I noticed that there was always someone in support crying when they walked out of the office. It didn't take long for me to realize that the people working in that support department really took things to heart and got very emotionally involved with the work. Typically, this is not such a bad thing when the emotions are positive, but it's very destructive when the emotions are negative.

A colleague who sat next to me would get involved in the regular issues and asked for help from senior colleagues. Most of the time, she struggled to fix the issues and I noticed that it was not because of the technical challenges, but because of the emotional ones. She would get bogged down because she couldn't find the answer in a timely fashion and appeared to panic. This appeared to cause a negative reaction from the support manager who scolded her for stressing out. Of course, this didn't help her situation so she ended up crying. I couldn't understand it until I started taking calls myself and realized why this was happening.

The type of software we supported had a billing feature in it that would submit medical claims to insurance companies. The office staff, our clients, would stress out when this billing did not work and would call our support line in a panic demanding that we solve their problem immediately. It was not unusual for us to be threatened with lawsuits and promises to get us fired if we didn't solve the problem pronto. The more I worked there, the more I understood that the medical office staff who could call us was themselves being pushed by the doctors who demanded that the medical billing be done on time. Their revenue depended on it. The medical office staff would convey that stress to us, the support people, and those of us who couldn't take it would break down. I soon realized that this was no way to solve technical problems. The technical work was challenging enough and the stress from an emotional customer only added to the problem.

However, I also noticed that not everyone in the support team got stressed by these emotional customers; however, the senior people who had been working on the team for a few years did not seem to be bothered at all. They were never stressed and I never saw them cry. To set the record straight, I only cried once, maybe twice. I asked one of the more senior support women how she kept so calm when the customer I transferred to her gave her a piece of his mind. My colleague told me that no matter how much abuse she heard from the customer, and no matter how dire the situation, the issue could only be resolved so fast. She said that no matter how loud the customer yelled and how much they were losing in billings, at the end of the day, she would go home to her family and forget all about it when she watched Seinfeld that evening. It's a mental thing. If you let it get to you, you won't be able to be analytical, practical, and technical in solving the customer's issue. My colleague's adage was that the customer didn't need a crying buddy, the customer needed a competent tech to fix the problem.

Fast forward five years or so and I found myself working at a small security software company, once again in the tech support department. However, this one was really small, with only three people. While working at another company, I was very impressed with the application that this small software company made, so I decided to apply. I really liked the software and was interested in learning everything about it. However, in my desire to learn, I made a big mistake. I took the work home. I set up a lab at home and did some testing in the evenings. This went on for a few months and soon I started feeling like I was getting burned out. The stress of taking the work home and doing the testing and tinkering with the lab in the evening was cutting into my productivity during the day. Sure, I was much more knowledgeable, but it cost me dearly in lost sleep and lost time with my family. From that experience, I learned a very practical lesson. Whether your office is at home or in an actual commercial building, when you are done with work for the day, be sure it stays away from your personal time, friends, and family. The time away from it is what keeps us sane so we can do the work better.

■ **Tip** No matter how hard you work in a day, one thing is certain. work will still be there the next one.

Make a Difference in Every Call

Have you ever wondered why customers call us for support? Is it because we have all the right answers all the time? Is it because they just want to get their money's worth from the maintenance contract they purchased? I think the answer is a bit more idealistic. I think they call us because they think we'll make a difference in their situation. They call us because they know that if anyone can solve the problem, it is the people who deal with the same type of problems and do it for a living.

With that idea in mind, don't let a call go without making a difference, even if it's a small difference. Make sure that a customer always gets something from you regardless of how small. After all, talk is cheap. Since we work in technical support, we know how to talk to customers and we know how to deliver value. Think of it as making your mark in the work. Don't let any call come in without making a small difference. The opportunities are endless and making your mark can come in many shapes or forms. All we have to do is listen carefully for the needs.

I used to speak with a customer from New York City who would always call me at around 8:30 AM EST to ask if I was in. Of course, I told him. After all, I answered the call. Then he'd say he just wanted to make sure and that he would call me back in 30 minutes. Then he would do the same thing again at 9:00 AM EST and ask if I would be available in 15 minutes. Finally, we would end up getting to the real issue close to 10 AM. This went on for a few months, until I finally asked him why he had to call just to make sure I was going to be in. Why not just call me at 10 AM EST?

The problem was that the computer on which our software was installed was in a separate building from where his office was, so he had to make sure I was going to be in because it was a long walk to that building. He didn't want to make the walk and then have to wait until someone could handle his issue. He wanted to ensure we would be available. "Well, jeez," I told him. "Why not just use remote control software?" I explained that our company had such a package, and it was just a matter of getting a demo, installing it, and then he wouldn't have to go anywhere. I also explained that if he liked it, he could buy it and I sent him a link to the demo. He used it and liked it. Eventually, he purchased a license and both the walking and the three or so calls stopped.

Of course, I didn't support the remote control software. I didn't sell it nor did I make a dime if he bought or not. However, I wanted to make a difference. My only regret is that I had not asked him before.

Support people have a huge advantage over most other departments. We get to talk with people when they have their guard down. They don't have to worry about us selling them anything or trying to convince them to buy our services or maintenance. We don't chase them to fill out a survey or anything of that sort. When we speak with customers, we usually have their undivided attention and what's more, they think we are the experts! You cannot buy that type of influence.

Because of this, we have the opportunity to help in many other ways other than just taking their call and opening an issue. We can also suggest ways of making the product work better and suggest ways they can look for help when they don't want to call or don't have the time to sit on the phone with us. We just have to be careful not to be pushy and offer help but not demand they take it.

For a company with many divisions of products, there are more chances to make a difference. Imagine a customer gets to our queue and he is in the wrong place. The typical response may be to just

17

ask him to call again and choose the right option the next time. Not a necessarily rude response, but not the type of response that will get us noticed for making a difference. In this type of erroneous call, the difference can be made by finding the right person to speak to and then transferring the customer there, or giving the customer the correct number to call. Whatever you have to do, just make sure the difference you make is a pleasant one. Imagine what the customer will tell his colleagues. You want the support at your company to be described as the best, rather than just another one in the bunch.

Making a difference in someone's situation may not even be something we do, but it can just be something we say. Is the customer stressed about something that you may know the answer to? Maybe you came across a similar case and you can provide a few positive words. As long as you don't compromise yourself and your company, you should do the right thing and offer some helpful words. Sometimes that's all it takes.

A few years ago when interest rates were very low, I called my mortgage company. I wanted to see if I could refinance my house at a lower rate. The first representative I spoke with pretty much told me I didn't have a chance. He was not rude, but he wasn't friendly either. He spoke as if he was an authority on the subject and I believed him. I hung up the phone all discouraged thinking I was going to be stuck with a higher interest rate for thirty years. Then I remembered what happens sometimes in technical support. Sometimes the person who answers may sound like they know everything, but there is always someone else who knows more or simply looks at the situation from a different angle and is able to come up with a better solution. I called my mortgage company again and this time I spoke with a fellow who looked at my situation and asked a few questions that the other guy didn't even bother to ask. He came up with a solution and I closed on the new mortgage 45 days after that—all because the second person decided to make a difference.

■ **Tip** You cannot solve every problem. No one can. But you always can make a difference, no matter how small.

Success is Up to You

In technical support, one of the most critical aspects of the work is getting the customer to think you are genuinely interested and capable of helping solve their problem. This does not mean that they care whether you are the one who will ultimately solve it or even if you are the one able to solve it from the technical side. What they want to know is that somehow you will get them an answer regardless of where you get the answer yourself. There is only one way to accomplish this: be genuinely interested.

In order to be an effective problem solver, you will need to achieve the following tasks:

- Take the problem personally

- Feel the same pain the customer feels

For someone else to believe that you really care about the problem, you have to take the problem personally. There is no other way. This is a matter of commitment and responsibility. Face the problem and put all your effort into it because your technical record depends on it. Look for answers wherever you can. Think of it in terms of points. Each problem you solve is points credited to your technical support account. Each problem that you cannot solve constitutes points against you. One good measure of success in technical support is how many problems you found answers for, but not necessarily how many you solve yourself. They should overshadow the ones where you did not find the answer.

Taking the problem personally means viewing it as a personal challenge, as something more than just a customer issue. It means that you view it as a professional hurdle and as something that stands in the way of reaching the top of your profession. Be sure to make every technical problem you face a personal challenge. When you achieve this, customers will notice and will trust you more than ever. However, you must be careful to not internalize the challenge to an unhealthy or dysfunctional level. There is a difference between taking challenges personally and letting the challenges wear you down outside of the office.

For example, I had a colleague who was very energetic and really got into his work. He was a pleasure to work with and his commitment was beyond what the customer expected. He was a very effective support person and learned immensely from his own efforts. Conversely, I also worked with a man who internalized the challenge so much that it affected his personal well-being. He often described how he lost sleep over a work situation and even developed health problems as a result. These two examples illustrate the difference between taking a challenge personally in a healthy fashion and internalizing challenges to the point where they cause unnecessary personal problems.

I realize this must sound very idealistic and you may be interested in something a little more pragmatic. Here is an experience from an issue we had once in the group: A colleague of mine took a call from a customer at a school district in Texas. He explained that our URL filtering software was not functioning properly and, as a result, the kids were able to surf out anywhere they wanted to and were not blocked. Kids being kids, they went to all kinds of inappropriate sites.

We checked the settings, files, logs, and URL database. It all pointed to a very common problem we had with that package. The problem was with the URL cache which disappeared every time the service was restarted, and there was no real way around it. Often we just told customers that the product would not work and to take it up with the salesperson. This time, however, we had really had it with such answers. We took it very personally. Here was a product we really believed in, yet we were not able to get it working properly because of the way it was designed. We also did not want to disappoint the customer.

We wanted to feel proud about our solution so we looked for a solution using other features. In an eureka moment, we found our solution. We built a cache internally by using a traffic generator and a list of bad URLs and grew the cache file to a size containing over 70,000 sites. We gave this cache file to the client. This meant that the product did not have to build up a cache, but would have it already and could block from the cache. Our solution was so innovative that this feature was built into the product. It happened because we got tired of giving the same answers to clients and took the problem personally.

In order to make your issue solving process a little more effective, you have to learn to feel the same pain the customer feels. Put yourself in their shoes. The customers are people too and, just like you, they have a job to do with repercussions when the job does not get done correctly. If they are calling you, it is probably because your product is the culprit. Try to see it from their point of view.

Imagine this scenario: the salesperson went out and sold them on a product that would solve a business problem. The product promised to replace the existing solution. The customer purchased and later found out that all the promises were not realized because of a technical problem. This is the reason we exist: to take care of those problems that are preventing our customers from reaching the full promises of our products. Sometimes the situations get even more drastic and affect our customers personally as well. This is when they want to find someone who really cares about solving their problem.

I had a customer whom I helped set up the same type of URL filtering solution as the school district in Texas. The only difference was that this time the school district was in the state of New York. The customer called me, explained that the URL filtering was not working, and that his boss had given him two days to fix the problem or he would be fired. To make things worse, he was in the US on a H1B visa. Needless to say, the customer was really worried. We worked on it for a few hours until we reached a solution and solved the problem. Amazingly, I was able to work through the problem faster and more efficiently because I felt like it was my own job on the line. Solving that issue gave me more satisfaction and sense of accomplishment than others because I was able to feel the same pain the customer felt.

Technical support success relies on technical and people skills. Neither is more important than the other and neither one can be improvised. The successful support person knows that inspiration in problem solving is enhanced when the issues are made personal and then the customer's pain can be truly felt. This may not be necessary in all issues, but you will know which ones require this work ethic.

■ **Tip** Showing the customer you truly care about their problem can be accomplished only by truly caring about their problem. This cannot be faked.

Take the Initiative

Have you noticed how some support people seem to always do the right thing and initiate change? Some seem to bring out positive actions that have transforming effects on whole support groups and their clients. Such actions may be huge or very small, but they are always proactive.

What sets superior professionals apart from mediocre ones is the ability to take initiative. This may involve such simple actions as proactively keeping the work going and making sure the needs of customers are met to putting new ideas in practice so as to improve the work itself.

The working environment of the technical support professional is changing dramatically and more than ever; the support person must strive to initiate change. It is not unusual for technical support work to be handled from home or remote offices where the support person may not have others physically around. In global operations, there may be only a handful of people scattered around per global region.

Also, groups are getting smaller and, with the advent of much more complex hardware and software technical products, people must specialize. This brings isolation to the work and even to the individual. For many of us, gone are the days when we toiled in long rows of cubes where we all took the same type of calls for the product and helped each other. There were team leaders and supervisors who called the shots and there was never any doubt of what to do or when to do it. Those were the early days of the technical support work. Now, with technical support viewed as an up-and-coming and evolving IT profession, the people who succeed are those who are able to work independently and get things done without being told to do so. This is what initiative is all about.

Initiative consists of three factors that must be present for initiative to occur. They are the following:

- Motivation is the drive, enthusiasm and inspiration that keep us going.

- Discipline is the control we have over the work, schedules and tasks.

- Action is the start of a process of change: the kick-start of new ideas and practices.

These definitions are not from a dictionary. They are the definitions we see every day in technical support professionals who excel in their respective technical specialties. Initiative is not easy to describe but it is obvious when observed. It cannot be managed or mandated. Initiative is inspired by internal and external forces. Motivation, discipline, and action are the internal ones. The external stimuli are usually others showing self-initiative but may also come from inspiring leaders who incite us to act. I have received such stimulus from mentors, colleagues, and even clients. I have also seen other colleagues act based on other external forces and demands. One of the strongest stimulants of initiative is need. Only those who have motivation, discipline, and action rise to the occasion to become agents of change. Those who lack initiative easily fall into lethargy and the work degrades. A colleague of mine once said that the job of management is to push the support people to act: to work and get issues closed and customers happy. I disagree. It is in all of us who support customers to act without being pushed to do so. Management is there to provide the resources we need to get the job done. I refuse, and so should you, to be pushed into doing what is supposed to be done in the first place. The minute you are pushed to do your duties is the minute when the work becomes an occupation and ceases to be a career.

Some support people appear to be naturally gifted with all the elements necessary for taking initiative while some of us are thrown into it and pretty much forced to act. I was once in that situation, forced to rise to the occasion. I survived it as have many others and grew wiser from it. It happened in

1999 when the small software company I worked for was acquired six months or so after I started. I only had two other colleagues: one in the same office and one in Israel. We were managed by a senior tech named Barbara. A few weeks after the acquisition, Barbara decided to go work for another company. This left my local colleague, Richard, and I pretty much on our own. Barbara was the one who directed us on the work, did much of our testing, and was pretty much the expert we relied on for our toughest answers. I was the newest one of the now diminished group. We hardly knew our new manager from the new company, and the manager did not know what or how we did our work or the systems we used. My colleague Richard and I were not inspired to take the initiative; we were forced by need. We survived it, carried on with work as usual, and initiated new practices that made our work a bit more efficient.

Taking the initiative also means putting ideas into action based on observed needs. I have a colleague in Spain who speaks multiple languages. Her group takes issues from all over Europe and she noticed that all our instruction files were written in English. Our customers struggled at times and this caused the opening of more issues. She raised the issue with management and nothing happened because, after all, it would take forever to translate all the documents. She had started writing the instructions in different languages as customers needed them. Eventually she was able to meet the needs of many of the customers who struggled with the English language. She was motivated to fulfill a need, had the discipline to carry it out in an orderly fashion, and took action to make it a reality.

Motivation allows support professionals to keep at it despite the obstacles and loneliness of the new paradigms in our field. It drives the tech working from home to keep doing great work from the home workplace and inspires the desire to keep learning and improving the quality of the work. Successful telecommuting would be impossible without motivation.

Discipline enables the support professional to control the work and the tasks, despite the load. Discipline requires commitment, self-control, and even self-regulation. It lets support people recognize the quality of their own work without being told by others. Discipline starts out as a work practice and eventually becomes a need. The need for someone to close so many issues a day; the need to tackle problems a certain way; and the fortitude to change the rules of troubleshooting when required.

It all culminates with action. Without action, discipline and motivation are mute. Action culminates in the end result of initiative. Forging ahead with change or with adherence to the status quo both require initiative. Change being the transformational power of initiative seems more glamorous, but adherence to business as usual without letting up also requires initiative, especially during organizational change or turmoil.

Our line of work is changing; more and more it requires individuals who are able to take initiative. These professionals will succeed and bring forth positive change to their groups, their companies, and their customers. Those who fail to act will fall by the wayside and become another casualty of our progressive profession.

■ **Tip** Never wait for a manager to push you. Take the initiative and make the manager praise you instead.

Specialize in Something

In technical support you need an edge. You need the ability to be better than everyone else in something. This allows your team to rely on you and for you to concentrate on and devote your efforts in a specific area. This is not to say that you will devote all your time to only one thing, but generally every member in a technical support team must specialize in an area of the technology the team supports, while also being able to take general issues.

The idea behind this topic is not to propose that you somehow try to get a leg up on your colleagues or try to reach job security. Job security may occur in the long run as a result of specializing, but the true reason for specializing in a specific area is that it allows for better utilization of resources within the support team. With more technologically advanced and complex products, the need for specialization is greater than it was when the technologies were simpler.

It used to be the case that it was possible to know everything about a product. I remember products like Lotus1-2-3 and early versions of Word Perfect for DOS. I remember how relatively easy it was for a tech savvy person to get to know the entire product inside out in a matter of weeks or months. Nevertheless, with an ever-expanding array of operating systems and modern enterprise hardware and software products, it is becoming necessary for synergic forces to come into play and allow for the technical dominance to take place by a group of support people, rather than by a single individual.

As a technical support professional, you know that your knowledge is very different from that of the end user. You know what goes on under the covers and recognize patterns and symptoms of how your product behaves when running properly and when a problem exists. Merely knowing how to use a product is not enough to make it in technical support; you also have to master the intricacies and hidden features of the technology. That is exactly the reason why it is imperative that complex products be divided up among a technical support team and that each member becomes an expert in a specific piece.

Now that you know why specializing is important, the question becomes how to select an area of specialization. When choosing your area of future expertise, ask yourself the following questions:

- What piece is in higher demand by customers?

- Which area is more likely to remain a key component in the future?

- Which area has the least number of experts already?

- What about the product do I find least and most challenging?

- Given my skills, background and interests, which area would I be stronger at and enjoy the most?

Make yourself a list and explore the different areas to see which one would be the best fit. You should probably consult with other colleagues and your management to make sure there will not be any objections or in case they have different plans for you.

After you decide on the area in which you want to become an expert, you will have to learn everything about it and gain the experience necessary to be the true and undisputed expert. The terms expert, guru, go-to person, specialist, and whiz are tossed around all the time, but their true meaning is not at all ambiguous. In technical support, the expert is the person who knows everything about the area of expertise, has the most experience, and can solve any issues and think critically and creatively about workarounds pertaining to that area. To put it in a different context, the support issue should not make it past the expert; otherwise, he is no expert. How do you go about becoming an expert in your newly selected area? Here the six steps that need be done in no specific order:

- Take as many support issues related to that area as possible.

- Read up on as many past support issues relating to that area as you can.

- Set it up in a lab environment; break it and fix it as many times as possible, changing the variables every time.

- Help as many colleagues as possible from your team with issues relating to this area.

- Read all documentation, ask the developers, and speak with anyone who may have further knowledge about this area to add to your own knowledge.

- Write down, share, and teach everything new that you learn about your area.

You are probably confused after reading the six steps and are thinking, "Where is the part where I get to hoard the knowledge to myself?!" There is no such thing. The expert, by definition, shares information; otherwise, he would not be an expert but an information hog. It takes much more than just information to become an expert. If that were not the case, you could just buy yourself a bunch of books about the Renaissance or any other topic and become an expert immediately. It is really not that simple and this is why we often call some people "experts" when they are really far from it.

You know who I am talking about. Yes, the guy or gal who has been supporting the same product for five or more years and does not want to give you the answers unless you get on your knees and beg. This is the same person who refuses to speak with customers and insists on having you get all the information so that he can just tell you the answer to give to the customer. Then he won't divulge how he reasoned through to the answer so that you can find it on your own the next time this problem comes up. On top of that, this person is so arrogant and makes you feel so stupid every time you ask a question that it gets to the point that you are afraid to ask.

As you can see, I worked with those "experts" as well and learned exactly how to spot them. You, on the other hand, are going to be a genuine expert who shares information, teaches others, and is not afraid of losing your edge because it takes more than merely knowing answers to cookie-cutter questions to be an expert. It takes a desire to learn and the wisdom to solve any problem, regardless of how difficult or obscure. Becoming an expert also takes a lot of practice, and that is why you have to see as many issues as you can and read up on the ones previously solved. You will also be at the top of your game by staying ahead of all the new developments in your areas of expertise. It also takes people around you to think of you as the expert. Once every area of your product has at least one true expert who can also take general issues, your support team will be unstoppable.

Once you become a true expert, you will shine for your knowledge, reasoning, intuition in problem solving, but most of all, your desire to help others on your area of expertise. For now, go out and find the area in which to become an expert. The sooner you find it, the sooner you can start reaping the rewards of your newly-developed expertise.

■ **Tip** With little effort, anyone can be knowledgeable, but it takes hard work plus dedication to become a true expert.

CHAPTER 2

■ ■ ■

Intricacies of the Field

Those of us who work in technical support view the work differently from those outside of it. We don't just have experiences about calling someone when we have problems. We are the ones providing the help. The question is where to take our field from here. Because technical support is still in its infancy, there is still much work to do in order for it to develop into a full-fledged discipline, even a young science.

In this chapter, you will read some basic themes that shape the work and the field of technical support. I have done my best to portray it as a discipline with some fundamental aspects that apply to all technical support people, regardless of the technology. Since technical support is relatively new, there is no research-based published literature specifically on the subject of technical support as a formal field or discipline from where to extrapolate support's intricacies to serve as a basis for this chapter. I had to research and develop the best way to explain it in a concise, easy format t along with providing some practical examples. This chapter covers the status of the profession, theories, functions, the case for a need of a common support vernacular and the science of the industry.

My main intention in this chapter is for you to realize that the work you do is not just an informal trade, but a real profession. We find ourselves at a crossroads where we must either choose to continue to be considered as a footnote in the scheme of things or else dedicate ourselves to the process of becoming a bona fide discipline and emerging science. Most professions went through the same process; the only difference is that they probably did it a long time ago. The following are already existing strengths:

- A large and growing body of practitioners.

- An influential and indispensable role in the course of our technologies.

- The beginnings of a body of knowledge.

- The realization that we are in this together, and a collective consciousness that we want our field to become more than what it now is.

I love this field and look forward to a lifelong career, just like many of you. Let's make the best of it and take advantage of this rare opportunity to make a change in our professional lives and future of all support professionals.

The good fighters of old first put themselves beyond the possibility of defeat, and then waited for an opportunity of defeating the enemy.

—Sun Tzu

The Status of the Profession

Like any very new trade, technical support still finds itself in the infancy stage. There is no formal degree. The theories on troubleshooting have been borrowed from other disciplines or developed informally by the groups who do the work. I am sure you have noticed how the typical training you receive when entering the field usually consists of either contract training or end-user training. The training is seldom focused on the actual troubleshooting of problems dealing with the nature of the work itself. The work, by its very nature, requires training and education, which includes theories and logic aimed at helping you solve complex technical problems. Some methodology exists but much more is required. There are entities, such as the Helpdesk Institute (HDI) and the Service and Support Professional Association (SSPA), which are making great strides to formalize our line of work by establishing norms, best practices, and even certifications. Nevertheless, technical support is still somewhat of an underground vocation to many because ours is a very new trade. I argue that it resembles an emerging scientific discipline, and I say this because the characteristics of a new science exactly match those of technical support:

- There is plenty of practical knowledge, it has just not formalized.

- There is some empirical evidence to support the science.

- There is no widely accepted theory.

- The jargon has not yet been established.

Have you ever noticed how every trade has a noun describing it? There are mechanics, carpenters, doctors, plumbers, lawyers, managers, and even dishwashers, yet we don't even have a noun that describes us. We are called technicians, analysts, support people, techies, helpdesk representatives, technical advisors, and even engineers, but we don't really have a solid, widely accepted noun for our trade. How is that possible?

Just about every other area of Information Technology has some recognition in academia. There is Computer Science, Software Engineering, Robotics, Telecommunications, and Systems Analysis, but there are not even community college degrees on technical support as a general discipline. There are currently some courses on computer systems support in scattered schools around the world, but there is not a distinct degree that addresses technical support as a multidisciplinary science. The existence of an accredited degree is essential for the discipline to be recognized as a capable workforce, and for academia to invest in research to advance the body of knowledge. Technical support is growing as a profession and we need formal research to keep us from having to reinvent the wheel in every technical support organization.

The people at SSPA and HDI are doing a great job and hopefully they will help bring technical support into the recognized place it deserves in the industry. It is my hope that in the near future, technical support can be viewed as a viable career option that young people can aspire to and prepare for in a technical school or can obtain a degree in. I did not grow up wanting to be a technical support person, but that was because I did not even know it existed. When more young people with technical and customer service inclinations learn that this profession is a viable option, the ranks are likely to grow to meet future demands. With the advent of more complex and advanced technology, the support people of the future will need a lot more technical skills and probably much more preparation than just on-the-job training like most of us have received.

The most critical thing we lack is a set of baseline theories on the nature of technical support work. Most of us just borrow the scientific method we all learned in elementary school and apply it to solving technical problems. It works fine for a majority of the cases but we need a better theory to solve technical problems. I know that there is someone out there with a great idea for a problem solving theory. There is probably also someone with an idea for a perfect noun to describe what we do.

Even still, the future of technical support looks very bright. More and more technologies are being developed every day, as well as more users who need help using those technologies. Unlike the people that used to stack punch cards or maintain vacuum tubes in the early days of modern computing, technical support is here to stay. In fact, the only reason technical support exists is because the technology got so advanced that it required specialized knowledge to answer questions from users and to diagnose and solve technical problems from the administrators of the technology. You can bet that as long as humans use advanced technology products, they will need someone to call on when that advanced product malfunctions or is simply too complex for the end users to know all about it. Indeed, our future looks increasingly promising.

Technical support is also going global. No longer do customers have to speak to someone from only one or two countries. Today, customers can speak to technical support people sitting anywhere across the globe. I've personally worked in groups with people in Latin America, Asia, and Europe. This is the beauty of our profession. It is both a technical and a people business.

■ **Tip** Every great human achievement in history started with a vision and the actions of its pioneers. In the case of technical support, all of us are the pioneers. Let us make something of it.

The Curse of the One-Eyed Man

Over the years while speaking with customers and handling thousands of problems, I was always amazed at how much my customers thought I knew. They were always amazed at the immediate answers I was able to recite as soon as they finished asking the questions. I felt sort of like a magician who could pull tricks out of thin air without looking things up, or so my customers thought. Customers would thank me for helping them and asked me how I did it. My answer was always the same: "I do this for a living. I would starve if I wasn't good at it." I am sure that many of them thought I was just being modest when in reality I was quite ordinary in technical support terms.

I have many colleagues who are much better than I am at supporting their respective technologies. Some of them have been at it for close to three decades or more. Imagine doing support for 30 years. It does not take a genius to know all the answers when you have to provide them to customers on a daily basis over and over again. In fact, there were instructions which I could recite in the dark, and actually did so many times when I was awakened by our after-hours call center with a customer on the other line.

This ability to learn by heart very complex sets of instructions is not a monopoly of technical support. Doctors, lawyers, mechanics, accountants, and pretty much any professional who does repetitive work learns that there comes a point when 50% to 90% of the questions asked by customers have been asked by someone before them and the answers are always very close, if not the same. When you reach this point in your technical support area of expertise, then you know that you have reached the pinnacle and you are indeed the expert. You have become the envy of every rookie who is just starting out in the technical support field. You are the one others look up to and go to for questions, because it will take you a lot less time to give them the answer than it would take for them look it up. The same goes for clients. Once they know you exist, they would much rather call you than mess with finding the answer themselves. You have become the proverbial one-eyed man in the land of the blind. What now?

Once you become the guru, there is no other way to go. You could try and move to another area in the company or move to a management position. Notice I did not say "move up" to a management position. Ironically, I do not consider management necessarily a move up or move down. It all depends on your aspirations. If you are in the software industry, you could go into Quality Assurance (QA), become a bug fixer (Level 2 support), or go into development. If you are in the hardware arena, you can go into testing, sales, development, and services. However, you will find that the work is much different.

For someone who is both a techie and a people person, there is no job like technical support. I have seen colleagues go into other areas only to come back as soon as they could to technical support. I have also seen others who make the transition and are equally successful in their new area. Yet, the obvious question remains: Is there anything wrong with staying where you are? Is there a stigma with being the expert forever, staying at the top of your game indefinitely? Certainly not and do not let anyone tell you otherwise.

If you are satisfied being the expert in your technology, than be the best expert you can be, just do not be idle. The problem exists in treating expertise as a destination, as a place where your career goes to die. This truly is a tragedy and a waste of potential. Before you accuse me of flip-flopping, allow me to explain.

We are, for a lack of a better word, lovers of technology. We remain in technical support because we are techies who find technology fascinating and intriguing, and we aspire to learn as much as possible about it. It is a passion of all successful technical support people. I have never met or known about a successful support person who is not in some way an enthusiast of technology and who does not love learning, talking, and tinkering with their respective products. This is why they became experts and reached the top of their areas. Nevertheless, once you reach your expert status, you must use your new powers for good, much like Superman or Wonder Woman. The expert has the responsibility to advance the field. You, as the expert, have three responsibilities that you must accept and exercise. These are:

- Teach and mentor others

- Find ways to improve your technology

- Contribute to the body of knowledge in your field

If you work in a group, you want at least one of your colleagues to ultimately be as good as or better than you. Do not worry about your mentee taking over your position. There is always a place in any company for good people. Also, it will probably take your colleague as long as it took you to be at your level. Additionally, you want someone to do the stuff you do not find enjoyable, so there may also be a self-interest motive behind this.

Since you are now the expert, you are well aware of the strengths as well as weaknesses of your technology. Who better to know what customers need and want than you? This is your opportunity to exert your expert influence and push for positive changes in your product; you will also be giving back to your company and benefiting your customers and colleagues.

As the expert in your field, you also want to leave your mark. You should have a legacy that stays behind even after you are gone. This is one of the most rewarding things you can do and it is one of the main responsibilities of the expert. Contributing to the body of knowledge includes documentation, articles in internal or external publications, new ideas and theories, patents, and even books on the subject. Whatever you do, just make sure that it will be of benefit to the future users and supporters.

The position of expert is not just a description or a designation. It is a responsibility that sets you apart from the rest. Once you achieve this status, make sure you don't succumb to the apparent comfort of stagnation.

■ **Tip** Expertise is not an achieved position but a new stage in your career.

The Paradox of the Solo-Solver

More creative and capable of solving random problems than any supercomputer, the human mind comes up with so many ideas at such a fast pace that sometimes working to solve a problem alone and uninterrupted yields more innovative solutions and workarounds than a group of similar minds. This represents a contradiction to conventional wisdom that states that synergic forces are at work in intellectual endeavors, including Information Technology. We all practice collaboration and see the benefits of working in a group bouncing ideas off each other. However, the truly hard problems that require a radically different way of thinking sometimes benefit more from the solitary mind. Why is this so? Perhaps it is a Darwinian principle that it is the fittest mind that is able to come up with the best solution or perhaps it is the unintended but positive consequence of uninterrupted individual thinking that yields the solution. Solving issues in a group works great for brainstorming, choosing among competing ideas, and filling in knowledge gaps, but true genius does not come from a committee; it originates with the individual. Technical support is not different. The truly great eureka solutions often come from individuals.

In the movie *Saturday Night Fever*, Tony while dancing with Annette, grows bored and tells Annette, "Oh, forget this," and starts dancing solo. In the work of technical support, sometimes the best performances have to be solo acts. For lack of a better term, I call this the solo-solver paradox.

I became aware of this topic while working with the best minds in my area of support. I noticed how when we had very tough issues the best solutions sometimes came from the individual, despite numerous conference calls to troubleshoot or brainstorm. It always came down to the individual with the brilliant, sometimes obvious idea that could not have come out of the group because of its nature. As a field, technical support is full of exceptional individuals who take it to a completely different level. In my own office, there is a PhD in Mathematics, several degreed engineers, and many other people with all types of experience in different fields. It all adds up to the quality of work they do for customers.

Why does this solo-solver know to go off alone and solve the problem? I propose the explanation that the genius does not realize that he is doing the truly exceptional. The solo-solver truly feels he is only following his passion and enjoys the challenge. While innovators, like Marc Andreessen, the founder of Netscape, or Steve Wozniak, who manually made the first Apple computer, may have known that they were making history when they set out to create the future of IT, the rest, I suspect, just enjoy the challenge. The trick is to know when to go it alone and when to do it as a group.

In technical support, we work in groups and sometimes in teams. The group consists of individuals working together and taking the same type of issues, all trying to lower the queue and get as many questions answered as possible. The team consists of individuals who own the work collectively but handle different aspects. The team model works well in complex technologies where no one person can answer questions for the entire product and its modules or components. The specialized individuals work in different modules, but are all responsible for the work. The group model works well where the work is homogenous and the technologies being supported are less complex. Individuals within a group compete, whereas individuals within a team collaborate. Neither model is better than the other. It all depends on the technology supported and the structure of the support organization. However, in both models, the individual is responsible for the customer on the other end of the phone. You as the individual, regardless of the structure, will come up with the ideas for the solution. However, the solo-solver comes up with the truly ingenious ideas. How does the solo-solver do it? The solo-solver does it in solitude away from the phones and distractions.

Creativity and inspiration do not lend themselves to partial attention. For you to be productive in these areas, you need to think, experiment, observe, and repeat all of this from different angles. This cannot be an interrupted activity. Otherwise, you will lose your frame of reference. I am sure that anyone can come up with great solutions with some creative time to themselves and overcome the needed challenge, yet I am not referring to the everyday solutions that we recite over and over. I am speaking about the issues that no one seems to have an answer for. These are problems that neither development nor QA can figure out. These are the problems that cannot simply be designed, analyzed, or debugged. These issues are the ones that seem beyond the limits of the technology, obscure, and keep you awake at night. These are the perfect examples that only someone from technical support can solve, someone who has a passion for the technology and a strong commitment to customer service.

To be a solo-solver is to live the essence of being a techie. Avishay Dinar, one of the best solo-solvers I have ever known, once solved an issue that I and others had been working on for weeks. All it took was for him to look at the problem, go into a lab for a couple of hours, and find the solution. The rest of us had been on conference calls, looked at knowledge bases, tried everything we could think of, and could never even reproduce the problem. His solution was completely off the wall but it solved the problem perfectly. The symptoms and cause were not even closely related. I learned afterward how he tested it, but I will never know how he came up with the idea to try the solution.

■ **Note** Great minds think alike, but true genius is a solo game. Everyone has the potential to be a genius in something.

Technical/Mechanical Support Style Theory

Most of us in technical support who find ourselves beyond the learning curve, and are now in the stage where we are comfortable with the technology we support, can classify our approach to work in one of two ways: mechanical or technical. Both are valid ways to get problems resolved and both can be equally successful in ensuring the highest level of customer service. You may consider yourself one of the two already or you may not even know your support style. Once you have finished reading this section, you may find that you are strongly mechanical, strongly technical, or a little of both. The two styles are defined in the context of our work in the following ways:

- *Mechanical*: relies on the design, knowledge, and understanding of the technology to explore problems and questions that determine the answers.

- *Technical*: uses technique, abstract thinking, scientific methodology, rationale, and even creativity for analyzing and solving problems.

The mechanical style of problem solving relies heavily on the design (the known) of the technology. If you are predominately a support person who uses this style, you would be more comfortable with knowing how the technology works under the covers and the cause and effect of the actions that trigger the problem. This style is heavily influenced by previous occurrences of the problem and relies on known symptoms to diagnose the cause. A mechanical-technical support person would be most comfortable with things that have been seen and documented. For new problems, as a mechanical troubleshooter, you would be inclined to follow the process that takes you to the symptom. As a practitioner of the mechanical style, you also prefer an automated approach to determining problem causation such as a formula, a process or a specified set of steps to follow. Anything outside of the norm may throw you off. The problems that most challenge you, and the ones you prefer the least, are the ones that are completely new since there is no precedence. In other words, if it's not documented and it's not in the knowledge base, log files, or product design, you are going to have a hard time figuring it out. In learning a new product, you would rather study manuals, blueprints, process flows, and previous issues before supporting customers.

The mechanical style may be found in support people who came from development and who have a background in the exact sciences, such as software engineering, mechanical engineering, math, and any other science that follows a distinct set of criteria such as accounting or biology. If you find yourself looking at logs files rather than asking open-ended questions, then your style is probably more mechanically inclined. This is a very productive way to look at the work and to handle the bulk of issues that come into a technical support queue. The mechanical style, by its very nature, is probably the one that yields the highest number of closed issues and the one that can answer the most questions, as long as they have occurred before. Support management would love to have as many members of the support staff as possible with this style because they are very productive and can be counted on to follow rules and not break with support policies. The support people with this style may also prefer to support the same technology over many years. They challenge is to solve the same problems faster and with better customer satisfaction.

The technical style is less concerned with the emotionless development of the technology and is driven by the challenge of the problem itself. This is the person who finds joy and fulfillment in the challenge regardless of the technology. If you are predominately in the technical style category, you are bored with routine questions and problems and want to be challenged. You want to be in unexplored territory. You actually get excited about new problems and can submerge yourself in exploring the answer without regard to how long it takes. This is the person who typically is considered an "out of the box" thinker and is usually the one who seeks to own the issues that the more mechanical styles do not want to spend time on. In a company with multiple products, this is the person who wants to learn them all and wants to be involved in customer problems that involve technologies outside of his expertise just for the challenge. The support person with a technical style is a true techie. He does not care for the technology as much as he cares for the challenges the technology poses.

The technical style also does not prescribe to a specialized area as much as to the technical support discipline itself, regardless of technology involved. This style is also much more creative and spontaneous than rigid. If you are a technical-style support person, you will follow the scientific method and may start hypothesizing about problems, but you are not afraid to jump around and skip steps to find answers. The thinking is also very abstract and may not even involve the technology at hand, but instead selective use of troubleshooting principles, such as listing possibilities rather than following designs. You may also successfully use these principles in other areas of your life and would be comfortable using your technical style regardless of the type of problems you are faced with. You would find reading manuals useless and prefer to jump into the technology and simply learn by doing rather than understand first and practice later.

The technical-style support person usually has a diverse background, and is more of a technical renaissance person rather than a specialized individual who knows everything about something. This person prefers to learn as much as needed about the problem and technology at hand, but his quest for knowledge can be limitless, depending on the need. In this style, you are not in love with the specific technology, but find a passion for the challenge regardless of the supported product. The background is less important than the principle of rational and creative thinking. You would be more inclined to write your own manual and support process than to follow one that you found limiting.

The technical style is needed in smaller quantities in support organizations because of the less prolific number of closed and resolved customer problems. Also, this style is rarer and people with these qualities tend to go for more creative lines of work. The tendency of the technical style is to devote full attention to a customer issue until it is resolved. A technical-style support person may not be able to handle multiple issues concurrently because of the demanding nature and the focused attention this style exerts on the issues. Support management prefers to assign the high-impact issues to this support style because of the issue to customer ratio. In large support organizations, this style may be given a high status because of the tendency to be of high impact to the customer base, and even to the addition of features to the product via better analysis of persistent problems. This style does not care about title or status, but rather about the quality of the challenge. Without appropriate challenges, this style would grow bored with a mechanical approach to support, would much prefer to seek change, and move across technologies in pursuit of the limits of support abilities.

Regardless of which style fits your support practices, the important thing is to understand yourself and for you to understand why others work they way they do. Both styles are present in most groups and together they make the support organization an effective one. Most of us may exhibit one style or the other depending on the situation, but are stronger in one of the two styles. Now that you know about them, see if you can figure out which one best fits your support patterns.

"And knowing is half the battle.

—G.I. Joe

The Avit Phenomenon

Solving complex high-technology issues demands equally highly developed skills. Solving them without possessing exceptional technical or mechanical talents or a passion for technology would seem rather difficult. Doing it and even thriving for over 25 years seems like a lifetime. However, it is known to happen. The equalizer is not luck or chance, but rather an exceedingly developed passion for customer service and a strong will to serve and make a difference, coupled with determination to get problem resolved.

Such is the case of a colleague of mine, Mr. Steve Avit, a mainframe technical support person, who embodies the concept of devotion over skill. Steve is the type of person who is not infatuated with technology. In speaking with him, you may even think he has an indifference for technology and anything that may seem overly methodological. He does not subscribe to the latest gadgets or to the advancements in computing, although he would very much like to. He is a mainframe guy who wants to know as much as possible, but because of his workload does not have time to learn more than required.

Steve closely fits the mechanical support model, but only in his approach to the work. The process is not what drives him. If you did not know his long track record in this field, you might view him as the type of support person who might stumble into support but quickly move on. Nevertheless, Steve has been at this profession almost half of his life, and he is very successful at solving issues. He has one of the highest customer service records I have ever encountered. He is constantly featured in customer referrals where he is described as a great resource to his company and an asset to the technical support department. At this stage in his tenure, some professionals may grow accustomed to the work and apathetic to the needs of customers. Yet, this is where he shines. You may be thinking that this sounds like an unusual phenomenon. It is unusual, but it is also invigorating in an unexpected way.

The strength that enables Steve to still go strong after 25 years is his obsessive quest for customer satisfaction that drives him to stop at nothing in search of a resolution. In my many years in this field, I have never seen anyone like him. He has a very strong Brooklyn accent and a loud voice, which may not seem so strange except for the fact that he lives and works in North Texas where New York accents are not exactly typical. I used to sit next to him and I could hardly concentrate. However, if I was a customer calling in for a support issue, Steve is the person I would want handling my issue.

In unavoidably overhearing his calls with customers, I could hear the positive change in his demeanor. Suddenly, he was no longer the loud guy you can hear across the support floor. During support calls, he turned into the perfect technical advocate who fought for the customer and genuinely put the customer ahead of any other priority. It was truly inspiring to hear his calls. He chased colleagues, developers, managers, and anyone he needed to in order to make it right for the customers. If he saw something inefficient in a process, he would have no qualms in going straight to the top in order to correct the problem. His less than tactful ways brought him grief on occasion, but he did not seem to care as long as it was a customer that stood to benefit. You may be thinking, "So what? I strive to satisfy my customers, too." The concept here is that someone like Steve Avit is a phenomenon. Someone with less than stellar technical skills should not last so long in this profession, much less be very successful at it. I am in no way suggesting that he lacks anything in the technical or mechanical department, but his strengths do not lie there. As in other areas of life, commitment to the customer can sometimes triumph over technical proficiency. Of course, neither Steve nor you can be oblivious to the technology being supported, but it is the secondary priority. The first priority is the commitment to the customer.

A support organization benefits from having people who are driven by a principle of service. These are the people who truly enjoy interacting with customers and the benefits of accomplishing a change in that customer's work by solving their technical problems. These are the individuals who lead the organization in their own way, and who point out the inefficiencies in the best interest of their customers. When asked why they are in technical support, they simply respond, "Because I love it." This devotion is a natural tendency of some individuals. It cannot be trained or managed into someone. It is truly an asset to have an individual who is highly motivated to pursue the interest of the company by aggressively supporting customers and not resting until those customers are fully satisfied.

Support people displaying the "Avit Phenomenon" are rare, but easily recognizable. I have only known three among my colleagues globally, despite many years in this field. One of them is from Chennai, India. Therefore, culture or country does not matter because customer devotion goes beyond borders and tradition. Yet I know there are more out there because I have spoken with a few of them when it was my turn to be a customer calling in for technical support. You may have one in your own support organization, most likely the colleague who gets the most kudos every month despite not being the expert. Or he may be the colleague who appears as a nonconformist and prefers to go against the grain as long as it is after improving the situation for customers. When you find one, listen to what he says to customers and how he says it. The whole tone of voice changes and you can vividly see that this is not only his job but also his passion.

Clients come first. It does not mean they are always right, but they always come first.

—Steve Avit

Support Demand Function

There comes a time when every new science must make sense of the concepts that sustain the new discipline. Technical support is no different. Just like every other body of knowledge, technical support exists to provide answers. Whether they are to problems or the simplest of questions, technical support provides answers at its most basic levels. We refer to the answers as resolutions. In order to make a logical definition of what goes into an answer, we must define a constant set of variables that go into arriving at a resolution.

The Support Demand Function is composed of the equation:

R_d=f(C, P, A, E, S)

The function is not intended to be a mathematical function, but rather a logical one. The principal variables that influence the resolution demanded by the technical support constituency, as depicted by R_d, where "f" means "is a function of" or "depends on," and the variable inputs are as follows:

C = Question or problem complexity

P = Precedent of the problem previously occurring (all other things being equal, there would already be an answer recorded for such problem or question)

A = Availability of the necessary working environment either local or remote to experiment or confirm

E = Effort devoted to the problem or question by parties involved

S = Severity level of the situation

Before you close this book and put it aside for the next year or so, please try to understand this simple, but powerful function. Also, read the following so that you see why the function is so powerful and understand all the variables that go into resolving an issue the way the customer demands.

The function is a generalized statement of the fundamental variables that go into solving a problem as demanded by a customer. The variables are complexity, precedent (pre-existence of similar or identical resolved issues), the necessary resources being available to enable the support staff to adequately address the problem, the effort devoted to the issue including its timeliness, and the severity level of the issue.

Any variance in the variables to the right of the equal sign must be met by a similar inverse adjustment in the other variables on the same side. For instance, if the complexity of the problem increases, one or more of the other variables must increase or decrease in order for the same resolution demand to be met. If there is no adjustment to at least one of the other function variables, the resolution demand will invariably have to change. Of course, this presents a problem for the person working the issue, because if the variables in the function are not adjusted correctly, then the customer would have to put up with a different level of resolution from what was originally demanded. Since our discipline is not yet accustomed to dealing with functions, allow me to illustrate the function in action.

Suppose that you get an incident from a customer who is in the middle of a project and needs the problem resolved in order to finish his project on time. The resolution demand from that customer includes dependencies for time, accuracy, and possibly even ease of implementation. The resolution demand is R_d, and this is not negotiable from his viewpoint because he has other constituencies that he is responsible to.

In order for you to work that incident, you will have to account for the complexity (C) of the technology as well as the complexity of the problem. In addition, the process to resolve the problem will be heavily influenced by whether there is a precedent (P) on that particular issue. The precedent could be in the form of a frequently asked question (FAQ), a solution document or just your memory. Also, the availability (A) of the customer and his environment are necessary to reach the resolution. If the customer is not available for you to gather more data from his situation, the resolution as demanded by the customer will be affected. If the customer placed high demands on the resolution, this means the effort (E) placed on finding the answer will be greater and vary with the value of the other variables in the function.

For example, if there is no precedent for the type of problem the customer is having, then the effort exerted by you will be greater than if there was a precedent available. Therefore, the variables P and E are inversely proportional. The last variable involved is the severity (S). If the customer places a high severity or priority on the issue, then the resolution demand will be affected depending on the severity level of the issue. Generally a lower-severity issue has a lower-resolution demand in terms of time. If the severity is increased and the resolution demand is to remain at the same level, then two other variables, such as effort and availability, will have to compensate for the higher-severity level.

Precedent and complexity are constants and generally cannot be affected by changes in the other variables. However, changes in the precedent and complexity have a positive and negative effect on effort. Severity also has a negative effect on effort. All the variables in the function also have an effect on the outcome, which is the resolution demand.

All other things being equal, the support demand function may be utilized to analyze situations and support offerings. It does not account for changes in any other external variables and assumes that all other things affecting problem resolution are a constant and remain static.

■ **Note** It is a beautiful thing to understand; to finally reach that point where you can say, "I got it!"

The Multidisciplinary Field

Picture the ideal technical support person. Think of the colleagues you admire and strive to model yourself after. Think of the highest performers in your support group and the ones who appear to close the most cases. Also, think about the colleagues who appear to be the most effective and close the toughest issues. If you could describe them in five words, what words would you use? I can think of the following words to describe the colleagues I admire, technology "know=it-all," a great communicator, or a great analyst. Maybe you came up with different terms, but chances are they are related to the preceding.

Technical support may appear to the rest of the industry as a one-dimensional line of work that only answers technical questions. This would be a simplistic way of describing technical support. For those of us in this field, it is truly a multidisciplinary profession. The different disciplines that merge in technical support are:

- Communications

- Systems analysis

- Education

- Group dynamics

Where is technology? Where is programming, mechanics, software, or computers? The subject matter supported is the variable. The specific technology supported can change yet we would still have the disciplines previously listed. Maybe you never thought about your work in these terms. Nevertheless, technical support comprises some level of each discipline. Think of it this way, if you suddenly find yourself supporting a completely different technology than you are supporting now, what things would you still do the same? For instance, if you are supporting software, like I am, and you are forced to start supporting some other technology that you may have knowledge of, such as auto mechanics, computer hardware, copier machines, television sets, or cellular phones, would you not do some things the same way as you do in software? I would, and I think you would also, regardless of the technology you are currently supporting. Let's look at the different disciplines as they relate to technical support.

We deliver the support to customers via some form of communication. However, the mere transfer of information is not all we do. The trick is how we deliver the answers and get the questions and information out of those we support. This is where our communications skills play a very important role in support. To add complexity to the communication requirements, we also have to be skillful in consumer behavior, customer psychology, conflict resolution, and a gamut of other fields we may not even realize. Communications plays an elemental role in our work. This is what sets us apart from development people in that we know how to communicate with the customer.

One of my colleagues was always amazed at how I handled a certain type of client: the one who wants to know every single little aspect of the technology and will not end the call. His questions are endless which can drive the support person crazy. My colleague would get frustrated and conference me in with such clients. I promptly answered the questions with as much detail as possible. Never using language over the customer's head, I would just talk and talk, and it was hard to shut me up. I would keep this up until the customer would thank me, say that he would read the manual, and call with any other questions if he could not find in the documentation.

This was the art of communications at its core. It was almost like reverse psychology. What the customer wanted was not the answers but an assurance that we knew what we were talking about, even assurance the knowledge could be found somewhere. Sometimes the symptom of a client's incredulousness is a constant barrage of questions. When we as support professionals understand and recognize different personality types, motives, and voice hints, then we can say we are on our way to mastering communications. I am not there yet and only managed to be successful with some types of customer communications. You may have mastered others. This challenge is especially present when we support customers from other cultures and global regions. If you are interested in learning more on this and any other subject, I urge you to go and study the established body of knowledge. The best way I know is to enroll in a "principles of" course at your local university or college. If you are short on time and would rather just read, then get the name of the book the course is using and read the book instead. You will learn from the official knowledge base and benefit from it without trial and error.

In technical support, we also continually practice the concepts of systems analysis. We take the troubleshooting approaches of dissecting a problem based on the systems involved and inspect the different pieces of the technology to determine the origin of the problem. Some call it root cause analysis and others just basic troubleshooting. However, there is already an established discipline so we are better off just building on the discoveries of others. The main thing to keep in mind is that we use root cause analysis in technical support and, whether we are aware or not, it is an integral part of our field.

Have you ever thought of yourself as an educator? Every time you speak with a customer and teach that customer something new, you are engaged in education. We may not do it in classrooms, and it may not fit the exact definition of a systematic instruction, but knowledge is transferred to our customers and other entities, such as internal services, partners, resellers, and anyone else who needs to know what we know. In some ways, we are teachers of technology. We dispel erroneous notions and eliminate doubt. We also impart, through our support practices, the necessary knowledge so that our respective industry progresses, so the new knowledge becomes part of the general body of knowledge. It is not all done by technical writers, despite what they may want to believe. It is done by the organic interaction of customer and support person.

The last interesting yet obscure discipline that support inherently adopts is group dynamics. This is a huge area of improvement and practice in our field. How does the group work, interact, learn from each other, and eventually progress? There are great examples of groups that excel despite roadblocks and other similar groups that fail miserably. Why does this happen? If we stop and learn a bit more about group dynamics, we find there are many aspects in that discipline, but all revolve around social relationships. This does not refer to just personal friendships, but to the relationships that members of the groups exert on each other. Some are mentors; others are the experts; some are the communicators, writers, academics, techies, and even the counselors of the group. These are all areas of group dynamics that play a huge role in our support groups. The proximity of the members, the nature of the work, and the need for collaborative practices are what make this discipline an integral part of technical support.

You do not truly know what you are talking about until you can describe it in one sentence.

—Dr. Norman Blackaby

The Vernacular of the Profession

What is it that sets professions apart from the informal trades? When a doctor or lawyer speaks with colleagues, do you think you will understand the jargon without being in their profession? Chances are we probably won't understand unless we are somewhat familiar with their profession. The lingo sets apart these professions from the rest of the laypeople.

If you ever go to court, see if you can understand what the judge is telling the attorneys. When you hear a policeman speak with colleagues about police matters, you'll realize that they are speaking a language only they can understand. They have their codes and radio calls, which are a mystery to most of us. When I go to my family doctor I usually ask him to dumb down the prognosis because, unlike him, I didn't go to medical school. Specialized terminology is not only for doctors and attorneys. Just about every profession has them, from architects, researchers, politicians, and even plumbers. In fact, a plumber or electrician can easily communicate with another member of the trade from a different company or region. Their jargon is the equalizer. Do we have that in technical support?

To some extent, our profession is developing the language particular to the work. However, until there is a general body of knowledge and formalized publications, such as professional books, trade magazines, associations, and any other entities that involve professionals from different industries, we will still be in disaccord with what the terms are. For instance, we all refer to incidents that customers open with different terms. Some of the names used are issues, cases, tickets, contacts, queries, and probably some other names that are particular only to some companies. We all have different systems for issue tracking so the process also has different names and stages. There are no established words to describe them. Even within companies and support centers, the vocabulary changes depending on the system used to track the issues or to take the phone calls.

How does the formalized standard lingo for a profession get established? It is possible that some professions simply use jargon to keep outsiders from knowing how simple their work is. Take some of the terms in economics, another young science. In the spirit of full disclosure, I majored in economics so I know some of the jargon of the field. For instance, take the term "marginal," which is used in a gamut of economic theories and models. In economics, "marginal" simply means one extra when speaking of dollars or units of production, supply, or demand. Many of the terms and theories have a meaning that we could all understand if it was put in simpler language. One example is the marginal propensity to consume. Another term is the price elasticity of demand. The first one means the more you have, the more you spend. The second means, if you need it, you'll have to buy it, but only if you think it's worth it. I may be oversimplifying here, but economists speak a different language so that they can make sense of their world. Economists have to make special terms that sometimes may seem pedantic, and unless you know what they mean, you will be at a loss when confronted with them.

In our case, we can start by adopting whatever the industry as a whole says we should. Most professional lingo starts with pioneering published works on the subject. Some of it comes from professional bodies that determine the best and most adept language to use. It is my hope that we have such a venue established in technical support before too long and that it encompasses all support work, not just what is inherent in the IT field. I hope that soon we will have a proper noun describing a member of our profession, a verb for our type of work, and a full dictionary for technical support. There are some attempts currently underway, but they are costly and probably not what we would consider as industry knowledge. They appear more as an attempt to sell yet another product, training course, or certification. Instead, I urge my colleagues to write and publish. Who better to know and develop the discipline as well as the professional vocabulary than the people actually doing the work?

I know there is a vast world of knowledge on this subject in the minds of practitioners of this humble, yet fulfilling profession. I recently visited several mainstream bookstores that carry thousands of books in their retail locations. I went in looking for books on technical support and found nothing. I visited online bookstores and found a few titles that were not written for the professional. They were apparently written for people who wish to learn about technical support, but not really intended for the practitioner. They describe what an ACD line is and the different support levels, even how to get out of technical support and become a developer.

It is time that we have our own respectable line of published works that help establish our professional vocabulary, processes, theories, models, and experiences. We need works that can be obtained for regular bookstore prices and not for ridiculously high prices so knowledge is available to all, not just people with money or an employer gullible enough to spend hundreds of dollars on a single book. I argue that our profession does not need certifications as much as it needs degrees, whether they are technical, bachelors, or advanced. We need people trained and learned who can meet the challenges of the next technology revolution, whether that be in quantum computing, robotics, or renewable energy. I want to live to see the day when technical support, or whatever it's called in the future, is a field where the practitioners have their own lingo, share common practices, and have processes based on theories and models arising from experienced practitioners.

I know there are colleagues working somewhere right now who have the next big idea on how to improve technical support. I have seen a few already. I used to think that I knew a lot about this work. Then I met colleagues who support different technologies in different companies. I was astonished by how much they knew and the great processes and models they work under. This type of progressive knowledge should not be hoarded by individual companies, but shared by the profession as a whole. We will only achieve this if each one of us gets the word out by way of published works, and gives everyone else a chance to accept, reject, critique, modify, and expand our ideas. This is how all the great disciplines started and ours is no exception. The only thing we lack now is the common medium and the pioneers, but I suspect that will not be a problem for long.

■ **Note** The difference between a dream and a real possibility is the time until you wake up.

The Expert Proletariat

When we think about our incredibly complex line of work and the boundless opportunities that await our profession, we realize that we are barely scratching the surface of what our field will become. Yet, there is one certainty that will most likely be a constant for future generations of supporters. The technical support profession is and always will be a necessity, but not the driving force behind the development, marketing, and evolution of the technologies supported.

I believe that technical support will be a contributory force behind the success or even demise of any technology company, but not the sole or even main driving force behind revolutionary changes in technology. Of course, this is not such a bad thing and there will undoubtedly be members of the technical support body who will inevitably invent and revolutionize technology. But as a subset of the industry, technical support will be limited to delivering the expert help, analysis, and responses to masses of constituents. The technological revolutions coming from support will be a matter of statistical inevitability. In other words, with so many people solving complex problems and answering technology questions, some breakthroughs are bound to happen. In such a huge field, someone has to come up with great ideas and inventions, even though this is not the main function of technical support. For those of us currently in this profession, this point is quite apparent and not one open for discussion, despite technological improvements arising from discoveries by support people in the course of issue and problem analysis. Nonetheless, I argue that we are moving toward becoming the expert proletariat of the 21st century.

Why are we the proletariat and not the aristocrats of technology? Is being a proletariat such a bad thing? What is a proletariat anyway? The proletariat or "working class" are the people who do the work, the ones who make the proverbial machine move, and the ones who by their labor allow the industry to carry on, and even progress. As in an attacking or defending army, the proletariat can be thought of as the infantry. The men and women who toil to win and who ultimately carry out the strategy of the generals. It is not a bad place to be, just not as glamorous as we might like. Yet, despite being the worker bees, we are not only labor but also expert labor. We are part of what drives ongoing sales and makes development possible. We take care of customers after the sale and enable the next renewal. Because of our discoveries, development teams can correct problems or take advantage of unexploited opportunities to make a better product. The way we do our work can affect whether our customers highly recommend or bad-mouth our company and our technology. Therefore, we hold a tremendous power in our work and together we can help drive the financial health of our employers and ultimately, ourselves.

We are left with the following questions: where will technical support make the greatest impact and is there any particular aspect of technology where we will be *the* driving force? Given the customer-focused nature of our work and the problem-driven characteristics that dictate the direction of the profession, it appears that we will make the biggest inroads in the area of product and technology usability and user satisfaction. We will also most likely play a bigger role in product quality. This radical move necessitates a mandate from company strategists, such as executive management and buy-in from development and marketing, to make technical support the link between the two. It is also likely that technical support will become a specialized area of industry as specialized companies are already providing support services based on the needs of customers and technology vendors. There are some pioneering companies currently doing support based on specialization and quality models, such as 100% work-from-home as well as routing customers to individuals to different places in the world based on required language and expertise. Some of these support pioneers work on different technologies regularly as demand dictates for different companies and types of customers. The new practitioners of this new industry sector will need to be experts, primarily in both technology adoption and systems analysis, with an inherent expertise in customer communications and synergic group skills.

The question is whether the efficiencies can also be achieved by the technology vendor. I am not referring to the outsourcing trend where companies go to places like India or China where labor costs are lower. The key here is expertise, capacity, and efficiency, not just costs. Whatever happens, I firmly believe that such a support model would work much better in a new technology where the support originates with a specialized company rather than having internal support groups get detached from the technology company, and then be forced to become part of a third party support vendor.

You may not want to be thought of as a member of the working class or member of the proletariat, but think of the well-respected professions that are made up of experts. Doctors do not make new medicines or drive medical discoveries. They are expert practitioners, just like us. They need communications skills; they have their own lingo; they do a lot of technical or systems analysis; and they educate and engage in group dynamics. They are the expert proletariat of medicine just as we are the expert proletariat of technology. The big difference is that doctors have a well-developed body of knowledge, theoretical foundations, schools, and a lot more respect, but fundamentally our work is no different. Out of our profession, many others could potentially arise as we perfect our own practices and see the need for other specialties. For now, we will have to work with what we have.

Technical support alone will not drive a technology company to success, but it will be an integral part of that success together with marketing, sales, development, and management. Technical support links the technology company and technology customer base in a manner that is more relaxed and focused than any other department within the technology company. You are the informal bond between the two and know firsthand the challenges faced by the customer base. You know more than just the technology implementation and usage challenges; you also know the strengths and weaknesses of the technology and even the customer. In a world where knowledge is power, this makes us a very powerful working class. Hence, we are the expert proletariat.

Live as if you were to die tomorrow. Learn as if you were to live forever.

—Mahatma Gandhi

One Last Note About Science

When you ask your colleagues how they go about solving problems, especially those annoying and obscure problems that require either a lot of in-depth knowledge or a lot of testing, you will get a vast array of answers. You will hear answers ranging from "I look at our knowledge base" to "I just jump right in until something works." Others may get very fancy in their approach and even cite specific systems analysis techniques, like "divide and conquer" and diagnosis formulation.

Problem solving did not originate with technical support. It has been around since man first started to run into problems and questions in the search for knowledge. I can only imagine how the first caveman figured out what mix of mud, ash, berries, water, and natural dye would make permanent ink for use on cave walls. Then someone must have improved on the idea and added color. Someone else must have figured out a way to make the ink more durable and so on. The process of problem solving forms part of, and is inherent in, intelligence. Humans have a monopoly on brain capacity, but we are also the ones with the best ability to create, improve, and concoct technology, ideas, and art—not to mention the manual dexterity to bring them to reality in physical form. Since all technology retains some level of complexity, humans needed a better way to conceive and solve the problems complex enough to require a system. This need gave birth to the scientific method, which we all use to some extent whether we are aware of it or not.

I strongly believe that the scientific method has been inherent in humanity's pursuit of answers to technical questions since the early thinkers and technologists. Nearly 5,000 years ago in Egypt, early pioneers of medical science figured out that by studying symptoms, observing cause and effect, and experimentation, they could come up with an explanation to the physiology of the brain and its relation to the heart[1]. Humans have always been smart and capable of understanding complex problems. They may not have had the technology of today, but that does not mean they were any less intelligent. In fact, we might argue that our immense body of knowledge in all aspects of the sciences is a direct result of all the compiled scientific facts of our earliest human ancestors. All this trial and error, guessing and experimentation, written and verbal understanding, and awareness must have resulted in all of us being more adept at acquiring and growing intelligence. As a fundamental task of our profession, what we do in technical support revolves around the scientific method and adheres to accepted scientific practice. Regardless of where this may lead in this still non-documented field of ours, the scientific method drives

---

[1] *Encyclopædia Britannica Online*, s.v. "Edwin Smith papyrus." `http://www.britannica.com/EBchecked/topic/179901/Edwin-Smith-papyrus` (Accessed November 8, 2008).

the best of our practitioners to find answers to questions and problems. The simple scientific method that we all learned in school has only five steps:

Question

Hypothesis

Experiment

Observation

Conclusion

Technical support, being a field in which the main foundation is troubleshooting, may make better use of the more complex[2] scientific method that best fits it and is published in the *Journal of American Society for Information Science*:

1. Define the question

2. Gather information and resources (observe)

3. Form hypotheses

4. Perform experiments and collect data

5. Analyze data

6. Interpret data and draw conclusions that serve as a starting point for new hypotheses

7. Publish results

8. Retest (frequently done by other scientists)

Do these steps look familiar? Except for the "publish results" and "retests" by other scientists, all these are steps that we use every single day in our daily exercises with customers and their problems. Sometimes we may think that this is stuff that only we do, but the reality is that scientists do these steps when searching for the next breakthroughs in technology and natural sciences. Of course, the use of the scientific method does not automatically make our discipline a science but I am confident that soon we will have a very diverse body of knowledge encompassing many other areas of study. Then someone, perhaps you or one of your colleagues, will think up a phenomenal theory or model that will be the basis for a new science.

When you think about your work, think of the big picture and how Albert Einstein must have felt while working as a clerk at the US Patent Office. Think of how Thomas Edison must have felt when his 100th attempt at inventing the light bulb failed, or to hit closer to home, how Colonel Sanders must have felt when the 1000th restaurant turned down his fried chicken recipe. You are on the brink of something new. You are a pioneer in a field that may someday be something huge and may give rise to the next

---

[2] Crawford S, Stucki L, "Peer Review and the Changing Research Record,", *Journal of the American Society for Information Science* 41, (1990): 223-228.

generation of technology and science practitioners. If you think the sciences are advanced now, just wait another ten or twenty years. Then we will really be at the brink of the greatest time in history in terms of scientific and technological enlightenment, a time that will undoubtedly dwarf the Renaissance, Industrial revolution, and the Internet in scope and global impact and advancement. This is where we will shine and truly realize the importance of our work.

Education is what remains after one has forgotten what one has learned in school.

—Albert Einstein

CHAPTER 3

■ ■ ■

Your Work Practices

Throughout this chapter, you will read about the approaches to technical support work itself. I try to derive conceptual principles based on practical approaches to the work. I also provide examples to illustrate the concepts in action. One thing I will not do is tell you how to do your work. I assume you are already good at supporting your customers. Otherwise, you would not be in technical support as this is not a field for the incompetent. Therefore, my approach is to fill in some of the potential gaps and give some practical advice that can be used by any support person, regardless of the technology.

All of the material contained in these pages is original. I included sources where necessary, but everything else is based on experience and observation. I welcome and encourage any and all critiques, commentary, and feedback as it will help improve our field. Keep in mind that I write from the perspective of enterprise software technical support, but as much as possible try to make the material applicable to any technology, whether software, hardware, or procedural support services. I urge you to read with an open mind because these concepts have helped me progress in my own support career.

This chapter provides you with:

- The work practices as well as examples.

- Practical approaches to these concepts.

- Potential actions for career and process development.

As you read, please remember that our field is still a work in progress and we still have a lot to do. I hope that the concepts written in these pages stimulate you to find ways to progress in your own support work as well as improve our field.

> *If there is no struggle, there is no progress. Those who profess to favor freedom, and deprecate agitation, are men who want crops without plowing up the ground, they want rain without thunder and lightning.*

> —Frederick Douglass

Write Down Anything New Immediately After You Learn It

When you are answering a question, troubleshooting a problem, or testing a situation and come upon a new discovery, write it down so you don't forget it. It will help you add to your arsenal of knowledge and build up a library of answers.

As a support person you are confronted with an array of problems and questions on a daily basis. It is very likely that those same questions and problems will come up again in the future. If you write the question down and document the answer, you will solve the problem immediately the next time it happens. It will also allow you to help your colleagues to solve their problems faster because you will have many of the answers already written down.

Nevertheless, it is not enough to just write the answer down. You have to write in a format that will be easily copied to an e-mail, a support system, or any other electronic format to answer the question for your customers. A good practice is to make a folder somewhere on your hard drive and catalogue the different types of questions so you can easily find them when you are pressed for time.

When I was doing software technical support, I had a folder populated with sub-folders arranged neatly by component, type of problem, and operating system. Inside the folders, I had simple ASCII text files with the answers neatly arranged and presented. The name of the file was the actual question and the content of the file was the answer ready to be given to a customer or colleague. For instance, when a customer asked me for the instructions on how to edit a report manually on ABCSoftware 3.0 system, I simply looked at the "*Report*" folder and opened the file *"Instructions to edit reports manually.txt"*. This file contained all the instructions and was worded like this:

```
Hello <name>,
Per our conversation, in order to edit a report in ABCSoftware 3.0:

1) Go to the folder:
C:\Program Files\ABCSoftware3.0\ABCReports\file\

2) Look for the correct xml file (report file) that pertains to the report in question. One
way to do it is to search under that folder for any file containing a string such as the
report name. Another way is to generate the report and right-click on the report data and
choose "View Source". There will be a string such as:

action=genxml&file=report23.xml
The report23.xml refers to the report file.

3) Edit the report (xml) file with MS Word and remove undesired entries. For instance, in
report23.xml, to remove a machine entry, delete the following lines:
 - <REC>
   <VAL>3.0.06.2333</VAL>
   </REC>

4) Save the file and refresh the ABCSoftware Console report and it will show up with the
changes.

Let me know how it works.
Thanks,
John Doe
```

All I had to do was copy and paste the entire file content into an email and add the customer's name. I saved time by having typed responses where I only had to add the customer's information. This practice alone allowed me to close a lot more issues than I would have closed otherwise. It also allowed me to help my colleagues faster so they could close more issues as well. It wasn't that I was smarter or knew all the answers; it was simply that I wrote them down and pulled them out as I needed them.

This is a simple system that you can use to minimize typing and to keep you from having to remember the technical details of the answer you gave to a customer months or even years ago. Keeping the answers to the problems previously encountered is really an extension of your memory, and allows you to build a body of knowledge for your product or the subject you support. Another advantage of this practice is that when you decide to leave your position to pursue something else, your colleagues don't lose all the benefits of having you around. The knowledge remains and can be used by them even after you are gone. This will ensure that you provide value to your employer long after you are working for someone else.

Why do you want to keep the answers in simple text files? It's easier to copy and paste into any other application such as Outlook emails, Word files, and any proprietary or special system you may use to communicate with customers and your colleagues.

A few years ago, the company I worked for was acquired and the product I supported at the time became a sensation. There were only three of us providing support when we were a small company. After the acquisition, dozens of salespeople and many more partners and resellers started to sell more product. During this time, the number of support people remained the same. We faced a huge increase in the number of support issues. We were extremely busy but were able to keep up because we had built the inventory of answers during the previous two years. Having the answers ready to send to a customer allowed us to answer question after question without stressing intellectually, because all we had to do was look for the correct file. Of course, this still required in-depth knowledge of the product, its components, the customers, and the common problems associated with the products, but it still allowed us to coast with many of the issues because they had occurred before and all we did was copy and paste an answer.

This concept of having answers ready to provide to customers verbally or electronically is very different than having the answers on a web site or support site for customers to access. Such a system doesn't provide nearly the same intelligence that a support person does. Additionally, many customers prefer to speak to a live person and frown upon having to find their own answers.

This section is not suggesting hoarding information and keeping others from getting their hands on your valuable knowledge. The temptation might be to make yourself indispensable by not sharing the knowledge with your colleagues and thus ensuring job security. My advice is to cut down on the menial tasks, such as typing out an answer to a question which has come up before. You will be more efficient in your work.

■ **Tip** If you get in the habit of writing down everything new you learn, eventually, you will have ready answers to most of the questions you encounter.

The Above-Average Performer

While working in technical support all these years, I have come across colleagues who consistently produce above average and always turn out high numbers of closed issues. These high performers could be considered average in technology skills and troubleshooting capacity. They are usually no more knowledgeable than the rest of the support group and do not work longer hours than anyone else. They are simply able to accomplish more in the same amount of time and with the same resources and capacity. I watched some of these colleagues closely in order to understand their work habits, and I was mesmerized at how simple their methods were. Their ability to produce more simply lies in their ability to work, for lack of a better word, smarter.

What exactly makes people produce more and work more efficiently? Must you enslave yourself and work like crazy without stopping or work longer than a support project normally takes? Is it something more inherent in individual style rather than specific activities? To answer those questions, we have to look at the typical colleague who produces at an above-average level. I never saw any of those colleagues work more than anyone else. In fact, they often worked less, but accomplished a lot more. They also did not seem to work incessantly. The secret to their success is in the approach to the work, rather than the activities of the work. In other words, the goal of the high producer lies in cutting out any activities that can be done automatically or by some more efficient means. Some of the innate characteristics of high producers are the following:

- Automate repetitive tasks

- Prepackage solutions

- Reduce typing

- Script client actions

The biggest area for improvement is to do away with repetitive tasks. These are the ones that you can do with your eyes closed and do not even have to think about. These tasks are a time-killer because they do not make appropriate use of your intellect. For such tasks, find a way to automate them. An example is to run a batch script to open all the necessary applications required to do your work. One of my very productive colleagues created a small script to search several knowledge bases for strings. Another colleague found a way to automate the generating, copying, and pasting of license numbers into emails to be sent to colleagues and then to record them in the support system. He was able to cut a process that normally took over six manual steps down to just one. This type of process efficiency may make more sense in a support job in information technology but even outside technology, support people can automate repetitive tasks. The trick is to find tasks in your daily activities where you can eliminate manual intervention and shorten the process to get more work done with the same amount of time and effort.

Another big item for support people is the solutions we send to clients. Think of all the frequently used solutions you have to email or FTP to your customers. Do you have to send multiple files or just one? Do you also have to send separate instructions and an additional email to let them know you placed it on an FTP folder? Solutions that are frequently sent to different customers should be prepackaged in a way that the customer can easily retrieve them, get instructions, and even install the solution. The package can include all the information you would otherwise use multiple emails to send files for. A well-packaged solution will also include instructions or additional solutions in case the main solution does not work correctly or in case something else goes wrong. Of course, this other unforeseen event would be something that happens regularly. I remember we used to package a solution with a link to a software patch in the event the customer had an older version. This practice serves a dual purpose. You get more accomplished by anticipating the needs of the customer and putting together the instructions, actual solutions, and contingencies while the customer benefits by getting the solution and any other potential issues resolved quicker.

I sincerely hope that typing goes away in the future and is replaced by a mechanism that can read then, type my thoughts without spelling errors, use proper grammar, correct my style and make me coffee, all at the same time. However, until that happens, I still have to type. Nevertheless, I do not want to type the same thing over and over again if I can help it. Much like automating the repetitive task, in this approach you try to eliminate typing by replacing it with an automatic typing function in your application or by typing your messages once, saving them, and using them over and over again. The issue tracking system I used for the last ten years has a feature in which I can record what I type and then replay it. Ever since I learned about this feature about five years ago, I have been saving data entry formats, email formats, and even entire situations that occur frequently. This saves me a considerable amount of time typing. For those of us who are not fast typists, this practice allows us to be much more productive and devote our efforts to problem solving rather than typing.

The last technique used by some of the top performers involves the use of scripting client actions to get logs, rules, application data, and any other type of data that you would otherwise have to guide a customer though or do yourself. This technique may need to be approved by your management, but is very powerful when used. Additionally, if it turns out to be a good idea, it can be incorporated into the product as a new feature.

Back in 1998, one of my colleagues came up with the great idea of creating a small script that would gather all the application logs, operating system information, hardware, resource output, and just about everything else we could possibly need to figure out the problem. This script alone allowed my colleague and me to support an increasing number of customers with the same resources, all because we did not have to talk customers through reading or emailing logs to us. It was so helpful that it later became a feature of the product.

Above-average productivity is within the reach of all of us. All we have to do is find ways to eliminate the repetitive tasks inherent in our support processes that are not directly involved in intellectual endeavors, such as troubleshooting and customer service. In addition to closing more issues, you will enjoy your day more by focusing on the problem and the customer rather than menial chores.

Few things are harder to put up with than the annoyance of a good example.

—Mark Twain

The Resource Collector

Few things are more annoying and depressing than needing information and not finding it, or worse not having any idea of where to look for it. Technical support is a business of answers and solutions. Customers ask, we answer. Customers have problems and we solve them. This is the nature of the answer machine, which is our profession. This is exactly why we need to have our collection of resources where we can get the answers we seek when those answers are neither ones we know nor ones we can experiment to find out.

What type of answers do we need resources for? Specifically, we need resources for answers that lie in facts. For instance, any questions that start with: "How many," "How much," "Does it do this or that" and "Where can I find," may be relevant only to your technology and the nature of your customers. In the course of doing support for your product, you have probably amassed a number of resources to answer the different questions previously cited, but in case you have not, then I recommend the following:

- Develop resources in different departments within your company

- Develop resources specifically within support

- Find resources outside of your company

- Be a resource to others

This topic does not have to do with troubleshooting or experimenting. What you are about to read is only about facts that you cannot find on your own, and that may not even be related to support, but customers might ask you anyway.

In answering a bunch of support questions daily, we inevitably get questions, such as "How much does the license (product or contract) cost?" This type of question is beyond the scope of many of the support groups in which I have worked. It was always someone else, like sales and customer service, who dealt with such questions. This is why you have to learn where those resources are and how to contact them to get the answers to provide your customers. I suggest asking someone who knows and then building your own database of resources of where to get answers. The "database" may simply be a sticky note on the edge of your monitor or a piece of paper taped to your wall. Whatever the record may be, be sure to record all the internal resources you can, and make sure they can also call you when those resources need help that you can provide. I have seen colleagues make their own small databases using tools ranging from simple notepad files to much more complex databases using Microsoft Access. I am very particular to the Contacts feature in Microsoft Outlook. How do you go about finding out who is who inside your company? The only way is to ask. Unless you work in a very uptight company where no one wants to help anyone else, I recommend just asking. After all, everyone in the company is on the same side as you are. At the risk of sounding overly idealistic, I firmly believe that everyone in any company is working toward the same goal: more customers, better service, and more revenue. I am not blind to the fact that there will be politics and differences in opinions, but your goal is service. In addition, I suggest not playing the game of politics because you will lose. Leave that to others. Your main concern is getting facts for you and for your customers. Shyness and fear of others is not in the realm of technical support. However, when going about obtaining resources, make sure that you run it by your manager or your mentor first. If you find them to be an obstruction, then I suppose just go to the source. If you are concerned that you may be construed as someone who goes around your manager, then just limit your resources to one level above you. In other words, resources at the same level as the next level above yours. I believe that among technical people we are all the same, so even when someone three levels under me asks a question or requires help, I promptly and happily assist. As long as you do not abuse the privilege, any technical person within your company should be happy to help. So I urge you to develop your list of resources within your company at every possible level and use diplomacy to get facts so that you can help your customers.

What about when you need help outside your company? What if you need answers that lie beyond the scope of your expertise or even your technology? This is truly a challenge of major proportions. The way you can overcome this challenge is to develop a network of resources with customers and support colleagues in other companies, as well as resources within your industry. As long as you do not violate any ethical rules within your company, you should be fine. If there is a doubt, then ask your manager. One way to cultivate resources is to develop partner relationships through friends, industry associations, and even with customers. Customers are not always the clueless people we may think they are. In fact, nothing can be further from the truth. The great majority of customers I had the pleasure of helping were usually experts in their field. I often received lessons in different aspects of software and hardware from customers who taught me a lot about technology while I helped them with my technology. Remember, these are people who are as passionate about technology as you are. If you maintain a good relationship with your customers, there is no reason they could not answer a simple question from you. Of course, they are not technical support, but a simple question now and then in the course of a support call is not a transgression. I once had the hardest time finding a Netware Server command. During the course of a call with a customer I mentioned it to him, and he told me how to find the command immediately. It turned out that he had been working with Novell Netware since the early 1990s. He knew so much about Netware and was so passionate about the technology that he gave me a long lesson about it after I mentioned my problem. I learned more about Netware from him on that call than I ever learned from the Netware help files and my own colleagues.

Another great resource can be found in industry bodies, such as technology associations, and even sources like Experts-Exchange.com and TechnicalSupportForum.com plus a bunch of other questions and answer forums out on the internet. While working on a project for our technical support department, I needed guidance on industry trends so I called Service and Support Professional Association (SSPA). They quickly answered my question in a very professional manner. There are plenty of other resources and people who are as passionate about technology as you are, and who are willing to lend a helping hand when you need one. Once again, unless you pay them, do not abuse the privilege.

In acquiring resources, make absolutely sure that there is reciprocity. You cannot always pay or afford to pay your resources, but you can serve as a resource to them or to others. We are all in this together. We are not salespeople competing for customers. We are just out to find answers to our questions for the sake of technology and to give us the extra push when we are in need of a fact. A favor for a favor is a good practice that most people would not object to. I still have ex-colleagues from all over the world who email or call me from time to time asking about quick facts on Intrusion Detection technology or TCP or IPv6 packet architecture. If I can answer them quickly and effortlessly, I gladly do. Who knows, maybe later it will be my turn to ask someone else.

> *Business, labor, and civil society organizations have skills and resources that are vital in helping to build a more robust global community.*

> —Kofi Annan

Work Smarter, Not Harder

The typical support team has multiple layers or tiers. Group dynamics keep everything going. There are the people with specialized skills who do everything to help the rest of the group. There are the less specialized ones who take all types of issues from customers, work them, then pass the issues they cannot solve on to the specialists. Then there are the ones who live in an ivory tower and refuse to speak and prefer to handle everything via email or IM. In case you are sensing a bit of sarcasm, you are right.

In technical support, the higher you go in the tiers or support ladder, the more that is expected of you. Also, the more you should strive to fulfill your role and live up to your position . . . and then some. Given that technical support is now more competitive than ever and support teams around the globe are always losing some ground to some other world region with more technical skills or lower salaries, the support teams must live up to their mandate. If it sounds like I am pressing a point, you are right again.

In order for a support team to strive for excellence, each member must strive for excellence individually. What is excellence? In our case, excellence is the act of delivering services that are better, cheaper, and smarter than that of the competition[1].If our support is going to be better, cheaper, and smarter than our competitors that means each one of us has to develop ways to meet those goals individually. That level of achievement only comes when we do what we are supposed to and more. In order for the support team to achieve excellence in the technical support delivered to customers, each individual team member has to do the following:

- Do the tasks listed on the job description.

- Find ways to do those tasks more efficiently.

As you read the preceding list, you might think this is too much to ask of anyone. After all, technical support work is not exactly relaxing; we are always full of issues and customer problems to diagnose and test. But we are striving for "excellence" and that means doing more than just what's required and

---

[1] "Excellence." Bloomsbury Business Library—Business & Management Dictionary (January 2007): 2895–2895.

expected. It's about showing our customers that our service surpasses anything they could have received from any other vendor.

I am not going to discuss how to do the tasks listed on your job description. You should already be doing that anyway. But doing those tasks more efficiently is what improvement is all about. No one wants to work more than they have to. This is about improving the way our work is done so that we don't have to work longer hours, but get more accomplished within the same number of hours. This could mean taking more calls, answering more issues, and helping more colleagues. It is all about high-quality productivity. Furthermore, the work has to be done with a high-quality result. We can all just take more calls and answer more issues, but if all our answers are wrong, it wouldn't make any positive difference. How do we get more productivity out of our days? There are only two ways to increase productivity without working longer or hiring more people:

- Use better technology.

- Use better processes.

- Make better use of the technology you have.

Now, I know that as support engineers we don't have a budget and we don't have the liberty to just buy more computers or a bigger lab. We also are not the ones who dictate processes (although we probably should be) or how things are supposed to be done. However, we all have the power to control how we do our own work.

How can you use better technology to do more? Think about the steps required to solve a typical issue in your line of support work. Do you use a lab? Do you send instructions? Do you make phone calls or receive them? All these tasks require some technology, such as a phone, a server, appliance, software, etc. Think of ways you can shorten the process to complete one of these tasks. I have a few colleagues who shortened their testing time from two days to a few minutes. It didn't require the company to spend any more money or even to adopt any new policies. All they did was create virtual machine environments. They set them up to a point where they are ready to run tests. When they need to run a test, they just make a clone of it and run their test. Before, they used to have to set up a physical computer with OS, software and all. I have other colleagues who, instead of reproducing a customer's environment, just ask the customer to take a virtual copy of their server, remove all the sensitive information, and send it in to support. This shortens the troubleshooting time by hours and puts the support person in complete control of the environment without worrying about breaking something.

Once I visited a client and when I approached their front door, I saw a group of guys outside the front door smoking and talking. When I got closer, I realized they were not talking to each other; they were talking on the phone. I checked it out a bit more, saw they had small wireless headsets, and that they appeared to be doing troubleshooting. I went ahead and walked in to meet with the customer. He was the head of IT for the company, so I asked him about the people smoking and talking outside. He said they were the internal helpdesk reps who, in order to become more productive, use wireless headsets even when they are on smoke breaks. He said it was odd at first to be talking to an internal customer while walking or smoking, but that it gave them more flexibility and improved productivity.

What about processes or the way we do tasks? How can we improve those? Think of it this way, our company needs us to answer customers' questions and solve their problems. Management gives us general and specific processes to follow. But for the most part, it's up to us to figure out the best way to do the work required. This could involve taking all the calls first, telling the clients we will work on the problem and get back to them, then working them out as fast as possible. We could do all the easy issues first and get them out of the way before devoting time to the harder ones. It could involve the way breaks, lunch, or even smoke breaks are taken in order to leave us more productive time to work the issues. It could even be a special process to work the issues themselves. Perhaps you are a very analytical person who wants to think about a problem first before looking at a solution database. Or it may be the opposite. You want to ask colleagues to discuss potential solutions and shorten the time you spend coming up with the answers. Whatever your process may be, do whatever you can to do more with the same amount of work.

■ **Note** You can produce more by working more. However, it is easier to produce more with better tools and processes than with a longer day.

Following the Watson Way

In the mystery novels by Sir Arthur Conan Doyle, the character Sherlock Holmes often mocks his assistant, Watson, because Watson is prone to hasty conjecture. Both Watson and Holmes are presented with facts, innuendo, and chances for observation, but it always seems that Watson makes quick decisions while Holmes takes his time to come up with all kinds of intelligent conclusions that could only exist in a work of fiction. However, what Holmes calls speculation, and seemingly careless inference, are not such bad ideas in the technical support world where we often do not have all the facts. In the novel, Holmes calls it elementary, but only because he has all the information. What he does not have, he makes up from previous knowledge or education. At a very fundamental level, Holmes makes the same type of speculations as Watson, but bases them on more and deeper knowledge. Therefore, in situations in which we do not have all the details and we lack complete knowledge, it is more advantageous to make inferences based on the facts and limited information at hand. In the scientific method, we call this "forming a hypothesis."

To the untrained, a hypothesis may mean making a wild guess. It may seem just like a wild supposition the same way Holmes thought of Watson's conclusions. A hypothesis is more than just conjecture and wild ideas of supposition. A hypothesis is the best answer formulated by experts when they lack the facts and the information to say that, without a doubt, that is the answer. A hypothesis is the starting point for experimentation. In technical support, a hypothesis is the point where we start formulating tests and trials to make sure that our "guess" is in fact a true fact.

In technical troubleshooting, we are trained and often forced to make conjectures based on incomplete information. Not every case will have a clean set of facts leading to a certain decision. Many times the information missing is something we are either forced to test ourselves or take a good guess at. But if you are an expert in your technology, does your opinion count more than that of the novice? Of course, our guess is more then just an uneducated crack at solving a problem. As experts in our fields, our "guesses" are nothing less than expert opinion and thus carry a lot of weight. I am not going to try and teach you or even propose to educate you on troubleshooting technical problems. You are already good at it. Otherwise, you would not be in technical support. However, I want to bring to light the art of conjecture, which in the hands of an experienced (or at least a well-trained) supporter, can be a hugely beneficial tool. Hence the next step in the scientific method, formulating a hypothesis, which comes after gathering information. We all go through these steps when the customer tells us what they did, how they experienced the problem, and afterward we analyze the logs and facts about the problem. We may not have the same level of intuition as Holmes, but we often find ourselves making conjectures based on real facts and data. We just have not proved it yet and we may not even have to. The main thing is that we should fix the customer's problem in the shortest time and with the least input of energy possible.

When presented with new situations, such as unseen problems and challenging questions, there are some things that will make your life easier, whether you subscribe to the technical or mechanical style of support. As discussed in Chapter 2, you are considered a mechanical supporter if your problem-solving approach is systematic, and if you are most comfortable with the known and the documented. You are considered a technical-styled supporter if you prefer the unforeseen technical challenges, feel more comfortable working from the symptoms alone, and do not necessarily follow the technology system, but rather utilize your own troubleshooting techniques. Regardless of your support style, you cannot derive a hypothesis without some information and enough experience.

For success in the Watson Way of conjecture to problem solving, you need enough experience in your field. If you have familiarity with the technology you support and you have seen problems and received questions that qualify you as at least an "expert in training," then your hypothesis will be made with sounds facts and a foundation in practice. The following are ways to derive valid hypothesis:

> Hypothesis based on information, facts, past experience, and even "gut feeling."

> Hypothesis based on similar symptoms and similar circumstances.

> Hypothesis based on what should be or deviation from the norm.

I would love to provide valid academic sources for the preceding, but I arrived at them from personal experience and observation. I am lucky this is not a PhD dissertation. Otherwise, I would fail miserably, but allow me to explain why I think that the "gut feelings" of the expert are enough for a valid hypothesis.

As experts, we have seen most of the problems our clients' experience. If we have not taken the calls for the problems, it's only because they have not occurred yet. As technical support people, we know what causes the problems, how our technology behaves, how the problems are manifested and, ultimately, how to solve them. We may not be right all the time, but we are always basing our decisions on some level of knowledge. Sometimes, we just do not remember all the details of the problems we have previously addressed, but we know that there is some correlation to something else. We have a hunch that tells us that the problem lies in some specific area. This intuition is not some metaphysical property that we have. It's simply based on our expertise. It is not entirely based on facts because we do not remember them all, but we know within us that the problem lies somewhere and we have a good idea where that may be. When we have nothing else, we should go with our gut feeling. When there are no options, no resources, no colleagues to aid us, then our instinct has to take over and guide us to the answer. I do not have any other explanation than that, but I sincerely think that it is a more valid way to a resolution than what Sherlock Holmes thought of Mr. Watson's conjectures. There may appear to be a fine line between gut feeling and wild speculation, if it was not for the fact that the person making it is an expert in the technology.

As the support person in your respective technology, you are free to make deductions based on your knowledge and experience. You are qualified to do so. No one else can, only you. Your time spent submerged in the technology has given you that right. Do not let anyone take that from you. It has been a trial by fire and you have earned your stars. Your expert inference, whether based on facts, experience, symptoms or even "gut feeling," is sometimes the only thing separating you from the answer.

An expert is someone who has succeeded in making decisions and judgments simpler through knowing what to pay attention to and what to ignore.

—Edward de Bono

Don't Be Afraid of the Tough Issues

Issues that appear very obscure and difficult are a blessing in disguise. Have you ever encountered a tough issue that everyone is afraid of because they feel they will be in over their heads if they attempt to solve it? Usually those issues are misleading and if you tackle them, you will develop a deeper understanding of the product. Also, you may have the chance to learn more than just about the specific product, like acquiring a deeper understanding of other technologies to add to your troubleshooting skills and, even to your resume. The ability to view every new situation as a chance to learn and become even better at what you do is a characteristic that separates outstanding support people from average ones.

Learning new material in technical support happens in different ways, but two major ways to learn new material are: first, by way of training and, second, by tackling tough issues and learning from the experience. It is also exciting to get into your product or technology and be lost. This is when you realize how little you know. From there on, anything you find out is new information and, thus, new knowledge. However, just because you have no clue how to handle the issue at hand, this does not mean you will just wander in the dark until you stumble upon the answer. The difficult issue must be tackled in an orderly fashion so as to be solved. Assuming this issue has not happened before and that you are the first one to encounter it, use the following six steps:

1. Understand the exact situation. Make sure you ask the customer everything you can until you have no doubts of what the issue is about.

2. Break up the problem into simpler problems or variables and attempt to solve each one individually.

3. Ask your colleagues to see if they have any ideas or hints you could follow.

4. If the problem does not make sense according to what you know of the product, find out how the product or technology works "under the covers." This will give you a better in-depth understanding and allow you to formulate better conclusions.

5. Recreate the situation in your internal lab as much as possible.

6. If you still cannot figure it out, go back to Step one and see if there is something you missed. A lot of times the issue is much simpler than we make it out to be.

The previous steps are a very simple approach that you may already practice. For the novice technical support person, the idea of handling a difficult problem seems insurmountable. Yet, this is how experience and technical maturity is acquired.

I once handled an issue from a customer in Asia. The problem had to do with a firewall software application that we no longer sold but were forced to support for a handful of global customers. This application was robust and once installed and configured, it rarely gave any problems. There were only two or three people in the company who knew anything about this software. When this issue came in, a few colleagues tried to solve the issue and could not. After some time, I was asked to help and I agreed to take on the challenge. The issue was perplexing because the application was behaving erratically despite the configuration being correct. It was allowing all the traffic, but was not allowing traffic in a very specific situation, despite having policies for it and having worked in the past. Immediately, I went to work and did the first thing that came to mind: uninstalled and reinstalled; unsurprisingly, the same thing happened. We tried installing from another software source and it behaved the exact same way. That was when I realized I needed to write down every possible variable that could be causing this problem. The following are the ones I came up with:

- Software source

- Policy and configuration

- Hardware

- Router configuration

- Host operating system

- Network client configuration

With this list in hand, I tried to isolate each one of the variables, and to my surprise the problem was with the operating system. But before I got to the operating system, I learned of the different ways the application can be installed. I also learned how to tweak the policies, generate and import the configuration files, how to generate and read router logs, and how to set one up in my own lab to recreate a customer situation. As you can see, I got more out of this customer problem than just a closed issue. If nothing else, I learned how to handle this type of issue and many others in the future. After I asked the customer to rebuild the operating system on the server, I installed and configured the firewall software the exact same way we had before. This time the application worked correctly. Had I not separated the problem into variables, the issue may not have been solved or it would have taken much longer. I learned a lot from that issue, including how the firewall application works, its interaction with the hardware, and some Cisco router commands. Now I feel as if I can solve just about any issue that comes my way.

■ **Tip** Next time you see the opportunity to work a seemingly tough issue, remember the following principle: average technical support people handle average issues but the outstanding support person handles difficult technical problems, overcomes the challenges, learns a great deal from them, and gains confidence in the process.

Find Your Zebra

As soon as I turned 26, I started feeling lethargic and quite abnormal. I just did not feel right. In the following five years, I went from bad to worse. I suffered from rapid weight gains and losses, to losing hair and skin problems. Life was quite an experience in my mid-twenties and only got worse in my early thirties. I went various doctors who treated the symptoms, but I never saw any real improvement. Then, I went in for a heart checkup. The cardiologist, Dr. Alan Taylor, looked at me and immediately saw something was wrong. I had been going to him for an annual checkup since my father nearly died of a heart attack four years before. However, that day Dr Taylor knew something was different from the previous times he amiably shook my hand.

That summer day the air conditioning was broken in Dr. Taylor's office. I had been waiting to see him for almost two hours because, unlike other patients, I was not in any immediate danger—yet while everyone else in the waiting room was sweating, I was freezing. When I finally went in to see Dr. Taylor, he immediately noticed the disparity. At that time, he was pretty overweight himself and was obviously overcome by the higher temperature in the office. When he shook my hand, I was cold. To me this was normal. My hands were always cold. He then proceeded to ask me a few more questions. He asked about my eating habits, symptoms, and then he said, "I think you have hypothyroidism." Hypo-what!? I had never even heard the word before. I thought he was just going to check my pulse, do a quick echocardiogram, and tell me to exercise, eat my veggies, and send me on my way. But, he tells me he thinks I have something I never even heard of before.

I remember he had an intern with him that day who was taking notes. She looked at him funny and then looked at me even funnier. The doctor turned to her and said, "Yup, Mr. Sanchez doesn't fit the type of person who would develop hypothyroidism, but I bet that's what he has." As they discussed a few things in medical lingo, I must have looked lost to them because they turned to me and smiled. Dr. Taylor then went on to explain that hypothyroidism is a condition in which the thyroid gland does not produce enough hormones and the rest of the body cells cannot metabolize energy correctly. This results in all kinds of symptoms, not unlike what I described and appeared to have. He said the biggest hint was my ice cold hands, which despite the higher than normal temperatures due to the broken AC, were still colder than his metal instruments. He also said that 99% of patients with hypothyroidism are older women. Of the men who have hypothyroidism, 99% are men over 50 yet here I was in my early thirties. Finally, he shared that although it was highly unlikely that someone my age would develop the condition, I showed all the symptoms.

At that stage in my life, I was willing to try anything. Luckily, technical support is not exactly a very physically demanding profession. I never had any energy, could hardly do any physical activity, and the symptoms were often very painful. What is worse, I got to the point where I thought it was normal. I saw older men, even much older men, with more energy and a better quality of life than I had at a much younger age. I could not understand how my wife could get up and do all kinds of activities while I could not even get out of bed. I am not talking about morning, but in the early evenings when I got home from work. Therefore, if Dr. Taylor said I had hypothyroidism than I was ready to try anything.

He sent me for some blood work and it came out that I had a Thyroid Stimulating Hormone (TSH) level of 7.5, a level slightly over what is considered the normal limits. I quickly made an appointment with an endocrinologist and was prescribed medication. As soon as I took the pills, I felt like a new man. I had more energy than ever before. I was active the whole day and have been ever since.

Every time I see Dr. Taylor, he jokingly calls me his "zebra," and tells the story to his nurses or whoever is assisting him that day. When they ask him why he refers to me as his "zebra," he goes on and tells the following anecdote, "If you are lying in bed at night on a farm and you hear a hoofed animal galloping and stomping violently right outside your window, what would immediately come to mind?" His nurses always tell him, "A horse?" and Dr Taylor replies, "Yes, a hoofed animal galloping on a ranch at night would surely be a horse, but could it also be a zebra?"

Forgive me for tormenting you with this story about my medical maladies, but just like Dr Taylor, technical support should treat root causes, not symptoms. In technical support just as in medicine, we should not discard any possibility, however remote it may seem. The consequences might not be as dire as mine were, but they may be severe nonetheless. Learn from my drastic experience and apply the wisdom imparted by Dr. Taylor: do not overlook the possibility of the zebra.

What is all wisdom save a collection of platitudes? But the man who orders his life according to their teachings cannot go far wrong.

—George Norman Douglas

The Knowledge Seeker

In *The Great Transition*, James Martin makes a point early in his book to establish that "constantly renewed and enhanced knowledge is the primary source of competitive advantage."[2] He goes on to argue that only knowledge which is controlled and closely held by the corporation, unshared knowledge, gives power in a competitive environment. How does this apply to technical support where pretty much all we have and deal in is knowledge? It works at several levels, but I argue that at the individual level, the

---

[2] James Martin, *The Great Transition: Using the Seven Disciplines of Enterprise Engineering to Align People, Technology, and Strategy* (New York: Amacom, 1995).

only concern is with the renewal and enhancement of knowledge that James talks about. Technical support practices and models are still in their infancy but technical support would benefit as a whole if we could share that which will improve our discipline. At the support-practitioner level, the two areas that will allow us to keep our knowledge renewed and enhanced are:

- Constant learning and development of skills.

- Improving the uses of information we already have.

I propose that as support people, we are naturally in a discipline that deals in and requires constant learning. This applies to all technologies, even the ones that are inherently more stable than others, such as mainframe platforms being more stable than distributed systems; diesel mechanics being more stable than gas and ethanol motors; and printing presses being more stable than new electronics computer printers. All these technologies, whether stable or ever-changing, require their support people to constantly be renewing their arsenal of facts, wisdom, and proficiencies. In other words, the people who support even very stable technologies have to keep learning and have to keep getting better at supporting those technologies.

How does one keep learning and developing skills even when already an expert? First, it is unlikely that anyone knows everything there is to know about anything. Technologies that require a support staff are usually complex by definition. Otherwise, the users would just figure it out on their own. If you think you know everything there is to know, find something you do not already know and learn it. Also, when you feel like you do not need to learn much more about the technology, then that means you have the required knowledge to find a colleague to teach what you know. Bringing as many of your colleagues to your level will force you to keep improving.

Effective technical support involves many skills that you can improve on, but not all are technical. Examples of non-technical skills are customer service, presentation, mentoring, time management, foreign languages, teaching, and speaking to name a few. All these will help you anywhere you go and can improve your effectiveness in your current support job, depending on the level of skills requirement. If you are wondering what skills you could develop, just think of the situations in which you were not as effective as you would have liked. There was a reason, and it was probably a lack proficiency in a specific skill. I have had that happen many times.

One of the software products I used to support was very famous in Brazil. The Brazilian customers were often handled by some of my colleagues based in that country, but I was there to assist when they needed help in the technical areas. However, when we had to speak with the customer, I was always at a disadvantage because I do not speak Portuguese. Some of the customers I dealt with from Brazil spoke English but most did not. If my Brazilian counterparts were out, and I had to give an update to the client or needed to request a log or file, I had to wait until the Brazilian colleagues were back or find someone else. That is when I realized I had to learn some Portuguese, at least enough to greet and let the customer know what I was looking for. To develop Portuguese skills, I went to my local public library and got some CDs on basic Portuguese. I learned how to greet, numbers, and a few other words so I was at least able to make out a word or two during Portuguese calls. My point is that the constant enhancement of knowledge, such as learning a few words and phrases in a different language, handling difficult customers, public speaking, or teaching a technical course will put you and your company in a better position in the marketplace. You too can improve and renew the knowledge that will help your company gain a competitive advantage.

The second way that we can help our company and our support teams gain a competitive advantage is by better utilizing the information we already have. Usually, the bigger the company gets, the more data there is in different places. You can get a leg up on your competitors by finding ways to transform the data that already exists into useful information to improve business processes or, in our case, to better support customers. To make the most out of the data you already have, the information should be:

- Readily available to those who need it the most. Information has to get to those who can use it, especially those who need it to drive the business and help the company generate revenue. In support, the people who are talking to customers need information at their fingertips in order to better service the client.

- Customized for the user. The information must be exactly what the user needs. Support people need contact information for those who can help provide answers and appease customers. They need to know what the customer is entitled to and for how long. The data provided to technical support personnel is not the same type of data that should be given to a sales person or a developer.

- In a concise format. The information must be in a format that requires no interpretation. Facts and numbers should be spelled out. If information is left up to the users to interpret, they run the risk of interpreting it in a different way than intended.

- Updated regularly so that it is not outdated. Information needs to be valid to be useful. It can only be valid if it's current. It can only be current if it's updated.

Each one of us in technical support is a knowledge owner, producer, and seeker. Technical knowledge changes when the technology changes. This constant updating and renewing ensures that we gain a competitive advantage in the marketplace and also allows us to help our company succeed.

For wisdom is a defense as money is a defense, but the excellence of knowledge is that wisdom gives life to those who have it.

—Ecclesiastes 7:12 (New King James Version)

Reinventing the Wheel

We have all gotten advice from someone watching us try something believed to be new, but that turns out to not be so novel. Someone tells us, "Don't reinvent the wheel," when attempting to create something or some process that already exists. After all, who wants to work in vain when someone already went through the trouble? What about improving what already exists in an effort to bring about more efficiency and perhaps a better product or service? This aspect of our work improvement can be called the constant reengineering of support processes.

In the context of your daily tasks to produce closed issues and happy customers, the support processes refer to how you do your work as an individual and as part of a support group. They are part of your knowledge and the efficient processes you put in place are a competitive advantage to your technology and your company. This is not to say that the processes you put in place are all formal rules and part of company policy, but rather any processes you utilize in the course of your support work, including the informal ones. We all take customer calls, work the issues, answer the questions, and do our testing plus a number of other tasks. The processes you use need constant revisiting to make sure they are at their optimal level of efficiency. I am not a fan of abstract explanations, so let me give you an example.

I recently led a project to look into a process of marking specific customers as "high priority" sites. I consulted with a colleague who works in the department that determines which customers are placed in this "high category" designation as it had lost some luster in recent years. We looked at the entire process and found that the current process involves a department that adds an average of three days to the site designation but that department adds no real value to the process, support, or the customer. We put together a small committee to reinvent the process and came up with a much shorter, more effective way to get sites designed as "high priority" using an existing infrastructure with more control exerted by the support engineers. We were able to shorten a process that took anywhere from three days to a week into one that takes less than one hour. In a few months, we will look at it again to see if we can improve it even more. This is an example of a formal process.

Informal processes can also be reengineered to save time and increase productivity. For instance, think of the things you do every morning when you come in to work. Is there something that you think could be shortened or improved by just making a few changes? As you learned in "The Above-Average Performer" section, one way to increase efficiency is to automate repetitive tasks. In reengineering personal informal processes, you can look at the non-productive tasks that take time in your day, and see how you can reduce the time they take or eliminate them altogether. One such task that used to take me time to figure out was which issues and clients I had to work on and when. I often found myself trying to remember what I had promised to do and for whom. I would write sticky notes and post them on my monitor, but that just did not work well. I also wrote down a list of the things I promised to do and when, but I often ended up losing the notes and then I spent considerable time trying to remember what I was supposed to do. Then it hit me. I realized that we have Outlook, which has a great calendar tool, so we all use it to set up conference calls, meetings, and other appointments. Now every time I promise to do something or call someone, I enter it in my Outlook calendar and it automatically pops up telling me what I have to do, regardless of whether it is to call a customer, work on an issue, test a scenario, or work with a colleague. This is just a small example of reengineering informal processes used at the individual level that can give us an advantage and form part of our knowledge.

In addition to making process more efficient by revisiting the steps and ridding them of the ones that do not add value or take up too much time, processes in the intellectual fields such as support require that a large part of the decision making is left up to the individual. Take for instance, a production line in any industrial manufacturing setting. The mechanized process carried out by the production staff must be fixed and non-flexible. Otherwise, the end product will not be consistent. Process reengineering in such a setting deals primarily with reduction in time, resources, and defects. However, in intellectual services, the processes must also include leaving the decision making up to the practitioner and to not codify every aspect of the process to the point where it inhibits the creativity and wisdom of the support person. This is a bit hard to explain without going into some examples.

Back in the mid-1980s I took up a summer job at a frozen food factory and started out sweeping the warehouse. After a few weeks, I was promoted to squeezing the button that sprayed tomato sauce on round dough pieces that eventually became pizzas. The entire production line consisted of more than 20 people doing all kinds of tasks. From the guy who put each of the round dough pieces on top of pieces of round cardboard and stacked them, to the tomato sauce button controller (yours truly) who also took each one of those round dough breads and inserted it onto the belt, to the guy who eventually took the boxes of finished pizzas back into a gigantic freezer, there were people doing just about everything you could think of from measuring the little cups of cheese, to the ladies putting on the outer slices of pepperoni. The process demanded exactitude. Any pizza that did not weigh exactly the right number of pounds was rejected. However, there was always a constant: the ingredients for the specific pizza we were making were always identical. All dough pieces were round, all cheese was white and fluffy, and all pepperoni were the exact same size.

The process to make pizzas obviously would be disastrous when doing support work. Despite this, there are support managers who try to codify the way issues are handled, how customers are greeted, and what information is to be gathered from customers. The only problem is that not all customers are fluffy and round, and not all problems are as consistent as tomato sauce. If you leave a pizza production line up to the individual, you will end up with tacos or hamburgers. Nevertheless, if you only provide guidelines and some levels of expectancy to the professional supporters, you will end up with issues in which the professionals are left alone to solve the problems in their own way. Intellectual work is stifled by rigorous guidelines, but flourishes in the midst of personal decision making.

Therefore, look at your current processes, especially the informal ones, and find ways to make them more efficient by removing those steps that take up the most time or do not add to the end product. As a support professional, you are a thinker and the bulk of your work and processes must involve thinking and making your own decisions.

Everyone is born a genius, but the process of living de-geniuses them.

—R. Buckminster Fuller

The Technology Contributor

In the course of your career in support, you will go through several stages. You will start out as a rookie, become familiarized with the technology, turn into the knowledgeable one, and ultimately learn so much that you will grow to be an expert. As an expert, the job changes a bit and will include mentoring others, handling only the hardest of issues, and even being involved in some strategic support planning for the future of the product. These are all great things for an expert to do, but they are still support-related.

If you find yourself at the pinnacle of your technology, then start contributing to your technology by advancing it. Instead of just being the mechanic or the technician, look to become the developer or the engineer within technical support. This is very doable and it is within your reach because you know the ins and outs of your technology. You also know how to use it and how it's used by others, plus the problems they face as well as the shortcomings of your technology. This requires a bit more vision and leadership than just remaining as the static support person who reached a limit and does not want to go any further. It is within the reach of everyone, but not everyone wants to do the reaching.

I am not talking about moving out of support and into development or product management. What I am referring to is the use of your experience and creativity for the advancement of your technology and eventually your company. This is probably not in your job description or in a support manual. This requires quite a bit of initiative and can only be done if you really believe in your product and want the best for its future and your customers. In addition, it also requires a development team that is open to the ideas of technical support, and sees support as a partner rather than just another technical department within the company. I am sure there may be other ways to do what I just described, but this is how I know it works within support.

To become a technology contributor in support you need the following:

- A need or gap in the current technology that is responsible for many of the support issues.

- An original workaround or solution that fixes those issues.

- A development director who is willing to entertain the new feature and incorporate it into the product.

The first thing that support needs in order to contribute to the technology is an answer to a problem of the product. Therefore, identify the most problematic areas of your technology and find a way to answer that necessity. Technical support may or may not be privy to the internal engineering designs of the product. In the software area, technical support may not have access to the source code. Nevertheless, there are still ways to contribute. You just have to have an answer to a pressing question posed regularly by customers. A few years back, I supported a security software product. This software package had a reporting module with dozens of reports. However, customers always seem to ask for one particular report that we did not offer. Given the data stored in the database from which the reports were derived, the report the customers wanted simply did not seem a possibility.

The next thing you will need is a way to resolve those frequent problems or requests from customers. In some technology fields, the development departments move faster than others. If you work for a reseller, your pull with the development department of the vendor may be less than significant. If you work directly for the technology maker, then your influence may be greater. Nevertheless, this is still no guarantee that they will listen to support. Therefore, the thing you need is a proven answer that the problem that customers are having can be solved with your invention or workaround. Sometimes the solution may be simple, highly complex, or even innovative, and thus be something that the development or engineering department may not have thought of.

Going back to my example of the report, I started looking at the problem a little closer and found a way to design a report that pulled from the database the necessary information. With some additional coding within the report itself and some formatting, I came up with a rough report that filled the need the customers had. Since our product had a feature of customizing reports, adding one more report was not a problem. However, this report was requested so much that it really needed to be a part of the actual reporting module.

The last factor needed to contribute to the technology you support as a development engineering director who is open to entertaining your solutions. Of course, I highly recommend that you let your own support managers fight your battles and do not get yourself involved in any politics. If you have enough rapport with your development department, then you could propose it. If it is a solution that can be incorporated into the product and the development people see it, rest assured that it probably will be. Additionally, if your company has a patent program and your new contribution is a patentable idea, be sure to file for a patent. Your company may even offer a monetary award if your contribution becomes a patent. Also, a patent does not have to be invented. It could be just an idea of how to improve a technology. You never know, it could very well happen and it might as well be you. So far, I have filed three patent proposals. None have been accepted by our patent office but I am confident that soon one will be. If nothing else, you will be contributing to the technology you are so passionate about and improving the competitiveness of your company in the process.

The report I created was well received by our development people and ended up as part of the product. You could do the same and much more. All you need is an answer to a customer problem and receptive developers, or at least support managers who believe in your idea and are willing to fight for it. You too can be a contributor and say proudly that such feature exists thanks to you.

One might think that the money value of an invention constitutes its reward to the man who loves his work. But I continue to find my greatest pleasure, and so my reward, in the work that precedes what the world calls success.

—Thomas A. Edison

Recognizing Opportunities

Have you ever seen colleagues who seem to be at the right place at the right time and land some greater achievements? Some even get promotions or advancements based on something that you could have easily done, perhaps even better? Everyone says that you have to recognize when opportunity knocks. The only thing they don't explain is how to recognize the knock. In fact, sometimes opportunity rings the door bell and we miss it because we are waiting for a knock.

What kind of opportunities are we talking about here? I think the opportunity is up to you. Opportunity is one of those things that depend greatly on the eye of the beholder. There are opportunities for all types of things, but it all depends upon what is important to you. For some people it may be a job promotion, more money, a new project, or some other form of career advancement. For other people it may be a way to do work that is more significant or to fulfill an innate interest, goal, or a lifelong dream. Whatever your situation may be, the opportunities are seldom presented to you on silver platters with a label that reads: "opportunity."

In this context, I want to emphasize opportunities that are substantial and will have an impact on you. This is strictly not about petty stuff, but rather things that will make a positive change in your career and your life. Opportunities are recognizable when they have the following characteristics:

- *Attainable*: This means the opportunity is within your reach. This is not a goal or some aspiration. This is a real situation that either crosses your path or you go in pursuit of. For the opportunity to be a good fit, you have to be able to accomplish and manage it.

- *Beneficial*: The fulfilling or attaining of the opportunity must bring some benefit to you, your career, your work, and your company. In personal terms, it must also bring some benefit to you as a person.

- *Interesting*: You have to have an interest in the opportunity. Otherwise, it just a prospect that is not for you. It has to fulfill you in some way.

- *Transforming*: The opportunity must also have the capacity to change you in some positive way. This is more than just a benefit but refers to a real transformation in the way you think, work, and are perceived by others. It can also refer to the impact you will have on your work, technology, and company.

Obviously, not all things that come your way are real opportunities. Some may be quite the opposite disguised as a good prospect. For instance, someone offers you the possibility to learn by participating in a project. However, is it a real opportunity or just a way to get you to work more? Of course, I don't suggest that you don't volunteer for extra work or anything of the sort. I am just strictly trying to explain what a real opportunity is and how to recognize it.

First of all, it has to be attainable by you in your present situation. In Texas, we like trucks. Truck salespeople know this and they usually take us for a ride, both figuratively and literally. You often see parking lots in Texas full of trucks whose owners bought with the idea that they were going to do something with it and just never did. I have a coworker who bought a truck with a towing package because he was planning on getting a boat. He never bought the boat but he has a truck with a towing package. The towing package was not an opportunity but rather the work of a skilled salesperson.

Consequently, the prospect presented must be attainable in the sense that you have the current credentials or capabilities to achieve it. For most of us, the change to qualify for the Olympics is not an opportunity, its pie in the sky. If someone offers you a job in software development but you don't have any programming skills, it may not be an opportunity unless you at least have the capacity to learn programming fast and the offer comes with the understanding that you will learn on the job.

The opportunity must also be beneficial, mainly to you. If there is nothing in it for you, then why would you take such offer? If there is some future possibility of obtaining some benefit, then it may qualify as a good opportunity. But be sure that it's a good chance and also that you don't leave a sure thing for a mere possibility. The benefit is also very subjective. What you view as a benefit may not be what someone else views as something good. Generally, anything that is attainable and will allow you to advance your skills, experience, visibility, or pay is probably an opportunity you should consider going for. If you get an offer of a promotion for a job no one else wants, that may be a sign that it's not a good opportunity, unless you can somehow benefit from it.

Why would you do something that is not interesting to you? If you don't have an interest in it, if it doesn't fulfill you in some intellectual or professional way, then it's not a good opportunity. You are more likely to be successful at something that you find interesting and stimulating than something you find monotonous. Even if a new project or position pays more, is attainable by you and would seem like a dream come true to most, if you don't have an interest in it, then don't do it. You would probably regret it. Life is too short to do things you don't enjoy and don't find some fulfillment in. One of my colleagues was offered a director position within technical support. He did not take it. For anyone else, it seemed like the perfect opportunity to advance and potentially do something better, maybe even make more money. However, it did not interest my colleague. He was more interested in working in supporting his technology. Becoming a director may have been interesting to some but not to him.

Finally, the opportunity has to be transforming in some way. If it's a chance to pick up a new technology to support and it will add to your arsenal of knowledge and expertise, then it may be a good opportunity. If it's a training session which includes stuff you already know, then it's probably something you should pass up. As support professionals, our work is repetitive. We take issues, solve them, and go on to the next issue. The issues vary but in a way, they are always the same. Transforming opportunities may seem like they would not be abundant in our line of work, but in fact they are. The project that requires volunteers may allow you the opportunity to learn something new that will dramatically change the way you do your work now. The class in some technique or aspect of technology may allow you to be better support customers. One that was very transforming for me was the university that came to our company and set up a small table in the cafeteria to give out information about their programs. I picked up a brochure and found they offered a PhD program for working people. After reading more about it, I found that it had all the four characteristics. It was attainable, beneficial, interesting and transforming.

Technical support may not seem like a field of opportunities, but it really is. Going for the right opportunity can take you very far and choosing the wrong one may end your career. Next time something comes your way, make sure you are able to recognize if it's a good opportunity that you shouldn't pass up or just someone trying to dump some work on your lap.

One dreamed of becoming somebody; another remained awake and became.

—Anonymous

The Approachable Expert

Do you remember how you learned the ropes when you started in support? Remember how hard you had it, and how long it took you to find out stuff when you had doubts? Remember when training was a foreign concept and you had to learn everything on your own, even as you had a customer on the phone waiting for an answer? If you had a hard time and don't want to live through those days again, what makes you think your less experienced colleagues want to go through the same thing?

You are about to learn one of my pet peeves. I have a disdain in my heart for experts who live in an ivory tower and are not approachable to less-experienced colleagues. The type of expert who takes pride because "he doesn't have to talk to customers" and makes you do all the running around, acting like a messenger between the customer and "his eminence," the expert.

We are in technical support because we like to be of service. We exist to help and make a positive change to others when it comes to our technology. Our regard for service must start internally and with our own colleagues. As you become an expert, it is very easy and comfortable to get on your horse, stop being of service, and just become a bouncing wall where others can get instant feedback. There is nothing wrong with that. The problem comes when you stop being helpful to your less-experienced colleagues and instead put them through stress on purpose with excuses that you would never give your customers. Examples are:

- "I had to go through the same thing when I started."

- "You are supposed to know this by now."

- "You have asked this question before, go look it up."

- "You need to think outside the box."

- "You got a manual and a lab, figure it out."

The expert sometimes even refuses to answer questions made by less-experienced colleagues, and can even go so far as to require that all questions made to him be in a specific format and accompanied by everything the rookie did up to that point, including all relevant accompanying documentation and logs. Does this sound familiar? I cannot imagine I am the only unlucky one that this has happened to. I am not proposing that there should be some guidelines for mentorship, but some experts take it to the extreme and seem annoyed when someone does not know the answer. I have done the same myself when I was the expert and deeply regret it. It was only when I became more experienced and was in a position where I could see other experts and how they treated the first-level support people that I realize that the expert has a huge responsibility that goes beyond being technical.

I propose that the expert, specialist, upper tier or whatever you call the top support people in your company adhere to the following:

- Treat the lower level support people as internal customers.

- Give quick answers when asked for quick answers.

- Explain fully or demonstrate how to find the answer when appropriate.

- Be proactive in helping, rather than reactive.

When I refer to someone as an expert, I am talking to a person within technical support. Also, I specifically mean the person with the title matching their level of knowledge; for example, a Technical Support Specialist, third-level support, or just someone whose title is higher up on the ladder of support titles. I am not referring to the frontline person who happens to be very knowledgeable or experienced, but rather to the person whose job it is to help the less experienced or lower-support-level colleagues.

The person whose job it is to provide answers and mentoring to other colleagues should treat the colleagues he is helping as internal customers. There has to be a formal sense of duty, not a feeling that he is doing a favor. You, as the expert, must bring others up to your level. It won't always work but you have to try. However, your colleagues have to know they can approach you, Otherwise, they will feel like they are bothering you. If you push them away, they won't come back. You will be the expert who refused to help them and they may resent you for a long time.

Also, people come to you when and because they need you. Let's face it, technical problems are not the hot topics of conversation we may think they are. Lower-level colleagues come to you when their customers are asking them for the answers, or, they wouldn't ask. Be sure to answer them. It may seem like you will be doing this for a long time, and you may think that those colleagues will grow overly dependent on you. This may happen until they mature in their support practices and realize they have enough experience to do it on their own. This transformation happens and it happens faster when they have someone to learn from. Therefore, answer their questions when they ask. No reproach, criticism, or rebuke. Also, as I told many of the experts in my organization in the past, if you are asked a direct question, give a direct answer. If you know the answer, don't beat around the bush, just answer it.

If your colleague has a problem with a customer and is stuck, or you see that he or she is going in the wrong direction, take the time to fully explain and, better yet, show your colleague how it's done and any pitfalls involved. Be sure to point out their mistakes and explain how to avoid them. They will learn better if you explain it to them in a friendly way where they can ask questions and dispel any doubts. They will appreciate not appearing like an idiot in front of a customer. Trust me, customers can tell when we don't know our stuff. They may not always point it out, but they know.

If you sit close to your colleague and you see him having a hard time with an issue, offer to get on a conference call with the customer and help him solve the problem. Both your colleague and the customer will appreciate you. It will also serve as a lesson and you can be sure that, the next time the same situation occurs, the lower level support person will know how to handle the problem. When I helped colleagues in this manner, I usually asked them to make a Frequently Asked Question (FAQ) out of it and post it where others could get benefit from it. This will provide the person you just helped with a written record and may even boost their self-esteem. Also, when someone else has the same question, ask the first person you helped to take the "expert" role and see if he can do the same thing you did.

The last thing you need to get in the habit of as the support expert in your technology is to be proactive in your approach to helping others. I don't mean to just tell them that you have an "open door" policy, but rather to act like the door-to-door salesman and pursue those who need help. Actively ask your less experienced colleagues if they have any issues they need help on and just help them. This works wonders and may give that shy person a way to speak up and allow you to coach them through the issue. I used to have this approach mainly because my group was global and I only had one colleague in the same physical location where I was. I would make the habit of asking different colleagues every day if they had any issues they were stuck on. Some would pass and some took me up on the offer. I always had a blast helping them through issues and seeing how different their levels of expertise, even though their job titles and years of experience were similar.

In our young discipline, we need to stimulate collaboration—not just lip service—but true attempts at helping each other work as a team so that we can provide better support to our customers and more value to our companies. Collaboration also helps lighten our loads as each one of us works smarter. The expert must not be someone sitting in an ivory tower looking over everyone else. The expert must be a person who is not afraid to get involved in issues with customers and less-experienced colleagues. Remember, just because we had a hard time getting to where we are doesn't mean others have to suffer as much.

...If you want to be great, you must be the servant of all the others.

—Mark 10:43 (Contemporary English Version)

PART 2

■ ■ ■

Working with Others

In this part, we will look at the way technical support people work with each other. There are sections dealing with groups, colleagues, leadership, and the way we interact and use each. We will explore concepts and ideas dealing with the way groups add value to support and individuals. Though the ideas presented may or may not fit your situation exactly, they should be close enough for you to make use of them and apply the concepts to your own support practices.

Group or Team: Which Is It?

Unless you work in a very small support organization, chances are you have colleagues you work with on a regular basis. People who do the same type of work you do and with whom you share the workload or different aspects of customer support. However, before we jump into a proper discussion about working within a support organization comprised of colleagues, it is important to understand the type of organization you work in. Let us start with the cluster of people closest to you: the collective you are a part of who you call colleagues. Is this collection of support people a team or a group?

We all use the words "team" and "group" interchangeably, but there are distinctions documented in management theory.

A group is defined as two or more employees who interact with each other in such a manner that the behavior and/or performance of a member is influenced by the behavior and/or performance of other members.[1] This describes a collective of individuals who work together and whose successes or failures affect the success or failure of others in the same collective. The work involved is long-term operational work. There are two types of formal groups: task and command. (Some informal groups exist and will be discussed in the Informal Groups topic later in this chapter.)

A team is a type of group that exists to carry out a specific goal or task such as a project.[2] A team may not be operational in nature and the team members do not carry out the same task. In a team, all the members are equally responsible for the success of the goal or task. There are three types of teams: problem solving, cross functional, and self-directed.[3]

The command group is one that exists because of organizational structure and is what appears on organizational charts. The group members report to the same manager and may have similar duties. An example of this type of group in a technical support environment would be a support group that supports a technology in which all members are taking issues from different customers. The group members all report to one manager or supervisor in a formal capacity. Most typical support groups fall in this category.

The task group is one that exists for carrying out a specific goal or task, such as working a support issue from start to finish and ensuring problem resolution as well as customer satisfaction. An example would be a support group comprised of both junior and expert supporters. The junior supporters take the issue to a certain level and then request help from the expert supporters who may do additional testing, further troubleshooting, and work with the junior people to resolve the problem. The work performed by each member is different, but the result is common to both. Not every task group is a team because of the operational nature of the work. The main difference is the responsibility of the members. Only in a team are all the members collectively responsible for the successful completion of the assignment.

The problem-solving team is usually a short-term task group formed to solve some predicament that an organization or a customer is facing. An example would be a team formed to solve an installation gone wrong at a customer site. The team may be comprised of people from different groups or from within the same group. The team only lasts for the duration of the problem. When the team resolves the problem, the members go back to their regular jobs and the team breaks up.

The cross-functional team is made up of members of different functional groups that come together to carry out some task, usually a project. The members all bring together their expertise in areas such as

---

[1] Marvin E. Shaw, *Group Dynamics* (New York: McGraw Hill, 1981).

[2] J.R. Katzenbach and D.K. Smith, *The Wisdom of Teams* (Boston: The Harvard Business School Press, 1993).

[3] James L. Gibson, John M. Ivancevich, James H. Donnelly, *Organizations* (New York: McGraw Hill, 1997).

development, technical support, marketing, technical writing, sales, etc.. The objective of having a team of people from different departments is to shorten the time it takes to complete the project.

The self-directed team does the work and the management, but without formal managers. The team members manage the team and its functions, such as duties and tasks by committee. This constitutes a very different approach to group dynamics and works quite well when the members are mature and trust each other. The self-directed team must ideally consist of mostly seasoned support people for this to work in our highly demanding profession. Having entry level members in such a group may not work as effectively as with more mature employees who already know the work and can check the quality of their team members.

Working among peers comes naturally to technical support personnel. The support work may need individual effort but this often takes place within a group environment. The type of group has an effect on the way the group views the individual member and vice-versa. It also has a big effect on how the group views management and the work as well as responsibilities and alliances. As a support person, the more you understand the group, the better you will understand yourself and your role within the group. When the individual support group members know how the support group should function, it makes it possible for the advancement of the group as a whole and for synergic forces to work.

Is there an ideal type of group to work in? I firmly believe the type of group matters, but I also think that it is more important for the individual group members to be aware and understand how the group should function in order for the group to succeed. The first step is to understand the type of group and whether or not it is truly a team.

Consequently, a team is not necessarily better than an individually-responsible task group or worse than a command group. It all depends on the task and how committed the members are to the group or team. A command group will work much better in situations in which numbers are needed. Take for instance a call center where all the calls are for a less-complex technology, where the objective is to take as many calls as quickly as possible. A command group with a manager who directs reports will work better in this type of work situation. Everyone does the same task and is responsible for the number of calls taken and closed. On the other hand, if this is a call center that supports extremely complex technologies, such as an enterprise software application with many modules, then a task group may work better. Each member specializes in a portion of the technology and all members work together to work the issues, and then pass them to the next expert, if necessary. The goal is to solve complex issues together; however, each member is responsible for their own portion of the support. The smaller groups of supporters who specialize in the same specific portion of the complex technology may be a team. They may work together and are jointly responsible for the closure of issues and solution of problems.

Working in a group is a great way for support people to get things done, and makes our job more interesting as we have others to learn from as well as teach. Understanding some fundamental aspects of groups and teams will make us well-rounded support people and allow us to function better within our respective groups.

No man is an island, entire of itself.

—John Donne from *Devotions Upon Emergent Occasions*, Meditation XVII

Informal Groups

Just about every support person works within a group. The group may be local or virtual but it would be unusual to have a support department of only one person. I have seen such situations, but only in very small companies with a handful of clients. Therefore, they are hardly the norm. Whenever you have people working together in close proximity, you will also have personal preferences for affiliation.

Friendships will develop in which a given person will prefer to hang around some other person, and so forth. The individuals engaged in these relationships form informal groups that are not sanctioned or structured formally by the technical support organization. Understanding why such groups form, and how they associate, will allow you to work better within the overall formal group and gain appreciation for the informal groups.

You probably see informal connections among individuals in your own technical support environment. There are people who tend to congregate or socialize with one another based on some interest or social characteristic. There are the younger guys who like to socialize, have lunch together, and even get together after work for a drink; the women who go to lunch together every Friday, or the men who like to hang around at each other's cube to talk about their new lawnmower or the work they are doing to their house. These are examples of informal social forces that have an effect on the way the work carries out, sometimes reaching the level of political maneuvering within the formal technical support groups.

Informal groups form naturally and are shaped by the need for humans to affiliate. Some of those social attractions include:

- Interests

- Friendship

- Social similarities

- Personal similarities

It is a fact that people with similar interests will orbit each other. After all, people like to talk and hear about things that interest them. Dog lovers like to hang around other dog owners, people with kids like other parents, and so forth. I, for one, like to talk endlessly about ranching and farming. I would like nothing more than to have long conversations over lunch about the proper technique to castrate a calf, raise heifers, or the best way to lubricate a tractor, but someone with no interest in ranching may not want to talk about such a subject during lunch.

Inevitably, people will become friends while working in a group. Such work friendships are very tight relationships, and when enough people become friends, the individuals become an informal group (friends) within a formal group (tech support group). You can always tell the friends from the mere colleagues. The friends bring each other stuff from home or give cards during Christmas, share lunch with each other, and do the sort of things that friends are supposed to do. Of course, this lends itself much better to local groups. Virtual groups also form friendships that can be just as strong as "in-person" friendships. I know people who I never met personally but who I consider close friends, people for who I would stick my neck out, yet have no idea what they look like.

The relationship based on social similarities is to some (not to me) one of the most obvious types of relationship to decipher; for example, the women colleagues who recently had children, the single-parent guys, the colleagues who live in apartments, etc. People socialize with others who share similar social characteristics. Yet the informal group bond formed by these individuals is not as strong as other informal groups, because they are based on characteristics beyond the immediate control of the individuals.

The most intriguing type of informal group is the one formed by individuals with similar personal characteristics. These characteristics are intrinsic to the individuals and completely under their control. These include features such as a contrarian nature, high inquisitiveness, high intelligence, modesty, introversion, and any other personal characteristic that may attract individuals to each other. When you observe individuals engaged in informal groups, this type is very captivating because it's amazing to see how similar individuals steer toward each other.

Why do we care about informal groups? Informal groups are important because they help keep the formal structure together even though they exist for the mere benefit of their members. Informal groups meet a very fundamental need of their members, the need to congregate and affiliate with like-minded individuals. Informal groups simply answer a human need for social interaction and association.[4]

When working in a formal group, you may notice that there is a lot of activity around a smaller subset within the formal group. The activity may be social or functional, such as non-work-related conversations or work cooperation among certain colleagues. The dynamics that you see happening within the formal group may, in fact, be an informal group functioning within the larger formal group. Informal groups affecting their larger formal group are not necessarily something to avoid. Sometimes good ideas and positive actions come out of a small group who gathered informally over lunch or a break to talk about work. Some of the ideas for topics in this book came out of such a group.

Sometimes an informal group exerting influence over the formal group can be detrimental to those who are not members of the informal group. Informal groups who are negative, anti-management, or simply not in line with the goals of the formal group will tend to destabilize the formal group, and may end up causing harm. I used to work in a formal group in which there were three members who were extremely negative about anything that management had to say. I sincerely do not think they meant to do any harm or were negative out of malice. It was just their personal characteristics or personality, but they were detrimental to the rest of the formal group.

Informal groups are an essential part of any collective and will form naturally given enough time. They are the glue that holds the formal groups together and keep the individuals engaged and interested. It is to your advantage to learn to identify the informal groups and the basis of their affiliation. Once you figure out how individuals socialize and associate, you will gain an advantage to help the formal groups solve its challenges.

Give every man thine ear, but few thy voice; take each man's censure but reserve thy judgement.

—William Shakespeare

What's So Good About Groups Anyway?

People generally gravitate toward like-minded individuals. Some like to hang around people similar to themselves and with the same personal characteristics. Formally, support people are usually grouped into functional products managed by a supervisor or team leader. What is the benefit of having a group over not having one?

Formal command and task groups are formed because of economies of scale.[5] Economies of scale is a term used in economics to describe the added efficiency when the production increases (the more gadgets produced, the cheaper the cost per gadget because of mass production). This concept also applies to specialized labor, such as technical support. The more people that learn to support a product, the less it costs per individual support issue. Additionally, unless the workload is very light, one person cannot do it alone. Technical support organizations need enough people to provide help to high numbers of customers and so on. We all know this. This is logic. What we may not know is that groups provide a much bigger benefit to the organization than just a composite of labor units. Groups alter the

---

[4] Kerwyn K. Smith and David N. Berg, *Paradoxes of Group Life* (San Francisco: Jossey-Bass, 1987).
[5] "economies of scale." *The American Heritage® Dictionary of the English Language, Fourth Edition.* Houghton Mifflin Company, 2004. 19 Jul. 2009. <Dictionary.com `http://dictionary.reference.com/browse/economies of scale`>.

motivation, needs, and initiative of the individual. This is also more than just synergy, the combined effect being greater than the sum of the parts.[6] This is organizational behavior in action.

The presence of a group, formal or informal, provides motivation in the form of stimulus and support to the individuals, which they would not otherwise have. Group motivation does not take the form of simple mental attitude. It involves a lot more, ranging from social behaviors absent in lone individuals to competitiveness that force and entice achievement. The lone individual in a support organization made up of just one has no peers to compete with, no motivation to excel against a group, and no stimulus to do better than anyone else. The absence of a benchmark keeps the individual more stagnant than if the individual were part of a group. Think of it like this, if you are alone doing a task there is little incentive to outpace yourself. The lack of colleagues to compare and pace yourself against may result in lethargy and diminished potential. Even the Lone Ranger was not so alone; he had Tonto to work with.

Specifically, how do groups alter the motivation of its individual members? Motivation is the psychological feature that arouses an organism to action toward a desired goal—the reason for the action, and that which gives purpose and direction to behavior.[7] In other words, being in a group makes you want to do things, more so than if you were alone. Think back to when you were the only one doing a task. Did it not feel cruddy to be alone with no one to bounce ideas off of and no one to share opinions and suggestions about the work? The group solves that problem by having others to share the fortunes or misfortunes of the delegated tasks assigned to the group.

A group also acts as a support system that allows the individual to develop the behavior to want to do the work. Behavior is a very difficult thing to alter alone. Behavior is the way you respond to something or act in specific situations or in response to others.[8] Can you imagine how hard it would be to want to slack off while working in a group? The other group members would surely point out your inability to carry your own weight. Aside from group pressures that mold behavior, there are also group dynamics that create certain behaviors out of the group itself, behaviors that were not present in individuals. For instance, the typical technical support group will have someone who is a mentor and who strives to show others the way to do or learn something via this type of group behavior. There will also be someone who may be the shoulder to cry on and who group members favor to confide professional, and possibly, even personal problems to. Look around in your group and find individuals with very specific behaviors who would not have them had it not been for the mere existence of the group.

The group also alters the needs for the individual members. As mentioned before, individuals in a group receive the motivation and challenge to work. For many, working in a group is more motivating than going it alone. This is especially true for highly demanding work such as technical support. However, the individual doing technical support also has specific resource and technical needs, which are met better by the group. Can you imagine trying to find all the answers by yourself? Working in a big enough group allows for most needs to be met within the group. The biggest command group I worked in had over seventy members. We had experts on just about anything. There was hardly any question, problem, or doubt that someone else had not already encountered. When the group meets the basic

---

[6] Dictionary.com. "Synergy." *The American Heritage® Dictionary of the English Language, Fourth Edition.* Houghton Mifflin Company, 2004. `http://dictionary.reference.com/browse/synergy` (accessed: December 11, 2008).

[7] Dictionary.com. "Motivation." *WordNet® 3.0,* Princeton University. `http://dictionary.reference.com/browse/motivation` (accessed: December 11, 2008).

[8] Dictionary.com. "Behavior." *Webster's Revised Unabridged Dictionary.* MICRA, Inc. `http://dictionary.reference.com/browse/behavior` (accessed: December 11, 2008).

knowledge needs, the individual members can start the process of reaching the next stage in their careers, enabling the group to progress. Thus, the needs of the group members are met and new needs develop to advance the group as well as individual careers.

Another very peculiar thing happens in groups that do not happen to mere individuals acting alone. Some individuals begin to gravitate toward informal positions of leadership. Leadership can take many forms but always has individual initiative at its foundation. This initiative aims to influence in some way the behavior or actions of the group. Some aspiring group members tend to become the technical leaders of the group. These experts take the initiative to be at the forefront of the group in matters dealing with the technology supported. Other individuals take the initiative to establish themselves as the ones who guide the group to make decisions or reach consensus. The leaders are political in nature and lead without authority through democratic means and with exceptional judgment. There are also the servant leaders who do things for others out of their desire to serve.[9] These initiatives would not be possible were it not for the existence of the group. In fact, it is possible to go so far as to argue that civilization would not exist without groups.[10]

Groups are an integral part of our work in technical support for many reasons. Companies have command groups for financial, administrative, as well as organizational purposes. However, groups take a life of their own and alter the behaviors and needs of the group members in ways that would be impossible without the group. Knowing and understanding the benefits of the group on our work lives allow us to better utilize them and make the best of the role we play within the group.

We must remember that one determined person can make a significant difference, and that a small group of determined people can change the course of history.

—Sonia Johnson, feminist, activist, and writer

Groups: What's In It for the Individual?

In technical support, as in just about any other profession or collective of individuals bound by some reason to form groups, the individuals must get something tangible and practical out of the group interaction. There are clear benefits to the organization, the group itself, and the customers. What about the individual? What does he get out of it? We know individuals gain motivation, needs, and initiative from being in a group but that is not all we gain. Let us look at some of the more tangible and immediate benefits that come from being in a group. These are:

- Context
- Security
- Information

Context gives you the ability to adapt to a situation rapidly based on observing others. If you have ever taken a new job with a new company, you realized that watching others has its benefits. Things

[9] Robert Greenleaf, *Servant Leadership, A Journey into the Nature of Legitimate Power & Greatness* (New Jersey: Paulist Press, 1977).
[10] Bridget Allchin, Origins of a Civilization: The Prehistory and Early Archaeology of South Asia (New York: Viking, 1997).

come at you so fast that it's not practical to remember every single piece of information you are told at orientation, or during the initial tour of your new company. This is where context comes in. Observing fellow group members allows you to learn faster than any type of training. Kids are great at this. You drop off a stressed out five-year-old on the first day of kindergarten, but at the end of the day when you pick the kid up, he knows everything about his new environment and his group. As adults, we learn the same way. The individual benefits from the group by learning to adapt to the new culture.

Recently, I saw an example of group context in my own family. My wife volunteers at a local hospital, but for some time she wanted to do her volunteer work in another department. She found out the name and location of that department's administrator, spoke with the administrator, yet did not seem to get anywhere. She tried again and the same thing happened. She stepped back and paid more attention to how people get things done and realized her colleagues went about it completely differently. It appeared that in order to gain acceptance by a person of authority, you have to be introduced by someone with some seniority at the hospital. She noticed that when her colleagues wanted some approval or admittance, they would summon a more senior group member and ask for an introduction. She tried this and succeeded where she failed previously, all because she learned from the context provided by the group. An individual also gains security from a group.[11] Just like in the wild where prey animals tend to find security in numbers, humans also find security in a group. The benefit to the individual lies in the perceived threat from managers, customers, and even other group members. The individual needs support that only the group can provide. In technical support, there are many threats and because we deal heavily in both the technical and the social aspects of service, the threats double.

To better understand this, let's look at an example that happened at the small company where I worked during the late 1990s. When a much bigger company acquired the smaller company we still remained a separate office with our own technology and were pretty much left alone. We were less than 20 strong in the entire US operation: only three of us in technical support, five in sales, two in channel sales, another two in marketing, and a few others doing administrative office work. We received word that the company that owned us was in talks about being acquired by a larger company. Rumors started flying about whether we would be affected, and if the bigger company would even keep us since there were support people in that company already and several competing technologies. I'd gone through a similar acquisition two years prior and had not fared so well; therefore, I was nervous. The companies involved in the acquisition did not say anything while everything was being finalized, which added to the anxiety. In this situation, it was the group that provided psychological support to the individuals. The sales people told everyone that we generated enough sales to be profitable to anyone acquiring us. The marketing people told everyone else that we were a leader in the industry and it would be insane to get rid of our technology or any people involved with it. We were very fortunate that the individual members of that group were positive and kept each other going during times of uncertainty. In the end, things turned out fine for everyone and we continued working well together. The support and security of the group does wonders in time of need.

The last big benefit that the individual derives from the group is the sharing of information. This information can take many forms and can have many purposes. As mentioned previously, the technical support group deals with both technical and social aspects. In the technical realm, we have information ranging from the minute technical details about the technology supported to the information about new releases and advancements in the product. The same goes for the people side of things. When one member speaks with a customer and there is something notable about the interaction, that individual will probably share the information with the group. Hence, the efforts of the group are really bigger than that of the individual members acting alone. These synergic forces enable the group to advance and

---

[11] P.K. Lunt, "The Perceived Causal Structure of Loneliness," *Journal of Personality and Social Psychology*, July 1991, p. 26–34.

individuals to prosper, potentially learning much more than if the individuals acted alone. Since we deal with technical aspects, this knowledge literally gives us the power to do our jobs better. When the group finds and shares information as an entity acting with different parts, the individuals benefit by the efforts of each other as a group.

The benefits of being part of a group are tangible and go far beyond the abstract. The abstract benefits such as motivation and initiative are important but the real question is, "What is in it for me?" Well, there is a lot in it for you. As long as your group is not dysfunctional in some way, you should get many real benefits out of being in a group. I only discussed three of them: context, security, and information, but there are more and they are there for the benefit of all the group members. Some of the other benefits are having someone to socialize with, the internal assurance of being part of a collective, and simply having someone to cover for you when you need to leave early for the day. Next time you find yourself within your group, observe and you will see the treasure you have at your fingertips.

Insanity in individuals is something rare—but in groups, parties, nations and epochs, it is the rule.

—Friedrich Nietzsche

The Vision of a Group

The success of the group and its impact on the overall organization depends on how well it performs and delivers some benefit to the company, customers, group members, and any other constituents with a vested interest in the group. The group's existence and its success depend greatly on the collective vision and how well the group lives up to that vision.

What is a group vision? It is very simply the act or power of anticipating that which will or may come to be.[12] The vision is the ideal picture that the group strives to become. Quite simply, the vision for the group is the bliss that the members see in their future. This image drives the actions and behaviors of the group. It is not a goal, but a purpose, an aspiration that the collective intends to live by. A vision is not a convoluted, abstract idea that requires an MBA to understand but is described in simple terms and with vivid imagery. Have you ever heard someone or some group say that their vision, or mission statement, is to reach full operational efficiency for the advancement of a brand? That type of abstract vision does not tell you anything other than they want to get better at something. A good example is Coca Cola's vision in regard to employees: "Being a great place to work where people are inspired to be the best they can be."[13]

Sometimes, it is hard for an individual to define a personal vision. How then can a group of individuals develop collective vision? Before we answer the bigger question of how to reach consensus on a vision that will satisfy all the individual members of the group, first we need to know what a vision is and what it is not. Vision is what drives the group and sets the ground for the actions and behaviors of the members. A vision has distinct characteristics in a group. In our case, we will apply it strictly to the

---

[12] Dictionary.com. "Vision." Random House, Inc., `http://dictionary.reference.com/browse/vision` (accessed: December 18, 2008).

[13] `http://www.thecoca-colacompany.com/ourcompany/mission_vision_values.html` (accessed: December 18, 2008).

formal technical support groups and the informal groups formed by the technical support professionals. The following are the main characteristics of a vision as it applies to a group:

- Communal

- Realistic

- Actionable

- Ongoing

- Transformational

A vision is not the same as a goal. The vision is similar to a personal life purpose but for a group. It lays the foundation for the strategic long-term decisions and actions. The vision is not something that will eventually be reached and thus completed, but rather the light-in-the-night that will allow the group to reach many goals and find its way when decisions become hard to make or when the group faces dilemmas.

A group vision must be communal. Communally-reached, agreed on, or shared visions ensure that no members are outside the vision. It would do the group no good to have one of the individuals in the group mastermind a vision for the whole group if the group does not share it. In informal and self-managed groups, the vision must come from the group members as a whole; otherwise, the members may not buy into it. This concept of a communally-reached vision is not the same as rebellion against the group's formal management nor does it suggest an anarchical approach to group consensus as applied to vision. The management in a technical support organization provides the goals and performance expectations as well as the metrics by which to measure the performance of the group. However, management directives are not the same as a group's vision and do not tell the group how to behave collectively. For instance, the vision for a support group may be to provide the best help possible in a reasonable time. Such a vision is only possible if the group members agree as to what "possible" and "reasonable" means; otherwise, the vision will result in confusion and prove detrimental to the group.

The vision in a technical support group, as well as any other group, must be realistic. It has to be within the reach of the group and within the limits of the organization. As discussed, the vision is the image of what the group wants to become, but the group must agree on a vision that will not be irrational or impossible to follow. For example, if the support group deals with a technology that is too complex or dynamic, the vision cannot be to make the technology simpler. A group that has most of its members close to retirement should probably have a different vision than a group of people just out of college or high school.

The vision must be actionable. Group members need a vision that is within their power to implement. A vision that lacks this characteristic is nothing more than a noble idea beyond the limit of what the group members can reach. Take the example of an elite group of engineers in a support organization. They developed the vision that the group will influence the rest of the support organization in doing everything that helps advance technical support and the skills of individual support people. This is actionable because it is within their reach as support people. It would be a different story if their vision included improving the sales organization. That is outside of their realm and therefore not actionable.

Possibly the most important aspects of a group's vision is to make it ongoing. A vision is not a fad or the strategy of the weak. It should be at the core of the group members' culture and belief system, and as such cannot be temporary. The vision is not something the group reaches, but something the group lives by, and a philosophy under which the group chooses to conduct business. Since a vision is an enduring belief and modus operandi, it requires simplicity. Making a vision so complex that it makes the members have to think too hard dilutes the vision and eventually the members run the risk of forgetting the whole thing. Therefore, for a vision to remain constant it has to be simple enough to adhere to, but powerful enough to live by. Technical support practitioners must choose a vision that is not subject to a technology or a type of management; otherwise, the vision may be affected by changes in either. Continuous learning is the ideal medium for keeping the vision ongoing.[14] By making learning and development part of the vision, the group ensures that there is always relevance to the vision as the members are constantly updated.

So far, we have not clearly mentioned the "why" of a vision. Up to this point we discussed what it is, what it is not, and four aspects the vision must have to be effective. The last one answers the question of the direct benefits of the vision upon the group. The whole purpose of having a vision is to guide the behavior of the group for transformation from a present state to a desired state. It is the institutionalizing of desired behaviors in the shared culture that embodies the whole purpose of the vision. A vision has to be transformational and bring the benefit of joined efforts to the ongoing results experienced by the group members. A vision that is not inherently transformational does not do much good since the group simply remains in its present state and no evolution results from the endeavor. The picture the group forms from itself must be different from the present. The vision helps the group move toward the attitudes and behaviors desired that the members consider ideal. This is why it is a vision and why the efforts are worth the effort. The support group adopts a vision to help it close more issues, become more relevant to customers, improve the cooperation among members, and utilize resources at a more efficient level.. The point is that a group does not develop a vision to remain the same; it does it to change and improve.

Groups develop a vision to guide their actions and behaviors. The dynamics of a support group, composed of technology, people, and service requires a vision to give the members the ideal picture to guide the members. Without the collective image of what should be, the group will not develop its full potential. It will be like travelling without a map or trying to build a castle without a blueprint. Success will come to those support groups that know where they want to go and have a good idea of what their future should be.

The bravest are surely those who have the clearest vision of what is before them, glory and danger alike, and yet notwithstanding, go out to meet it.

—Thucydides

Group Communication

Technical support is in the business of knowledge and answers. The members of the group impart solutions to customers, solve issues, and come across ideas that the group as a whole finds beneficial. Since knowledge and solutions are our business, the more knowledge and solutions we have, the better we are as individuals and therefore as a group.

Communication is a vast academic and professional field with many theories and models. However, in this context we are concerned with communication as it relates to group cooperation and collaboration. Individuals in a group sharing information foster a unified awareness that make it possible for the group members to move forward and develop that awareness to its fullest. The challenge in a support group is reaching unified awareness through communication in a timely fashion. Given that technology is dynamic, the timely dissemination of information across the group members means the difference between the group acting in unanimity to get the solutions to customers and the chaotic environment that results when group members are unaware of findings by their peers. Improper

---

[14] Strasmore, Martin. 2007. "Strategies to create leadership development." *Fairfield County Business Journal*, 2007, 22. *Regional Business News*, EBSCO*host* (accessed: December 22, 2008).

communication in a support group minimizes synergy and prevents customers getting timely solutions for their support issues.

The communication in a technical support group has more challenges than other types of groups because of the rapid change in information and new advancements in the technology, which can vary greatly depending on the group. The three main communication models in a technical support group are:

- *Parallel Communication Model*: This is the type of group communication in which the group members exchange information real time and in person or with the use of technology, such as voice and video conference. Examples of this type of communication are face-to-face group meetings, but can also include less formal means such as discussions among the group when they are in close proximity.

- *Non-Parallel Communication Model:* This is group communication where the members share information with a delay such as via email distribution lists or an online forum. The group members share replies and advancement to the original posting.

- *Event Driven Model:* This model occurs when the individuals in a group share communication only when an event happens and the event triggers the need to communicate the information. This type of communication is one way and does not elicit a response, as is the case with the Non-Parallel Communication Model. An example of this communication occurs when an individual finds a defect in the technology and communications it to the rest of the group.

The ideal situation is for a technical support group to utilize all three models with frequency. One of the models may constitute the predominant form of communication depending on the structure, size, and dispersion of the group members. Smaller, localized groups depend primarily on the Parallel Communication Model. However, globally dispersed support groups with members in different time zones will inevitably use the Non-Parallel Communication Model as their primary source of group communication.

Yet, all groups have some form of the Event Driven Model because this is the natural context of technical support. When a support person encounters a new problem or solution of some significance, the inclination is to communicate it to the rest of the group. When the events that trigger the Event Driven Model become too many, they may become disruptive. When this happens, the events that trigger the Event Driven Model naturally become the type of information that comprises the agenda for the Parallel Communication Model. In other words, when the notices of new problems or solutions become so many that they disrupt the normal course of business, the group should set up a special meeting to review these new discoveries. Furthermore, the absence of any communication model is a recipe for disaster as communication is the foundation of a support group. Without it, the individuals are just working on their own, and their actions and behaviors most likely do not affect anyone else.

Two years ago, I had the opportunity to mentor a colleague in another technology. Initially, she told me that her main issue was that she was getting no help from her group members so she asked me for advice on how to transform this situation. The first thing I asked was the schedule of group meetings. She said they had none. Then I asked how she communicated her questions to the others in the group. She said she did not send them questions. It immediately became apparent that her problem was communication and that her "group" was in reality just a few individuals supporting a common technology but far from being a real group. My advice to her was to institute a weekly group meeting (Parallel Communication Model) and to use it as a live forum to exchange information. She did and the group benefited from her initiative.

The benefits from communication in a technical support group go far beyond the mere exchange of problems, bugs, and solutions. Group communication also fosters personal relationships and trust. The building and preservation of a group culture is through the Ritual Communication Model as proposed by James Carey.[15] The individuals in a group are engaged in communication to foster the morale and meaning of the group. The French have name for this, "esprit de corps," which is the feeling of camaraderie among members of a group or an organization.[16]

Look at your technical support group and see what type of communication models you have. If you lack any of them, see if they may be necessary; remember that unless the group is small and localized, all three are of some relevance. If you and your peers have no real form of communication, I urge you to take the first step and initiate it. Be sure to get approval from your management if you deem it necessary. You now have a basic understanding of the reason and benefits of group communication. Remember that as support people, we trade in problems, answers, and solutions. Share those with your peers and your group will be on its way to becoming the best it can be, armed with a strong foundation in knowledge sharing.

Take advantage of every opportunity to practice your communication skills so that when important occasions arise, you will have the gift, the style, the sharpness, the clarity, and the emotions to affect other people.

—Jim Rohn

The Involved Group

Working in a support group, you may notice that many of the things you and your colleagues do on a daily basis do not seem to make much sense. Some of the steps we have to follow or questions we have to ask customers appear to have no technical or even service merit. I am not trying to instigate a revolt, so do not misconstrue my statement because unreasonable procedures happen even in the best-managed support organizations. The idyllic condition is one where the group knows the reasoning behind the procedures and even involves itself with deriving them.

Look at a normal day for you and see if you can identify a process or two that you do simply because someone higher up thought it was a good idea or has some other justification unbeknownst to you, and possibly your colleagues. In fact, your immediate manager may not know either, but this is normal, especially in a large organization. Why does this happen? Aside from the truly nonsensical and unjustifiable, there are multiple valid reasons. The main ones are as follows:

- *Reporting*: Higher-level managers and those who make resource decisions in the company need to have useful information with which to make decisions. Some of the things you have to do that do not make much sense may be because of reporting requirements. Some of the fields you have to fill out in the problem tracking system or in the issue reviews are simply because there is a need to track and report on these things.

---

[15] Carey, J.W. "Chapter 1: a cultural approach to communication" in *Communication as Culture: Essays on Media and Society.*(New York: Routledge, 1988).

[16] *The American Heritage® New Dictionary of Cultural Literacy, Third Edition.* "esprit de corps." Houghton Mifflin Company, 2005. `http://dictionary.reference.com/browse/esprit de corps` (accessed: December 22, 2008).

- *Standardization*: The bigger the organization, the more need for standardization. In the case of larger support organizations that handle multiple technologies by different support groups, some of the things required in the systems are there simply because some other group needs them, and everyone else is stuck with them. In my office, most copiers use three-hole paper because the mainframe groups require it for their documentation and manuals. It does not make sense for non-mainframe groups to have to print everything on 3-hole paper, but we need to standardize. Since there are only a small number of copiers, it is mostly this type of paper we use.

- *Financial*: Businesses are in business to make money and saving it is equally important. Procedures in support groups are ultimately financial because we provide a service that customers pay for in some way and we, as company employees, utilize resources which cost money. A company I worked for required that we enter a personal code for every fax and phone call we made. This did not make much sense to me or my colleagues in 1996, but since there was no VoIP calls probably were more expensive than they are now, and using a personal code was just a way to avert unnecessary or personal long distance calls.

- *Legal*: Many of the apparently silly things we do are because our company does not want to get into any legal trouble. In civil law, there is something called the Principal-Agent Relationship which basically says that a Principal (employer) is responsible for the actions of an Agent (employee) when the Agent is acting on behalf of the Principal.[17] In other words, if you get it wrong while supporting a customer and cause bigger damage, it is your employer who is responsible. This is a very strong incentive for companies to adopt procedures to limit or prevent liability even when those procedures make no sense to technical people.

Now we know why some of the things we do are justifiable, but that still leaves us with a void: how to be aware of, and even involved in deriving, the things we do. The answer to that question is for the group to adopt a high-involvement culture. A high-involvement group culture is one where the individual members participate in the identification of the group's problems as well as the resolutions. The high-involvement group does not wait for management to tell them everything, but rather act proactively as a collective to fix the shortcomings. This type of group engagement may occur in any group and is not limited to technical support. A good example is a special team formed at the Trenton, Ohio plant of Miller Brewing Company in 1991.[18] Miller conducted a pilot for a self-regulated, high-production team. The team formed at the plant managed itself, had all the relevant information, and made procedural decisions based on sound data. The team had freedom to decide on production metrics, processes and even their own management. The team was clearly empowered and allowed to decide their production levels and methods. The members made their own policies, sometimes in conflict with company policy. By 1992, the team took 30% fewer labor hours to produce a barrel of beer.

Your company may not allow such a pilot to take place in a technical support environment, but there are still a few practices that your group can engage in to transform into a high-involvement group.

---

[17] Henry R. Cheeseman, *Business Law 2ⁿᵈ Edition* (Englewood Cliffs, NJ: Prentice Hall, 1995), p. 513–527.
[18] Richard Welling et al., *Inside Teams* (San Francisco, CA: Jossey-Bass, 1994), p. 66–78.

The conscientious and successful adoption of these techniques will eventually lead to a high-involvement group. The practices are as follows:

- *Find out why*: Make it a point of asking the reasoning behind the new and current procedures that do not make sense to you and your colleagues. The more the group understands the reasons and benefits of the procedures, the more inclined the members will be to do a better job at it. Knowing the reasons behind a procedure may increase commitment and satisfaction.

- *Adopt and improve*: When a new procedure comes down to the support group, the group should improve on it whenever possible. No one knows how to improve support work better than the people already doing it now. Therefore, look for ways to make the procedure better and more efficient.

- *Report the results*: After adopting the new procedure, be sure to let whoever originated it know how the procedure worked and how your group's improvements made a difference. When your group reports the results, it will make those in charge think a bit more the next time, and they will get some opinions before just pushing new procedures down to your support group. The main idea is not to wait until someone asks for the report but to have proactive reporting on the part of your group.

We all do things we may not understand or even like, but we do them anyway because we are told to do so. When the group understands the reasons behind the new procedures and put the high-involvement techniques in practice, the members of the group will be more inclined to increase engagement and advance the group to a new level of efficiency.

A small group of thoughtful people could change the world. Indeed, it's the only thing that ever has.

—Margaret Mead, American cultural anthropologist

The Open Group

Working in a support group allows the individuals to learn from each other and grow together in technical expertise as well as personal skills and even professional ambitions. Learning and developing together is an inevitable, but positive, part of progressing as a healthy group. Individuals in the group act as a sounding board for each other, because they become each other's mentors and apprentices. Most importantly, they check and balance each other's behavior and status within the group. This information transfer among group members is the openness of the group. The group members provide feedback to each other continuously in all areas of the work. The individuals exercise their openness with each other both formally and informally. Meetings and peer reviews are examples of the formal openness, while commenting on a colleague's handling of an issue over lunch is an example of the informal honest peer feedback.

In *The Fifth Discipline*, Peter Senge identifies two types of openness, participative and reflective.[19] Participative openness refers to the sharing of ideas, feedback, and simple "freedom to speak one's mind" that individuals exercise in the context of the group. Participative openness, Senge explains, leads

---

[19] Peter M. Senge, *The Fifth Discipline* (New York, NY: Currency Doubleday, 1990) p. 276–281.

to people speaking out and reflective openness leads to people looking inward. In reflective openness, the group members question their decisions, thinking through any other views the group shares about the work and the world.

While the participative and reflective openness models certainly apply to any support group, they are descriptive in nature; technical support needs a model adapted to the line of work and the complexity of technology coupled with the service aspect of the profession. Because our profession deals heavily in the accuracy and reliability of information, being forthcoming within the group is paramount. You and your support colleagues would not get far by keeping vital information about your technologies from each other, and you would even cause detriment if you did not point out fallacies to your co-workers. Therefore, we need at least an active model for technical support and another one that deals with frankness in a hierarchical structure. These are called the Cooperative Supportive Analysis and the Hierarchical Cross-Differential Openness models.

Cooperative Supportive Analysis occurs when the group engages in a mutual analysis of the work and events affecting the work or the working conditions of the group. In this case, the "freedom to speak one's mind" becomes a collective effort and allows the group to vent, resulting indirectly in the group supporting each other emotionally and personally. The group members find comfort in each other and evolve the analysis of the discussed event to a point where they reach a collective decision or where they placate their concerns. At its core, this is the essence of a group: a faction where people change their reality by the mere assembly of the minds confronted with the same challenges and circumstances.

In late 2007, the group I was in became the center of a divesture to another company. We had no information other than the fact that it was happening. No terms, conditions, details, or any other calming particulars reached us. We did not know the future of our own jobs and technologies. In the midst of this uncertainty, we carried on our work as usual and began discussing our situation in our weekly meeting as well as a small weekly newsletter. The individuals in the group became more open, argued many points, provided their insight and ideas about our future, and the group even came to a point where we were looking forward to the change. It was an amazing transformation from apprehension to positive expectation. However, this only happened in the technical support group. The development groups, also affected by the divestiture, did not demonstrate Cooperative Supportive Analysis and, as a result, were left in droves.

In the Hierarchical Cross-Differential Openness model, the degree to which the group members speak their mind is inversely proportional to the differential hierarchical space between the group member and the highest-ranking member in the audience. The individual volunteering the information or feedback will consequently not stick his or her neck out if the biggest shot in the audience is someone who may take offense or simply not want to hear the feedback. To put it in different terms, you only speak your mind when there is no danger of a higher-up taking offense; the higher the most senior person in the room, the less likely you will be to risk putting your foot in your mouth. This model is nothing more than rationalizing the individual who tries to protect his position and job at the expense of candidness.

Here is an example that illustrates the core of the Hierarchical Cross-Differential Openness model. Suppose you have a weekly meeting in which you want to tell your colleagues that the new procedure for entering development requests is too cumbersome and whoever came up with the idea obviously has never filled one out. You already went through the process yourself and you think your colleagues will want to blow off some steam since their work, like yours, is now as a result a bit more complex. The only member from management who typically shows up is the immediate group manager. However, just as you are about to speak up about the new procedure, the VP of Support walks into the meeting and sits down across from you. The VP is two levels above your manager. Do you go ahead with your input about the new development request procedure, mention it but keep it neutral and brief, or do you just keep your mouth shut? Some would keep their mouth shut or change the tone to be more objective so as to not offend the VP. In this example, you may think, "Heck, I don't care who it is, I'll speak my mind," and while this is a personal preference, it is quite the opposite of what the majority of people would do in such a situation. However, technical support people have a talent for recognizing and anticipating tense and socially ambiguous situations because we do it constantly in the course of our work. Some say that the squeaky wheel gets the oil, but it is also true that in many situations, the squeaky wheel gets replaced.

When individuals in a group speak their mind, it sets in motion a very peculiar dynamic that changes the group and provides support, cooperation, analysis, and reflection. We work in our groups constantly and share so much that openness is an integral part of our modus operandi. Keep that in mind next time someone in your group speaks his or her mind. Notice the models at work and try to improve your technical support group in every way you can. The collective starts with the individual acting for the benefit of all.

> *In all my public and private acts as your president, I expect to follow my instincts of openness and candor with full confidence that honesty is always the best policy in the end.*

> —Gerald R. Ford

The Group Crisis

A group consists of complex individuals, all with different backgrounds, motives, expertise, and personalities. These complexities sometimes result in predicaments that affect the effectiveness of a group. When these predicaments became so enormous as to change the basic group makeup, affect more than just a handful of members, or cause a shift in fundamental purpose of the group, the situation becomes a crisis. The crisis is not always perceived as such but its effects are quite real and sometimes traumatic.

According to Merriam-Webster's Medical Dictionary, a crisis is a psychological or social condition characterized by unusual instability caused by excessive stress and either endangering or felt to endanger the continuity of an individual or group; especially such a social condition requiring the transformation of cultural patterns and values.[20] Concisely, a crisis occurs when a group is stressed out and in risk of disbanding. If you work in a group, eventually the group will face a crisis and the better you understand the reason for the crisis, the better you will be able to help the group come out of the crisis and resume normal operations.

Technical support groups face different types of crises and the solutions vary as much as the crises themselves. The two types of crises that are most detrimental to technical support are:

- Political crisis

- Civility crisis

At its core, the political crisis in the technical support group is simply a problem with the work not getting done because of people not being able to work or agree with each other. The problem with a political crisis is that it arouses emotional intentions in the participants that have the potential to destroy the personal ties among the group members and eventually the group itself. In a support group, the political crisis starts by having at least two people of authority, expert or delegated, on opposite sides of an argument or policy. Typically, the disagreement ends without a crisis, but when neither one of the

---

[20] Dictionary.com. *Merriam-Webster's Medical Dictionary*. "Crisis." Merriam-Webster, Inc. http://dictionary.reference.com/browse/crisis (accessed: December 29, 2008).

parties wants to give up or find mutual ground it may lead to a fractioning of the group with some going to one side and others to the opposite side.

In the past, I was a party to one of these situations when two support groups were merged into one. Once we were a single group, we started fractioning almost immediately because the original group I was in had to support the product that the other group was quite experienced with. The conflict occurred when one of the guys in my original group put a few issues back in the queue after taking ownership of them, but thenseeing they were too much for him to handle. The leader from the experienced side balked at the idea and started accusing the group member of passing the issue to others without any due diligence, of being lazy, of unprofessionalism and even of trying to sabotage the more experienced side. Of course, I jumped in and the whole thing evolved into a small political crisis.

To fix a political crisis in a support group, one or more of the following must happen. The instigating parties to the crisis must work it out without involving the rest of the group. Management must intervene and put an end to the group members taking sides. The group members must refuse to play the political game and simply ignore the disagreeing parties for the benefit of the group. Anytime you see signs that a political crisis is brewing within your group, put an end to it by pointing it out for what it is.

A Civility Crisis is a situation in which at least one group member is so uncivil that his or her rudeness causes gratuitous stress on the other group members to the point that it threatens the stability of the group. The behavior may cause so much stress to individuals that they call in sick out of fear of facing the uncivil group member, change groups, and may even leave their job. The behavior varies from deviant or impolite behavior, all the way to plain bullying and abuse. Such situations are awful to watch and are even worse to experience. Incivility also costs the company a lot in lost productivity. In workplace research[21] dealing with uncivil behavior, researchers found that 22% of those experiencing the causes of uncivil behavior intentionally decreased their work effort. Ten percent reported absenteeism. Twenty-eight percent lost time avoiding the rude colleagues. Fifty-three percent wasted company time avoiding the uncivil colleagues. Thirsty-seven percent reduced their obligation to the company. Forty-six percent considered changing jobs. Twelve percent actually changed companies just to avoid the uncivil behavior.

While working with a support group in India, I had the chance to mentor and advise some of the people in that group. One of the women in the group confided how stressful it was for her to work with a particular male colleague who had a higher position within the group. She assured me this was not a single incident, but rather systematic. I asked other people and a few of the women told me the same thing. It appeared that this male colleague yelled repeatedly at some of the women colleagues. Since I was a mentor to the entire group, I approached the uncivil colleague and he denied it. I elevated the situation to management, he was reprimanded, and this behavior was not seen again.

The solution to the Civility Crisis varies and may range from mild dialogue with the uncivil party and a petition for the behavior to stop, to the escalation to management and the Human Resources department. As a group member, you are amidst where everything happens and you can spot crises long before they reach outside the group.[22] No one should have to fear going to work because of a rude or abusive colleague. It threatens the individuals as well as the integrity of the group. As support people, we have enough to put up with dealing with customers' technical problems so we need not face stressful situations with colleagues. If you experience or know someone who is going through a situation with rudeness or abuse, take action immediately and do not let it go on. Bring it up to your management or HR, if necessary.

It is up to everyone in the group to maintain it and keep the group from falling apart. Working alongside colleagues is one of the great rewards and satisfactions of technical support work. From time

---

[21] Lynne Andersson et al., "Assessing and Attacking Workplace Incivility," *Organizational Dynamics.* Vol. 29, no.2, Fall 2000 p123–137

[22] Giovinella Gonthier, *Rude Awakenings-Overcoming the Civility Crisis in the Workplace* (Chicago, Ill: Dearborn, 2002) p. 53–57.

to time, the group may become threatened by a political or uncivil crisis. It is up to all of the members to keep the crisis from causing the detriment of the group.

Character is not made in a crisis it, is only exhibited.

—Robert Freeman

The Constructive Group

In order for a group to continue ahead and be productive, the individual members must all be of the same mind; they do not always have to agree but concur to adopt a plan of action. Nonetheless, getting all the members in a group, especially a large one, to exercise communal assent presents a huge challenge that must be shared by everyone in the group. A single member who does not share in the common vision of the group may cause the demise of the entire collective. It sounds fallacious to think that one person can bring down a group and cause its demise, but it happens in technical support groups everywhere. The downfall of the group does not always mean its termination or disbandment. In a formal or command group that experiences corruption by one or more individuals, the structure will remain intact but morally the members may be miles apart. That is why the group members must always keep the group constructive. A constructive group is one that produces positive results and keeps its members amicably working with each other.

Take the example of a support group who had just a handful of moderately motivated individuals who all worked well together. They kept their queue clean and customers happy. They also worked well with management and other groups within the same support organization. The workload got a bit heavier because of a new product acquisition, and the local management hired a new person to join the group. The new person was technically impressive. He knew everything about the operating systems and relevant technology, and picked up the new product at a very rapid pace, which was even more remarkable due to the lack of training. However, the new fellow had a huge issue that became apparent almost immediately. He strongly and negatively criticized the company at every chance and with anyone he could. It was amazing to see this new hire talk badly about his new employer, even to company veterans he'd just met. Soon, the members of the group, who previously worked harmoniously, were bad-mouthing the company and the local management. One person alone corrupted a group of individuals who apparently were not even aware of it. After a few months, the manager fired the new person but the group was never the same again. I still exchange emails with him because, personally and technically, he is great but a detriment to a professional group nonetheless.

The responsibility to keep the group constructive falls to everyone in the group, not just management or the leaders within the group. Every member has several key responsibilities to keep. These obligations are typically not in any employee manual or formalized job description, but are more part of a personal and group ethical agenda that ensures the group remains positive and productive. The following are the responsibilities bestowed upon the individuals within the group.

Every individual must encourage group moral and social cohesiveness within the group. Every group member should reach out and communicate to the other members when something appears morally incongruent with the ideals of the group. The same goes for the social fabric. The group members in a constructive group must remain socially intertwined with one another so that straightforward communication takes place. This does not mean that people in the group must be best friends, but it does mean that some social interaction must exist even within a very individualistic society for the interest of the group.

The people in the group must also allow the expression of dissent. Disagreement in the group is normal, may lead to the perfection of ideas, and is a natural course of the democratic concept. The group exists for a purpose, to provide answers and solutions to customers. Every person in the group supports those customers; therefore, everyone has some level of expertise in their own right. However, the presence of disputes must not lead to animosity. Every member must ensure that every voice is heard but in a positive manner.

When there are disagreements, the members must foment discussion in order to resolve the disagreements and reach a state of harmony in decision making. You and your fellow supporters do not have to engage in anything fancy or formal, all you have to do is talk and discuss. Some people are naturally more assertive than others are and may feel that they have to always have their way. Others have a passive personality that prevents them from affirming their will. As professionals, we must also understand that a collective must reach an accord and it is up to everyone in the group to watch out for these individuals and prevent them from imposing their will or not have their opinions heard.

As in the example with the corrupting colleague, there are people for whom nothing seems good enough, and they seek to destroy and corrupt the opinions, views, and work of others in the group, management, and even the company. You and your group colleagues must impede destructive negativity in the group. Destructive negativity is the attempt by someone to initiate discord by highlighting a negative criticism or argument based on nonprofessional reasons. Disagreements are fine as long as they are objective, within reason, or simply move the group to a better state. Disagreements become destructive negativity when they:

- focus on personal attributes that go beyond the professional.

- are based on distorted, subjective negative opinion.

- are not shared and seem unreasonable to the rest of the group.

- seek to ridicule someone based on personal dislike.

- aim to sway others to have a negative image of someone or of the company.

When you see anyone in the group exhibiting any of the criteria cited above, make sure to put an end to it immediately before it infects the group. If the group allows this type of negative behavior, the individual exercising it will continue until others adopt his way of thinking. You must understand that destructive negativity has no place in a technical support group. We are supposed to embody optimistic and proactive reactions for our customers and cannot tolerate the corruption of our own support groups by people with personal agendas.

The support people working in a group must also keep things in perspective: This is a profession and a job. There is no need to get personal or destroy personal relationships just to get your way. Your focus is customer satisfaction and the pleasurable experience of working in a support group. Let's remind each other that technical support is a job, and we do it because we love it but also because we have to. As members of a technical support group, it is up to all of us to keep the group constructive.

Have regular hours for work and play; make each day both useful and pleasant, and prove that you understand the worth of time by employing it well. Then youth will be delightful, old age will bring few regrets, and life will become a beautiful success.

—Louisa May Alcott

Support Group Development Cycle

Have you ever looked at different support groups and wondered why some groups are highly efficient while others are not? How some groups seem to work so well and never appear to have any problems while others are a constant struggle? Have you ever tried to compare your group against another? When we look at a support group to analyze their performance, behavior, and expertise, we must take under consideration the stage of the group's development cycle. Groups, just as individuals, progress and adapt to their customers, mature, learn, and dominate the technology they support. All groups, including technical support groups, grow, peak, and plateau through similar stages. Tuckman[23] describes group development in four[24] initial stages:

1. *Forming:* the initial stage when the individuals come together to form the group.

2. *Storming:* the stage at which the individuals within the group start to develop conflict. The formalities established during the Forming stage give way to the normal operations of the group and frictions within the group arise, causing the "storming" among the group members.

3. *Norming:* at this stage the group members become aware of each other's strengths, weaknesses, and work to keep the team together. They form rules for interacting with each other.

4. *Performing:* this stage is one that not all groups reach but it is characterized by the group being able to act independently and in harmony. The individuals work seamlessly together and so well that they become highly efficient. This stage takes years to reach and requires a high level of maturity from all its members.

Tuckman's group development model fits ideally with what happens in a technical support group from the social perspective. Nevertheless, it requires something a bit more comprehensive that includes the technology variable into the equation. Immature, and even mature, groups experience different dynamics by the sheer introduction of new technologies into the support mix or because of acquisitions, requiring fast growth that changes the stage and even add more stages and internal forces within the groups. The bottom line is that technical support groups require an extension to Tuckman's paradigm that encompasses the expansion of the membership in the group and changes in the technology supported.

For a technical support group, the stages require the inclusion of the improvement of the technology as well as the growth of the company. Both of these aspects affect the development of the support group and force it to create and adopt new practices and behaviors to meet the demands placed on it by the user body as well as the technology. The following stages describe the typical technology that originates in the small company, but also includes the typical new technology either acquired or developed in the big company that necessitates a new group to support it. The following are the stages as experienced by the typical support groups:

---

[23] Tuckman, B, "Developmental sequence in small groups." *Psychological Bulletin, 1965*, 63:p.384–399.
[24] Tuckman added a fifth one ten years after developing the initial four. The fifth one was "Adjourning" or disbanding of the group but it does not generally apply to technical support groups. Adjourning fits short-term project-based groups much better than our typical support group.

1. *Entrepreneurial stage:* This is where it all begins. In any new technology, whether it is a new software application or a revolutionary tortilla-making machine, the company that invents it is small and new. The growth is organic and tends to be quite informal in nature. The demands on the new support group are small as the customer base is small. The individuals in the group devote their time to get very familiar with the technology, and usually provide a superb level of service to the few customers who adopt the new technology. This can also happen within a big company that comes up with a new technology.

2. *Acquisition stage:* If the new entrepreneurial company is good enough and survives the initial stage, typically it gets acquired by a larger, more established company. A few good companies do not go through this stage because they remain independent and simply grow organically on their own. For the acquired companies, the support group goes through a process of adapting to the new company and its processes. It is not unusual for many members of support groups in the Information Technology (IT) field to go through at least one acquisition.

3. *Expansion stage:* -Due to adoption by the industry, the technology supported faces increasing demand in this stage. The support group is forced to expand its membership and faces exploding growth in the customer base. This is often somewhat of a traumatic stage for the original group members as they observe the high level of service present in the Entrepreneurial stage morph into a lesser quality of service during the expansion stage. Because many of the members in the group are now novices in the technology, the more experienced members are at odds on how to handle this new growth and may become isolated. They remain purely technical and turn into the experts who, because of the growth in the customer base, are now required to handle only the toughest of issues, leaving the newer members to fend for themselves with little or no technical leadership.

4. *Stability stage:* The technology and customer-base growth level off and the group membership stabilizes. The group members become much more accustomed to one another and more comfortable with the technology. The advancements in the technology maintain it rather than advance it, and the requirements on the support group are less than in the Expansion stage. At this stage the group develops new ways of doing support more efficiently, and works on documentation and expansion of support tools to aid customers. The technology's end-users are also more mature, and the type of questions and issues are mainly for maintenance and operations, rather than adoption, deployment, and orientation. At this stage, the support group members begin to contribute to the technology itself and propose new advancements and features to the product.

5. *Competence stage:* The individuals in the group become very proficient in the technology and in solving issues. The group as a whole is mature and capable of solving most issues with the use of troubleshooting techniques and testing. There are few new customers and the questions are often advanced in nature. The group diminishes in membership because the needs of the customers are less than the capacity the group provides. The company sees that it can do away with some of the support members and only the most proficient or more

advantageous to the company remain in the group. The individuals who remain in the group are authority's on the technology; work so efficiently that they solve a very high percentage of the issues within the first call; and exercise a very efficient way of handling the tougher issues.

6. *End of life stage:* This is where the product dies and becomes obsolete or replaced by a newer technology. The group members may adopt and support the newer product, get pulled out and placed with other support groups, or simply done away with by the company. However, the group members retain their experience and when placed in a new group or adopting a new product, they maintain their level of proficiency after a short period of adjustment to the technology. The strength of the group is not in the technology but in the skills and maturity the group acquired during the entire process. The technology is a variable but the maturity level easily transfers to the new technology.

Understanding the stages of development in a support group allows us to analyze the needs and management required for the group. What works for a group at the Entrepreneurial Stage will not work for one in the Competence Stage. Trying to compare the two groups is also futile, because they function differently and have different needs according to each stage. Looking at your support group and trying to determine the stage will give you a different insight into your understanding of the work, your colleagues, and yourself.

There are no great limits to growth because there are no limits of human intelligence, imagination, and wonder.

—Ronald Reagan

The Successful Group: An Inventory

While working in your support group, you probably wonder if your group is achieving its full potential and living up to the expectation of the people forming the group as well as management and customers. There are no easy answers to these questions, but there are many symptoms and characteristics of the present stage of your group that provide clues as to the effectiveness it provides to the group members and to its constituencies. You may find that your group is in good shape and on its way to becoming a model for your industry, or perhaps you find that your group is dysfunctional in some way. Such a label is not gratuitous, but rather derived from observing certain aspects of the group members' behavior and achievements toward each other and, ultimately, to the customers.

In order to proceed with the evaluation of your group, we need a simple inventory to help guide your observation. The following points provide basic yet important insights into the functioning of the group. As you read them, analyze your group and your colleagues' behavior as objectively as possible. Your reality may or may not match that of the other group members, but it is a start.

Cohesiveness

The first aspect that you must observe is the cohesiveness of the group. This refers to the unification and camaraderie of the individuals. There must be solidarity within the group because without it, none of the other measures of success are possible. The question is whether the group members see each other as necessary to the success of the group and to what extent. In addition, does the group form a social as well as professional relationship among its members, or are they disinterested in what happens in the group and prefer to work independently of the rest of the members? The measures to this question are as follows:

1. *Not cohesive*: There is no bond among the members, social or professional, and the individuals for the most part act alone. They are just a group in name but not in practice. The members of this group are there because of management mandate, but not because the group functions truly as a collective.

2. *Somewhat cohesive*: Some of the group members seek each other and have a professional attachment that for the most part keeps them united. Some members may act alone in situations, but often act in solidarity when it is in their best interest. This group does not reach its full potential because of the tendency for some to not completely integrate into the actions of the group.

3. *Cohesive*: The majority of the individuals in the group seek each other socially and professionally. The individuals face structural, operational, and technical challenges together and only act independently when it is in the best interest of the group, the company, or the customer. This group functions at a level of professionalism, and even when the individuals are forced to act alone, they retain their camaraderie with the other group members.

Collaboration

Collaboration is how well the group members work, help each other to find solutions, and face the challenges posed by forces internal and external to the group. It is a group effort and requires commitment from the individuals involved. Though it takes many forms, collaboration generally deals with the individuals making an effort beyond their own workload to mutually help each other in times of need. In other words, some individuals provide help in some situations then receive it in other situations. Collaboration also involves group effort to solve common issues and problems, but also mandates the absence of selfishness on the part of the individuals. The collaboration levels are the following:

1. *Non-Collaborative*: The individuals in the group do not genuinely help each other, sometimes even when asked for help. The more senior members typically give useless answers to those who ask for assistance. Those asking for help soon tire and cease to ask, opting to find their own answers. When they reach the senior level of expertise, they treat others as they were treated.

2. *Semi-Collaborative*: The group acts together to find common solutions and to help each other when in some situations and by some individuals. For the most part, only some individuals are helpful and truly desire to help, but the rest of the group acts egocentrically and prefers to allow the members in need to fend for themselves. When asked why they act selfishly, the members argue that it is how they learned; therefore, others must learn the same way.

3. *Collaborative*: The group acts as one and each colleague genuinely is there to help the next. When asked, the group members respond with helpful solutions or with an offer to help research the question. This group is the ideal situation for the new support person as the group provides the most support possible, enhancing the development of the individual's technical expertise and self-confidence in customer-facing skills. When common problems affect the group, the members unite and handle the problems together using each person's strengths.

Sympathy

A healthy group requires some level of sympathy among the members for it to function properly. This understanding and consideration for colleagues allows the development of strong personal ties to the individual and allows everyone to work in the best interest of the group. Sympathy prevents elements in the group to sabotage the efforts of their associates. It does not mean that you have to approve everything your associates do, but you should support and cooperate with the search for solutions and be genuinely interested in your group's efforts. The group sympathy levels are the following:

1. *Apathy:* Group members lack authentic interest in each other and their work. The members are indifferent to the goals of the group and the achievements of challenges faced by other group members. The apathetic group is characterized by members showing lethargy and lack of concern for the objectives of the group even when directly asked for participation. The members may be forced to collaborate but their hearts are not in it.

2. *Considerate:* Group associates are thoughtful of each other and their work, and may go so far as to truly care for others and their work, but such concern is not uniformly adopted within the group. Members are selective in who and what they sympathize with and to the extent. A considerate group is characterized by the members respecting each other and their right to involve or decline involvement in each other's issues as well as the group's goals and challenges.

3. *Empathy:* This level of sympathy is the highest level possible by a group and is characterized by individuals with a very high sense of purpose and maturity as well as genuine understanding and compassion for each other. The associates are kind to one another and agree in principal and practice with the goals and efforts of the group. They function so well together that this congruence allows them to reach higher levels of efficiency than that of Considerate and Apathy groups. This is typically a mature group with several years of harmonious work. The individuals know each other well; know each other's strengths and weaknesses; and do everything possible to complement their colleagues' work. Although rare, this group exists typically in legacy-type technologies. The members typically reach this level of sympathy because they have gone through a tumultuous time together and possibly lost much of the group to layoffs and other crises.

After reading the descriptions above, select the value that best describes the situation of your group for each of the three behaviors: cohesiveness, collaboration, and sympathy. The possible values for each of the behaviors are 1, 2, and 3. Then add the values to get the inventory result. Possible overall values are from 3 to 9. A brief description of the values and their consequences follow.

Total Value = 3 — The Dysfunctional Group

After reading all the descriptions, if your group best fits the value of 1 in each the behaviors, then you and your colleagues are currently not operating truly as a group. It is merely a conglomeration of individuals because the essence of a collective is not present. The individuals do not want to work together, do not know how, or simply do not care. They also do not help each other and do not care for each other. There is little that the group can accomplish collectively. This group would be better served by some management intervention, training, and the emergence of a leader within the group to set the tone of the group's purpose.

Total Value = 4–5 — The Struggling Group

The group with a combined value of 4 or 5 is in the process of improving if it's a relatively new group, or one with a recent infusion of new members. If the group has been around for a few years, then it may be struggling because of strong discrepancies among the membership and those differences are impeding the group's healthy advancement. The group has problems of culture and the group members have not yet all realized the value of the group. The individuals need to meet more often and speak among one another on a regular basis. Only through constant communication and fellowship will the group be able to further develop the three behaviors.

Total Value = 6 — The Idiosyncratic Group

This group has very positive elements but the members are still in disagreement in some aspects of the group's vision. Some members act alone and others in the collective, but they all know what is best for the group; they just fail to consistently act in the group's best interest. The idiosyncratic group would greatly benefit from additional exposure to the "big picture" in regards to the impact the group members collectively make in the group's vision, support organization, customers, and company. This group is on its way to reaching its full potential and just needs more agreement among its members.

Total Value = 7–8 — The Healthy Group

If you score a 7 or 8 in the sum of the three behaviors it means your group is healthy and is working at an optimum level. If the group members work in multiple geographical regions and even time zones, then this is most likely the highest score it will reach and the best level possible. If the group is small and all in the same office, the group can improve, but small differentiations in the actual work, and in levels of expertise, are keeping the group from reaching a score of 9. The small, local group at a score of 7–8 needs small cultural modifications to reach the summit of group behavior. Ideally, all that's needed is for the members who are not entirely cooperating to adhere to the group's vision and mandate.

Total Value = 9 — The Communal Group

This group is typically small, very experienced, localized, and very mature. The members are usually older and in very stable technologies with little change. A score of 9 is much harder to achieve in a geographically distributed group. This level of group behavior escapes most groups, but yields the most productive support work. It should be the ultimate goal of any established group. Age or maturity alone does not guarantee the communal group. The individuals have to be of equal mind and pull their own weight as well as care about each other enough to rate at this level.

The inventory you just read is a simple yet effective approach at analyzing your group's present situation. It provides some insight into three major behaviors and it should allow you to assess the status of your group.

The business schools reward difficult complex behavior more than simple behavior, but simple behavior is more effective.

— Warren Buffett

CHAPTER 5

■ ■ ■

The Technical Support Colleague

In the support line of work, the dependence and relationship among members of the group has a direct impact on the overall group success. Specific individuals vary in their productivity and styles, but the collective work has a direct impact on the entire organization.

In this chapter, we'll explore some of the topics relevant to the relationship between you and your colleagues as well as a few theories dealing with observed behaviors and personal characteristics. The content is a brief but solid foundation on which you can build your own style for dealing with coworkers. Specifically, the concepts discussed in the chapter include trust, solidarity, conflict, and performance vs. productivity.

Paradoxically, coworkers are the cause of many of our successes and failures in technical support. Despite our profession being one that rewards and measures individual effort, the successful alliance with colleagues often produces positive results for the individual and detrimental to all involved when the social and professional ties fail to materialize.

The main reason that support coworkers don't reach their potential is often not because the individuals are incapable, but rather because the members fail to work as one team. Even when each member possesses all the individual attributes to be an independent success, if members don't work together, the group will falter. Success starts with the relationship with your colleagues.

The topics presented in this chapter made me think of all the wonderful colleagues with whom I've shared a great portion of my life. People whom I admire, respect, and grown to favor. Others who I never understood despite knowing and working side by side them for years. I finally came to the realization that, at a personal level just as in a family, colleagues should be accepted and not necessarily understood. To you, all the wonderful people who toil in this profession, I offer the next few pages in the hopes that like me you come to realize that the only people you can lean on in the successes and struggles of your labor are your support colleagues.

■ **Tip** Anyone can work with you by doing as you do but it takes someone with a bit more commitment and sharing to be a colleague.

Work on Trust

Next to your own knowledge and expertise, the best resources you have are your colleagues; the people who work with you and share the workload of supporting customers. These are the people who make you strong and who allow you to reach beyond your limits by extending what you know into what they know. Collectively, you can all come up with ways to solve the customers' problems. In order to work effectively with your colleagues, you have to trust them and they have to trust you. Trust is not something you can just give or get; trust is something you and your colleagues have to earn, and eventually adopt as a norm in your dealings with each other. Trust, at its most basic level is the firm reliance on the integrity, ability, or character of a person or thing.[1]

Developing trust is not something that can be taught or achieved via training. It is something very personal and subject to emotions and personal judgments from both sides. There are people who worked for years side by side and still cannot trust each other. Conversely, there are people who out of necessity needed to trust and developed this emotion very early in their relationship. In technical support, we live by trust and fail by lack thereof. Think of it this way, customers place their trust on us because we command trust by our mere position. But internally within our support groups, we cannot always depend on our own knowledge to solve the problems brought on by customers. We must trust that our colleagues will help and that their advice and technical assistance will be valid.

Trust among technical support colleagues comes through interaction, communication, and simple relations. Often because of proximity, colleagues learn to trust each other. In the case of people working in different offices, inevitably the coworkers must communicate so trusting relationships evolve. Trust is most prevalent among coworkers who have learned to adapt to each other's style and personalities. There are several aspects of adaptation that aids in the formation of trust among individuals. If you are relatively new to your group and wish to develop trust, it is necessary to follow these adaptations. They may also be helpful to the associates who have failed to develop trust by other means.

In order to begin building trust with your colleagues, you have to initiate it by lowering your guard. This may seem counter-intuitive, but so is the idea of trusting someone else—especially in an individualistic society where personal reliance is the central inspiration; making yourself vulnerable to others may seem like a weakness rather than a basis for trust. However, your colleagues, much like yourself, will only disclose needs and desires if there is a sense of mutual trust.[2] Also, remember that you are in this together, so the more you and your colleagues know about each other, the better off you will be in helping customers, and the more issues you will close. The most successful support groups are those who work together and take advantage of each other's strengths. Otherwise, why have colleagues? There is absolutely nothing wrong with your colleagues knowing your weakness and you knowing theirs. In fact, it is a positive thing since at least you know what now to ask and what to help others on. It is amazing how some support people are afraid to disclose to others what they do not know as if somehow this was a cause for shame.

To build trust the coworkers also need to share more than is required. I am not referring to adverse sharing, such as rumors, or destructive sharing, such as gossip. People who seek to gain and build trust must build a rapport based on information sharing; ideally, this information is of interest to other colleagues and will help them perform better or somehow gain some kind of advantage.. If your coworkers share information about the work and the technology, it should foster trust. If someone is willing to share information, it means they trust you enough to use the information and for your benefit. An example of information sharing that fosters trust is you telling a new colleague about the intricacies of the support group, the technology, or the dealings with other groups. Obviously, the new colleague

---

[1] "trust." *The American* Heritage® *Dictionary of the English Language, Fourth Edition.* Houghton Mifflin Company, 2004. 06 Jan. 2009. http://dictionary.reference.com/browse/trust

[2] D.G. Pruitt, J.M. Magenau, E. Konar-Goldband, and P.J. Carnevale, "Effects of Trust, Aspiration, and Gender on Negotiation Tactics," *Journal of Personality and Social Psychology* 38, no. 1, 1980, p. 9–22.

would learn in due time, but the advancing of information, as long as it is positive in tone, will foster the reliance of that new colleague on you. This forms the beginning of a trusting relationship.

In developing trust among colleagues, it is imperative to form camaraderie among the individuals. Individuals who trust one another will tend to trust others around them. Coworkers who trust one another will also be more comfortable in trusting management, because fallacies and shortcoming are readily known among trusting individuals. For this reason, it is in the best interest of any support management to build trusting relationships among reports. In a recent study, only 38% of employees in American and Canadian office workers felt their management was honest and only 27% felt management cared for them as individuals.[3] Such low numbers in trust have their origins in coworkers not trusting each other. Therefore, trust among support people is desirable and of benefit to everyone involved: colleagues, management, and customers.

Risking your technical advantage is the last item in developing trust with your coworkers. This last requirement of trust is the hardest for many people in technical support. Technical prowess is our business and our niche; how can we risk it? The answer is simple. Initially, trust is a one-way street. You have to give in order to receive. If your colleagues are people of integrity, they will reciprocate your gesture. If they are not, then you still win because you know their character and no one can blame you for being distrusting. Additionally, your strength is trust. Others may abuse it, but your trust is a strength nonetheless. A good support person does not fear losing any technical advantage because technical support is much more than just technical facts; it is the application of knowledge and troubleshooting skills.

Relying on others' trust complements you and your colleagues' relationship. If trust is lacking, then it is up to you to initiate it. We are all in this support business together, and it makes no sense to work with people you do not trust.

All I really want is one outside opinion. They say, he who has two watches never knows what time it is—you have to pick one person and decide to trust them.

—Richard Price

Respect Among Colleagues

There are few professional satisfactions as gratifying as working among people you admire and respect, individuals who share your ideals and passion for the profession. The ideal technical support work environment has all the general aspects for a congenial work relationship with others of the same thought. However, one facet must exist for support colleagues to work in harmony, or at the very least in accordance with each other. This aspect of the work is respect. The word respect refers to an attitude of admiration or esteem.[4] Although admiration represents the idyllic approach toward colleagues, esteem is the most appropriate stance since it is the most neutral and the appropriate cultural occurrence in technical support.

Respect among colleagues embodies the professionalism of the parties involved. There cannot be a professional atmosphere without respect among the practitioners. At our specialized level and vocation, respect typically comes naturally from customers and other constituencies who look to support people for help, but among support coworkers, it usually requires earning.

---

[3] G.W. Kemper, "Managing Corporate Communication in Turbulent Times," *IABC Communication World*, May-June 1992.
[4] "respect." *WordNet® 3.0*. Princeton University. 08 Jan. 2009. `http://dictionary.reference.com/browse/respect`.

In a social context, people give respect by the mere fact that some people deserve it out of civility or cultural norms.[5] For instance, young people may respect colleagues who are older just as men may respect women, and vice versa. Personal upbringing and cultural contexts may also account for the giving of respect to some members simply by their age, gender, or other factors that are outside of personal merit. However, this unearned respect appears wrong to some. Raz argues that bestowing respect on individuals without merit subjugates the respecting individuals.[6] Regardless of which idea of social respect you subscribe to, respecting others based on norms of civility is the professional thing to do while keeping in mind that granting such respect should not bind you from making objective decisions and choices regarding the interaction with your colleagues.

Among support colleagues, respect based on technical merit is something that we cannot demand but rather must give out of recognition.[7] Unlike a situational or positional demand for respect, technical experts derive respect because of personal talent and out of acknowledgment. No one will simply respect you because you are in technical support; you have to earn it. Think of a new support person coming into the group. He or she may have excellent credentials but that alone seldom gains that person respect. The experienced supporter knows that the only thing that matters is how well that new person can learn the technology, service customers, and cope to close issues. The efficacy in which a new coworker manages to deal with these three requirements determines the level of respect technical colleagues provide. We have all seen the new guy that comes to the group with all sorts of certifications, only to find that he falls short on the technical merit and struggles to pick up the technical requirements of the job.

Respect in the technical sphere represents more than just going to the expert or the person that can help you. Respect denotes the uplifting and promoting of the person subject to esteem.[8] Ethical respect does not consist of only going to someone and paying false piety or lip service in order to get your answers and nothing else. This amounts to hypocrisy and is unhealthy in a support center. Respect among support colleagues, especially to the experts in the organization, must be a true and ethical admiration and even veneration of the individual. Admiration or respect are not to be given away without merit, but if a support associate provides value to the support organization, serves those around him in a straightforward manner, and helps in the progression of the group than that person deserves respect. Anything self-serving from the recipients may be described as respect, but is truly insincerity.

This brings us to the real question: How do we earn respect in technical support? Since respect is a cognitive behavior, there are ways to inherently command respect and to claim it via actions. The first way we can claim respect in technical support is by giving it. You give respect and others will give it to you. This is not always the formula, but those who are ethical in their professional practices will inherently reciprocate the esteem initiated by you. Behaving in a civil manner with your colleagues and exercising deference is a proper way to initiate respect.

To earn respect in your current situation, do something that is beyond your required duties and make sure it provides value to others. The general notion is that a person's authority or delegation deserves respect. Rawls asserts that respect comes automatically by position or agency.[9] However, in our case of a technological driven context, it takes more than a position to gain respect. A manager position has regard among supporters, but not necessarily respect. If that manager provides values and earns the admiration of the reports then respect is the next logical step but it still requires earning. Senior-level support people are in the same situation. Just because a support person has a higher position in the support ranks that person does not automatically merit respect. Earning respect does not equate to

---

[5] C.F. Cranor, 1983, "On Respecting Human Beings as Persons," *Journal of Value Inquiry* 17: 103-117.
[6] J. Raz, 1989, "Liberating Duties," *Law and Philosophy*.
[7] A.W. Wood, *Kant's Ethical Thought* (Cambridge: Cambridge University Press, 1999).
[8] Anderson, E., 1999, "What is the Point of Equality?" *Ethics* 109: 287-337.
[9] Rawls, J., 1982, "The Basic Liberties and Their Priority," in *The Tanner Lectures on Human Values*, vol. 3, Salt Lake City: University of Utah Press.

doing what you are supposed to; you must do something beyond what is expected of you in order to merit admiration. Will answering the phones at your required allotted times gain you respect? Probably not, but visiting that customer to fix his problem in person on your way home probably will get you closer.

Another way to gain respect is to act in an altruistic manner with your colleagues and customers. There are many ways to achieve this. Specially, they are:

- Make others look good. There is nothing more rewarding and constructive to others than to honor them in some way. Perhaps by giving credit for work, offering sincere praise in front of others, and talking well about them with colleagues. Such actions make you look selfless and earn your esteem and respect by others.

- Give more than asked. In the technical environment in which we work, there is always the need for information. If someone asks you for something, make sure and provide more. Great service is not only for customers, it also works with coworkers.

- Teach others what you know. Look at people who obviously hoard knowledge. Do they seem respectable people or selfish individuals who opt for apparent job security? Teaching and mentoring others allows you to interact and to gain the respect of those around you. It does not take a lot and the returns are fantastic for everyone involved, even for your company and customers.

Respect in our profession represents success. Because of the nature of our work, only the best behaviors command respect, and those behaviors are nearly impossible to fake with people who work around us. Admiration, esteem, and even veneration are necessary among support colleagues. These behaviors keep us professionally healthy and in harmony with our coworkers.

Leaders who win the respect of others are the ones who deliver more than they promise, not the ones who promise more than they can deliver

—Mark A. Clement

Coworker Solidarity

As individuals, we want to be part of something and feel a sense of belonging. This sense of identification goes beyond the structural and organizational links between members of a group or a functional silo. What we want is to feel identified with others around us and for our coworkers to identify with us. If we are successful or struggling, we do not want to be alone. It is often said that misery loves company, but so does fortune, struggle, and any other human notion of sentiment. We want, and even need, solidarity with our coworkers in order for us to feel that sense of community and belonging. Solidarity is defined as a union of interests, purposes, or sympathies among members of a group; fellowship of responsibilities and interests.[10]

There are several reasons why we need to be of "one mind" in technical support. The main reason is to increase quality and efficiency in our work. The role we play serves a higher purpose in our companies

---

[10] "solidarity." *The American Heritage® Dictionary of the English Language, Fourth Edition.* Houghton Mifflin Company, 2004. 09 Jan. 2009. <Dictionary.com `http://dictionary.reference.com/browse/solidarity`>.

and our industries and fields from bicycle assembly support to mainframe software. When we understand that purpose and act in solidarity to serve the best interests of our companies and customers, then the increase in quality will come as a direct result of the synchronized motion of our efforts. Think of the real boat with individuals forming a rowing team. They row in the same direction with similar efforts and in synchronized fashion. When the support organization learns to work as if we were in a real vessel using our individual efforts to move it forward, we could take that vessel anywhere.

Solidarity in common terms is simply being "on the same boat" as your colleagues. In other words, sharing the same situation and accepting the same faith. In fact, this is exactly what we are in technical support. We are a bunch of technical people who happen to all be on the same proverbial boat. Our profession sits in its infancy and all of us will benefits from its development and advancements. In the typical support group, the coworkers work better and feel stronger in their personal ties when they support the same product and have similar interests and passion for the vocation and the technology. Solidarity is what drives some professions to organize and form labor unions in order to bring change and right some imbalances. Luckily, technical support is in no need for labor unions; at least in the near future. Nevertheless, at the local support group level, the individuals must be of the same mind to deliver the best support possible to meet the demands and satisfy the users of the technology. Aside from the reasons provided by people analyzing technical support offerings and the decline of support quality, [11] the main reason quality declines or does not materialize in support departments is due to the lack of solidarity among the engineers providing the support. I have studied different support groups and find that the most successful groups with the best issue closure numbers, best customer satisfaction, and the least problems, such as friction among coworkers, are the groups in which the colleagues think alike and share interests, purpose, and are sympathetic to each other. Just imagine how unlikely you would be to go the extra mile in providing great technical support if you were in disagreement with your peers about how to provide the actual support. Colleagues who are not rowing in the same direction in the proverbial boat are causing the boat's demise.

One industry article reported that the economics of technical support are complex and being lousy at it can hurt a company as much as being great at support. This is due to the inherent cost of supporting customer; great support costs more cutting into profit margins while lousy support turns away customers resulting in less revenue and market share. [12] However, one aspect that article did not explore was the relevance of shared aims and solidarity for support personnel on quality. The quality level of support is not entirely dependent on cost; it also has to do with the mentality and the collective efforts of the individuals providing the support. If the support organization aligns with the rest of the business and understands the value it provides and how, the efficiency levels in support increase. [13] Consequently, a support organization that ignores the industry and business their company does will be less capable of providing the best quality of support to their users. Therefore, solidarity of support coworkers includes the people outside of support. [14]

How harmony and cohesion effects quality in technical support eludes most people except those who are intimately familiar with this field. Some even propose having trainers and troubleshooters handling customer issues together as a solution to increasing efficiency and service levels in a helpdesk. [15] But is it not that what the typical supporter is? After all, when we help customers we are telling them how

---

[11] Dodd, Jeff. 2004. "Tech Support Going, Going, Gone? (cover story)." *Smart Computing in Plain English* 15, no. 8: 56-57.

[12] Albro, E. (2006, January). Why Isn't Tech Support Getting Better?. *PC World, 24*(1), 15.

[13] Goldrich, M. (2002, October 28). Does your technical support add value to your business?. *Westchester County Business Journal, 41*(43), 27.

[14] Gray, P., & Durcikova, A. (2005, Winter2005/2006). The Role of Knowledge Repositories in Technical Support Environments: Speed Versus Learning in User Performance. *Journal of Management Information Systems, 22*(3), 159-190.

[15] Hubbard, A. (2002, May). The Help Desk Paradox. *Mortgage Banking, 62*(8), 102.

to do something, training, or trying to figure out the root cause of their problems by troubleshooting. We do not need specialized roles within support, but rather the unification of purpose among those who do the support. We need that sense of belonging and the common desire to help. Only then will our quality improve; not because we need to learn anything new or device a new process, but rather because we will all be pushing in the same direction.

To improve solidarity, promote the following practices among your support organization body:

- Understand the business you are in and the role your support efforts play in improving that business. Then promote this knowledge among your colleagues.
- Support management and colleague-initiated initiatives for improvement. Be careful not to think of all new initiatives as just some new idea or change imposed on you. There should be a reason why. Find out and then help promote it.
- Finds ways to harmonize with colleagues and share work and personal experiences.
- Take initiative to start solidarity among your support coworkers. Do not wait for management to initiate it. Be the Lech Walesa[16] of your support organization.

As support people, we are all in this together. Our profession still has a long way to go with a very bright future. We will achieve more in the way of quality and efficiency when we all work coordinated with our colleagues. Solidarity represents the fundamental movements in our working circles. Once we get into that habit, we will become a community in harmony with one another.

Truth is not a matter of fact but a state of harmony with progress and hope. Enveloped only in its wings will we ever soar to the promise of our greater selves.

—Bryant H. McGill

Teach Them How to Fish

Recently, one of my former managers explained why technical support people should be more like construction workers. He worked in construction before coming to the support field so he knows enough about both subjects to compare them. He says that construction workers strive to teach each other so that everyone knows the same thing. In other words, colleagues share information on how to perform certain tasks such as making joints, raising walls, and leveling floors. The construction workers benefit when their colleagues are at the same level of expertise because that way, they can work together and achieve more as a group. When one individual does not know what the rest knows about the work, it causes delays. Since most things are done in groups, such as putting on a roof or pouring a foundation, one person's inability to perform may delay the entire construction project.

In technical support, we also need to strive to teach our colleagues what we know. The benefits are mutual and serve to spread the knowledge as well as advance the organization's goals and efficiency. However, the sharing of information to other support colleagues is not something that takes place on a regular basis. The crude reality is that most people who know something special about the technology

---

[16] Beyer, G. (2006, January 16). What Ever Became of Solidarity? (Cover story). *America*, 194(2), 11-14. Lech Walesa started the Solidarity movement in Poland in 1980 which lead to the demise of communism in that country as well as social, political and economic reform and all because he promoted common values.

hoard this knowledge and fail to teach others. The reasons why this happens are many, but it is a sign of a still immature support organization that has not yet promulgated a culture of knowledge cooperation among its individuals. It is easy to blame the individual directly, but in the case of a support organization the acts and behaviors of the individuals are the symptom of the organizational culture. This begs the question, how can the culture promote the proliferation of knowledge sharing?

First, organizational culture is the specific collection of values and norms that are shared by people and groups in an organization and that control the way they interact with each other and with stakeholders outside the organization.[17] The individuals and their practices form the organizational culture, not the other way around; it starts with the individuals behaving a certain way that gives rise to the collective behavior. When support people come to the realization that the best way to work is by sharing information and teaching each other, the culture changes and the practice of collaboration in learning is adopted as part of the culture. Culture does not come by mandate from management, but is enabled by management. The best support organizations are those in which management allows the people to flourish and cooperate, thus adopting behaviors conducive to greater efficiency. The supporters interact with each other in constructive ways to elevate each other's skills. These behaviors are informal as is the nature of organizational culture. The individuals in a healthy culture do not wait for all answers to come from management; they engage each other to come up with their own solutions and solve their problems.

The unhealthy learning culture in a support organization is recognized because the individuals constantly complain about training. Those of us who deal with support people on a daily basis recognize this behavior immediately. The individual often says, "I have not been trained; therefore, I cannot perform" or "I am expected to solve such and such issues but received no training." Does this sound familiar? In this support organization, the problem is that the people "in charge" are not initiating the learning practices required to make the individuals learn and develop well enough to deal with the support issues. The people in charge are not necessarily the managers. They are almost always the technical leaders in the group and the highest ranking supporters, such as the senior or second-level support people. When new individuals come into the group, it is up to the technical leaders in the group to get them up to speed, not by formal training but by the act of sharing knowledge constantly until the new person acclimates to the support work. Formal training may be present but the technical development of the support person comes from those around him sharing what they know in an amicable manner and without holding anything back. When the sharing behavior is inherent in the individuals, the acclimation continues at all levels until the new support people become experts, or at least very proficient in the technology to a point where the individual knows where to find answers.

The knowledge sharing organization culture starts primarily at the top with the technical experts. They are the ones who must set the tone and share what they know so that others may also become experts. The expert who does not want to share or refuses to teach others everything the expert knows is a hindrance to the organization. When asked a technical question by someone with less experience, the expert who pushes back or gives useless answers should be removed from the organization by management. The ideal expert is one who shares at every opportunity and seeks out to help the rest of the support people. The expertise, when properly leveraged, allows the expert to close many more issues and help many more customers via helping other colleagues with their issues. When the rest of the support organization sees this behavior, they will mimic it, and the behavior will becomes part of the organizational culture.

Helping others with their issues has two major benefits, the increased efficiency of expertise and the sharing of knowledge with colleagues. Think of how much you learn when someone else with more expertise helps you work an issue. This type of learning is much more effective than formalized training because its hands on and deals with true customers situations. Additionally, it is unlikely that the expert will have to help you twice with the same type of problem since you will remember from the first

---

[17] Charles W. L. Hill, and Gareth R. Jones, *Strategic Management* (Boston: Houghton Mifflin, 2007)

instance. You can also share this knowledge with others so that they benefit from your experience. Moving others to develop desirable behaviors in support via examples and sharing of knowledge comprises the real role of the expert. In the enviable support organization, the experts share what they know proactively and cordially and entice others to do the same. Consequently, a positive organizational culture is initiated where everyone shares and no one is desperate for answers.

If you are an expert who hoards information, think of what you are doing to improve your support organization. If all you do is limit yourself to work your own issues, then you are doing a disservice to your colleagues. If you are not an expert and are not helped by those with expertise, you can also initiate a positive culture. It takes considerable more work, and it requires changing the behaviors, but it is doable. I strongly suggest speaking with your management and with the technical leaders in your support organization to explain why it is in everyone's best interest that they start sharing what they know. Remember, it is the expert's job to teach others how to catch that proverbial fish.

> *Give a man a fish and you feed him for a day. Teach him how to fish and you feed him for a lifetime.*

> —Lao Tzu

Personal Conflict

While working in social situations and surrounded by colleagues on a daily basis, it is almost certain that eventually you will have a personal disagreement with someone. Sometimes, given the right circumstances, personal disagreements escalate into friction then downright conflict. The source of friction is usually irrelevant, but the detrimental effect it has on you could be catastrophic because your feelings and attitude toward your colleagues, and theirs toward you, tend to negatively change. In the technical support environment, we usually work in close proximity to one another in cubicles which are sometimes no bigger than our closet at home. Thin three-inch dividing walls separate us from our neighbors; therefore, it is hard not to interact within your local work area. Under specific conditions, it is likely that disagreements among coworkers develop into friction and result in quarrels that sour the social work environment. Nevertheless, the issue is to try to avoid personal disagreements, but if you have them than you must effectively deal with them.

In order to explain personal friction and conflict, we must understand the different types of major conflicts that exist among technical support people. The types differ greatly in how they affect the actual work performed by the supporters. Conflicts fall into two major categories, personal and professional. The personal conflict involves matters not directly related to support work but have to do with some disagreement involving differences in opinions or facts about anything other than the actual work. Professional conflict is any escalated disagreement about the actual work or work-related processes. The big problem with conflict is that eventually it all becomes personal. When things get out of hand, the squabbling parties personalize even disagreements over professional matters. There comes a point we lose our control and become so eager to prove our point or discredit the other side that we stop at nothing and engage in truly despicable practices.

What we are talking about here is not simple disagreement or professional debate, but blatant clashing of people. This incompatible behavior may include heated arguments with offenses from both sides or simple stern disagreement with deep personal impact. There are huge differences between disagreement and clashing conflict. Personal and professional friction among individuals leads to negative consequences, such as animosity and even hatred, and has four characteristics that support people must avoid at all costs. When any of these distinctive factors are involved, the individuals move beyond the professional boundaries and into destructive territory. Colleagues that witness such quarrels must put a stop to them, even if they are not directly involved. The four characteristics are the following:

1. *Personal*: Anytime an argument or disagreement gets personal, things have gone too far. You know when something goes into the personal domain because it involves attributes of the parties involved that are beyond their control. Examples are "John, you are a loudmouth who can't keep quiet even if. . ." or "Jane, you look like a mortician with your long, pale face. . ." Another hint that things are getting personal is when the quarreling parties start accusing each other of failures that are not entirely their doing or not directly out of malice. For example, "John, if it wasn't because you goofed up and did not call the customer we wouldn't be in this mess!" or "Jane, am I supposed to believe that you are so slow that you couldn't do this alone despite me showing you over and over?" Anytime personal attributes enter into the argument, things are escalating so it's best to end the argument at once.

2. *Offensive*: While arguing, individuals tend to attempt to hurt each other citing derogatory comments or even name-calling. Examples are "John, you idiot, didn't you realize this was going to happen?" or "Jane, you are dumber than a wet noodle!" There is no room for offensive statements in a professional environment. The support person who acts in this way will alienate those around him and is sure to get animosity in return, which only aggravates the situation. The biggest problem with offensive statements is that people remember long after the quarrel settles, therefore its destructiveness lasts even after people make up.

3. *Irrational*: Arguments that progress to the ridiculous may not appear offensive but are very destructive. When people go into making ridiculous accusations while arguing, they embarrass themselves and the people with who they are arguing. I once had a difference of opinion with a colleague in a meeting in which he accused me of being an optimist to a fault and not living in the real world. Obviously, like everyone else, I can be positive or negative depending on the situation and the matter at hand. My colleague's irrational comments got personal, offensive, and irrational all at once. Instead of arguing the facts, he opted to attack me with irrational claims about my optimism, which did not help his argument.

4. *Emotional*: Quarrels that go into the emotional realm cease to be controlled by the parties involved. An argument where people start crying or get angry will go nowhere fast. People who get emotional during an argument tend to lose control of their temper and are bound to explode. The argument may result in cursing and could even get physical. Such emotional behavior will only lead to resentment and broken friendships, if not losing a job or even jail.

To avoid the type of conflicts previously described, you, as the technical support professional, must always remember that you are in a professional setting. There is no place for disagreements to become personal or offensive. If you know that your personality type may conflict with a colleague of yours, then limit your interaction to professional matters only and do not get into personal issues. When you sense that things are about to get out of control, then walk away or change the conversation. It is preferable to leave things as they are than to risk having a sour experience. Remember, these are the people with who you have to work every day; there is no need to have animosity toward them.

A quarrel is like buttermilk, the more you stir it, the more sour it grows.

—Bolivian Proverb

The Power of Criticism

Most things we do in technical support may be done in a different way by other people. The troubleshooting of an issue could go differently if done by someone else with a different set of qualifications and approaches to the technology. The way we approach a customer, or the things we say or do with the data we gather, may be construed as lacking merit by someone else within our circle of coworker, even when we are sure it is the best approach. Passing judgment on someone else's work may be appropriate with the right individuals but detrimental with someone who does not accept criticism or views it negatively. Consequently, the criticism we provide, even with the best intentions, may come across harsh and condemning, if not presented the correct way. When properly administered, criticism is a very powerful tool for technical support professionals that helps us grow and mature as supporters, and allows us to provide that benefit to others.

Criticism is a serious examination and judgment of something.[18] In some cultures, criticism carries a negative connotation of judgment and disapproval that may result in people feeling shame rather than anger when receiving criticism.[19] Western and eastern cultures view criticism and its consequences differently depending on how personal the criticisms are made and perceived by the recipient.[20] Therefore, when dispensing criticism, we must be sure we are not causing undue duress to our colleagues. How can criticism help us grow? The answer is simply by making us aware of what we are deficient on and can improve. Even when the criticism is no more constructive than a disparagement, we may get an idea of what others think of our work and of the intent of the criticism.

Benefiting from criticism is much more complicated than simply accepting constructive criticism and turning down or ignoring destructive criticism. We really can learn from both. However, the way we do it may be a bit counterintuitive. First, constructive criticism is defined as criticism or advice that is useful and intended to help or improve something, often with an offer of possible solutions.[21] Receiving such criticism would be great but may not always be volunteered by our colleagues in technical support. Additionally, the definition of constructive criticism implies that the person dispensing the critique is better prepared or, at least, more experienced than us to opine on such matters. Otherwise what grounds would you have to criticize someone else's work? Nevertheless, adding value to a colleague's work by means of critical analysis does not require a higher level of expertise, just a different point of view.

Among support people, there is also the possibility that criticism may not always be positive or proactive. There will surely be colleagues who will tear you down for no other reason than you do not do things as they do. This is especially true among people with conflicting personalities who are highly opinionated for no other reason than to disagree or hurt others. The smart supporter who can keep his cool and does not sway under harsh destructive criticism can also learn a lot from it. It seems

---

[18] "criticism." *WordNet® 3.0*. Princeton University. 21 Jan. 2009.
[19] David Yau-Fai Ho, Wai Fu, and S.M. Ng. 2004. "Guilt, Shame and Embarrassment: Revelations of Face and Self." *Culture & Psychology* 10, no. 1: 64-84.
[20] Cohen, Dov, and Alex Gunz. 2002. "As Seen by the Other . . . : Perspectives on the Self in the Memories and Emotional Perceptions of Easterners and Westerners." *Psychological Science* 13, no. 1: 55.
[21] "constructive criticism." Webster's New Millennium™ Dictionary of English, Preview Edition (v 0.9.7). Lexico Publishing Group, LLC. 21 Jan. 2009.

unorthodox to think that we can learn from people who try to destroy our spirits with negative criticism but the fact is that we learn a lot from the people and not from their technical or service suggestions. The following are examples of negative criticism and what we can learn from it:

- *Personal criticism*: Critiques that place the blame on you and not your skills or actions. This is probably the hardest one to ignore as it borders on insulting and is, at minimum, offending. However, what you can learn is that the colleague making the criticism simply does not like you, or has some personal divergence with you. This type of criticism says a lot more about the person making it than about the target of the criticism. When confronted with this type of situation, you will know who the problematic people are and who you need to be wary of. You can try and approach the critic and try to find out what is causing this disconnect. It may be just that the person is simply socially incapable or there may be some other hidden reason why he is criticizing you harshly and personally. The proactive way to deal with this type of criticism is to immediately confront the critic and ask that he or she be more constructive and stay away from personal criticism.

- *Demanding change*: This type of negative criticism in technical support carries an imperative tone and demands that you make some change to satisfy the critic's view of what should be. Of course, there is no reason why you should change simply based on criticism, but it will give you an insight into what your criticizing colleagues think of you and your work. It will also give you a good idea of what bothers them about your actions so much that they demand change. To deal with this criticism, analyze the specific change demands and determine if they have some rational reason and potential for validity. There is a possibility that the request has merit, but is just communicated in the wrong way. If you see the same criticism coming from multiple colleagues, it may be something that you need to look into further. If the criticism is made in a spurt of emotion and isolated, it is possibly just your colleague talking more than is prudent.

- *Blaming*: This type of criticism is the most destructive as it places someone directly in the line of fire. Charging a colleague with the culpability for something that goes wrong is only asking for trouble and little good can come out of such criticism. If you are the object of this type of criticism, the best thing to do is to bring it to your manager for resolution. When a coworker blames you for something that goes wrong, there is no reasoning with such criticism. You will learn about your coworker's personal values and professional ethics, but that is about all the possible benefit you will get out of it.

Chances are you will not satisfy everyone regardless of what you do and how well you do it. There will always be critics of your work and handling of support issues and customer situations. Colleagues will criticize you, sometimes fairly and sometimes not. Regardless of how you are viewed and the type of criticism you receive, you can learn from your colleagues and about your colleagues by listening to their positive analysis or even their condemnation. The trick is to remember to keep an open mind and not lose your temper. Take it all in and retain the good. You will grow as a person and you will gain an insight into the motives and behavior of your colleagues.

You can't operate a company by fear, because the way to eliminate fear is to avoid criticism. And the way to avoid criticism is to do nothing.

—Steve Ross

Comforting the Demoralized Colleague

Occasionally, you will come across a colleague who feels disheartened and requires some uplifting by someone more emotionally robust; that colleague might even be you. The specific reasons are not as important as the fact that your coworker requires some cheering up in order to go back to being a productive member of your support group. As a responsible and amicable support fellow, you can take the lead and provide some well-chosen words of reassurance to your dismayed associate. As a professional supporter and colleague, you should not wait for anyone else to step up. If you wait and see, it is likely that no one will and your colleague's depression may very well prove contagious and others will come down with the same malady.

In a profession such as ours that encompasses multiple technology industries, it is almost guaranteed that events of an adverse nature will trouble our work environments from time to time. It may be because of a downturn in the economy, economic cycles within the industry, or more microeconomic factors, such as the acquisition, bankruptcy, or a management-related episode that causes grief to those in the support organization. As support employees, we are not safe from any matter affecting our employers and may feel the brunt, justifiably or not, of the problems that our companies are going through. Many of us experienced the possibility of layoffs, changes in management, acquisitions, and other drastic changes that deflate our spirits. Fortunately, the feeling is all in our minds and emotions. We can change our perception of the situation by looking at it from a different angle. This is where colleagues are the key.

Despite technical support being a very individualistic line of work, colleagues do work things out among themselves and often are the best source of positive reinforcement when faced with dire circumstances. Remember that ours is a very intellectually demanding profession and the wrong mindset greatly affects the service and quality of the support offered to clients. What is worse, it may also spread to other support colleagues and the entire department could catch the same gloomy outlook. Since you understand the importance of a colleague when it comes to providing words of encouragement, you will need to pose particular questions to your colleague in a clear, calm, and rational manner. When your coworker sees that you are serene about the outlook of the situation, he or she will find comfort in your mere confidence. The questions to pose are the following:

- *What is the worst thing that could happen?* Phrased in a rhetorical tone, this question invokes reasoning. Talk with your colleague and try to answer in a mature fashion what is realistically the worst possible outlook for the situation at hand. For some strange play of destiny, I have found myself in these situations more times than I care to remember, such as the five acquisitions and divestures in my support career. There are truly hard times when it seems like your professional world is coming to an end. The possibility of finding yourself out of a job is terrifying to many. But what is truly the worst thing that could happen? I was once laid off after the reseller I recently started working at was acquired and they no longer needed the newer people. Three colleagues and I got the ax. It was one of the worst feelings, if not the worst, feelings of my professional career. This happened on a Thursday, but by the following Monday I was working at another company for a higher salary.

- *Have we been through something similar before and came out okay?* Posing this question requires that you and your colleague have some history together in the same job, at another company, or at least that you have some knowledge of other similar situations which had a positive outcome. You certainly do not want to bring up a comparable situation in which things turned out terribly. Comparing analogous events and their repercussions is a very healthy way of managing stressful changes. If your experience proves that things should reasonably turn out fine, your colleague should find comfort in knowing the possible odds. I remember a discussion at the office when the gas prices were very high in late 1997. Everyone in the group was speculating the demise of our personal gas budgets. One of the colleagues calmly pointed out the similar situations in the 1970s and 1980s where gas prices went up and eventually came down.

- *Will this be temporary or permanent?* Anticipating if the situation has a potential to be permanent or is only temporary drastically changes the outlook of the coworker who finds solace in certainty. For support people, one of the most stressful situations consists of issue loads larger than the group can effectively manage. Support colleagues may give in to stress and declare the workload as something to be very anxious about; however, large issue loads are typically temporary and eventually come down. Analyzing the increase in issue volume as a symptom and trying to rationalize possible causes, such as a new release of a product, new sales efforts, or the cyclical time of year when customers have more free time to call in support issues, will help calm distressed coworkers.

- *Do we have other alternatives if this situation continues?* If all else fails, talk with your colleagues about a possible contingency plan. If you think about this question, this is what we do in our support work naturally; we find possible alternative solutions to problems. Suppose that you work in a large organization but your group has a terrible product that may be in jeopardy of being taken off the market. What would the alternative be? The answer may be looking for a support position in another technology elsewhere in the same company. It may be moving into another line of work temporarily until you can find another suitable support group to join. The main thing is to find an answer to the possible continuation of the stressful situation.

Of course, you should not feel that it is entirely your responsibility to appease members of your support group who find themselves in the doldrums. You should also talk with your manager and explain the need for some uplifting from him. Sometimes hearing positive assurance from the delegated authority reassures colleagues that things will turn out all right. You can also find people who went through similar situations with positive outcomes and ask them to speak to your group. Finally, summon help from the other supporters in the group to help reinforce the "bright side" to your depressed colleague. An effective support group is like a well-oiled machine, but a member in despair throws a monkey wrench into the whole thing; therefore, avoid it at all costs.

> *Just as despair can come to one only from other human beings, hope, too, can be given to one only by other human beings.*

> —Elie Wiesel

Understanding Your Colleagues' Behaviors

While working with your support colleagues, you will undoubtedly notice how much they differ and how differently they react to different situations, sometimes without making sense to you. This manner of reacting to an event and conducting oneself form the behavior of an individual.[22] The big challenge is

---

[22] "behavior." Merriam-Webster's Medical Dictionary. Merriam-Webster, Inc.

that the causes of behaviors are very diverse; however, understanding the behaviors of your colleagues and their causes will help you understand their performance and how to best work with them.

To understand the behavior of your colleagues, you will need to recognize the different behavioral patterns present in support people and figure out what drives the specific behaviors. Of course, to study behaviors in a support group, we will need to look at behavioral research in the workplace. Behavioral research states that employee behavior is a function of individual and environmental variables as proposed in 1936 by German Psychologist, Kurt Lewin, in his famous formula B=f(I,E).[23] What this says is that even when the behavior manifests itself in different ways depending on the individual, there are some basic principles that are the same for all human beings. Behavioral scientists generally agree on the following:

- Behavior is caused.

- Behavior is goal-directed.

- Behaviors that are not directly observable are also goal-directed.

- Behavior that can be observed is measurable.

- Behavior is motivated.

Because behavior is caused, the actions that your support colleagues take, such as arriving on time (or late), helping each other (or not), going the extra mile (or stopping a few feet into it), and documenting effectively are all caused by something in the individual. For instance, getting to work early everyday may be caused by your colleague's desire to get an early start on the work for the day, but it could also be caused by the perceived danger of downsizing. Your colleague is afraid that he may be next and thinks that by arriving early, and showing what a good worker he is, his chances of being laid off will decrease.

Behavior has a purpose even when it appears hard to figure out. People do things for a reason regardless of whether you think they are right or wrong. Some coworkers like to take the easy cases first while others would rather tackle the hardest ones. There is a goal in mind for each individual. The goals may be the same but the approaches are different. Once you understand why the people in your group behave in such a manner, it will be easier for you to figure out how to best collaborate with them. The fact is that everyone does something for one of two reasons: to get closer to something or to get away from something. Take the coworker who exercises religiously every day after work. He may want to be fit or maybe he wants to not be obese. The colleague who smokes five times a day may want to savor the nicotine or maybe he just wants to keep off the pounds. The same can be said for any other behavior present in your support colleagues whether it be training, mentoring, arguing or gossiping. All behaviors have a goal. What about behaviors we cannot easily observe, such as thinking or troubleshooting? Actions that we cannot simply observe also contribute to achieving the individual's goals. A support person who is thinking and remembering solutions in his head does it because he wants to attain his goals of solving issues or finding answers.

The good thing about observable behaviors, such as picking up the phone to call a customer or letting the phone ring off the hook and not answering it, is that they can be measured. These measurements serve to compare and derive metrics. Why would you want to compare and derive metrics? The answer is simply to predict performance. For instance, your coworker takes 20 support issues per day and he closes at least 18, which comprises a closure rate of 90 %. However, you notice that if he takes 30 issues per day, he can only close 20. That is only a closure rate of 66%. You can make a prediction that if he takes any more than 20 issues his closure rate diminishes. Evidently, this is a very

---

[23] Mitchell G. Ash, "Cultural Contexts and Scientific Changes in Psychology," *American Psychologist*, February 1992, pp. 198–207.

simple way to rationalize an observable behavior and predict future performance based on a small sample, but statistics aside, measuring behaviors allow us to predict performance.

The most important aspect of behavior in dealing with colleagues is the concept of motivation behind actions. When you see that a coworker is exhibiting a certain behavior, there is a central motivation behind the specific behavior. It is reassuring to know that motivation is behind good behaviors, but certainly detrimental in the case of negative ones. The motivation behind the behaviors observed of your colleagues may not even be rational to you but understanding their motivation will give you a broader understanding behind changing and eliminating undesired behaviors while reinforcing desirable ones.

Allow me to illustrate with an example that happens in many support groups. It is almost 5 PM, which, in most places, is the end of the work shift. The support line phone rings with what appears to be a valid support call. You notice that most of the people in the group do not pick up the phone, while a few select people do go ahead and answer. You may ask yourself, "What motivates some coworkers to leave a customer hanging?" Along the same lines, "What drives others to forgo a few minutes and take the call anyway even when it is the end of the day?" The answer is their motivation. No doubt it will be different for all of them, but fundamentally the reasons are similar in nature. The ones who do not want to take the call are motivated by more free time, others may be late for some other activity after work, while some simply are tired and do not want to take another call; all are perfectly valid motivators and possibly justifiable in their own way. On the opposite spectrum, the people who go above and beyond, even if it means working after their shift ends, may also be motivated by all types of reasons. Also, just because they display the desirable characteristics does not automatically mean their motivation is desirable. It could be they just do not want to go home, they may have an unhealthy work habit that makes them want to work after their shift, or hopefully they simply want to live up to a level of excellence when it comes to customer service.

When it comes to why people do things, it is helpful to look at the causes of behaviors. Remember that people do not act without motive or reason.

We are all serving a life sentence, and good behavior is our only hope for a pardon.

—Doug Horton

The Customer Within

Have you ever stopped to think what would happen if you treated your coworkers the same way you treat customers? What if your colleagues expected and received the same level of service from you as your outside customers receive? In the support group, customer service is not just for external constituents, but also for internal associates. Imagine if within the support organization, you could go up the higher tier of supporters and receive similar treatment as the actual customer who buys and uses our products receives from you. Wouldn't that be something?

Before you close the book and think I'm out of my mind, please allow me to explain. The support organization, by its very structure, is designed to make sure we use all of our skills and experience to the maximum level possible. The design I am alluding to is that which has multiple tiers. The first one handles the bulk of the issues; the next one handles the issues escalated or transferred by the first one, and so on, until eventually getting to someone who can actually make design changes and package the solution in a future model, version, or product release. This type of organizational structure ensures that everyone in the tiers exhausts their expertise and resources before the problem passes to the next tier. It is not a new concept and just about every profession has some form of similar structure to extract the most of the individual contributors. For example, if you go into an emergency room at a local hospital you may first have to see a nurse, then a nurse practitioner, then an emergency doctor, and eventually a specialist and so forth until you get to the individual who can cure your ailment. However, when it comes to technical support, the big problem with this structure is that the higher you go in the tier, the more the colleagues become isolated and, in many cases, the higher tiers become "untouchables."

In this context, we define the "untouchables" as those upper-tier colleagues who do not speak or deal with customers directly, who only want to consult, do not want to own any of the tickets, and who treat lower tiers with at least some level of demeanor. These "untouchables" are very hard to deal with from an organizational perspective as they hold the bulk of the specialized knowledge and experience but typically do not share it freely or willingly. I am not suggesting this is done out of malice because I have known many colleagues in this situation and they are great people who truly believe their "way" is the best one. Nevertheless, the paradox is that they are technical experts, but they are terrible supporters as well as a detriment to their support organization. What is worse is that they have no idea of the harm they are causing.

Of course, some of the unapproachable colleagues may just appear to be distant or unfriendly but may, in reality, be willing and even happy to help you. However, since our perception guides our behaviors they will continue to be "untouchables" in our eyes until something happens; either we discover we had the wrong perception or they pleasantly prove us wrong.

By this point, you should have a good idea if there are "untouchables" in your upper tiers. Now the problem becomes what to do about it and how to improve the negative behavior. If you are in the lower-level tier and look up to someone for answers but that person fits the preceding description, then the following will help you approach these colleagues:

- *Contact the person directly.* The best way to get an answer from someone who has it is to go directly and simply ask. Too many times, upper-tier colleagues feel "special" because others make them feel special, not because they claim to be.

- *Demand specific answers.* When approaching an upper-level colleague who fits the description of an "untouchable" upper tier member, a good way is to be very specific about what you are asking. Do not make the mistake of asking for opinions or just feedback because you will not get your colleague's attention in that manner.

- *State specifically the timeframe in which you need the answer.* Typically when a support person goes up to a higher tier for answers, it is because there is a customer on the other side requesting the help. This is not a voluntary request for available time, but rather a very real demand for help. The customer will not wait around until you and your colleagues develop the rapport needed to understand each other. You need to ask for a specific answer by a specific date or within a very specific timeframe.

On the other hand, if you are an upper-tier supporter and fit the description of the "untouchable" colleague, you have to do everything in your power to change that perception of you. The following are ways you can change the perception others have of you:

- *Proactively help.* This is not an easy thing to do especially if you are the subject-matter expert. However, if your colleagues think you are unapproachable, the only way to remedy the situation is to prove them wrong and show them that you are approachable and proactive. You start by asking them if they need any help and volunteering new information as you learn it.

- *Communicate often.* The more your lower-tier colleagues hear from you the more they will get acquainted with your style of communication and of providing help.

- *Treat them like customers*: The upper tiers exist to help the lower tiers and solve the problems the less-experienced colleagues cannot. The performance of the higher tiers is reflected on how much the lower tiers are stuck on issues very much like the performance of technical support is reflected on how much difficulty our customers experience when getting help with our technology.

Efficiency in technical support is maximized when everyone works at his or her capacity. This means that the first tier of support people take the first round of problems and the upper tiers the more complex or difficult problems resulting in everyone being utilized at their technical capacity. The problem arises when the upper tiers are difficult to access, either because of their own behaviors or because of wrong perceptions from their constituents. Regardless of which support tier you are on, your role is to help the customers and to be there for your support colleagues in the capacity that best utilizes your talents.

Our business is about technology, yes. But it's also about operations and customer relationships.

—Michael Dell

The High Performer Vs. the High Producer

Support people are typically measured by the output they produce in terms of customer satisfaction and the quality and quantity of resolved technical support issues. Look around your own technical support group and you should be able to identify two types of behavior that stand out in individuals, which makes them very important to the organization for the work they do and the value they add to the group. These are not the only desirable behaviors in a support person but they are quite sought after because these behaviors often determine the success of a support group to achieve the goals of the technical support organization. The reason they are included in this chapter is because you must be able to identify the behaviors as they naturally occur within your own support group. We will get to the reasons later.

The two behaviors are high performance and high production. You may think these two items don't seem like behaviors at all, but they are indeed. The reason they seem vague or general is because there is not one specific action which makes either one. You may think these two are the result of behaviors, but in fact they are actions in their own right with different approaches depending on the individual. The point is that they always exhibit similar characteristics, even when the means are different. Individuals exhibiting each, or both, perform specific actions which together result in the two behaviors.

The two behaviors of high performance and high production sound very much alike, but in terms of technical support they are quite different and have very different characteristics.

High Performance is the behavior of producing the best work possible and always above average. The supporter that practices this behavior usually solves the most complex problems with the best results, least effort, and in the shortest time. This is quite a feat especially when surrounded with other capable individuals. The high-performance individual is the one who can resolve seemingly even the most complex and difficult problems. High performance will typically be the result of experience, exceptional troubleshooting and reasoning skills, and a tendency to take on challenges that confound others.

The colleague with the high performance behavior is not simply the one who knows the most, but rather the one who utilizes what he knows at its fullest. The natural tendency is to think of the expert of the group as the high performer, but this is far from the case. The expert may know more but that expert also has to put out innovative, numerous, and timely solutions to be considered a high performer. In short, the high performer is the colleague you would go to with problems which are beyond your level and from whom you expect a timely and accurate solution.

High production behavior, on the other hand, is the act of closing a lot of issues, answering many problems, taking a high percentage of the group's calls, and answering the most customer questions as possible. The high producer does not have to answer the most complex questions, only the most number of questions. If you look around your group, you will see that there is at least one person who seems to always close the highest number of cases, incidents, or issues month after month. Their record is consistent enough to be more than just a good month, so it is a learned behavior that makes that person a high producer.

In my years in technical support groups, I have seen this behavior only a handful of times. In every single one of the cases, the approaches and techniques were different, but the result was always the same. These individuals always closed the highest number of issues regardless of the month or even technology supported. Yes, you read right; even when these individuals went from one product or technology to another they produced among the highest number of closed customer issues. This is what leads me to conclude that high production is a behavior independent of the technology supported.

Now comes the good part. Why in the world would you care about the high performers and the high producers in your group? The answer is quite simple: These behaviors are reproducible. All you have to do is figure out who in your groups have these qualities; once you find out exactly what makes them high performers and high producers you can do the same and achieve similar results. Allow me to give you an example. I have a very dear colleague in Spain whom I worked with in a support group a few years ago. This colleague was consistently among the top three issue closers in a team of over 70 people worldwide. He was not regarded as the expert in the technology, but he closed a lot of issues every month. He later moved to a completely different technology in a whole different industry. He continues to close a lot of issues and ranks among the top producers in his global support organization. I observed him for some time, read his issues, and also asked him what made him close so many incidents. He shared he has one underlying principle; he makes it a point to speak to as many people as possible. Sounds overly simplistic if not, well, downright strange. However, by speaking to a high number of customers he stacks the odds in his favor because the more people you speak with the more chance you will have to close an issue.

You may be wondering if there is a preference or an advantage to being a high performer over a high producer, or vice versa. Nevertheless, each behavior is valuable depending on the context. The high performance behavior is ideal with a mature technology and customer base or in a technical support group with multiple tiers and where there are support people who are new to the technology. The high performer allows the rest of the group to focus on the less complex, easier issues. Consequently, the high producer is very desirable in a young technology, new customer base or a popular, hot-selling product area with a high number of incoming issues.

Understanding the two behaviors previously outlined will allow you to better understand your colleagues and mimic the desirable behaviors you see in others. There are many advantages to being a high performer or a high producer, but the main is that individuals with these behaviors are very valuable to their employer and customers. Therefore, if you want to become more valuable in your current role, find a colleague exhibiting those behaviors, and do as they do.

Don't lower your expectations to meet your performance. Raise your level of performance to meet your expectations. Expect the best of yourself, and then do what is necessary to make it a reality.

—Ralph Marston

The Self-Sustaining Colleagues

Richard came from small support group at a startup tech company in which a handful of supporters took care of a small number of customers in the best way possible—often with issues closing in the first call and with those calls answered on the first ring. The technology was new and innovative, plus the customers loved it, and the technical support they received was so prompt, courteous, and accurate that customers often commented on how superior the support was compared to other companies. This was taking place at the height of the internet and Y2K bubbles in late 1998.

Because of an acquisition, Richard and his colleagues found themselves absorbed by a much bigger software technology company that was accustomed to absorbing smaller companies to fuel growth and expansion into new subsets of the industry. The small support group was allowed to continue with normal operations but without a local manager. The group thrived and was quite successful in dealing with the new volume of issues generated by new customers of the much bigger sales force in the new company. The support group was successful and needed only administrative management; it was truly a self-sustaining group.

Just like Richard and his colleagues, the self-sustaining support group is one in which the technical support continues despite changes in the organization, management, customer base, and even when the company changes. In order for a support group to become self-sustaining, it has to go through some drastic change, such as an acquisition, dramatic increase in call volumes, changes in management and pivotal changes in the technology supported. In other words, the group does not realize it is self-sustaining until it is faced with adversity; otherwise, it is business as usual.

The self-sustaining support group has certain characteristics that differ fundamentally to the groups that collapse when faced with unexpected or dramatic change. The group is self-sustaining because it can function independently of anything else happening around it, and even when they are left without proper care from management or technical leadership. This type of group does not require any external technical or managerial input for it to function and deliver high-quality technical support to customers. The characteristics that make a self-sustaining group are the following:

- *Small size*: The size of the self-sustaining group may be as small as two or as big as 20, 30, or perhaps more. The importance of the size is that it has to be small enough for the group members to defy chaos when the change occurs. In the case of being left without direct managers, if the group is beyond what can be controlled internally by the members themselves, the group runs the risk of collapsing in disarray.

- *Harmony among group members*: Drastic organizational and business changes have the negative effect of causing undue stress on group members. The self-sustaining group is one in which the members remain congenial to one another even under stressful situations and uncertainty. In this group the members generally share the same vision for the future, the understanding of the current situation, and the needs of the customers. But most of all, the members have no disagreement about their priorities on how to go about delivering support to customers.

- *Strong internal processes*: In order for the group to be self-sustaining, it needs to know what to do and how to do it. This knowledge and methods comprise the processes the group utilizes to deliver the support. When the processes are proven strong and reliable, the group members depend on the processes to carry out the work, in spite of anything else happening around them. With reliable, specific, and proven processes, the group continues with the business even amidst chaotic changes in the organization.

- *Resilient culture*: The members in the self-sustaining group share the same mentality of going forward with the business. They may be under stress but have a firm, entrenched belief that they must keep doing the work. A good example of this is when Richard, along with a few colleagues, became manager-less after an acquisition in the middle of Y2K. They knew that they had to keep providing support as they always had. It certainly mattered that they faced radical changes, but that was secondary to the desire to keep providing great support to their customer base. Many years after that, and in a much larger group, they went through a very similar situation for the fourth time. However, the majority of the group did not share the resilient culture and the members simply grew disillusioned and stopped providing adequate support.

- *Technically mature*: The group that proves impervious to chaos and forced transformation will typically be quite knowledgeable in the technology. It would be quite difficult to be an amateur in the subject matter and still be self-sustaining. Of course, being technically mature in the technology does not equate to being an expert; it simply means that the group is beyond the learning and experimenting phases of learning the technology. It also does not mean that the group is self-reliant, as the self-sustaining group may need to go outside of the immediate members for technical answers.

In your technical support career, you may eventually face drastic change at some point. Your group might make it through the transition unscathed, may barely survive, could simply disappear, or be outsourced. It is in these times of transition that the true self-sustaining groups shine and rise to the occasion, proving to be incredibly valuable to the organization.

Aside from providing value in times of change, the self-sustaining group is one of the most desirable group traits because it succeeds and requires little or no external input to do so. When change has passed, all the group has to do is sustain the success and be on their way to achieve great long-term goals. The individuals go on to be positive influences in new groups and grow individually with their new earned war scars and valuable experience.

I have a great belief in the fact that whenever there is chaos, it creates wonderful thinking. I consider chaos a gift.

—Septima Poinsette Clark

Dealing with the Impossible Coworker

Working with others doing technical support and helping customers is probably the most rewarding aspect of our profession. When you and your colleagues work harmoniously together to carry out the goals of the organization, the work becomes more enjoyable and meaningful. Nevertheless, there are people with whom you will simply clash at a personal or professional level. With some individuals, you will just have no luck despite what you do and with who even reasoning will not work. In such situations, tensions rise and you may eventually engage in a heated argument in which you lose your cool. Thus, your colleague becomes the difficult coworker.

The collision with the difficult coworker is more than just the occasional disagreement or heated argument with your support buddy that you later forget and carry on as usual. With the difficult coworker, you genuinely have a problem. It is nothing rational; it is simply a clash of personalities. The reasons why you clash with a coworker are not as important as the fact that there exists a true dislike and downright loathing of the other person. What is so awkward is that both you and your difficult coworker have no problems with anyone else. The problem is just you and that coworker.

Given enough time and prolonged festering, the coworker goes from merely difficult to downright impossible. What is worse, the presence or proximity to that person causes you undue stress and may even affect your health, both physical and mental. Situations become more stressful for a party if one of the coworkers has some advantage over the other. Such advantages may be things like seniority, better title, physically bigger or more imposing, higher authority or position, and better and more fomented personal relationships with the other coworkers.

If you or one of your close colleagues is experiencing this situation with someone else, the best thing to do is to get away from that other person and just accept it for what it is: an impossible relationship. Things probably won't improve and the effort and aggravation are not worth the potential benefits so it is best to put some distance between the two coworkers. How that distance is achieved is something that should be discussed with your manager or your human resources department. Some possibilities include the following:

- Moving to another seat or side of the cube. Having a few feet between you and the impossible coworker may be all that's required. Also, not having to see that person may remove the stress.

- Move to another department or support group. If you think it necessary to make a bigger change, then making the move to a position somewhere else within the company will certainly get that coworker out of sight.

- Leaving your job and moving to another company. This is certainly the most drastic of the options but your mental stability is more important than any job. Additionally, everyone should have an agreeable working environment, especially in our profession where we have to put up with enough stress from dealing with technical customer issues.

Notice that I did not recommend speaking with the coworker or the usual private meeting to try and reach an agreement between the two. The reason I did not resort to this solution is because the impossible colleague is one you have something stronger than just a disagreement with. There is blatant hatred or loathing from that person to you, and nothing you can do appears to change that. This type of situation is unusual and hopefully will never happen to you. But if it does, it is a source of tremendous stress; I know because it happened to me.

The first time I was at a small internal helpdesk at a telecommunications company. Almost as soon as I joined the helpdesk, there was a coworker who seemed to go out of his way to aggravate me. His demeanor changed as soon as I entered the room. Other coworkers even noticed that his face would change with an expression of anger as soon as he saw me. I never understood why and I don't think he did either. The local management spoke with him and tried to reason with him. It did not seem to make any difference. He just had it out for me and I never knew why. All I can think of is that there was something in me that reminded him of something negative. Maybe I looked like his school bully or perhaps he had a bad experience and I reminded him of it. Whatever the case, it was clear to me and even to management that the situation would not change and I should just accept it. I was not thrilled with the position or the pay so I decided to interview with other companies and found my dream job soon thereafter.

A few years later, I saw a similar situation with two of my coworkers. They were great guys and I truly enjoyed working with both of them. However, one of them could not stand the other. It was more than just sarcastic remarks now and then or the occasional personal problem. The guy just hated the other coworker. It got to the point where the impossible coworker would not speak to the other coworker, except to mistreat him. Management got involved but it did not do any good. Along with other coworkers, I tried to reason with him, but nothing worked. There was an inexplicable hatred from the impossible coworker to the other.

You may think that the situation may be handled without having to make a move by completely ignoring the person. However, the person will still be there and your aggravation as well as peace of mind will be affected by not being able to work in a harmonious environment. Peace of mind is what you are going after and not necessarily keeping your pride.

If you ever find yourself in a situation with an impossible coworker or even if you are the impossible coworker, try and find the cause of the disdain. If you cannot find any sensible reason why this is happening, then it's time to put an end to the relationship, even if it means parting ways. Life is too short to work in a stressful environment.

Man's enemies are not demons, but human beings like himself.

—Lao Tzu

CHAPTER 6

■ ■ ■

Leadership in Support

Why do some people seem to move the masses or at least their cube neighbors with just a word? What is it that makes others spill their guts and yet not entice a single person to even lookup and respond? During my career, I asked these questions many times when I saw seemingly powerless people say a few words and have the big shots follow. This sort of influence is a personal power that emanates from something bigger than simple knowledge or authority. This is called leadership.

The leader is very different than a manager. People have to obey their manager or risk their jobs. On the other hand, a leader captivates the will of the people and drives them to do things they would not have otherwise done.

Of course, leadership is not the monopoly of support; we just see it there often. My most admired colleagues were not the brightest or the most knowledgeable. After all, if you work at something long enough and have a decent intellectual capacity, you can become an expert in your field. Possibly, you may also get someone to do what you ask willingly. True power comes from mobilizing others to follow your lead and comply with your requests simply because it was you who asked and not anyone else. It doesn't matter if you have the brass to show, people go where you lead them because they see something in you they admire, want, or benefit from. This is what leadership is about: moving people to action.

In this chapter, we explore a relatively new discipline, which teaches us a great deal about human nature and the power of persuasion and influence. The chapter includes several topics from the existing body of knowledge in leadership such as existing leadership models, as well as some new theories, such as pragmatic leadership, which I previously developed for a research paper I wrote in my doctoral studies in Business Leadership. The original research paper is quite lengthy and involved so I rewrote the main aspects of it for this chapter and applied it to technical support.

Take all you can from this chapter and use it immediately as leadership requires practice and a lot of patience. As you practice your leadership skills with those around you, you will realize the power of leadership.

You can judge a leader by the size of the problem he tackles. Other people can cope with the waves, it's his job to watch the tide.

—Antony Jay

What Is a Leader?

The word leader is tossed around quite a bit, especially with management and higher-ups. The word has even been used to describe objects and behaviors. For example, an innovative product is often called a leader in the industry and upper management are said to be executive leaders. Yet, leadership is a field of study that is expanding and developing a very broad body of knowledge. This brings us to the main question of this topic: What is a leader? Is it your local manager, your CEO, or is it the support person who closes a lot of technical issues for customers? Under the common definition of the word, all those people could be called a leader and often, they are. However, a leader is someone with more than just authority, knowledge or power.

The word "leader" is quite common yet everyone uses it to describe someone or something different; typically when that someone or something stands above the rest. However, the term is used in the study of leadership to describe someone who "directs the activities of a group toward a shared goal."[1] In short, a leader is a person who influences others to action. That action, of course, implies positive or progressive action. We typically wouldn't use the word leader to describe a villain, a bad influence, or an evil doer.

In our field of technical support, a leader is also a person who leads others to action. That action can be anything that provides some positive experience or an added value to the lives, work, and practices of support workers. The leader is always a person. A thing, product, or company does not entice others to action, regardless of how the idea is pitched. A leader is a formal term used in the technical jargon of leadership science. Therefore, whenever I refer to a leader, it is always a person. This will help understanding of what a leader is and does, and how a person can become leader.

First, let's look at how you can recognize a leader. Leaders everywhere are typically very easy to spot. They are at home, at work, and in church, pretty much anywhere where people congregate and do things together. There is a very simple way to locate the leaders in your workplace. Look around your technical support group and find the person or people others follow. The person who says "Let's do this or that" and others go and do it. Now, I know what you are thinking. I imagine you are immediately thinking about your manager. However, a leader is almost never a manager. The reason a manager is not a leader is because people have no choice but to follow and obey the manager. The manager has delegated authority, so he does not really influence other people; he directs other people because that is the manager's job. Nevertheless, the manager can also influence other managers, and may even influence or inspire action in direct reports, but it would be very hard to pinpoint what is real unbiased influence and what is just being influenced by the manager's authority. For this reason, when we refer to a leader, we do not refer to a manager.

A leader is someone who influences others to action via inspiration, example, direction, or service. Leaders influence other individuals like them. The people who follow a leader do so out of choice, not obligation. Think of a colleague in your technical support group that has influenced or inspired you to do something. The leader is the support colleague who inspired you to treat customers better. The leader may be the coworker who always brings a cake for others on their birthday and influences other to have a good time. The leader may be the support person who revolutionized your support group by bringing and teaching you new ideas and ways to solve support issues. The leader may be the colleague who always goes out of his way to go beyond the job requirements, achieves outstanding customer

---

[1] Gary Yukl, Leadership in Organizations (New Jersey: Prentice Hall, 2006), 21. In this definition, Yukl quotes (Hemphill & Coons, 1957, p.7) and is only the first of 10 definitions and the one that best describes leadership as it takes place in technical support.

satisfaction, and entices others to do the same. The leader may be someone with lots of knowledge or someone with lackluster knowledge but still manages to get you and others to act.

Why do you need to know about leaders? In a nutshell, everything gets done because of leaders. A leader who influenced others to come together and start a venture most likely founded the company where you work. A leader possibly initiated the idea for the product you now support, and makes your life a little better every day with or without your knowledge. Leaders move the world and initiate change. Again, we are not talking about managers or executives. We are talking about people just like you who want to see a difference in the world or who are moved by a need to help, transform, or improve the work and lives of others. Try to think of a nation that does not owe its independence or freedom, at least in part, to a leader. Can you think of any? Social and political movements throughout history have been as a result of someone leading others to action. Many South American countries owe their independence to a single man, Simon Bolivar. All the ex-Soviet republics owe their independence to Mikhail Gorbachev. Billions of lives are shaped by the leadership of religious leaders, such as Jesus, Moses, Mohammad, Buddha, and others. Our way of life and thinking in the West originated from Socrates. The very way you do your work, and possibly even what you know about the product you support, is most likely a result of a leader.

What is a leader? A leader is the person who influences you to do things either by inspiration, service, or direction. If you cannot think of who inspires you in your technical support organization, there is a possibility that you may be the leader.

A leader is best when people barely know he exists, when his work is done, his aim fulfilled, they will say: we did it ourselves.

—Lao Tzu

The Leader: Made or Born?

A question that has entertained leadership researchers is the one of whether there is a possibility of learning leadership or whether there are innate characteristics that predispose someone to become a leader. Some people seem to have a knack for influencing others to do things while others just can't see to make anyone do anything. I'm sure you have seen it your own support group, family, or circle of friends. There is usually one person who directs action and others seems to always follow. I was always amazed with my parents. They always seem to have a group of followers. As a child and teenager, there were always people at my house willing to follow the lead of my parents in many areas of their lives. People became Christian, married, started businesses, and ran for office because of my parents. In particular, my father has a way with professional matters and matters of the church. My mother is a modern life, Mother Teresa, helping just about anyone and influencing and changing their lives in the process.

If I didn't know better, I'd say that my parents were simply born with a leadership gene. Your parents or someone else you know may be the same way. Some people appear to be naturally fit inspiring people to action or change. However, leadership is a learned set of behaviors that allow you to drive transformation and achievement in others. My father was heavily involved in politics as a young man and he learned leadership behaviors, which later my mother picked up. If leadership was an inherited genetic trait, the children of leaders would themselves become leaders, and this is hardly the case.

Leadership in technical support occurs when you learn the following behaviors:

- Self-belief
- Assertiveness
- Servitude
- Independence

First and foremost, you have to believe in something in order to lead others. You cannot borrow those beliefs and just use them at face value. True self-belief is always original, hence the word "self." This is not to suggest that all self-beliefs are different. Inevitably, there will be people who have the same self-beliefs. However, for the most part, self-beliefs originate from experience and from success. Examples of self-belief include the confidence that you can go into any situation and make the best of it. This may be a core self-belief for many that can truly only come from the success of having achieved it to some extent. It would be very difficult to believe that you can do anything if all you know is failure; otherwise, it would be self-delusion. Technical support professionals with self-belief in some area of their professional lives will have some basis for their self-beliefs. I have a colleague who believes she can go into any situation where the customer is upset or very negative about our support, product, or company and turn the customer around. Can you guess why she has this self-belief? Yup, you guessed it. She does this all the time.

Another important aspect of leaders in technical support is their assertiveness. In this context, I use assertiveness to describe self-confidence and poise. This is probably the hardest thing to achieve, especially in our profession where we are always faced with new experiences and complex and demanding situations. As a supporter, if you wish to lead others to change, action, or service you must have some level of poise and confidence in the topic you are asking or influencing others to do. After all, would you follow someone who seems to doubt what he is preaching? As support people, we are experts at sounding assertive to customers, even when we have no idea what we are dealing with. This self-confidence is the nature of how our line of work deals with constituents. Think of how many fewer issues you could close if your answers sounded doubtful to the customer? However, being assertive with our own support colleagues is a challenge because they can spot a fake a mile away, after all they are in the same line of business as we are. Therefore, assertiveness has to be genuine. Just like self-belief, assertiveness is the result of successes, not failures.

Servitude in leadership is a mystery to many. In fact, the concept of servant leadership sounds like a paradox to many unfamiliar with the study of leadership. However, serving others in a manner that improves their life, work, and well-being is a type of leadership. The concept of the servant leader begins with the desire to serve others first.[2] It is important to note that servant is not synonymous with follower in the same way that master is not synonymous with leader. These terms are often misconstrued and this is why the servant leadership concept is hard for many to comprehend. Why is servitude a necessity to a leader? The reason is that leading others is a selfless act in benefit of someone other than the leader himself. Therefore, the leader acts in servitude when he leads. Additionally, a servant leader typically leads through service and influences those he serves. Nelson Mandela, Martin Luther King, and Mahatma Gandhi sought to serve their respective constituents via their leadership. In your situation, there may be someone who helps you and others achieve your goals by offering their help. In technical support groups, the coworker who prepares trainings but is not required to do so is a servant leader. The colleague who offers to help others solve problems even though it is not part of their job description is a

---

[2] RobertGreenleaf, Servant Leadership, *A Journey into the Nature of Legitimate Power & Greatness* (New Jersey: Paulist Press, 1977), 27. This leadership model originated formally with Robert Greenleaf but was described in essence by Socrates and many others since.

servant leader. Hopefully, you will also become a servant leader and improve the working lives of others in some constructive way.

The last behavior necessary for a leader in technical support is independence. This behavior does not mean that you are free to do as you please, but rather that you developed the autonomy to act so that others may follow. This is also irrelevant of your job requirements for you cannot dictate if others will follow just because of a job requirement. Independence comes through achieved results and a sense of initiative. Initiative is also independent of your obligations. Initiative is a chain reaction that starts when you are empowered. Most likely, that empowerment came from another leader or a very good manager. People do not follow just anyone. The leader is someone who stands above the rest because of their ability to entice others in a particular direction. It would be almost impossible for others to follow someone if that leader did not have some level of independence.

The behaviors I just described are not genetic and not natural. You have to learn them from experience. Therefore, leadership is learned. To become a leader in your support profession, industry, or support group you must develop the preceding behaviors and use them to entice others to action and eventual improvement of some sort. Leadership is learned and anyone can do it.

A good leader takes a little more than his share of the blame, a little less than his share of the credit.

—Arnold H. Glasgow

The Major Leadership Models

When you think of the leader in your support group, who is the first person that comes to mind? Do you think of the person in charge, the most intelligent, the one with the most charisma, the most money, or the person with the most experience? The simple answer is, the leader is the person who makes things happen by getting others mobilized toward a single goal. The beauty of leadership is that anyone can be a leader because there are so many ways to inspire others to action. The trick is to identify the leaders and the role they play within your local group and within the entire support organization.

There are three general types of leaders. In leadership studies, the following three types are referred to as leadership models:

- Transactional leaders
- Servant leaders
- Transformational leaders

Let us begin with the transactional leader and the characteristics that make someone recognizable under this leadership model. The transactional leader influences followers by providing instructions to follow to achieve something.[3] In technical support, we may think of them as mentors, technical advisors, and team leaders. However, the transactional leader may or may not have the title to go with it and often is an exceptional peer who others follow because of his ability to provide concise instructions to achieve an objective. This type of leader is called transactional, because he offers leadership through transactions or small developmental or operational changes. The transactional leader may be the peer who advises you on career choices, on handling customers, troubleshooting issues, or even on dealing with other colleagues. As a result of that transactional leadership, you as a follower change and progress.

---

[3] Bernard M. Bass, *Leadership and Performance Beyond Expectations* (New York: Free Press, 1985), p. 12.

This type of leadership is very individualized and the followers follow as one rather than as a collective. Also, the message and goal for each individual is different. Look around your peers and see if you can identify the transactional leader.

The second type of leadership model is that of the servant leader who aspires to serve first and attracts others to action as a result of that service. Technical support by its very nature is full of people who serve others by way of technical answers, help, and instruction. This fact alone does not make us servant leaders. We are in the business of service, and influence others to action by helping them, but this does not necessarily elevate us to the role of leaders. If it sounds like I'm speaking in riddles, please forgive me. The very man who coined the term servant leader tells us that there is not an easy way to tell who a servant leader is.[4] Nevertheless, look around you and try to find the individual whose help and whose services enrich everyone else in the support group. Here again, the servant leader is not the guy or gal with all the expertise, for all of us know the subject matter expert who holds information back instead of disseminating to others. Obviously, that would not be a servant leader, but a selfish expert. In addition, the servant leader does not necessarily move others to action as much as the servant leader enriches others by his actions. Typically, the servant leader serves and helps colleagues without really being required to do so. The servant leader does not imply a lower position or title. Anyone can be a servant leader, regardless of how high he is in the job ladder. Therefore, the servant part does not equate to lowly or junior roles but rather to service and value through assistance.

One of my dearest colleagues in one of our India support centers is a prime example of a servant leader. Mike is the type of guy who would go out of his way to help a colleague even when it was not his responsibility to do so. Mike would view it normal and possibly even as a volunteered duty to help others with anything ranging from testing solutions to taking issues over as well as anything else that did not have to do with the work itself. The entire group was made richer by Mike more than any other person. In fact, he was the go-to person because of his high level of service and great demeanor. Other colleagues started going to him for help to the point of almost completely ignoring those people whose job was to help. What made Mike to special? In a nutshell, Mike is the embodiment of the servant leadership model who enriches others by way of his service and at the same time influencing their actions.

The last leadership model, and the subject of many books and research, is the transformational leader. The transformational leader brings others together and inspires them to achieve results that are greater in scope than what could have been achieved without the leader's motivation and guidance.[5] The changes are typically progressive in nature, meaning that they service to improve some aspect of the followers' life, work, or belief systems. Transformational leaders through the ages have been responsible for the course and progress of history. Leaders like George Washington, Martin Luther King, Jr., Queen Elizabeth I, and Mikhail Gorbachev to name a few have all been transformational leaders. How does transformational leadership apply to our technical support profession? Because of the early stages of our profession, transformational leadership can help technical support progress in scope and knowledge. As discussed earlier in the book, we don't even have a proper name for our practitioners. I won't venture out to propose a name because I am in the same boat as many of you, but I am absolutely sure that there are colleagues out there working in some support center who are already thinking about how to motivate and persuade others to revolutionize and transform our field. It is just a matter of time but it has to happen eventually. It is my truest desire that you are that someone who reads this paragraph and

---

[4] RobertGreenleaf, *Servant Leadership, A Journey into the Nature of Legitimate Power & Greatness* (New Jersey: Paulist Press, 1977), 56-57. Greenleaf states that there is no easy way of knowing who the servant leader really.

[5] J.C. Wooford, Vicki Goodwin, and J. Lee Whittington, " A field study of a cognitive approach to understanding transformational and transactional leadership," *Leadership Quarterly*, vol. 9, no. 1 (1998) pp.55-84.

identifies with transformational leadership. Our profession, given its age and growth, is ideal for leaders who mobilize others to progressive change.

As mentioned, leadership is the act of influencing others to achieve something. Learning about the different major leadership models will allow you to identify leaders, and hopefully help you become a leader yourself. With the current status of our technical support profession, the time is ideal for you to start making some positive changes and adding value to our field by enticing others to positive change.

The true test of a leader is whether his followers will adhere to his cause from their own volition, enduring the most arduous hardships without being forced to do so, and remaining steadfast in the moments of greatest peril.

—Xenophon

The Pragmatic Leader

In the previous segment, we looked at the three major leader types as proposed in the field of leadership studies. The types of leader are:

- A transactional leader directs on the steps necessary to reach a goal. In technical support, this type of leader would be typically known as a mentor.

- A servant leader enriches others by way of their service and help. A good example would be the person in your group who is known as the go-to person and who goes out of his way to help others and improve the group in the process.

- A transformational leader inspires others to take meaningful action to change the status quo and result in impacting changes.

A big challenge to these three models is the lack of a guiding principle that is follower-centered. All the models focus on the leader and his actions, but not one of them starts with the follower and the desired results from the follower's perspectives. To fill this need, we need a fourth type of leader that does not conflict with the other three and that still offers another approach to leading others. The pragmatic leader fills those requirements.

The basis for the pragmatic leader model came from the philosophy of William James in 1907 called pragmatism, which states that truth is whatever is practical. For the sake of brevity and without getting into a discussion on philosophy, pragmatism is a way to determine what is truth without having to rely on rationalism or empiricism; rationalism being the philosophy of truth by reason and empiricism of truth by proof. [6]

The pragmatic leader has one simple test that consists of leading others only in and when his followers will attain some practical benefit from his leadership actions. In others words, the leader has to lead others with the intent to provide some usefulness to the ones he leads. This pragmatic leader model synthesizes William James's pragmatism for the use of leadership, but provides a test to leadership actions regardless of which of the three major leadership models are used.

---

[6] William James, Pragmatism and Other Essays (New York: Washington Square Press, 1975),16-17. In Lecture One: The Present Dilemma in Philosophy, James describes the disconnect that philosphers have with the real world. He puts forward the argument that while philosophers argue on what they can imagine or set to prove, it is only the real experience that has any real meaning since it is, in fact, the true reality.

The pragmatic leader in technical support leads others to action only when the results will have some practical consequences to the followers. During one doctoral class I took, Professor James C. Denison once said that a leader is someone who plants trees he will never live long enough to sit under. However, this is not the case for the pragmatic leader. In your support organization, you may identify leaders who drive progressive change, enrich colleagues through service, and mentor coworkers in order to achieve some goal. From those you identify can you make out which leader drives practical change?

Allow me to illustrate the concept and make the distinction between a pragmatic leader and a non-pragmatic leader. John is a leader in his call center and others typically follow his lead. He is known for driving others to new initiatives and programs. His latest leadership challenge was motivating people to wear Hawaiian shirts on Tuesday. He promoted the idea within the colleagues in the cubes next to him and then to the entire product group. It eventually got so big that now the entire support center wears Hawaiian shirts on Tuesdays. Mary, on the other hand, is not as charismatic as John and does not even own a non-dress blouse. She doesn't quite care for Hawaiian shirt Tuesday and rarely gets involved in such wacky initiatives. However, she is held in very high regard by just about everyone in her support group. She is not exactly the most expert or experienced in the group. What she does have is a knack for instructing her colleagues on how to close more issues. She analyzes people's queues and past issues and figures out ways in which they could improve their efficiency in order to get more issues resolved. Many come to her for advice and she tells them exactly what to do to achieve higher issue closing rates.

Based on the previous two examples, who do you think is the pragmatic leader? If you picked Mary, you would be correct. She provides leadership with the intent to provide practical value to those who follow her as an advisor or mentor. She fits the description of a transactional leader and also of pragmatic leader. John is clearly a transformational leader, but not a pragmatic leader because his guidance does not lead others to any practical benefit other than looking like Fantasy Island cast members.

Pragmatic leaders are effective and if you follow one, you, as a follower will receive practical benefit you can take to the bank. Practical leaders take us where we need to go and allow us to realize value relatively fast. In technical support, because of the fast-moving nature of complex technical products and support processes, we need pragmatic leaders to take us to where we need to go, rather to where they, arbitrarily, want to take us.

To become a pragmatic leader, ask yourself, "How can I influence others to action that will result in something of practical value to them?" If you start with this question, you will be on your way to becoming a pragmatic leader. It doesn't matter which of the three leadership models you subscribe to, if you are a pragmatic leader, the usefulness to your followers will be your guiding principle.

At this point, pragmatic leadership is still a relatively unknown way of looking at follower-oriented leadership. It is a very proactive and productive way of looking at influencing others to achieve value. It is my hope that you will become a pragmatic leader and think of the practical value you will deliver to your followers as your guiding principle.

The leader has to be practical and a realist, yet must talk the language of the visionary and the idealist.

—Eric Hoffer

The Linda Effect

Some time ago, I was asked to take over the technical support delivery for a support group within the same company. I knew little of the group and even less about the product. The move meant stepping down in hierarchy, but it was presented to me as such a challenge that I could not refuse the offer. I looked at the statistics for the group, the locations, number of support people, and the characteristics of everything from the product, tools, people, and processes. As I latered learned, the group's main issue was that of execution. They knew what to do, but they just didn't quite do it collectively and in unanimity.

The first thing I did when I took over the support delivery for the group was to implement a new process to take phone calls from customers and issues from the queue. It all went well the first day, but less than two weeks into the new process, the unassigned issues in the queue were so backed up that by the Monday of the second week we had issues left unassigned from the previous week. The problem was nothing to do with availability of people, resources, or even knowledge. The group just did not mobilize to take the new issues. I was strongly considering sending out an email to the entire group asking each person to pull at least one issue from the unassigned queue. This would effectively eliminate our unassigned load.

I was in the process of discussing the possibility of the email with my counterpart when an email went out from Linda, one of the supporters in the group urging others to take some unassigned issues and urging them to put a stop to the uncontrolled growth of the unassigned queue. She made it very clear in the email that this was not her place to be urging members of a global support group, but she urged people to work together and make the queue reduction a reality. This group had members in group different locations with offices in Argentina and the US across three time zones. Within a few seconds of the email going out, people started to respond saying they were taking issues and specifying the issue numbers. I read the email in amazement knowing quite well that she beat me to the punch, and also ecstatic that this colleague took the initiative to persuade others to act in harmony for the benefit of all. By the end of the day, the group had taken 57 very complex issues and managed to drastically reduce the unassigned queue size. It was very inspiring to watch colleague after colleague join in the action and take issues here and there. Linda herself took at least five or six. At least 15 colleagues participated and all got a valuable lesson in leadership when a colleague inspired others to action.

As a manager wishing to bring improvement to the group, I knew that effective change must come from within the group itself. I can direct until I'm blue in the face but it is preferable to have a peer lead the group to act than a manager. The peer is typically much more inspiring and lasting than a boss. During that exercise with Linda, I was reassured of the true power of leadership in technical support. Initiatives happen for the group and by the group. Support people should not have to wait for all calls to action to come from management. Every group should have at least one leader who moves the group along and keeps it motivated. The Linda Effect refers to the positive and snowballing impact that a single action creates. The action is initiated by a single act of leadership and results in a change in behavior which leads to a change in attitude. This has the potential to lead to a change in culture. To put it in a more theoretical way, we can express the Linda Effect as follows:

$$LE = fA(b_g)$$

or the Linda Effect is a function of a single action on group behavior.

Having action originate with a peer has several advantages seen by the initiative taken by Linda. Those advantages are the following:

- *Credibility*: The type of credibility that a peer can bring to an initiative is much higher than what any manager can bring to the initiative. The reason is that the support peer is someone who is already doing the work and is no stranger to the challenge, the resolution, and the rewards.

- *Knowledge*: The peer who calls others to action has the knowledge of the work and how to get it done. It is not enough to just have knowledge of, but rather the leader should have *direct* knowledge of the work and how it gets done. This can only come from someone who is doing the work firsthand already.

- *Sharing:* The leader who opts for influencing others to do something is not only knowledgeable and has he credibility, but will also share in the action. Therefore, he will be a leader as well as a follower, and the rest of the followers feel more related to the leader as a result.

- *Validity:* The leadership actions from a peer are more valid than anyone else's because a peer should have better insight into the work; consequently, the leader has more relevance when he is a peer than when he is something other than a peer. For instance, think of an executive or upper-management member with whom you have had some contact and received direction. You typically do what you are told, but that person doesn't necessarily inspire you to do anything others than what he asks. The concept of being inspired by the leader is a function of validity, and that validity only comes though experience and some exposure.

Take Linda's example of initiative to drive others to reach a positive and useful action as a prime example of the technical support leader we need in our field of technical support. She showed great transactional leadership and proved to be an excellent pragmatic leader. Every support group would be enriched and achieve a much higher level of performance and excellence if each group had a Linda to initiate action in the rest of the group.

A good leader is one who can tell another how to reach his or her potential; a great leader is one who can help another discover this potential for him or herself.

—Bo Bennett

Characteristics of a Support Leader

The origin of leadership has been established as being something that is learned rather than acquired from genetics. No one comes to the world being a leader. Leadership is a learned behavior that only comes through very specific and coordinated series of experiences. Leadership forms part of a need for humans to move, to act, and to synchronize their efforts. The only problem is finding someone to guide them. Humans are not the only beings where the masses follow a single individual. Cattle follow an individual to water. It is usually not the bull or the biggest cow. It is not the most aggressive or the best looking, or the youngest or the oldest. It is usually just one of the individual cows that establishes itself as a leader and where it decides to go, the others follow. I have observed, though not scientifically or with any systematic inquiry, that a new herd of cattle will run around disorganized and in a confused fashion. This typically occurs when they are brought to the pasture from a sale barn. These individual animals usually come from different ranches and are sold to the highest bidder in an auction. I have personally purchased several herds over a few years and noticed the same type of behavior. The livestock is bunched up in a trailer, taken to a new pasture, let out, and then left on their own. They are herd animals so they stick together, but don't always know where they are going or what they need to do. The first instinct depends on whether they are hungry, scared or thirsty so upon being let out of the stock trailer for the first time, the herd will run, eat, or drink. A few days later, the herd follows a clear leader who takes them to the grazing spots, to the shade of trees, or to the watering ponds.

Technical support groups are not so different. The newly formed group is at first disoriented and does not know exactly what to do, but soon someone emerges that sets the pace for the actions and, usually, behaviors of the group. The new leader need not be a manager and he seldom is a member of management. Because the field of leadership is still relatively new, there just is not very much written in the niche of technical support leadership. However, in my experiences with different support groups in different technologies and companies, I noticed the following characteristics of the typical technical support group leader.

- *Necessity*: The support leader is usually pushed into the leadership role, not by desire but by necessity. A leader steps in only where there is a leadership vacuum because there cannot be two conflicting or competing leaders in a single group. One will eventually leave either by force or from lack of support. There can be multiple leaders who lead in different areas of the group, but not leaders who compete. Leadership is seldom about competition but always about influencing others to action.

- *Confidence*: The leader who rises in the support group, does so only if he has confidence. People simply do not follow someone who has no confidence. It would feel quite awkward and cause detrimental results if the leader did not have sufficient confidence that his leadership would accomplish something. Many people try to be leaders, and this is where they almost always fail. It is counterintuitive to attempt to inspire confidence in others when the leader does not have confidence in himself, the followers, or the goal he is trying to instill in others.

- *Honesty*: The leader has to be honest. There just is no substitute for honesty. Candor and openness are essential to building the honesty that others can see in you as a leader. As a follower, you would not want to follow someone who appears to be hiding something from you or who is not clear and leaves doubts in your mind. We follow leaders because they make us feel good, first about ourselves and then about them. Being true to the group and doing so in a consistent basis will allow you to be a trusted leader that others follow.

- *Integrity*: Just like honesty; there is no substitute for integrity. Leadership, at its most fundamental levels is nothing more than credibility made into action. In other words, people follow leaders because they trust them and because the leaders offer a viable opportunity and a credible alternative to the status quo. If the leader's integrity is questioned, even in the most minimal way, the leader's efficacy fails. The great leaders in history may have had many faults, but lack of integrity was not one of them. If you think about it, the difference between a great leader and a crook is integrity. A few years ago, the CEO of the company I worked for was indicted for presenting untrue financial information about revenues. In other words, as a company, we were cooking the books. The CEO was someone I admired and respected, even if I did not know him personally and never spoke with him. He never heard my voice and probably did not know my name but he had a follower in me. I believed in him and toiled daily and gave it my best effort because I believed in his desire to transform the company and improve it. I know many of my support colleagues felt the same about him. When we learned about his lack of integrity, our heart was broken and we ceased to follow him. As of the writing of this book, he sits in jail. One mistake and he went from being our leader and our inspiration to a convict and someone we regret having followed.

- *Initiative*: As a leader, you must not only have the necessity, confidence, honesty, and integrity but you must also have the drive to lead people. The role of a leader is not an easy one and there is no silver bullet that will turn you into a success in leading people. Because leadership is a learned behavior, I am giving you the tools but you must have the drive to take action first and then inspire others to follow your example and to turn your message into execution. Many people have all the characteristics listed in the previous bullets but are still not leaders. I have had support people tell me that they have done everything right and asked others to action, but nothing happens. For example, I once had a very frustrated colleague who seemed to fail over and over at becoming a leader. I asked him about what he did and he explained that on the most recent attempt, he put all the ingredients in place to mobilize a group into addressing a problem with a customer. Yet the colleagues he invited did not bite and failed to follow him. After a few more questions, I realized there was one integral part he did not do. He did not act first, but rather expected others to act so that he could follow. He had the intention but did not have the drive. Without initiative to be a leader, you are something akin to a manager or supervisor. Initiative is the stuff that all leaders are made of. Picture the *Washington Crossing the Delaware* painting by Emmanuel Leutze from 1851, but without George Washington at the forefront on that boat. Now you can you understand why a leader is called just that?

Generally, all leaders have the same characteristics that make them stand out and the subjects of followers' inspiration to action. If you tried to establish yourself as a leader and have not been successful, see if you missed any of the characteristics previously outlined. Amazingly, technical expertise or title is not one of them. This means that leadership is not the monopoly of experts, managers, or big shots, but rather of a select type of individual who moves others to action and change.

A leader is someone who helps improve the lives of other people or improve the system they live under.

—Sam Houston

Leadership Development

So you want to be a leader? If the idea frightens you, I suggest you move onto another segments of the book with less direct involvement, but if the idea of becoming a leader has even the smallest appeal to you, I suggest you keep reading. I will provide you with the concise steps to get you on your way to establishing yourself and being recognized as a leader, regardless of the group or even the field. This is a book about technical support; therefore, I assume your interests lie in this profession. However, even if your field is different, the steps of leadership development are generally the same so you should get some value out of this reading.

Leadership education and training abound. All you have to do is an internet search to find about 38 million hits on the phrase "leadership development." There are classes, trainings, workshops, seminars, books, and even software that promise you everything necessary to become a leader or improve your leadership skills. Is leadership development for people who aspire to a leadership role really that complicated? Keep in mind that when I refer to the "role" of leader, I am not referring to a management or executive position. I am referring to the actual leading of people to action via influence. This is the essence of leadership, but since the word is used for so many functions, it is hard to pinpoint how others use it. However, rest assured that this is how the field of leadership is typically taught in leadership studies PhD programs.

Becoming a leader is not some secret to which only some are privy. You don't have to have a PhD in leadership studies to become leader, although I am certain it helps. In technical support, there are specific steps required to become a leader and lead others to action via positive influence. The steps are as follows:

- *Genuine interest in people and their success*: Without an interest in the benefit of others and their success, there is not much you can do because you would lack the credibility. As a follower, you can spot a fake leader faster than a $3 dollar bill. People are not easily duped into following a leader when that leader does not have a genuine interest in their welfare and success. Just think of the politicians and presidents who come and go. Some of them are quite gifted as politicians, but terrible as leaders. In technical support, the colleague who takes a genuine interest in customers and his peers is easily recognizable by actions and consistency. Therefore, if you want to become a leader, you must connect to people by taking an interest in them. The interest has to be true to be effective. Consequently, if you don't have an interest in people and their success, you don't have any business wanting to become a leader.

- *Find a gap in your group or organization*: The next step is to find a void in the current leadership of your support group. There is usually something that you could lead, where there is no one that has filled that role. The space to be filled may be in training, mentoring, technical, social, or just about anything else worth doing. Find a void and work on filling it. The reason you want something that is not currently filled is quite obvious: you don't want to compete with anyone for a leadership role. Of course, this is assuming the current leader is effective and brings good to the organization. If you are still interested in a field that already has someone leading it, offer to help and collaborate with whoever is the current leader. There is nothing wrong with having multiple people lead as long as they are not at odds with each other. However, I strongly recommend you stick to the areas where there is no one already. You can be more effective and there is more opportunity to excel. Once you indentify the need and opportunity for a leadership role, then it's time to start making some plans to create some impact.

- *Find something to mobilize people around*: Once you find the leadership opportunity you want to fill, you must find something to mobilize your followers around. At this state you may not have any followers yet. Depending on the leadership role you identified, there is a chance you won't have any followers until you take action first either by example, or by selling yourself as someone who can be followed. Followers are quite astute and they will only support a leader who will return some value to them in some form. This is why you have to find some specific action or concept to mobilize potential followers around. This can be your vision or your goal. It may also be your plan of attack or strategy, but it has to be something precise. Unlike other literature, I am not going to suggest you write the action, vision or goal up, and tape it to your refrigerator because that action must be something you personally decide to do; otherwise, it won't work. *Take bold actions to move others*: After your find the area around which you want to mobilize, you must take actions to influence others. This is the main idea of leadership and not an easy task indeed. If it were easy, there would not be thirty eight million hits in the internet on the subject. The actions you take are your initiative and when others see this, and if they are also interested, they will follow. It is amazing how people follow a leader, even when they know their leader is not the best or the most capable. However, what people need is something to follow so you have to start making your plans towards this goal. The bold actions you take should be substantial but the ones you ask your followers to take should be much smaller. Start gradually and your followers will soon be capable of performing much bigger actions.

- *Develop others and help them take over.* -The movement does not belong to you. You chose to become a leader because you wanted to see a result and influence others to carry out the actions to achieve the goal or vision. Eventually, you will want to pull out and go to the next challenge. This is why you must find someone to take over your work. There are few things worse than having your efforts undone by a less than capable individual. Back in the early 1990's, I started a small tabloid-format magazine publication which competed in a very special niche market. I did great and mobilized the niche market segment into looking at their market as something more and my publication helped this niche to think of themselves in a new light. After a year and a half of publishing this small magazine and enduring a good level of success, I sold it to a much respected member of that market segment. Within three months, he ran the business into the ground and ceased publication. Later, I realized that I failed miserably to develop the new owner to take over and the results showed. It is no different with technical support. If you are going to hand it over to someone else, make sure you prepare them and groom them for the challenge.

Becoming a leader is not easy but it is very doable. The steps above will help you be on your way to becoming a leader within your support organization and even other parts of your life. This is not the property or within the realm of a privileged few. Anyone can become an effective leader who makes a positive impact to the lives and work of others. Follow the steps to leadership development as previously described and start making an impact on your colleagues.

"The first duty of a leader is to make himself be loved without courting love. To be loved without "playing up" to anyone—even to himself."

—Andre Malraux

The Situational Support Leader

Leadership is a very young and complex social discipline with only a few models and theories. The three major leadership models are servant Leadership, transactional leadership, and transformational leadership. A new and, hopefully emerging, theoretical model of leadership is pragmatic leadership. However, other ways of looking at leadership are quite flexible and consist of a leader taking at least two possible avenues to mobilizing people to act. This is the theory of situational theories of leadership, which suggests that leaders understand their own behavior, that of their followers, and the issues at hand to come up with a best approach to the leadership challenge. [7] Of course, these were not exactly written for the field of technical support, but the value in them is that it provides another way to look at the use of leadership in the technical support group.

As a technical support leader, it is very likely that you will move from group to group helping out and leading your peers out of challenges. If you move from group to group improving them, soon you

---

[7] E.A. Fleishman, "Twenty Years of Consideration and Structure," *Current Developments in the Study of Leadership*, ed. E.A. Fleishman and J.C. Hunt (Carbondale: Southern Illinois University Press, 1973).

will gain a reputation as an effective leader and the ideal person to bring in when positive change is needed. As you can imagine, what works in one group may not work in the next. Technical support groups have all types of complexities, which vary from the level of experience of the group members doing the support, the knowledge level of the customers to the complexity of the product. For each situation you encounter in your career in technical support leadership, you will undoubtedly need to adjust your leadership style and practices to fit the situation.

As a support leader going into a new situation, there are different variables that you have to take into account when deciding how to lead the group out of whatever challenge they are in. Of course, this is assuming that you are brought in to improve a situation and not just merely to sustain a successful support group. You probably would not need a leader for that but a good manager or administrator. Let us assume you are called in to perform a turnaround of a group that is facing challenges in their delivery of support services to customers. In order to proceed to lead them, you will need to determine the following about the group you are about to lead: maturity of the group, maturity of the product, and internal and external challenges. From these variables, you will need to determine the appropriate style to use in leading the group and the possible outcomes and adjust accordingly.

The maturity of the group is quite obvious but it has a huge impact on the overall challenges to any support group. If the group is comprised of people who are inexperienced in the support profession and relatively new to the technology, then you will have a much different challenge that a group that is made up of industry and support veterans. The way to handle the two is quite different. With the rookies you will want to utilize a lot of direction and reaffirmation of the desired behaviors. At no time should you leave them alone because it would be relatively easy for them to adopt undesired support practices. On the other hand, with a seasoned group of support veterans, you will have a lot less direction, and possibly more overseeing and correcting of ingrained undesired behaviors. Therefore, your leadership style with these two types of group maturity would be quite different and mixing the two would bring catastrophic results. Imagine if you treat the group of support newbies as if they were veterans. If you were to assume they already know what they are doing and just trust that they will do the right thing you would be disappointed. Also, if you try and micromanage the support veterans you will demoralize them or even drive them away. In a word, the relatively inexperienced support person needs a lot of direction and guidance while the experienced supporter needs some recognition, some overseeing, and possible correction.

The maturity of the product also has a lot to do with determining your leadership style. A product life cycle will dictate how aggressive the group needs to be in meeting the new challenges. For instance, a new up-and-coming product will typically be selling like hotcakes, especially if it's an industry leader or a hot new technology. The group that support this type of product will need a much different approach than the group that support a product on its way out, such as one that is reaching an end of a life cycle. The new, hot product will have a lot of demand for features and very likely a very new user-base as well as many more defects than a more mature product. The leader guiding the support group with the up-and-coming product may need to concentrate more on volume and productivity, and may also face the challenge of creating new processes and correcting existing procedures on the way. The leader of the mature product may simply need to maintain the current levels of service and productivity, but often with a declining set of resources as the organization shifts existing people, money, and tools to a newer product.

Another determinant to the type of leadership style you will adopt has to do with the challenges the group faces. Internal challenges may vary from support policies, resources such as tools and systems, staffing levels, and skill levels. The variance and deficiency of any of these variables in the internal challenges will dictate how the leader influences the group to action. As a leader, you will have to move your group to improve the challenges and turn the problems into opportunities. The internal challenges are ones you can typically control and have the higher impact on. The external challenges are something you will have to live with because they are external and typically cannot be changed by the support group, but there are still ways to deal with them. External challenges include the level of knowledge of the customer base, the volume of calls into your support group, and the behaviors of the customer calling in for support. These are just a few of the challenges but certainly the most typical. External challenges are not solved by the support group or by you as the leader, but they can be controlled to some extent. Customers who do not know enough to be helped by the support group may need extra instructions in order to get the support person to help them with the right information. A high volume support group will need to be led to find ways to cope with the volume using more efficient processes. As a leader, you will have to adapt your style of leadership to meet the internal and external challenges.

Situational leadership offers a viable and flexible way of addressing the need for flexibility by the leader. Once you learn to cope with the different leadership challenges and promote sound initiatives that lead to an improved state for the support group, you will be in great demand because leaders who are effective in different situations are very hard to come by. The more groups you lead, and the more situations you encounter, the better you will get at leading support groups to success.

One secret of leadership is that the mind of a leader never turns off. Leaders even when they are sightseers or spectators, are active; not passive observers.

—James Humes

Leading by Involving Others

When we thing of a leader, we typically think of a single person who making things happen either by personal power or because of favorable circumstances. Mahatma Gandhi, Rudy Giuliani, Bill Gates, Pope John Paul II, Joan of Arc, and many other leaders throughout history are thought of as a solo act when in fact they were part of something bigger; they just happen to be the ones that made things happen. Leadership deals with people and their actions. It has little to do with inventing or being the first at something. Leadership is all about promoting a vision within others and collectively making that vision a reality. The leader is the catalyst that makes change happen, but followers are the ones that actually do most, if not all, the work. There is no such thing as a lonesome leader. Leaders, by definition, need someone to lead; otherwise, they are just individuals.

Leaders involve others to make things happen; to drive change and make things better. As a leader, you need others to do all sorts of things from making decisions to go and do the actual work that needs done. Without having delegated authority, you can entice others to action by involving them and motivating them to participate. The technical support group is a great chance for a good leader to make things happen. However, you must understand and learn how to involve others to help bring the vision to fruition. There are different levels of involving others in the typical support group to carry out special projects and initiatives to bring success to the group. The different ways to involve vary from the non-involvement to the granting of power to go do.[8] The following look at each of these individually:

- *Autocratic decision*: t=This is the most dictatorial and undemocratic way of doing something. In fact, it is not considered participative at all since people are not consulted and one person without regards of input makes decisions that affect others. This is the realm of managers, so it is quite unlikely that a leader would never act in an autocratic fashion. An example of this would be a new manager who comes into the support group and unilaterally decides to change a process without taking any input from anyone. I am not implying there is anything wrong with a manager doing this, but a leader typically does not act autocratically.

---

[8] Gary Yukl, *Leadership in Organizations* (New Jersey: Prentice Hall, 2006) p. 100-101.

- *Decision via consultation*: -In a consultation, a manager asks others within the support group for input, opinions and suggestions, and then makes a decision. The manager uses the input from others in the consultative capacity, but the decision is made entirely by the manager. There are situations in which the manager will need to do this, and though this is good management it is not something a leader will do regularly since it does not involve influencing others but rather just taking input and making the decision unilaterally, much like the autocratic decision.

- *Joint Decision*: This is the typical situation in a leadership exercise where a support person faced with a challenge summons peers to come together and make a decision jointly. The leader does not have the final words and everyone makes the decision to action jointly and without anyone having more power over the group. This is the most democratic way of reaching a decision and going into action. In a group of your peers, you, as the leader, must guide the meeting or decision-making process, but not make it for the group. Instead, you must influence the democratic process. I use this method regularly with my peers, and have found it to be one of the best ways of accomplishing something. People like to be included and listened to. I have also found that there is much more acceptance of a decision when the group has a say in making it. If you use this type of involvement, you will find that others will start mimicking you with their own projects. I once invited a dear colleague of mine to a series of meetings in which we worked on a project to develop a training session. A few months later, I was invited to listen in on a similar process and noticed that my dear friend Ross used a great way to elicit participation and consensus. After the meeting, I commended him on the style and he told me he learned it from me. I was unaware but very flattered, and happy that my actions influenced his leadership style.

- *Delegation or entrustment*: -This is the most powerful way of involving others and creating future leaders. It consists of assigning tasks or entire projects to someone in the support group and removing yourself from the decision making and even the work involved in the task or project. When you, as the leader, share your power with a colleague, you are in fact reproducing yourself and soon you will have other leaders within the group. It may sound like you are creating your own competition, but there is no such thing as competition in leadership. In fact, it is your duty as a leader to create others like you. In a way, a measure of your success as a leader lies in how many other leaders you have helped develop. When you delegate a task of project, you set an expectation of performance. As long as you have provided the right level of instruction, the colleague you delegated should deliver. If that colleague fails to deliver, be sure to understand what challenges he or she faced. It is quite possible that the person simply has no interest in leading, as anyone can be a leader but leadership is not for everyone.

Leaders depend on others to get involved and make things happen. The type and level of involving your use in your leadership style determines if you are a manager or a true leader. It is also a sign of great leadership when you help develop other leaders within the support group. Not everyone is cut out to be a leader, but when you find that someone follows your lead than you know that you have truly achieved the goal of every leader; to involve others and incite them to lead others.

People ask the difference between a leader and a boss. The leader leads, and the boss drives.

—Theodore Roosevelt

Cultivating Leaders Within the Support Group

There is nothing more gratifying and humbling than to help develop others into leaders within the support group. Anyone can develop managers and support people with training, but developing leaders is a true challenge because it involves much more than just cognitive skills; it also involves a high level of maturity and ability to move others to action. Anyone with delegated authority can give orders, but it takes a true leader to have others follow without being required to. This is where you, as the leader within your support group, take responsibility for bringing others to your level and ensuring that there will be someone to mobilize the colleagues after you move on to the next challenge.

Helping your colleagues rise up to the leadership challenge only comes after you have proven yourself as an effective leader; someone who rallies the group and helps create positive results. If you are not a leader that influences others, there is little chance of having others want to become like you. After all, people mimic those who they admire. When you start cultivating others to take on leadership roles within the group, you must make sure to get the right people involved in appealing and significant tasks and projects. In addition, you have to make sure you only involve those who show the potential to become leaders just like you or who may surpass you. However, just what type of person makes an ideal candidate for a leadership role?

The ideal candidate for a potential leadership role is someone who is liked, respected, dynamic and progressive and, of course, has the right skills for the role. We must make it clear that a leadership role is not a position but an informal role within the support group. You may hear the word leader or leadership used interchangeably with manager or management, but the two concepts are very different. The leader has power to influence people's hearts without delegated authority, while a manager has the authority to give out orders but may not have power over their hearts. In other words, the leader is someone we are inspired to follow without really having to while the manager is someone we have to obey, or at least comply with, but who doesn't necessarily inspire us. Don't get me wrong, there is absolutely nothing wrong with being a manager. A manager is necessary for decision making, planning, controlling, monitoring, evaluating, delegating, and enforcement within the support organization, but this chapter revolves around leadership so that is our focus.

Once you found your ideal candidate for the leadership role, give him or her a few small tasks to accomplish using the power of leadership, such as putting together a collaboration call and moderating it. You could also give the new leader a small project consisting of preparing a short training with the help of others in some area of interest to the leadership candidate. The new leader will prove himself by being able to summon others to help create or pilot the new training. This may sound trivial to a tested leader but to someone who has never done it before, it's a big task. Of course, after the new leader gets going on the delegated project, you will need some way of assessing his or her success. To do that, you must do the following:

- *Promote your new junior leader.* Keep in mind that you already made a name for yourself by taking the bold moves, inspiring others to action, and making things happen. Your new leadership candidate has the huge benefit of having you in his or her corner. As the mentor leader, you should promote the new leader to others within the group, management, and even outside the group. When you promote your new candidate, some of the respect that others have for you will rub off on the new leader making it easy for him to gain acceptance, elicit participation, and eventual followership from the support group members.

- *Provide constant feedback and guidance*: Just because you had to run through brickwalls and stumble through your leadership development doesn't mean that your new protégé has to suffer the same way. You must help the new leader find his way to becoming like you, just like the same way you helped others within the group learn how to support the technical aspects of you technology. Just think of how much easier it would have been if someone had showed you the ropes early in your leadership development.

- *Provide gradual detachment*: The new leader will soon reach a point when he doesn't need you anymore. This may be easier with some individuals than with others, but as the mentor, you should gradually detach yourself and let the new leader stand on his own. Support people are experts at this concept because that is typically how we all learned to do support and how we develop into technology experts. At some point during our career, someone taught us how to support and we eventually got good enough to stand on our own two feet. I assure you, there is nothing more gratifying than to see your protégé take over the leadership from you. It may sound like there would be jealousy involved, but leadership is a very altruistic enterprise.

- *Be there when needed*: The new leader may be out on his own but he will still need advice from time to time from you, the person he admires and who helped him get to his present leadership role. When your apprentice needs help, guidance, or just a sounding board, you are the one he will seek. I still go to my career mentor, Diane, for advice even though I do not work with her anymore. She always lends an ear and is ready to provide guidance. I also speak with those I have helped develop into the leaders they are today. They have surpassed me by leaps and bounds, but it is humbling to know they still consider me someone they can get advice from when they need it.

-

In your leadership calling, you will inevitably have to develop leaders just like you. It is only natural and the way this discipline works. All true leaders do it. This is the way true leaders leave their mark in the world and also in their support organizations. All the great movements in history came via leaders and their apprentices. Christianity, the Renaissance, democracy, and socialism to name a few were the work of leaders and the ones they cultivated. Your support group is smaller in scale, but can benefit from the same concept. Therefore, being successful in leadership inevitably involves developing others like you to carry on your work after you move on to the next challenge.

The final test of a leader is that he leaves behind him in other men the conviction and the will to carry on.

—Walter Lippmann

PART 3

■ ■ ■

The Support Organization

In this section, we explore the ways we work in support such as structure and processes. The topics covered vary in scope but follow a common line of thinking. It is not meant to be advice for you to go and try as-is but rather to serve as a foundation for you and derive your own answers and ways of adopting the work presented here. The section covers many areas of the organization and may or may not describe the reality in your company; however, it should provide intellectual stimulation to get you thinking about improving your work.

■ ■ ■

CHAPTER 7

Support Roles and Behaviors

The topic of support management could fill a whole book and much more. I don't have the luxury of devoting this entire book to the topic, but rather included ten topics that deal with the roles, management, and some behaviors in the support organization. The topics are by no means exhaustive because there are endless possibilities for research in this area. Specifically, the chapter covers topics such as the role of support managers, systems theory, recognition and management support strategy and other topics of interest to the support practitioner.

As mentioned, our profession does not yet have the formal inquiry enjoyed by other more mature disciplines, so we need to take the existing research applied to general management and organizational behavior and synthesize it for technical support. With some adaptation, the existing published literature works quite well.

The roles of supporters and their managers do not vary much among organizations; therefore, generalizing the roles and descriptions allow us to predict some level of uniformity to the field as a whole. Additionally, management theories work quite well in the support discipline because of the group organization and the still flexible management structures that exist. Our field needs a way to simplify the roles and establish common ground, so that we can all understand the fundamentals that drive our behaviors as practitioners. Establishing a foundation is not a small task; this chapter is an intrepid and humble beginning that I hope will be greatly expanded and developed by those who eventually take up the research questions posed.

The chapter also explores the topic of recognition in the support group as well as an ingenious way to tackle low performance independently of the rest of the performance spectrum. The work is entirely qualitative and put into a context that is easy to analyze and derive value from.

■ **Tip** A good manager is someone who is able to take it all in stride, turn around, fight adversity, strive to maintain harmony and still manage to derive value and work out of people willingly.

Your Excess Value

If you are reading this book, it's most likely because you are a support practitioner, a support manager, or somehow involved in the technical support profession. However, regardless of your role in the support organization of your company, you are, in fact, a support contributor. This is because you and your colleagues work together to achieve happy customers one support issue at a time, meaning even if the company has a support organization the bulk of the support work will still rely on us. Of course, you already know this as you live it every day and this is your profession. However, how do you view your role in the organization? Is it a one=way street where you give your hard work and get little in return or vice versa? Is it, as some describe, a battery that gets replaced when it wears out or runs out of juice?

Undoubtedly, you work with others who at times feel abused, neglected, exploited, and potentially even combative toward the organization. It happens to all of us at some point in our careers. This is normal. Nevertheless, the reality is far from this perception. Allow me to explain in a bit more universal way. Organizations exists to serve, produce, or somehow provide a good or service. But an organization is not self-sufficient. It needs people to do the work. Corporations, sole proprietorships, or partnerships are merely legal entities, but they cannot provide a single service or good to a customer. These legal entities need people to do the actual work. Support professionals all belong to some organization, regardless of how big or small. We work within the entity and the entity relies on us. The value of the organization is its ability to create revenue, maintain customers and market share, and create new customers, so that new streams of revenue sustain the organization for the near and long future. As a support contributor, you ensure the survivability of your company. This is your role.

When you work in support, unless it's a big organization with many technologies or products, you probably remain in the same situation for a considerable duration of your tenure with your company. This duration and consistency create a name for the support department. Obviously, experience makes you better and more efficient at your job. This added efficiency adds value to your organization as more customers experience the added benefit of dealing with a support person who is knowledgeable and can solve the issues at an efficient pace. You become an asset for your company by being able to do the work better, faster, and with greater customer satisfaction than someone who just came into the organization. This concept forms the notion of value that relies on assets that produce more than they consume. I am using the terms "asset," "produce," and "consume" quite liberally, so please don't think I am advocating anything other than the concept of value that workers bring to the organization in excess of what they get paid. In effect, this is what Adam Smith described when referring to the "invisible hand,"[1] because just as we are acting in our own self-interest by working for the company, so is our company acting in its self-interest by having us as employees. In simple terms, we need the company and the company needs us. We view the value we get from the company in the form of benefits, salary, and satisfaction as higher than the physical, intellectual, and time sacrifice of working. The company sees the value we provide as something of more value than the salary we receive. Therefore, we win and the company wins as well.

In terms of value and labor economics, your role to the company is a valuable one; otherwise, they would not keep you around. The company receives value from your work in excess of the value it provides to you. In turn, you view this value as greater than the sacrifice you put into receiving it. In other words, the salary, benefits and satisfaction from your job exceed the sacrifice you give in exchange. Eventually, the sym biotic relationship between your employer and you, the employee, becomes such as win-win situation that you must approach your job as a means to live and ensure the success of your company. When you company succeeds and thrives the value flow continues and even grows. The company is not out to get you, nor are you trying to bilk your company. In effect, the relationship is a mutually benefiting situation. Therefore, your role as a support person is that of providing excess value to ensure the continuation of the value flow to you.

The question is: how do you ensure the continual delivery of excess value to your support organization and thus your company? The following are some ways:

- *Perform at or above the company's expectations*: the labor market is not one of perfect competition. There are people at all levels of knowledge and abilities to provide value. If you do not perform at least to the expected levels, someone else will. This is a fact of a free market economy and, unless you are part of a labor

---

[1] Adam Smith, *The Wealth of Nations* (New York: Bantam Classics, 1976), p 537–568.

union, the company can find someone else to replace you.[2] The company knows how much you really cost as a resource. Your salary is only part of the total costs, because there also benefits, training, taxes, and facilities that must be considered when assessing the true cost of a labor resource. By performing the preceding expectations, you are decreasing the possibility that there is someone out there that could replace you.

- *Help to ensure continual value from company assets*: the company depends on its employees to ensure the protection of its interests. The company also derives value from the things it invests in, such as equipment, licenses, and processes. As an employee, you must make sure that the value derived from such assets is in excess of their cost. An employee who uses resources at its optimal levels is far more valuable than someone who wastes resources. Imagine if you hired someone to wash your dishes at home and that person leaves the water running while not in use and you end up with a large water bill. Would it not make more sense to either get that person to turn the water off or simply get someone who will look out for you when it comes to water bills?

- *Find ways to improve the excess value that you provide*: as a technical support professional, there are many still unexplored ways to increase the excess value you give the company. I am not advocating that you increase the number of hours or days you work, but rather the improved use of your skills and assets as well as the development of new ones to increase the excess value you provide your organization. The reason I do not think that you simply work longer hours or weekends is because you also must provide value to yourself in some way without that value having to come from the company. For instance, taking training to acquire a new skill or ability will allow you to provide excess value to your organization, but it will also add value to you as a professional.

At a very fundamental level, your role in your support organization is to provide more value that what you receive. This is how you improve your odds of becoming the type of contributor who is valuable and hard to replace. Attaining this level of professional value as an individual contributor comes through increasing the value the company receives from your labor.

Perseverance is the hard work you do after you get tired of doing the hard work you already did.

—Newt Gingrich

The Contributor Role in Regard to Management

All of us who work in organizations work under a manager. Some work under a team leader while others work under a matrix model of management; most work under a single manager who is in charge of the work and the people. Such a manager is also in charge of most activities and processes related to the contributors under his command such as training, scheduling, operations, and performance. But, how are we supposed to view relation to a manager in the technical support field? Is our manager the

---

[2] This does not necessarily imply outsourcing as that is a different topic which is not entirely related to excess value.

ultimate boss; do we work for him; what do we owe him in terms of obedience; or is our manager simply the one charged with keeping us productive?

The role that individuals have with their management varies depending on the industry, type of job, organizational size, and education of the contributor and manager. I mention education because unless the report and the manager have some knowledge of formal management, both are just going to make up their own definition of the role as they go along. Picture this scenario: You work in a small company doing blue-collar type work, such as a production floor or mechanic shop. You have no formal management education, but you are a hard worker and a top producer. The company owner or plant supervisor offers you the position of shop manager. You take it, viewing it as a promotion and a reward to your hard work and dedication. However, you still have no formal management education, and you think that being a manager is having everyone work for you and viewing you as the boss. You start viewing those who report to you as your workers and soon develop a sense of entitlement and demand their obedience. You start using phrases such as, "You work for me" and "I don't pay you to sit around." Eventually, the production of the shop remains constant or perhaps improves, but you now become "one of them" and a separation between the reports and you develop. Of course, it could also go the other way. You continue to behave and act as the best performer and soon just find that the shop is falling apart, because you had no idea how to manage a group. Does this sound like it could only happen in a blue-collar scenario or could it also happen in support organizations?

As the contributor, however, you work for the company, not an individual. Your fiduciary duty to the company and the manager is to make sure that the benefit the company gets for your labor is adequate. The manager is responsible for making sure you perform and contribute to the overall success of the organization. As a matter of hierarchy, you owe adherence and compliance to your manager. He is the one who will review your performance and you must make sure he knows what you are doing, how, and to what levels. He is also there to support your efforts to improve yourself and help improve the value of the company via proactive actions as it pertains to your work. As a matter of civility, you may want to show respect and esteem. When it comes to professionalism, you also want to give loyalty and hard work, all within company policy. However, you are not necessarily required to, nor should you be forced to. I am not suggesting anarchy or rebellion toward your manager in any way. I have worked in places where the manager was so feared that you would think he was the owner of the company when in fact he was only in charge of a few reports and their production. I have also reported to managers who exemplified the utmost professionalism and aptitude in the role. Both had an effect on my view toward them, the work, and the company. Needless to say, I worked much better under a professional manager than under a dictatorial one.

This brings us to the responsibilities that we as support professionals have toward our manager. The responsibilities are quite simple and effective. The following list shares these roles:

- *Adherence*: we must be in-line with our manager in the sense that he is ultimately responsible for your work. Apathy has no place in your relationship to your manager. The adherence should not just be superficial. In order to be successful in your role, you must also believe and be completely committed to your manager's initiatives, so that your group improves. If you don't personally believe in your manager's initiatives, let him know but adhere to them anyway. You should also not cause others to rebel or become indifferent to your manager.

- *Compliance*: your manager imparts the directives given to him for the group. It is up to you to execute the directives and for your manager to make sure this happens. This is where you become either a valuable resource to your manager and/or the company. Failure to comply with directives makes you someone who your manager needs to manage more closely. Subsequent failure to comply with directives leads you to become a hindrance to the group and the company. Look around your support group and you will notice that the most productive and desirable colleagues in terms of performance are those who comply with directives, especially those who do it beyond what is required. This is where the extraordinary excess benefit to the company makes those colleagues highly valued.

- *Productivity*: in the end, you have to produce at or above expectations. If you do not meet the expected levels of production, your role diminishes and you may be at risk of losing your job. However, you should not let the fear of losing your job affect your productivity one way or the other. I once spoke with a highly productive colleague who always performed more than anyone else in the group. He explained the techniques he used to close the most issues, plus the tips he put into practice which allowed him to manage his queue effectively. However, above all else, he said his motivation for performing was the fear of getting fired. I admire high performance, but cannot agree with doing so out of fear of losing your job. Our line of work is stressful enough as it is. If fear of losing your job is your main motivator, I urge you to find a more positive motivator, such as providing more value to the company and the customer or simply the motivation to perform.

Our role as support professionals in our interaction with management must be a healthy one in order to be sustainable. Our managers are there to make sure we perform and to make sure the company realizes the benefits in our labor. Our managers have other roles as well, but this is the core of them. Knowing our responsibilities as reports is invaluable, so we can take control of our careers and know if we are providing excess value to our support organizations.

Good management consists in showing average people how to do the work of superior people.

—John D. Rockefeller

The Role of the Support Manager

Just about everyone who holds a job has a manager. With the possible exception of free agent consultants, CEOs, and some contractors, the rest of us report to a manager from whom we get direction and orders and well as performance reviews. This concept should not be foreign to anyone who holds a support position. Support managers exist in call centers throughout the world and their roles should be relatively uniform in contributions and expectations.

The topic of management, unlike technical support, enjoys a multitude of researchers and writers. There are enough management books to fill an entire library and theories abound with some making more sense than others.[3] The role of a manager should be relatively the same regardless of the industry and level within the company. This applies also to technical support organizations, regardless of the size and technology. Of course, management is a social science so there are no absolute truths and different management theories state the role of the manager in different terms. For instance, the classical school of management,[4] which refers to the early writers in the subjects, such as Mooney and Taylor among a few others, proposes that the work of managers consists of a process made up of different tasks that all

---

[3] Daniel A Wren, *The History of Management Thought* (New York: John Wiley & Sons, 2005) p 231–239.
[4] James D Mooney, *The Principles of Organization* (New York: Harper and Row, 1947) and Frederick W Taylor, *Principles of Management* (New York: Harper and Row, 1911).

culminate in the managerial role. It also states that the tasks and ultimate process is subject to adaptation, depending on the needs of the organization and environmental circumstances.

- Another view of management states that management consists of three fundamental roles: decisional, interpersonal, and informational.[5] This is the management theory that best describes the role of the support manager. Because technical support is a disciple that deals with people and their problems, this model of three fundamental roles, when applied correctly, has the benefit of addressing the core functions of the support manager. Mintzberg did not specifically address technical support as he deals more with managers at the executive level, but the roles still apply. Let us look at each one independently, but in a synthesized manner applied to support.

- *Decisional role*: this is the core of the support manager's role. Because our professional requires making constant decisions and applying different processes to increasingly complex situations, the support manager exists, to a large extent, to make decisions. For instance, every company that provides technical support to its customers has policies on how that support should be executed and the limits and coverage of that service. However, because we deal in highly sophisticated products, technologies, and processes, the practitioner often faces predicaments that only the manager can resolve. Think of your own situation and the many times in which you had no idea which way to go. There is a point where the knowledge of the technology ceases and where no level of customer service can make a decision for you. It is in these situations in which your manager has to step in and make the decision for you. As a supporter, you should never have to make a hard decision as it relates to the delivery of your service to customers that places you in jeopardy. This is the role of the manager. If your manager refuses to make the decision for you, then the manager is an ineffective one and has no business managing because it is his job to do so.

- *Interpersonal role*: the manager is the personification of the company in the eyes of the reports. When we think of our company as an employer, we usually think of our managers, not the CEO. We work under a person and this is how we make sense of our employers. The manager also serves the function of bridging the gap between those external to the group and you, just as you bridge the gap between the customer and the company. Even within the organization, your manager is there to help you navigate the organization and get you in contact with others. This is a very crucial role, especially in a large company where technical support may just be a small subset of the customer facing departments. At no point, should you be confused or incapable of reaching someone else in your company because it is your manager's role to fulfill that need. Of course, that is as long as your need is reasonable and leads to some productive end. Take for instance the need to reach a salesperson to fulfill a customer's request for a demo. If you don't already know where to go and don't have a list of salespeople who can help, it is your manager who you should go to fulfill this interpersonal role.

- *Informational role*: the manager has to be able to disseminate information to the reports that he gets from upper management. Employees need to know certain things that they can get from their managers. This is a very simple concept, but

---

[5] Henry Mintzberg, *The Nature of Managerial Work* (Englewood Cliffs, N.J.: Prentice Hall, 1990).

one that sometimes eludes managers at all levels. Your company and support organization has initiatives, policy and process changes, and news that need to get down to you. There may be multiple ways for you to get the information, but the main one should be your manager. If the group manager does not disseminate any and all information he receives that was intended to go to the group, then he is not living up to the role. You are a constituent to upper management and as such you are entitled to know any actions and decisions that affect your work and the customers you serve. The manager is the conduit that gets the information to you. Naturally, the information flow is like a two-way street. There is information that you get from customers or from the work itself that upper management needs to know about. This is where your immediate manager comes in. You pass the information to your manager and he passes it on to whoever needs to know and can do something about it. This is one of the ways that an organization can keep up with the market and competitors—by sharing information internally from sources outside of the organization. As a customer-facing employee, you can provide a lot of information about what customers want, need, require, and deserve. Upper management will only know if you provide the information to your manager.

The role of the support manager is essential to the success of the company. The support manager is a facilitator and serves to make our jobs more productive by making decisions, providing a face to the company, and making sure information flows from top-to-bottom and vice versa. Hopefully, your organization's managers are living up to their role and ensuring your support department succeeds in providing the best technical support possible through you, the supporter.

The difference between management and administration (which is what the bureaucrats used to do exclusively) is the difference between choice and rigidity.

—Robert Heller

The Nature of Management

Why do we need managers? What is it that they bring to the organization that cannot be done without managers? How many managers do we need? All these are questions that arise in just about any support group. It is only natural for people to ask these questions when they perceive their management structure to provide little or no value. However, this is just a perception and the mere fact that you have a place to work every day and the tools necessary to do it points to the fact that someone had to make it happen. Why do we need managers? We need managers because when you have two or more people doing work, any type of work, the efforts of the workers need to be coordinated so that they do not conflict, overlap, or negate each other. It may sound too simple and you may think that managing the work of two people does not require any management. However, what about twenty people or two hundred? Imagine the amount of chaos that could envelop if there was no one to coordinate the efforts and the needs of so many people. This is where the managers come in.

You can pick up any management essentials book and they pretty much all agree about the nature of management. There are four functions of management: planning, organizing, leading, and controlling. You may think that your manager does not do all these things, but the work you see from a manager is only a small part of what he really does. You typically only see the leading and controlling. You rarely see the planning and the organizing.

The next question is, what purpose do these four functions serve and what do you and the company get out of it? They serve the purpose of reaching the most productive levels possible out of the same resources. After all, unless you are a volunteer and get nothing for your work, the company pays for your labor and it needs to ensure that it gets a benefit from such labor. In a nutshell, the four managerial functions assure that the company gets its money's worth from you and you benefit by making sure that your efforts are in-line with expectations; overall, that you are a productive employee by contributing to the success of the organization.

- Even though the four functions are generally the most accepted ones by the greatest number of management science researchers, other functions may be added or modified depending on the company. For instance, some add the function of hiring, staffing, interviewing, training, and many other functions which vary depending on the company and organization within the company. However, the four functions are typically the ones that managers perform at different levels of management from the executive to the front line managers. The following look at each function individually as they apply to technical support groups:

- *Planning*: there are only a finite number of support people in any given support group. The manager has to determine how to allocate the supports to best meet the demands from customers and others constituencies within the company. The scheduling and the proper allocation of resources such as labs, tools, and even vacations require planning. It would be very difficult for the group as a collective to plan everything effectively, because it would necessitate the absence of bias which would mean that individuals act in their self-interest. The presence of a manager to take care of the planning eliminates the bias that the individuals have. Planning as a function is transparent to you because planning is something the manager does alone or with other managers, but rarely does it happen in conjunction with the group. Therefore, it may not seem apparent to you, but planning does happen in just about every managerial setting.

- *Organizing*: the allocation of resources takes a lot of organizing. Your manager has to make sure that the people and other resources are organized in a way that ensures the highest possible benefit to the organization. For instance, the skills present in the support group may vary and some colleagues may have skills that others do not. Ensuring that the right skills are present when customers are more likely to require help with these skills takes organizing. The organization of people and resources allows the manager to prepare for the demands placed on the support group.

- *Leading*: leading in managerial terms is not the same as leading in the leadership discipline, since the latter deals with the study of influencing action in others without delegated authority. In management, leadership refers to the actual executing of the plans the manager prepared and organization that he designed. The execution is the actual delivery of the plans and organization. Without leading the group to perform, the manager has no role. The support manager also receives directives from upper management and those directives have to be rolled out to the support group. The level of efficiency in rolling out the directives determines the success of the overall initiative.

- *Controlling*: after the execution of the plan and the implementation of the organizational structure that your manager designed, the next steps are to make sure everything goes as planned. This is where the controlling function kicks in and the different performance measurements set in place have a chance to decide if the optimal levels of efficiency are being met. In other words, your manager has to make sure you and your colleagues are doing the work he planned for you in the way that he organized and implemented it. It is quite easy to just roll something out and hope that it happens. In a perfect world, that would be all a manager has to do, but in a complex work environment such as a technical support group, controlling the execution guarantees that everything does not fall apart. This may sound quite logical to you as a worker in technical support, but just think of the nature of your work. You have to take new issues in the form of support calls, work on the calls to resolve them by helping the customer, and then on top of that you have to implement any new plans from your manager. Therefore, to reach the level of efficiency required by the organization, the manager must control the execution and make adjustments, if necessary. If no controlling takes place, all the work put into the planning, organizing, and leading will be in vain.

Managers play a vital role in any organization by aligning the resources—in this case, support people—with the needs of the organization. The nature of management is to plan, organize, lead, and control. These four functions work at all levels and, when done properly, can help management determine the successful implementation of organizational directives.

When a management with a reputation for brilliance tackles a business with a reputation for bad economics, it is the reputation of the business that remains intact.

—Warren Buffett

Systems Theory in Support

Technical support groups do not exist in a vacuum. We work to help the company by helping our customers with their problems. The outlook of our profession is bright and we must find ways to make it better every time. It will be a long time, if at all, before machines support customers as effectively as us humans. Therefore, our demise will not come from technology as it did for many manufacturing professions in which automations and robots eliminated the need for actual people. What threatens us is the inability of our practitioners to progress and look at the work as something that can be improved and transformed.

Sometimes I hear colleagues in the profession complain about how management exploits them and how little training, money, resources, time, help, or just about anything else that can be cited as an excuse to doing their job appropriately. This is their reality, but it is not the same for everyone. The most successful colleagues in the profession do not complain; they take action. They know that the only reality is the one they make and with that mentality, they go and perform beyond their expectations. I have carefully analyzed what makes these colleagues so much more effective at supporting customers than other colleagues.

The colleagues who help their managers succeed seem to outperform those that fight their managers and refuse or, at least, put up some barriers to the progress of their support groups. Essentially, the reason effective practitioners perform beyond what is expected of them is that they use a systems theory approach to work and interact with customers and management. I know that this may sound a bit farfetched because I am mixing a theory that was not meant to be applied to technical support work, but was meant to explain the ways different parts of a system work together. However, the application of systems theory works very well in technical support.

According to systems theory, a system is a group of elements that individually establish relationships with each other and that interact with their environments both as individuals and as a collective.[6] In simpler terms, a system is a bunch of things working together well. When applied to management and the working of a support organization, understanding the bigger system in which a support department resides in, helps the practitioners, understand how they affect and are affected by changes and modifications in the overall system. In a sense, we have control over our little part of the system and with that we can affect the other parts. I am oversimplifying a few aspects of the systems theory for the sake of applying it to technical support and to make sense of why understanding it helps us increase our own effectiveness as well as that of our groups.

Support managers must understand, and typically do, the bigger systems that the support group resides in. For instance, within a support organization there may be a support group for a specific television model "T." If the manager of that support group does not grasp the importance of the success of his group to the overall company's success then he will not take actions that lead to the success of the model "T." When customers are not satisfied with the support received from that specific support group, they may stop buying any more products from that company. When this happens, the retailers may not want to carry any more products from that manufacturer and the company that makes television model "T" may be forced out of business.

The same goes for the individual supporters. If we do not think about the bigger implications of our work, then that work may cease to exist because of our very actions. If we provide less than adequate support, our customers may decide to buy a competitor's product simply because their support is better regardless of the product or technology being less capable. As individual contributors, you should help your managers carry your support groups to success. The first way is to perform. The support manager has the following general functions: plan, organize, lead, and control. However, without us actually doing the work very little is going to happen, regardless of how much effort the manager puts into it. It is only when individuals do what they are supposed to and help promote the directions of the manager that the support group succeeds. The way to get colleagues to perform and promote the initiatives is for the colleagues to understand how their work affects the entire system. Good support work has the potential to reverberate throughout the economy. I have seen colleagues solve support issues which where hindering the production of planes, tractors, cars, music CDs, and many other products and services throughout the economy. By solving those support issues my support colleagues made something possible that had challenges otherwise. Additionally, our support work sometimes makes the difference between our company selling more products and technologies or losing market share. This is how we affect the system and we can affect it with our individual actions. Think of it as a collective made up of individuals who work in agreement to make a change in the overall economy.

The best organizations are the ones where everyone works together to achieve the best results possible and affect the system as whole. Support groups do not exist only to solve issues; they also influence customer behavior, help increase sales, lead to the elimination of defects and, ultimately, create happy customers who will tell others of their experience and create a cycle of growth in the customer base. This is the power of systems theory applied to technical support, and only those colleagues who understand their place in the system will truly surpass everyone's expectations. Once you understand this concept, your role as a support becomes a bit larger and more impacting.

Managers need advocates that can help champion the initiatives of the organization. Those who can influence others to action are the leaders of the group. The manager can only go so far so it is up to the leaders within the group to help drive the change.

---

[6] Steven Cavaleri and Krysztof Obloj, *Management Systems: A Global Perspective* (Belmont, CA: Wadasworth, 1993) p 15-16.

Lots of folks confuse bad management with destiny.

—Kim Hubbard

Managing Behaviors

Some time ago, I had the chance to work in a support group where the group members had unusual practices that did not equate to the best customer satisfaction possible. I joined the group as a manager in charge of the processes and was tasked with helping make the group more productive and effective. Of course, I knew hardly anything at all about the group, and even less about the technology. If this sounds unusual to you, rest assured that this is the way many role changes take place in a big company. The group had been described to me as removed from the rest of the company and one that had performance problems. I immediately took it as a challenge and happily accepted the new role. When I started working with the group, I realized that it was one of the best I had ever seen. It had lots of people, a lot of resources, one of the best growth rates in the company, and the technology was a market leader in the industry. This group had everything going for it except for one thing: the behaviors. Human behavior is a very complex subject and we will do it little justice by simplifying it, but for our purposes, we will have to generalize it as the actions and conduct that support people do on a consistent basis.

The more I worked in the group, the more I realized that the origin of all the challenges faced by the group had to do with the small behaviors that are second nature to all support professionals worldwide. Behavior is anything a person does. Going by this general definition, the simple things that a support person does, which lead to the eventual closing of an issue, are the things that make up the individual's approach towards the work. The behaviors I am referring to include simple things, such as calling a customer, asking a customer to close an issue, following up a phone call with an email, or simply putting the customer first in every interaction. If these behaviors are missing from the support equation, then the support does not get done in a way that is most conducive to the success of the group. Enough individuals miss the behaviors and the group ends up as a failure. The group I was involved with was not there yet, but still needed a modification of behaviors.

Modifying behaviors leads to a successful and healthy organizational culture. In individuals, behaviors lead to practices. Once the individuals form a collective, practices lead to culture. As a new manager, identifying behaviors in need of modification is the first step in managing the behaviors of a support group. To indentify behaviors as a new manager you must find them in two ways, by asking and by observing. The way to ask is by setting up individual meetings with each person in the group you are taking over. If you are already working in the group, and know about what the group does, then a meeting with each individual will not serve for anything more than a way to set responsibilities and expectations. However, for a manager who is not familiar with the group, the individual meetings provide a wealth of information as you get to find out about the individual and his practices while at the same time introduce yourself and get some rapport going.

The second way to learn about the behaviors present in the group is by observation. You can listen in on calls, read the documentation on issues, simply stand in proximity to people, or make your rounds to see firsthand how the individuals behave toward customers, the work, and each other. What you observe will help you determine the behaviors that are causing the individuals in the group to falter. What is so interesting in this exercise is that rarely are the problems due to lack of capacity, technical skills, or willingness to perform. Bad behaviors are simply developed by the members of the support group. The members get so used to exhibiting them that they come to see them as normal, thus the only way to correct them is to instill the execution of proper support behaviors. Changing behaviors is fundamentally a retraining in support practices that force new behaviors, which leads to proper practices and, eventually, a proactive support culture.

Once you find out the behaviors that bring detriment to the performance of the group, you will need to plan the best way to change those ingrained behaviors. Your plan of action requires that there is no negative effect on the support operations. You will have to include the way you will roll out your directives, and how you will organize the group and the resources to execute on those directives. The way you typically go about implementing changes to collective behaviors is by putting into practice processes that allow the supporter to repeat the desired behaviors over and over. You will have to put the plan and organization of resources into effect little by little, so that the impact is not forceful and drastic enough to disorient the support group. The whole process of managing behaviors takes time and a lot of corrective action. The most important stage is the one where you control the work to make sure the plan is executed correctly, and that no one is reverting to the old behaviors. The danger in going back to old behaviors, because of the apparent failure of the new ones, is that they will be perceived as incapable of working. You may not have another chance to implement them correctly and still get people to buy into the whole initiative.

Because management is not entirely a solo act, you will need people within the group to champion the changes with their peers. As the authority in the group, you need to develop others who can help you implement the changes. This is all for the progress of the group and it starts with the proper behaviors. In a very basic sense, almost all successes and failures can be attributed to the behaviors of the individuals in an organization. These individual behaviors go on to form the practices that people perform and make the best decisions for their companies. Once the practices become uniform across the organization, then you have the beginnings of a culture.

Always imitate the behavior of the winners when you lose.

—Anonymous

The Davila Cycle

Working in your support group long enough will allow you to realize that not everyone performs equally. The team where everyone works equally well is very rare and is, characteristically, what we described as the communal group in Chapter 4. Most groups are not as perfect as the communal group and also have discrepancies in the way the group members work together. As a colleague and a manager, you must understand that the group has its deficiencies, but also has strengths. Rarely is there a group where everything is dysfunctional or far than ideal. I have never encountered it, nor have I ever heard of a single support group where there were no positive elements that kept it going. Nevertheless, most support groups will have elements that do not do their fair share in taking on new issues or closing existing ones. Of course, issue handling is just the core of the support group's work, and there are other tasks in which people will have a chance to underperform.

As a manager, you have to do something about the discrepancies of the work distribution among the members of the group. As a group member, you want to see some element of fairness in the allotment of tasks and do not want to have to work more than someone else who may be abusing the system. Allowing an imbalanced allocation of work has the detrimental effect of demoralizing hard workers and empowering laggards. The big challenge lies in rolling out changes in the process that will permit everyone to carry a balanced load. You can try forcing people to take a quota of work units such as issues or calls. However, you will soon find that the high performers will find a way to do more than what is expected of them while the low performers will find their own ways to do as little as possible to comply with the quotas. This is also not a very efficient system, because it creates a vicious cycle in which the groups do not progress in their development due to the fact that the fundamental problem of work distributions has not been addressed.

Another possibility is the use of a queue or call monitor to take all new issues and then redistribute them to the rest of the group. However, this does not work very efficiently, because you end up with a support person who is not doing support work, but more administrative work. Additionally, the group comes to rely on one person doing all the initial contact with the customers and may not put any effort into taking new issues that are not given to them. Therefore, how can you ensure that work is distributed across the group properly?

First of all, you must accept that there are exceptional support people who will always do more than what is expected of them. You must also accept that some people require more direct and intense management than others. Some support workers do not do all they can for different reasons, many of which make sense only to them, and become their veracity in justifying low performance. However, as a manager you have to be very objective in your actions and must find the best way to determine how the work gets allocated. Consequently, you also have to figure out a way to get the low performers to work more and, at the same time, allow the high performers to keep doing their thing. This is where the Davila Cycle comes in.

I once had the opportunity to work with a manager named Jose Davila. We worked in a matrix model in which he was in charge of the people while I supported the work. If you are not familiar with matrix organizations, the supporters report to two managers, but for different reasons: one for the hierarchical and personnel side of things and the other for the actual work and processes. We both shared a group of support people with discrepancies in the allotment of work. Roughly half of the people performed at or above expectations and the other half at below or way below expectations. At the same time, their personal queues remained relatively uniform across all the members. This told us that the people who took a lot of issues also closed a lot of issues, and the people that took very few issues also closed very few, all while their total individual queue sizes remained relatively constant. Based on statistical information about the number of new issues taken, like issues closed and queue sizes, I came up with the number of issues that should be allocated to each group members if, and only if, everyone performed at the exact same level. I also found that about half of the group performed in the upper half and about half performed in the lower half; ranges varied so much that it was hard to believe these were members of the same group. I needed a way to cluster as many people as possible around the average and to target only the low performers in any new improvement initiatives without placing them all in some sort of disciplinary action.

At this point, Jose came up with a brilliant yet simple idea that addressed the problem with surgical precision. His plan was to address only the lower half of the group as determined by a weekly issues report. The whole cycle starts with the manager assigning issues to the lower half until they meet at least the group average. The average was determined by taking the prior week's number of new issues and dividing it by the number of members in the group. Every week, the performance leveled across the group and only the lower half was addressed. In addition to this, because there were more issues taken on average by each member of the group, the people who were accustomed to take more issues would get a chance to work on their queue size and lower it. Because the queue size from one-half of the group got smaller, they had more time to devote to other ways of improving the group and the work. In result of devoting more time to things other than issues, the number of issues taken by some would decrease qualifying them to the issue assignment exercise by the manager. By keeping the cycle constant, the average of issues taken per supporter remained the same, but the standard deviation decreased so that there was little variance between the actual issues taken per individual and the group average. The real benefit consists in making underperforming support elements come to parallel with the over performing elements, making for a more uniform group on the upper half. In other words, it helped improve performance in people who needed it while leaving the others alone.

Because of the Davila Cycle, you can also make improvements in the average performance of the group by only focusing on the underperforming members. It only takes a little effort from the manager, but brings sustainable benefit to the group as a whole and to the customers who received much better support as a result.

When a team outgrows individual performance and learns team confidence, excellency becomes a reality.

—Joe Paterno

The Price of Recognition

Mark just wanted one thing in his tenure to complete his career. He had a good position, salary, and benefits. He had the respect that he needed and felt he had it made. However, there was one more thing that he had always wanted; something that he hoped for and even one of the reasons he had worked so hard for several years. He viewed it as a reward and a pinnacle of achievement. Years went by and he never got that which he longed for. All he ever wanted to affirm his career was for the CEO of his company to come by his cube and tell him what a good job he was doing. That was it. No money, promotion, or stock—all Mark wanted was the recognition of the highest executive in the midsize firm. He told his manager, his colleagues, and some of those close to the CEO, but he never got it.

People have different motivations, and in our profession it's usually not money, or at least not entirely money. If we cared for money, we would have chosen another profession that deals with it. A manager has to understand what drives people to perform and what motivates them to produce even more. Making the mistake that it's always money blinds us to the opportunities that abound for making others feel accomplished. In fact, we have all heard of different studies where researchers ask people about their motivations, and we are surprised to hear that most just want better working hours or the ability to make their jobs more varied and interesting. As a support professional, regardless of whether you are a manager or not, knowing what motivates your colleagues is essential to understanding how to influence them positively.

One of the main motivators in the support organization is the concept of rewards. There are many factors that influence the way people view rewards and there has been a lot of research on the subject. The following conclusions came from the research of Edward Lawler:[7]

- We are satisfied with a reward depending on how much of that reward we receive and how much we feel we should receive. This means that if we work hard and receive less than what we perceive to be fair, it will have a detrimental effect on our satisfaction.

- Our satisfaction depends largely on what we see happening to others in a similar situation. If we see a less productive worker get the same or better rewards than what we receive we will have a tendency to be less satisfied with the rewards because we may see it as unfair. Consequently, if we see others also being rewarded equally, we will have higher satisfaction than if we see them being rewarded unfairly in comparison to us.

- Our satisfaction with rewards depends on the satisfaction we receive from internal and external sources. For instance, we gain satisfaction when we do a good job. The rewards we receive may bring us more satisfaction if we are also satisfied internally. If we receive more satisfaction from external sources than satisfaction from the rewards we receive internally from our employer, then our satisfaction from the reward diminishes even more.

---

[7] Edward E. Lawler III, "Reward Systems," *Improving Life at Work* (Santa Monica: Goodyear, 1977) pp 163-226.

- We differ in what we want in the way of rewards and the importance we give to the rewards. Not everyone will value a plaque the same way just as not everyone will be satisfied with a gold watch. Some people would prefer a video camera or a gift certificate over a piece of jewelry.

- We value some rewards because they lead to other rewards. If we receive a reward that increases our potential for another reward, we will tend to value it more.

Rewards are excellent ways to motivate group members and help increase the performance of the group. Also, a manager does not have to be the one always giving out the rewards. In fact, sometimes they don't even have to be valuable rewards at all.

One of the groups I the pleasure of working with had a large number of members distributed all over the world. I was the top support person in terms of title, but there were a high number of people that closed many issues and made the group very successful. Many of our top producers felt a bit disgruntled, because they were not receiving the reward they wanted: recognition and respect. Based on this knowledge, we changed the weekly meeting to be half technical and half social and gave it the format of a show. We called it "The Support Hour" with me as the moderator. I interviewed people of interest to the group and even members of the group to speak about themselves in order to promote the social interactions among colleagues. However, the best part was the monthly recognition awards we gave out. To do so, we ran monthly issues statistics and chose the top three producers in several categories, such as most issues taken, most issues closed, and most calls received from the ACD (Automatic Call Distribution) system. People actually looked forward to their reward of recognition and appreciation for their stellar work. When I told others outside the group about the nature of the rewards, they could not believe it. The rewards were all virtual, consisting of a PowerPoint slide over LiveMeeting, with a picture of a golden telephone headset with their names in gold, silver, or bronze lettering along with their achievement. For instance, the "Golden Headset Virtual Award for Most Issues Taken during the Month" had the name of the colleague along with the number of issues they took. The other awards were done in similar fashion. All the colleagues were getting was a few minutes of glory in the eyes of their peers. It cost us nothing, it did not require a budget and the winners were always very happy to attend to receive their reward. Because of this simple act of honoring those who strive to produce above average performance, the group members looked forward to receiving a similar award, fulfilling their desire for recognition.

Again, everybody wants something out of their job, but it is not always more money. Learning to reward support people for their performance allows you to encourage the desirable behaviors in the group. You don't have to be a manager and the rewards don't even have to be tangible, but they do have to be meaningful. It's a win-win situation for all involved.

All awards and recognition, here and abroad, are to be cherished as recognition by your peers of what you have done in and out of magic.

—Paul Daniels

The Management Support Structure

Bill worked in a call center. He liked the work and truly enjoyed helping out customers. This was his first job out of college and he really wanted to make this his career. However, when he got stuck with problem situations he quickly found that he was on his own. He found the irony staring at him in the face: the helper cannot find help for himself. A few bad experiences later and he called it quits.

Support people are the embodiment of help. We assist, teach, explain, train, and offer just about anything else that customers require in order to get technologies, products, or processes working properly. However, have you ever wondered who is supposed to help us when we are stuck? Helping others with their problems is no easy task and requires a lot of skill—both technical and social, not to mention patience. However, most of us do not have a support structure for ourselves. We are the ones who help others, but what happens when we need help ourselves?

The support organization faces the challenge of being too externally focused. We always lookout for the customer and make sure his needs are met both in terms of quality and timing, which are very positive values for an organization to have. What about the needs of the support organization's internal workers? Picture this: you take a call and the issue turns into a complex situation in which you require guidance as to what to do next. You go to your colleagues, but they are busy. You try to get a supervisor and they are nowhere to be found. You try to find anyone with either the authority or the know-how but still come up short. Now what? Of course, this is somewhat of an extreme, but it happens to us at least once in a while.

The answer to the problems of having support people stuck in situations beyond their control is to have a structure that keeps them from getting into those situations, but to also get them out when they happen. The structure is two-fold. It has to come from the group itself and from management. The support organization is hierarchical in nature, because of the different skill and experience levels and is well prepared to assist. The different support levels are a prime example of a structure in which supporters become wedged between demanding customers and technical situations beyond their control and knowledge, but have a way out preventing any one person from being over their head in an issue. Yet, having the correct tiered structure only goes so far. The support group also needs the proper management structure to sustain the work efforts and a way out of difficult situations.

This is not organizational design or bureaucratic structure, but rather a blend of organizational flexibility and procedural configuration that provides a support person with a place to go in the event of difficult situations. It also has the ability to be reconfigured depending on the volume or need of the organizational demands. This hybrid form of management and process comes from managers. There is a management theory called Contingency Design Theory that states that the organizational design, technology, and management should fit the demands of a situation.[8] However, that theory is not particularly developed for the support organization. Our demands are a bit more bit more basic, but at the same time require flexibility and presence from authority figures.

After some debating about the actual needs of the support group, I concluded that what we really need is a form of internal structure from management that allows us to go to a number of managers and be treated as customers. The management structure has to be such that there is always a manager available to provide assistance and that the management culture is more supportive than authoritarian. Such a choice lies historically with the individual, but in this case it needs to lie in the culture, because support people need consistency regardless of what manager they go to. Therefore, the management support structure is a flexible process and organizational design approach that provides a constant level of support to the members of the group. Here are the processes, players, and how it works:

- *The local frontline managers*: they provide assistance and guidance to the support group members whenever difficult situations arise. It does not matter which manager the member approaches, they all provide the same level of assistance and decision-making authority. The frontline managers have their own formalized authority structure with their own groups. However, when it comes to providing help, assistance, and decision-making authority to support group members they support everyone, regardless of whether the constituent is in their authority group or not.

---

[8] Gibson, James L.; Ivancevich, John M.; Donnelly, Jr., James H., *Organizations* (New York: McGraw-Hill, 2000) pp 378-379.

- *Decision-making and assistance process*: the process is simple and flexible. The support person in need of assistance approaches the closest or readily available manager first. The manager provides the assistance or decision-making authority immediately. The process is a top priority for the managers as they are reviewed based on how available they were to the support members.

- *Management training*: the managers receive the same training that prepares them to provide assistance to anyone regardless of the group they are in. The level of assistance must be constant as to prevent the support people from going to the same manager every single time. Any manager should be able to provide the same level of help and the same decision when faced with a similar situation.

- *The mid-level manager*: the frontline managers report to this manager. The mid-level manager also acts as a support figure to the supporters and has to ability to make higher decisions over broader matters. In the case of the frontline managers being occupied with assisting group members, the mid-level manager steps in and provides assistance where needed.

- *The supporting manager culture*: frontline managers are there to facilitate the movement of issues by the support group members. The managers understand and strive to help. Their priority is serving customers through the support group since they strive to provide assistance to the supporters whenever it's needed.

The management support structure may already be practiced in some support organizations. I have never personally seen it in the magnitude described here, but it would make for a very assistance-oriented organization in which the role of the manager is to facilitate and make sure the customer gets the service in the most expedited way possible.

A manager is an assistant to his men.

—Thomas J. Watson

The Fallible Manager

Having a manager is a fact of work life. We all need some level of management, regardless of our position in the support world. Some have team leads, others have supervisors, and others report to a formal manager who takes care of the resource needs as well as performance management for the support person. Whatever the type of manager, the fact is that all of us have to report our actions and work to someone else. Like it or not, the support manager plays a vital role in the success and, sometimes, failure of the support group.

Not all managers are created equal. Some are great at helping their reports develop their full potential while others simply go along trying to keep the group from falling apart; others are simply detrimental and have no business managing people. Of course, the latter are few and far between, and usually don't last in their positions as long as upper managers are not blind to the effect that a manager has on production and morale. Every support colleague deserves the manager that will allow him to develop into a productive member of the support organization, while at the same time increasing the excess value the company derives from the supporter. After all, organizations need people to do the work, and the more work a person does, the more benefit the organization will derive. However, this brings us to a good and fair question: just what exactly makes a good manager? Is it the one who provides the most benefit to us as supporters? Is it the one who tries to save as much as possible for the company? Is it the one who drives us like slaves into ever increasing productivity? The question is not an easy one, because it all depends on who you ask. The manager is always going to appear fallible to someone. Just ask different people in your organization about a manager whom you perceive to be effective. Most will undoubtedly agree with your assessment, but there will eventually be someone who finds some fault with the same manager you admire. It's a fact of life that you can't please everyone. Yet the question still remains: what makes a good manager? The real answer is "it depends on who you ask." Nevertheless such a general answer doesn't satisfy anyone.

We need an objective view on an effective manager who lives up to the role. First, a good manager is the one who can manage the resources of the organization he serves. He works for the organization and is bound to protect the organization's interests. He is not there to make friends or be influenced by anything else other than productivity. The good manager takes a dollar input and turns it into two dollars, by managing it effectively and gaining value in the process. That concept applies to any industry because managers exist to be the eyes, ears, and hands of the company. The better the manager is able to deal with the resources entrusted to him, the more efficient that manager appears to be in the eyes of upper management. The benefits of a good manager are not only in the reputation, but essentially in the benefit his actions bring to the organization in the way of increased revenue or decreased expenses. This is the most objective view there is of a manager.

The characteristics that make a good manager are few, but yet very powerful because they allow the manager to consistently get the best output from the same input. The following are the attributes of a good manager:

- *A focus on performance*: the best manager is usually not the friendliest or even the most versed in management knowledge. The best manager is the one that can perform consistently and deliver the most benefit with the same amount of resources. In fact, the manager is the catalyst that makes the most with the least. Management is focused on utilizing the resources at their maximum and providing a good return to the company's investments in the support group.

- *The one who makes the best decision consistently*: the core function of a support manager is decision making. Without decision making, the manager is pretty much useless. His decisions have an impact on the efficiency of the organization and are capable of making the difference in any given situation via decisions.

- *Detached from the reports*: the best manager is the one who can make objective decisions about his group without having any vested interest in the individuals that report to him. Since the core function of a support manager is decision making, anything that clouds the judgment of the manager is, therefore, undesirable. This includes personal relationships with those he manages. Anytime a manager lets a personal relationship influence his decision, the organization loses.

- *Some formal management education or experience*: management is a learned skill. A good manager is made, not born. In management, experience allows the person to provide some prediction to situations. The best managers are the ones with the most experience. I have yet to see a new MBA graduate with no management experience make a great manager immediately. However, proper education in management comes in very handy and allows the manager to grow and handle complex roles with ease.

Contrary to what you may have heard, there is no perfect manager. All have faults whether professional or personal. The level at which the manager is capable of delivering value to the organization is directly proportional to the effectiveness level of the manager; therefore, the better the manager, the more value he delivers to the company.

I wouldn't say I was the best manager in the business. But I was in the top one.

—Brian Clough

CHAPTER 8

■ ■ ■

Structures and Tiers

As a department within a technology company, the support organization requires some form of order to make the best use of resources. Our field of technical support has relied on the tiered structure for many years now, and it has proven very effective. There are other possibilities that may well prove even better, depending on the organizations and demands placed on the support professionals. The current state of the support structure is heavily dependent on the predominant support model of tiers based in knowledge and experience.

This chapter devotes most of its content to the possibility of other models, in addition to the tiered structure. It also touches on some variations of the tiers and ends with the best recommended approach to the structure. I also included a couple of topics on the practicality of informally modifying the structure at the supporter level by initiating the practice since this could have a profound effect on the organization. Additionally, you will read about the concept of technology vs. skill as applied to the support structure, the service-oriented structure, the performance-driven structure, and other advancements in the way the support groups take shape.

In the next few pages, you will reason and think through the endless possibilities, repercussions, and opportunities with each structure model and theory. The ideas presented in this chapter are meant to provide long-term value to you as a support professional, either in the contributor role or the management position. You may not have the power now to make a decision on the structure of your support department or even local group, but someday you may choose to move into a position where you can. This chapter will provide a foundation on the structure possibilities and the opportunities available with tiers.

Read the following pages with an open mind. Before this book, most of the material has never seen the light of day in the exact way that it's presented here. I went back to organizational theory and applied some of the concepts with a bit of synthesis to technical support. We are at the brink of a shift in the acceleration of the knowledge and discoveries in our field. From here on, we will be on the cutting-edge of organizational development, and even coming up with our very own organizational structure theory. This chapter is a beginning, a very humble one, but a new start nonetheless. Just remember that it takes time for an industry or discipline to progress, and it only happens if the practitioners strive to come up with the new ideas to start a dialogue then revolution. As with every other human endeavor, it takes time and ideas to move the world. Technical support will be no different.

Every vital organization owes its birth and life to an exciting and daring idea.

—James Bryant Conant

The Structure Dilemma

By its very nature, support work carries a complexity that cannot be easily explained in one same model. Because this discipline is relatively organic in its inception, and because we don't yet have a well-established body of research based on practice, it is quite difficult to assert or even attempt to claim the best structure for the technical support organization. Some models exist that appear to work well in many unrelated organizations. Organically, the tiered structure arose out of the need to specialize in specific areas of supported technologies with multiple levels of specialization and even support approach. Most of us, at some point or another, worked in a tiered organization where the all the new customer calls or issues came in and the first or frontline tier worked them all. From there, the harder issues that required a more advanced set of expertise transferred over to the secondary tier whose members worked the customer problems until resolution or until they run out of options. If this second tier could not handle the issue any further, than the issue transferred to yet a higher tier with individuals who have an even greater knowledge, expertise, or specialization. This is the basic concept of the tiered structure.

Obviously, the tiered model of support lends itself well to only the most complex technologies, where problems can increase exponentially in difficulty by changing certain parameters or elements. Such support includes software, computer hardware, complex machines, and complex processes. Supporting a process is something we don't typically associate with technical support, but the processes such as the tax code, service contracts, insurance claims, and legal advice centers all deal with incredibly complex processes not unlike what some of us deal with in the technology side of support.

The tiered structure model grew out of necessity. The very concept is little more than the filtering of issues, problems, and calls in sequential order until the correct person with the necessary skills solves the problem. From a labor perspective, it's what Adam Smith described as the pin assembly.[1] Smith saw the need for the elaboration of a single item in manufacturing to be broken down in stages, each mastered by a different person. This separation of labor is exactly what enabled the rise of the Industrial Revolution and the modern manufacturing process. It is unlikely that Adam Smith had the support-tiered model in mind when he came up with his theories. But what we are doing to support work is in fact in the tiered model.

The problem with the tiered structure in support is that while it allows for the maximization of excess benefit from internal resource skills internally, it does little to accelerate the supporters' development and climb into the upper tiers. Nevertheless, it is also highly inefficient externally where the user of the support service needs to get to the correct tier immediately rather than be subjected to the filtering mechanisms of the tiered structure. Phil Verghis presented quite a differing option in his Savvy Support model,[2] which allocates the correct resource to the customer's needs immediately. Verghis states that the best way to structure the support organization is not merely to stagger the skills in an effort to satisfy each customer and protect the higher skilled resources internally, but rather to provide the customer with the highest-skilled resource from the start. Under the Savvy Support model, the supporter benefits because the work is more challenging and all the petty, repetitive questions go away by solving them. It is a promising concept and one that could revolutionize our profession, but perhaps only in the most complex of technologies. Verghis does not make any applicability claims, but from the text it appears that it would apply to highly complex technologies. It is not entirely clear if the Savvy Support model would work well in less complex technologies or in the support of processes, but there is also no reason why it would not.

Therein lays the predicament of the modern support organization. How do we structure our resources to be both to the highest benefit to the organization and to the customer? The tiered model

---

[1] Adam Smith, *The Wealth of Nations Abridged* (West Valley City, UT: Waking Lion Press, 2007) pp 3-12.
[2] Phil Verghis "No More (Support) Tiers!: Savvy Support" Verghis View Newsletter April 2008. `http://www.verghisgroup.com/publications/verghis-view-april-2008/` Accessed April 26, 2009.

favors the support organization internally from a business approach to cost-benefit of hired resources, but the Savvy Support favors the customers by saving the time it takes to reach the right person and shortening their time to resolution. The Savvy Support model also favors support professionals by presenting them with the correct level of challenge. Consequently, these two structure forms are not the only possibilities. Undoubtedly, many others are not yet documented in research or mainstream literature.

You may be thinking about something unclear from both structure models; the inclusion of the interest of the company and the potential for unjustly assuming the interests of you, the supporter. What we need is a contingency model in structure. It would be highly risky to assume that there is a one-size fits all when it comes to structure unless that structure model was itself not structure, but rather a theory. The complexities in support staff, technology, customers and organization are far too great for anything short of a flexible structure theory that can adapt to all of them. Enter the support contingency structure model that states that the structure of the support organization must be molded into the structure that best fits the interests of the organization, staff, customer, and the technology. There is absolutely no reason why a company cannot define its own structure independent of any research or documented structure model, as long the constituents are accounted for and their best interests met at a reasonable level. For instance, suppose your company offers free support to a small, inexpensive, but highly complex machine. Your organization must structure its support to provide service that is in line with the benefit it derives from the sale of the machine from the organization's perspective. The company must also provide staff sufficiently capable enough to solve problems in the least amount of time for the customer. The staffing must also be capable enough to solve problems in the complex technology, but be affordable enough to not be counterproductive and cost more than the profit realized from the sales of the technology. Simply, all the support contingency structure model resolves is that the structure of the organization follows the best approach possible by ensuring the most benefit to all the parties involved.

Structure in the support organization is still in its infancy and we have a long way to go with researching the most suitable approaches to our wide array of technologies and customer needs. Many support organizations in the industry are currently innovating in this realm of the support field. It is only a matter of time before the great breakthroughs see the light of day.

This organization is created to prevent you from going to hell. It isn't created to take you to heaven.

—Henry Cabot Lodge, Jr.

The Tiered Approach

The tiered support structure seems to be a polarizing topic when discussing support organizational structure with visionary colleagues. People either love it or hate it. It evokes negative sensations in those who started and grew their career in the communal support group as described in Chapter 4's conclusion. There are several arguments, but the main argument is that the tiered support structure isolates members within the support groups and silos them to the point that they build a barrier between those at the bottom and those at the top. In a recent intellectual exchange on ideas about structure and process, an admired colleague and manager explained that the ideal support group should have no tiers, and that the members within the group find the best way to exchange information and trade issues, so that the problems are always handled properly. The members in the group develop an informal structure in which the issues are worked in a way that no one is ever stuck with an issue he or she cannot handle.

I thought about my colleague's argument and realized that he fundamentally described an informal tiered structure in which colleagues help each other without the need for formal separation by skill and experience level. Yet, the tiers were still there; they just were not structurally defined. I also came to the conclusion that since tiers are in use by the majority of support groups, there must be something to them. Of course, it is also true that just because the majority use a structure it does not necessarily mean it's the most efficient or effective one. Yet, if you think about it, the tiered support structure is organic in nature and the rational approach to specialization. Doctors use it, police officers use it, and the military is full of hierarchies. I am not suggesting that any of these other fields have anything to do with support, but the hierarchical approach to labor and activity has its merits. In organizational theory, there is a theory by James Mooney that he called the Scalar Principle,[3] which says that the effort across an organization is naturally coordinated and that it exists in every organization for it provides the practicality necessary to be functional. Mooney went on to explain that the scalar nature of the organization served to grade duties and separate them into a hierarchical structure, depending on the importance and responsibility. He developed this theory primarily for the purpose of defining authority, but also included the idea that responsibilities should be scaled in a way that different players take different levels of assumption of accountability in order to reach a functional goal. The theory goes into a lot of detail, but at its most fundamental level it is describing what we know in technical support as functional tiers—each with the responsibility for different levels of technical accountability for the purpose of closing issues and solving customers problems.

Mooney wrote about what is essentially the hierarchical functionality in responsibility in 1947, which shows that tiers or a scalar approach is nothing new or equivocal in concept. The tiered approach is a valid and old-enough approach to pursue, but we sometimes go about it all wrong. In support organizations, we take a tiered approach as it relates to technical difficulty, but not in a scalar undertaking of responsibility. We normally think of the first tier as taking the easy-to-answer questions that do not require much thinking. As such, we staff the first tier with people with minimal skills and often with little consequence as to responsibility. According to Mooney, responsibility should be the driving factor behind the scaling of functions, not skill. Of course, this is not to say that we will staff our first tiers with the most skilled, but simply states that skills are not the driving factor in filling the tier.

The tiered support organization is only a structure model and says nothing about process. You can make the analogy that in organizational theory, structure and process are much like hardware and software in computing. The structure by itself will do nothing. Structure requires processes to move the parts and get everything working. Even the best structure could fail miserably, if the processes are not the correct ones to move actions. This is why the argument that the tiered structure is essentially flawed because it forces customers to put up with clueless supporters is irrational; it is not up to the structure, but to the process as to the skill level of the personnel. The structure is the skeleton while the processes are the muscles and nerves. The structure determines the shape of the support organization and the processes determine how the shape moves and functions. We blame all the problems associated with the tiered support model to the structure alone, but fail to see that the wiring of the structure is what really drives the success of the structure and not the structure itself.

The tiered support organization is alive and well in many companies and functions quite efficiently in most that I have seen, along with where I have worked. It does not work in places due to poor processes or poor implementation of processes. Recently, I had a chance to hear yet another argument, among many, against tiers. The support colleague explained that such a structure is full of holes and flaws because the frontline people, of which he was part, end up with the all the issues while the upper tiers don't do their fair share of the work. His support group had recently migrated from a three-tier structure down to a two-tier structure. As someone who has, for most of my career, worked in the upper tiers of the support organization, I immediately spotted the problem with the implementation of the tiered structure the colleague was referring to. It was very obvious to me, yet he still had no idea in his

---

[3] James D Mooney, *The Principles of Organization* (New York: Harper & Brothers, 1947).

mind as to why the multitier approach did not work. It all came to an end when I asked him, "So how did you transfer issues to the upper tier?" to which he replied astonished, "We were supposed to transfer issues?!"

The tiered support structure is popular and successful in many support organizations. It is, at its most fundamental level, a way to apply the Scalar Principle to multiple responsibilities in the support group. The structure is sound and organic in nature, but it needs the right set of processes to make its promises of increased efficiency and efficacy a reality.

> *The organizational architecture is really that a centipede walks on hundred legs and one or two don't count. So if I lose one or two legs, the process will go on, the organization will go on, the growth will go on.*

> —Mukesh Ambani

Technology vs. Skill

Our most widely used organizational structure, the tiered model and its variants, usually revolves around the grading of skill sets and, ideally, responsibility levels in regard to a single product or technology. In other words, all the members of a support group, as typically organized, support the same product. In a one-product company, this is not an issue, but in a larger enterprise with multiple product offerings, the problem becomes a bit more apparent. People with different roles within the support organization perform multiple functions from taking initial calls, helping clients with functional questions, writing new documentation, and even visiting the customer on locations in the pursuit of the solution to the reported problem and an issue closure. After seeing this separation by product, one wonders if one person does the front level or tier-one support for one product or technology, why couldn't the same person do it for other products? What about something that requires a longer learning curve, such as upper tier support? Or, what about specific types of support, like those dealing with a specific area that all products share? How do we arrange support people when there are multiple products present? Is such a question even possible considering that most of the technologies that would even qualify for having a dedicated support group are going to be so technically complex that generalizing across products would be unmanageable? As someone who has done support for multiple products concurrently, I must say that this is not an easy task, but it is possible. Suppose it was also possible in your situation, would you arrange them by product or by function?

That last question is the toughest one to answer, and the one that has some solid research behind it. Fortunately, organizational researchers tackled this question for us decades ago. In the *Harvard Business Review* article, "Organizational Choice: Product vs. Function,"[4] the authors explain the dilemma faced by organizational managers in deciding how to structure the organization by the specific product those groups work in or by the function within the group that the people undertake. Many other research papers and dissertations in the management and organizational theory fields targeted the question from different perspectives, but the article is still one of the pioneering research articles on the subject of structure.

The specifics of the dilemma are quite simple to understand, but incredibly difficult to resolve. Take for instance, the typical support organization in a global company with an array of product offerings. Product A has a marketing team, a product management team, a sales team, a services team, a

---

[4] Arthur H Walker and Jay W Lorsch, "Organizational Choice: Product vs. Function," Harvard Business Review (November–December 1968).

development team and, of course, a support group. Within the support group, multiple tiers all do different tasks requiring different skill sets, but as it relates to the same product. The other possibility would be to devise a structure in which all marketing people for all products were grouped together and managed accordingly. In other words, the grouping would be by function. The same goes for sales, services, and development—any other role that may arise would also be grouped by function or role. However, these two approaches may be fine for a general role, but what is a support group to do when there are multiple tiers within the same group? Could we as support people view our work as merely a function that can be flexible in the technology supported?

This is a question I've debated for years. I have spoken with a few colleagues in India, Costa Rica, and the Czech Republic, and they assure me as they move from product to product that picking up new technologies to support becomes easier once done often enough. Being the skeptic that I am, I have to agree that it may become easier to move from product to product, but can you really become an expert in different technologies with such ease? The truth is there are many companies doing this already. All you have to do is carry out a simple Internet search; there are literally hundreds, if not thousands, of outsourcing companies globally that do technical support for anyone without an internal support department, but with a complex product with customers in need of help. The technologies these companies can support vary greatly from computer software and hardware to machines, books, and systems. It is truly an amazing feat because many of these companies have made their processes so efficient and technology independent that they can take any new complex product and become very good at it very fast. As if that is not enough, they have supporters doing multiple technologies at the same time. Undoubtedly, these are very talented individuals with exceptional learning skills and social and service cleverness to match.

This brings us to the question: is it possible to arrange support workers by function rather than product? It most certainly is. However, support should be arranged by skill rather than function or by technology rather than product. There are different skills necessary for support, but having a certain skill, such as queue management or customer follow up, does not necessarily require for the person to master the product supported. There is a possibility that an individual with a certain skill set, such as administrative skills, to manage a number of queues for different products. It is also possible that someone with elevated logical skills to handle multiple products by simply learning fast and having the skills be his main asset, and not necessarily the product knowledge. This is quite a theoretical approach, and it is not clear that any company has attempted such a structure for an internal support department; however, it would make for quite an efficient support workforce. To some extent, these are in place in offshore and outsourcing operations around the work, so there is a huge possibility in this field to bring about new support methodologies.

The arrangement of the support structure by technology does not equate to a structure by product. A product and a technology are different things for multiple products and could share similar technology. A support professional with capacity in the general technology may serve as a support professional across multiple products. Take for instance, the software support field in which having skills in operating systems, networking, or even hardware allows the practitioner the ability to support a range of software products to some extent. The rest of the knowledge is more of a specialty, but having a core set of skills could potentially help. Nevertheless, the concept of structure by technology would have a harder future in the more complex products where prominent levels of in-depth knowledge are required to support effectively.

The question of arranging the structure of the organization by product or function is not a new one. It has been debated for many years and experimented with mixed results. For the support field, I must conclude, there is hope for arranging the structure by field across multiple products. However, doing the structure by technology may prove more difficult as the complexity of the product increases.

Once an organization loses its spirit of pioneering and rests on its early work, its progress stops.

—Thomas J. Watson

The Service-Oriented Structure

The work we do in technical support has many implications on the overall product success of the company for whom we provide the support. When the support is of the highest level, the existing customers are less resistant to purchase additional products or services from the company. When the support lags behind the expectations of the customer, then the implications for our sales cycles will be negative as it pertains to the importance that customers place on our service after the sale. On the negative end of the spectrum, we may hear about the loss of sales because customers perceived our support to be inferior to the competition while on the positive side, we may never hear anything. After all, no one calls support when everything runs smoothly. For this reason, it is imperative that support provide the best effective service the very first time the new customer interacts with us and every single time after that. This proposition may sound too optimistic and even aggressive, but it must become a reality if our company is to gain a competitive edge over the rest of the market.

The trick is to make sure we deliver the highest level of service every single time the customer calls into our support center. Because of the many factors involved, we typically focus heavily on the technical skills yet service quality often lags behind technical quality. The main reason is that we structure our support centers for technical efficiency and effectiveness, efficiency being the ability to do things right, and effectiveness being the ability to do the right thing. However, we do not really structure our support centers for service excellence. There is a monumental difference between the two concepts. For example, why is it that customers often complain that when they call our support centers they speak to someone who asks mind-numbing questions without really stopping to understand the problems first? Some of it is due to technical competency of the supporter, but a lot has to do with the service skills the colleagues possess. The other problem lies in how we arrange the structure to deal with the first issue contacts.

Consider this scenario: the typical group consists of people with differing levels of technical knowledge. We often divide them in tiers with the less technically talented people in the frontlines and leaving the people with the most knowledge and, typically, the most experience in support in the higher tiers where service matters less than technical expertise. There are a few modern trends debuting in the support field ranging from Verghis' Savvy Support[5] to the double tiers with functional knowledgeable people in the first tier to the more in-depth knowledgeable members in the second tier. All are quite commendable and promising. Nevertheless, one thing is missing: the concept of providing the best possible service in the most crucial stage of the support process. Savvy Support wants the most knowledgeable people in the first tier receiving the first customer call. I happen to really like the Savvy Support model and think it would be a great way to provide support; however, I am also not blind to the fact that it could very well be cost-prohibitive to the support organizations that must also deal with the realities of economics. In addition, the most knowledgeable person is not always the best servicer. Those who are both knowledgeable and high quality, service-oriented supporters do not come cheap or in masses. We have all seen the expert who knows all about the technology, but possesses the service skills of a medieval torturer.

---

[5] Phil Verghis "No More (Support) Tiers!: Savvy Support" Verghis View Newsletter April 2008. `http://www.verghisgroup.com/publications/verghis-view-april-2008/` Accessed April 26, 2009.

What we really need is a structure that exists for and produces service excellence. For example, in the archetypal support group there is always someone who exemplifies the best of support by providing the absolute best service consistently. All you have to do is look at the statistics and you will find, at least, one person who time after time successfully handles the most customers, closes the most issues, and receives most of the kudos in the group. Amazingly, if you look closely, that person usually is not the most knowledgeable. The fact is that the best support people are not always the most technical, but they are always the best servicers. The best people in support are the most productive, carry the organization, and make customers happy by providing the best solutions at the best time possible. This is the essence of service. I am not suggesting that the specialists or experts are not good servicers. What I am saying is that the best servicers are not always the most technical, but are typically the most productive, which is what counts in technical support.

The way that we structure our support organization to provide the best support and service possible is by concisely structuring our tiers and processes to put the best service people in strategic positions in relation to customer interaction. For instance, the person who speaks to the customer the first time and the last time should be the most service-oriented person in the organization. Because this is a relatively new concept, we need an example from another field. Suppose we want to sell the most products with the shortest sales cycle possible. The salesperson who closes the deal must be the absolute best expert in the art of closing. You wouldn't send in the person who prepared the sales proposal to close the deal, just because he knows the most about writing a sales proposal. You want the best person for the job. The person who creates the lead and sets up the first appointment should be the best at doing such a task. You don't want a closer to do the cold-calling; the job should go to the most efficient lead producer. The same goes for support. The first tier supporter should be the best at understanding problems and making customers feel at ease while at the same time providing some technical value. You do not need the absolute best expert taking the first call, plus the absolute expert probably won't do it anyway. What I am proposing is a structure in which the best servicers are in charge of the customer interaction throughout the life of the support issue, call, or ticket; then having the more technical but less service oriented people at their disposition. The best service people would be keen to sales people who use sales engineers to provide the technical expertise, but not necessarily initiate or close the sale just support it. The same goes for a highly complex technical issue in which the best servicers are in charge of the process and the technical gurus are there to support them. In the event the customer wants to deal directly with the technical expert, this is directly enabled by the servicer and under the servicer's direction.

The concept of structuring the support group with the best service-oriented people is counterintuitive, but the reality is that the best customer service-oriented people are usually the most successful in the support profession. Of course, this is with the implication that they are not technical neophytes, but can hold their ground on the technical realm, though not necessarily at the expert level.

Reduce the layers of management. They put distance between the top of an organization and the customers.

—Donald Rumsfeld

The Meaningful Support Structure

Why do we work? What do we get out of it? Is it only about the money or is there something more? Our jobs are the source of our livelihood and intellectual fulfillment. We have the jobs we have because we obviously derive some value, benefit, and relevance to the alternative. For technical support workers, our jobs are more than just a way to make money. Our jobs define who we are as realized individuals and provide meaning via service.

Support jobs are evolving from the early days of answering the phone to take functional questions on a specific technology, product or process, and little else to now becoming vibrant career choices with all types of alternatives. The modern support position ranges in function f4rom a focus on customer service to a very progressive engineering/support purpose in which you can fulfill many roles from training, technical writing, on-site services all the way to strategic leadership. This is not the same career that some of us went into. Support is crossing the helpdesk boundary of yesterday, providing a valuable business service, and helping our companies gain a competitive advantage.

One thing has not changed. Support is still, at times, a stressful job. Nevertheless, in recent years technical support management introduced in specific segments of the practice the concept of Quality of Work Life, which is intended to provide meaning to our jobs and allows us to grow as individuals.[6] In other words, we are no longer just a resource with knowledge to fulfill a specific need in the technical realm, but we are viewed as individuals with needs and wants who are given the opportunity to develop as much as we can with the help and support of our companies. Only through ostering individual development can our companies make the best use of us, as employees and technical resources, and realize the potential that we are capable of. When our potential becomes reality, our companies grow, our economies expand, and our countries prosper. It all starts with the way our jobs are designed and structured as to make the best use of us and, in turn, allow us to make the best use of ourselves.

If you work for a company that has a Quality of Work Life philosophy, then you are in a very good place. It is up to you to take advantage of it and allow it to take hold of your work and professional life in order to start paying dividends for you, your family, company, and customers. The following are these ways:

- *Take every possible opportunity offered*: your employer offers you benefits for a reason: to help you develop and grow as a professional and as an individual. Very few colleagues take advantage of any of these benefits, such as tuition reimbursement, flexible work schedules, work from home programs, training, career mentoring, professional development paths, and even time off for volunteer work. When taking advantage of these opportunities, go with the ones with the most promise and long lasting benefits first. For instance, if you want to improve yourself by way of education, go for the biggest return for your effort. The trick is to really measure the return. Allow me to explain, suppose your employer offers tuition reimbursement for technical training, college, or certifications. Most people would go for the certification because it appears to offer the most return for the effort in the least amount of time. However, a certification does not offer the most benefit overall. The most benefit would come from that which has the potential to keep on giving long after you exert the effort. That could only come from technical training or from a formal academic degree. Choose the training that has the potential to offer you career benefits for months, or even years, into the future. A college education is by far the most benefit you can derive from any type of education program because a college degree stays with you for life. In the Information Technology industry, there was a huge dilemma for years back about what was more beneficial: a Masters of Business Administration (MBA) or a Microsoft Certified Systems Engineer (MCSE) certification. If you reason through this dilemma, the answer is quite clear. The MBA lasts for a lifetime while the MCSE only for a few years. Education is only one of the possibilities in a Quality of Work Life adherent company.

[6] Richard Kopelman, *"Job Redesign and Productivity: A Review of the Evidence,"* National Productivity Review, Summer 1985, pp 239.

- *Hold nothing back*: You may also make your own opportunities by demonstrating the value you bring to your position and to the company. Share innovative ideas and take actions that will get you ahead. This does not mean that you complain every chance you get, but rather that you provide some value in every chance you get either by supporting company and management initiatives or by going the extra mile in everything you do. A good way to take initiative is to find a niche and develop it, but also to contribute to projects and programs outside your immediate area. The company may host cross-functional groups or mentoring opportunities in which you can participate. This will allow you to grow and develop your current position and gain value that you can then use to your benefit as well as that of your colleagues and employer.

- *Always be on the lookout for ways to grow*: Career satisfaction is not an accident. Those colleagues who excel and progress are always looking for the next chance to gain a new skill, position, or advancement. You need to be in constant motion. Make it a point to learn something new every day or every week. Look at other support groups to see if there is something you can contribute while at the same time learn from. It does not always have to be doing the actual support. You can also work in the background of support, making sure the support people have what they need. Especially in large support organizations, opportunities abound in everything from support systems, communications, and processes all the way to special projects in which someone with support experience has a better chance to succeed.

The meaningful support structure is not something formalized by a company or support department. This structure is created when the company provides the opportunities for a more meaningful career, but it only becomes meaningful when the employees actually take advantage of the opportunities and do it so often that it becomes a part of the organization's culture and morphs into an informal structure among colleagues helping each other succeed. People follow what they see. If they see you growing and searching for advancement in your career, they will be tempted to do the same. It starts with the individual and ends with the group.

Culture does not change because we desire to change it. Culture changes when the organization is transformed; the culture reflects the realities of people working together every day.

—Frances Hesselbein

The Reactive/Proactive Tiered Approach

We don't often think about working in tiers as more than a structure in which one group of people take the easier, frontline issues, the next tiers handle the harder issues, and so forth until the problem reaches all the way up to someone who can bring resolution. We are so used to a progressive increase in difficulty paradigm that we no longer view it as anything more than that. It has become a fact of support work; the higher up you go in tiers, the harder the issues get, and the more knowledgeable the people tend to be. Typically, the only people who make it up the higher tiers are those for whom the technical challenges cease to be so they need to face the next level of difficulty. This presents us with a couple of problems. The first is the reactive nature of our work that does not change as we go up in tier. The second is the lack of uniformity in the tier paradigm, but not all support organizations do it the same.

This leaves only a few possibilities for solutions. The best outcome would come directly from the support workers showing those in support management the benefits of the approach. For now, let us discuss the two problems in more detail.

The nature of our line of work is very reactive. Customers call us with questions and we respond with answers. They try our answers and if unsuccessful, present us with new questions. No one ever calls our support line to just tell us how great things are going. We only hear from our customers when problems arise. This is the nature of the work and there is, realistically, not much we can do about it. Checking up on customers to be proactive and preempt a problem is by far not what most support people do today. There are some strides in proactive support. Most come from specific players in different industries, such as computer software and production line equipment. These advancements mostly consist in anticipating problems based on intelligence built into operating systems and maintenance software. Aside from that, technical support is still very much focused on solving problems when they occur and only when we are told about it by a customer. I say this is a problem not because there is something wrong with it, but because it tends to get us into a one-mode view of "wait and see" for the next problem to come. Reactive, after all, works well in many other professions. Medical doctors typically see only sick patients. Mechanics usually work on cars when they need fixing. Lawyers see people when they are in legal trouble. As you can see, reactive is not a bad thing, but it is a problem when we want to look at our tier work in a proactive way.

The other issue we have with tiers is that the profession does not have any uniformity in how tiers are used. Some support organizations treat the level of the supporter as a role and not a title. In other words, you could be a Junior Support Technician as opposed to a Senior Support Technician and still do a role in a higher tier than someone who is a Senior Support Technician. In such a model, the tiers are not according to title but according to insight knowledge into the technology. The problem with this approach is that you have no idea what to expect and from whom. You may have a higher-ranking person with specific demands that go with the title, but the tier dictates something completely different. Conversely, you can have a lower-ranking support person who happens to have a lot of experience and is placed in a higher tier. The job description for the title demands work that is well below that required by the tier. Such a paradox may happen for many reasons, but mainly because of poor negotiation skills with management. If you think this rarely happens, all you have to do is move around.

The other possibility may happen when you have a formalized title that goes with the tier; these are the titles such as a Support Technician I, Junior Helpdesk Rep, Technical Support Representative 3rd Level, or some other title that clearly implies the tier it belongs to. Overall, this type of title by tier is preferable, because it allows the formalization of the role and function as well as implies clear demands by job description on the role. If you don't live up to the title you get demoted. If you prove yourself in the current title, you get promoted into the next title and, consequently, the tier. The only issue is that it only happens in some support organizations. Others, for the most part, just do whatever fits the organizational management.

Some time ago, I came to the realization that as players in our profession, we must standardize some way to do our work in a manner that is consistent. We know that tiers are pretty much the norm. There is no way around it. Some like them and some do not. The fact is we have them and they are a norm, be it by role or title. However, the responsibility within the tiers is what we need to be consistent about. I do not think all support organizations are going to magically change just because they read it here, but we can do it at the supporter level. What I propose is the reactive/proactive tiered approach. It works by focusing the roles and is the way to improve the interaction and functionality among the higher and lower tiers.

Suppose all support organizations had only two tiers: junior and senior. The reactive/proactive tiered approach would treat the junior tier as reactive and the senior as proactive. The junior tier reacts to the customers demand, works the issue, solves the problems it can, and communicates any progress to the customers and any other stakeholders. The senior tier, on the other hand, should be constantly on the lookout for opportunities to help, mentor, train, and take over issues from the junior tier. The senior tier should be more proactive in its approach. These are two distinct ways of looking at problems. The junior has the ability to search and the senior the ability to research. This may sound like splitting hairs, but the junior tier should be able to take issues and do complex searches, perform some level of troubleshooting, and engage in some level of intuitive problem solving. On the other hand, the senior tier should be doing the in-depth research into problems and coming up with only the most complex and inventive solutions, not in a reactive mode but a purely proactive one. It requires a fundamental shift in the way the senior tiers look at support work. It is no longer just the fixing of issues when they come to us, but rather us going to look for them, preempting what those problems will be, and staying ahead of them so that when they do surface, a solution will be waiting. The bottom line is that the senior should not just be a more experienced junior, but the senior should be a whole new way of looking at the role. A proper analogy would be a junior tier as a doctor and a senior tier as a medical researcher.

I know some companies are already experiencing and innovating on the reactive/proactive tiered approach, but it has yet to catch up to the whole profession. In fact, the whole idea is counterintuitive in today's support organizations because the higher the supporters go up the tiers, the less the role changes; it is only the problem's complexity that changes when it should really be the role that shifts. The shift to the reactive/proactive tier has the best chance if it comes from the ranks. Only if we start acting our roles under the mode will things change and the profession will see that this has promise. By the way, this is how the whole concept of tiers came to dominate the field.

> *The problem of social organization is how to set up an arrangement under which greed will do the least harm, capitalism is that kind of a system.*

> —Milton Friedman

The Performance-Driven Structure

We talk of tiers, groups, levels, titles, roles, and just about anything else we can do to divide the support profession into people with different amounts of knowledge, experience, and possibly even drive. One thing we rarely see is the grouping of support professional according to their level of value, efficiency, or even mere production. For some reason this never crosses our collective mind, or perhaps it has, and it just escapes us all. Think about this scenario: within the same tier or level of support colleagues we are all expected to do the same type of work. We are given the same tools and probably very similar salaries. However, if you look at statistical production reports, it will become very apparent that some people produce more than others over the long run, sometimes even for the short run. If you have access to stats for the group you work in, go and study them and you will see my point. If the group succeeds it's because the work of a segment of colleagues who pick up the slack for those who underperform. Obviously, this is simply not fair. Yet, fairness aside, the problem is with the structure. Support structures are there only for experience, knowledge, and capacity but not for performance.

For example, perhaps you work in a group with 20 people all at the same level or tier. You are expected to produce roughly the same work over the long run. Logic says that each person should do roughly about 5%of all the work produced on the group. However, after a year, the typical mark for the term "long run," the numbers show that five of the group members accounted for 50% of the total group's production. The other 15% did the other half of the work. In simpler terms, 25% of people did 50% of the work while 75% of people did the other 50%. Go and look at your stats to see if something similar is happening in your group. Most likely, it is.

Whose fault is it that a percentage of people in every support group are underperforming? Is it management's, the underperformer's own fault, or is it the structure? We have the structure to blame. The current tiered or technical-level structure that dominates the profession does little to account for productivity, which consists of number of issues closed and number of customers happy. Other production metrics may include number of Frequent Asked Questions (FAQ's) written, number of sites visited, number of trainings delivered, and just about anything else that we can measure. The reality is that group people must account for how much work they actually do. We keep them in the tiers even when they are obviously a detriment to the group and many times think of the high performers as a nice anomaly, but not something that we should have as a norm. To this, the answer is the performance-driven structure.

The best people in a support organization are those who produce the most and drive the most value to the organization and the customer. The opposite is also true; the worst people are those who produce the least and derive the least value. The fact is that unless the underperformers really screw up and simply produce the very lowest results, they probably will remain in the organization. The performance-driven structure attempts to keep the high performers and bring everyone else to their level. The people who are not producing appropriately, even after some fair effort from both the organization and the supporter are demoted in the structure. In simpler terms, the performance-driven structure rewards the high performers and punishes the low performers. It accomplishes the purpose in the following ways:

- *Defines performance objectively*: the term "performance" may mean many things to many people. The performance-driven structure dictates that performance should be defined with both qualitative and quantitative metrics. Numbers are only one of the factors. The reason is that numbers do not always tell the whole story. One supporter may close ten issues daily and another colleague only one. However, the first one answered the easy and well-documented questions that would have taken the average supporter two hours. The other answered one question in a day that would have taken anyone else a week. The way that performance should be defined is by looking at the number of issues closed, minus the reopens and the quality applied to each. The difficulty level of the issues should also be taken under consideration when analyzing the performance of the support professional. For determining the performance for the group, analyze the issue closure and quality then find the standard deviation. One standard deviation to the right of the group mean constitutes the standard performance. Anything to the left of the mean should be considered underperformance. If you are not familiar with statistics, I suggest brushing up on it briefly so that you understand the significance between variances from the mean. [7]

- *Sets expectations clearly*: the performance-driven structure requires that expectations be set very clearly from the start. The main expectation is that everyone will strive to produce the best performance possible in numbers and quality, and that over the long run the productivity should be divided closely among all the group members. The expectations should also include consequences of not performing at par with the most productive support colleagues. The prospects for not performing must be very clear so that there is no doubt later. People will be demoted if they don't perform.

- *Rewards and punishments based on the first two*: the performance-driven structure is not all about demoting those who do not live up to the best in the group. It is not a way to dethrone any high performer, but rather for the mean, or average, of the group members to be as close as possible to the average of the top performer with the least standard deviation as possible. If these terms are

---

[7] Terry Dickey, *Using Business Statistics* (Menlo Park, CA: Crisp Publications, 1995) pp 99-107. Dickey's book is easy to understand and presents a very complete view of the statics required to run a simple analysis of the performance-driven structure.

unfamiliar to you, it simply means that everyone must produce, on average, as many issues of high quality with as little difference among the group members. For instance, if the top producer closed ten issues on average per day, everyone else should close very close to ten. Seven, eight and nine are close to ten. Four, five and six are very far from ten. Of course, there is a whole segment of statistics devoted to statistical significance. For our sake, we just want to make sure that there are no colleagues that simply are not contributing equally.

The structure comes in maintaining the relative performance of the members of the tier or level. No person should ever be too far from the top performer. If someone does fall behind, then that person should be demoted as they cannot sustain the productivity requirements of the performance-driven structure.

Executives owe it to the organization and to their fellow workers not to tolerate nonperforming individuals in important jobs.

—Peter Drucker

Common Mistakes from the Upper Tiers

It's a fact that support people will always have different levels of specialization. We cannot expect for everyone to make it to the highest level of knowledge either because of capacity, effort, or simple preference. Support colleagues should not be treated as if there is something inherently wrong if they don't aspire to become the senior level, if they simply don't desire it. However, we should organize the structure in such a way that we give people the chance to become very proficient at their technical and service level. There is no reason to push the supporter who prefers a more direct interaction with the customer role to a higher technical tier, if that is not what he desires. It is also counterproductive because people tend to do better at jobs they enjoy. [8]

There are several common mistakes we make when we think of the structure of our support jobs, and how they typically pertain to tiers. These are the following:

- *The higher the tier the more valuable the supporter:* it is true that the higher tiers bring a different value to the issues—not necessarily a more desirable value, but just a different one. In this context, value does not equate complexity or level of solution. Value simply refers to the ability that the organization can qualify the return on the investment, not quantify it. We make a mistake by simply thinking that a senior-level supporter is somehow going to bring more value to the organization than a junior level one. For example, suppose we pay the junior-level colleague $1 for a unit of production, such as a closed issue and a happy customer. The senior-level colleague, because of higher salary, lower issue volume, lower resolution rate, and simple skills demand, will fetch $2 for the unit of production. Suppose the organization charges, hypothetically speaking, $1.50 for each unit of production. In this scenario, the junior-level colleague makes $1 more value for the organization than the senior one.

---

[8] Paul Osterman, "How Common is Workplace Transformation and Who Adopts it?" *Industrial and Labor Relations Review,* January 1994, pp 173-176.

- *The lower the tier, the less knowledgeable the person*: there is a belief that the higher the tier, the more expertise that exists in the supporter. The simple explanation is that not all levels of knowledge are identical. In technical support, our goal is to get a customer to continue to use our products and technologies in the least amount of time possible. This has less to do with simple knowledge as it is with skill. Junior-level colleagues are typically experts in getting customers up and running in the least possible time. This is necessary because of the higher call volume in the junior levels. I also want to clarify that I only refer to a hierarchical approach to tiers and levels, because that is how the industry treats it.

- *As tiers increase, so does respect*: many colleagues have the notion that somehow respect increases with tier or level. However, this is a mistake in reason. Many of my most admired support colleagues are in the customer-facing tier. Some of my dear colleagues and friends in Europe speak anywhere from three to five languages. This is why they are customer-facing, because they can communicate with just about anyone. My good friend Paulino España speaks Arabic in addition to English, German, Spanish, and several other languages. If that does not command respect, I don't know what does. Of course, such gifted individuals are hard to find, but there are many skillful people in every tier. Additionally, respect is earned, not just freely given. Anyone in any tier may be well-respected because it has little to do with the support level and everything to do with the individual and how they perform their work.

- *I moved up, so must others*: this one is a huge mistakes often made by the people in the senior-level tiers. We often think that because we decided to take on the best challenge, it should also be the goal for everyone else. The fact is that it is very possible that people who remain in the same level are just in their dream job and quite content. More technically challenging work is not everyone's goal. I know many colleagues who thrive in the interaction with customers. They would much rather talk with a difficult person than deal with a complex technical situation. Respect those who choose to remain in the initial technical level so long as they are productive and of value to the organization.

The support profession when comprised of tiers and levels is much like the various levels of an academic institution. The Bachelor's Degree holder has gained some level of exposure to the body of knowledge of his chosen field. The Master's Degree holder learned to use and apply the concepts and theories in the body of knowledge. The Doctoral or PhD Degree holder creates the body of knowledge that the Bachelor learned, and the theories and concepts the Master used. The higher we go in tiers the more that is expected of us. We can either learn to adapt to the next challenge or learn to do the best job possible at the level that we enjoy.

The mistakes we make in the hierarchical-tiered model in support all revolve around the idea that we all should eventually make it to the very top. This is just not true and hardly sustainable. Imagine if everyone in your support group eventually made it to the highest level or tier available. There would simply be no one left to do the easy support questions. We must learn to live and let live when it comes to support tier progression. A few years ago, I was very disappointed when I heard a dear friend and colleague tell another colleague something to the effect of, "Geez, you've been in this job for five years and you have not made senior level yet." Needless to say, I had a short conversation with him.

We are a fact-gathering organization only. We don't clear anybody. We don't condemn anybody.

—J. Edgar Hoover

Wiping Off the Tiers: The Flat Structure

Unless you work in a very small support organization or one that is very organically structured, chances are you are directly familiar with or work in a tiered support environment. We are accustomed to it and have come to think of it as the only viable option for a support structure. But what if there was a different way? What if we did not need a distinction between people according to technical expertise, specialization, or experience? What if we were all the same or somehow viewed as all the same under a single group? There are a few people in the field who think the best way to go about providing support is to do away with tiers or levels and just put everyone under the same umbrella with the same expectations and demands. Unfortunately, such an idea is not widely published or practiced, because if it develops and catches on it could prove to be a technical support utopia.

As you know since you work in the support field, a lot of what goes on in a tiered environment has to do with power struggles, technical arguments, process changes and adaptations, and a lot of plain politicking. The Level 1 people complaining they don't get enough help from the Level 2, or the Level 2 complaining that the Level 1 doesn't do enough, and so forth. You can probably tell I've done my fair share of work in the tiered environment. Let us just face the facts; tiered environments are chaotic at times despite having a structure that is supposed to provide order and hierarchy. The tiered supporters typically act in self-interest in order to progress to either make it to the next tier or to complete their daily support tasks. We should just consider it the norm in support operations. A lot of it could be blamed on the tiered structure, but it really is just an inevitable result of having people together who are not equally treated by management and with differences in title, responsibilities, and roles. If you don't believe me just look at any other social structure you belong to such as school, church, club, and even family. People tend to compete with each other and, at times, act in self-interest because it's simple human nature.

Yet the question is still open. Would things work better if we collapsed the tiers and made a socialist system out of the support group where everyone is the same and the group looks out for itself? Is being collectively responsible for the work fruitful? Would we get more productivity out of such a tier-less structure than of a tiered one? Would the individuals enjoy their work more and would customers experience a higher level of customer service and technical benefits out of such a structure? I consider myself lucky enough to have worked in this environment and also observed a few others who are incredibly successful in a flat structure. Therefore, the answer to the previous questions is, absolutely.

When I think of the flat structure, I think of a group of incredibly talented people whom I know from a previous position. They support a highly complex mainframe software product and have been at it for many years. There are only five or six in that group, but they produce more closed issues and happy customers than a group of thirty or forty people combined with a similarly complex technology. They are exceptionally bright and know their technology in and out. They look out for each other and are jointly responsible for the success or failure of their group. They take the commitment to the collective very seriously and will typically not view a problem as a challenge, but as an opportunity to shine. There is hardly anything they have not seen and they have the customer service skills to match. They typify the communal support group, described at the close of Chapter 4. However, they are not the result of mere structure. They are the end result of the tiered structure.

Exceptionally good support people don't grow on trees. They are scarce. Exceptionally gifted individuals only become so when the environment, their experience, and the customers are in the right balance to allow the support person to mature positively and with the desired behaviors. There are plenty of support people with many years of bad experience just as there are plenty of support people with years of limited experience. As in any profession, the really good people are coveted by companies who need the top producers, the top team players, and only the very best that the correct environments produce. Therefore, it will be very hard to just hire someone with exceptional skills and work ethics right off the street. These people are not easily let go by their employers. Even in recessionary times, you may interview ten people and maybe one comes close to exceptional. I know, I recently helped interview one who went and did more in his first month on the job then the rest of the local group did in a year in terms of discovery and innovation.

Because of the challenges of getting the right group together for a flat structure, I have come to the realization that such a structure is the result of a dwindling tiered structure. In other words, after the tiered structure goes through its ups and downs and the group becomes depleted of its dead weight, the only people that remain are the very best. The ones who the support organization couldn't afford to let go or simply give up to other companies or departments. The flat structure is the evolution of the tiered environments that dwindle down to the core of the competencies of the group. It is like the white dwarf star that went from being a bright sun to collapsing onto itself little by little, until all that remains is pure energy. Its days may be numbered, but the flat organization is at its highest peak of excellence and comprised of members who are nothing short of the very exceptional that the profession has to offer.

The person who figures out how to harness the collective genius of his or her organization is going to blow the competition away.

—Walter Wriston

The Hybrid Support Structure

The current predominant structures in the technical support field are mostly based on technical expertise and skills. The easy questions are answered in the first level, the hardest ones on the second level, and so forth. This is the current reality in support work in most organizations. Because this is a very fast moving discipline with innovations coming out constantly, the next obvious structure model is one done around variables other than technical expertise. The advent of support communication technologies, such as live chat, remote control tools, video conferencing, and even the possibility of virtual support inside the customer's own environment necessitates the development of a structure unlike any that we have seen, at least in the average support organizations.

The customer no longer wants to be a customer. He wants to be a partner. Not because he dislikes the term or title, but because he wants more commitment from us as vendors. The customer wants a relationship that ensures his survival in case things go bad and he needs to rely on someone at a level higher than a mere provider of technology. He wants someone to be in business with him, not only in name but in loyalty. Think about this, the success of a customer could well be in the hands of a support person when you consider that many of the processes and business decisions are made based on technologies supported by someone. Businesses depend on complex applications such as SAP, PeopleSoft, and SalesForce.com among countless others to provide vital business information and intelligence, which could make or break their business. When faced with such high stakes, why would a customer want a vendor? What the customer wants is a committed partner that can help him be successful. Because of this, the progressive technical support organization needs to innovate in ways that allow the relationship between vendor and customer to develop into more than just a sale or service contract, but more of a joint-venture. This may sound farfetched, but I've been on-site with customers when the systems fail and money and jobs are at stake. I have seen the distraught faces of customers when the technology their jobs depend on fail and they see their demise coming. I once handled a support issue in which the customer was so stressed by the failures of our technology that they had no other recourse but to sue us in order to get us to comply and fix their technology issues. Technical support is no longer the stuff of techies and nerds, but a real necessity in business. For many of our customers' business, the technology they get from us is not a luxury, but a necessity. Therefore, how can we structure our support model to best accommodate the business necessities of our demanding customers?

The best way to achieve our goals in meeting customers' needs and expectations is to utilize a hybrid model which is a combination of structure models that best helps us address the needs of our customer base. There are several possibilities that we can choose from. We have somewhat of a limited body of knowledge in the field of technical support structure but, at least theoretically, we can come up with several possible models from which to choose the hybrid model. The trick is to figure out the combination and the level of adoption of each model. Generally, the following models offer the best options from which you can make up your own structure. This is, of course, assuming you have the power to do so or at least the ears of those who have the power to decide. If nothing else, the following will serve for you to reason about the possibilities in structure. The options are the following:

- *A simple tier structure based on technical expertise*: the most prevalent structure in technical support, at least in the typical support group, in which the members are tiered into their respective levels by way of technical expertise and experience. This particular model works well in the majority of support groups with the exception of the very small or the very experienced. It also works best in complex technologies, processes, and systems.

- *The Savvy Support*[9] *structure*: Philip Verghis came up with this idea and it holds a lot of promise as long as the support organization finds a way to get potential supporters of the highest caliber to remain interested in supporting frontline issues. The concept relies on using the best and most capable support people to handle the initial calls without going through a frontline tier. It sounds very promising, at least in theory. Time will tell if it proves to be a successful model. This model should work well in a small, but highly demanding customer base for only the most complex products and processes. It would be prove catastrophically cost inefficient in the less complex support demands where the customers do not pay much for the support.

- *Technology vs. skills structure*: the support personnel provide support based on skill or technology. Supporters provide help for a specific technology regardless of how many products adopt the technology. This structure works best when the technology remains intact and exists in the different products in the same form. If the technology is customized as is the case in some software products, the structure by technology may prove to be a bit more problematic. The structure by skill suffers a similar fate. If the skills can be ported across technologies and products, the value of the structure becomes highly promising as the same support person can handle a wide arrange of products, technologies, and systems as long as they employ the same skill.

- *The service-oriented structure*: this approach concentrates the customer relationship in the hands of the people with the best customer service skills, rather than the people with the most technical skills. The purpose of this structure model

---

[9] Phil Verghis "No More (Support) Tiers!: Savvy Support" Verghis View Newsletter April 2008. http://www.verghisgroup.com/publications/verghis-view-april-2008/ Accessed April 26, 2009.

is to provide the highest customer service possible by having the technical resources at the disposal of the customer service people handling the customer relations. A proper analogy is the auto dealer service department. If you have ever taken your car into the dealer for service, you notice that the person you deal with is the service manager, not the mechanic. In fact, chances are you have never met any of the mechanics who actually do the work on your car. The service person handles the relationship with the customer while at the same time directing the technical work in the background for the benefit of the customer.

- *The meaningful support structure*: this theory puts the growth and development of the support person as its primary goal. It is not concerned with how the work gets done but in how the structure allows the individuals in the support group to delve into other fulfilling activities; in addition, it handles support issues in order to make the work more meaningful. This comes from the Quality of Work Life[10] philosophy, which states that the purpose of the job design is to allow the employees to grow and develop via rewarding and meaningful jobs. This structure can and should be tied with any of the other support structures chosen to be part of the hybrid support structure.

- *The proactive/reactive approach*: the customer facing tiers are, by nature, reactive and wait on the customer to propose the problem. The frontline tier reacts accordingly. This is the typical role of the support organization today. However, in addition to the typical reactionary function of the frontline tier, the upper tier, second level, or senior support people act completely different to what is customary in the support field. They are proactive in their approach by looking for problems before they even happen and strive to look into the future using their expertise as well as industry knowledge. This structure theory will go well with the tiered structure and with the service-oriented structure. It is still quite theoretical, but promises to take the support profession into the next level of disciplinary evolution, and possibly into a real approximation to the organizational and functional scientific realm.

- *The performance driven structure*: Should be part of any of the others when used in conjunction to derive a hybrid structural model. The structure deals with the ultimate purpose of support, to produce closed issues and happy customers, while at the same time delivering value to the support organization. This is the most objective of all the structure theoretical models presented as a possibility of this hybrid structure model.

- *The flat structure*: A bit of a misnomer as it is the culmination of a support career rather than something that can just be built into a structural design. It symbolizes the utopia of technical support, and brings the most productivity to the support organization. It is flat, not because it finds no user for a hierarchical design, but because it is beyond the tiers and levels. It is truly the promised land of technical support structures. The support group does not start in the flat structure; it ends there. The flat structure goes well with the Savvy Support model and already assumes most of the other models, naturally, with the exception of the tiered model.

---

[10] Richard Kopelman, "Job Redesign and Productivity: A Review of the Evidence," National Productivity Review, Summer 1985, pp 239.

- *The divide by channel structure:*[11] Depends on the presence of specific channels of support such as chat, email, or phone. The customers are limited to one of the communication mediums and divide the support personnel according to the medium. This may prove the best in very low-cost support organizations or for technologies or products in which customers pay very little for support in relation to the product price or industry norm.

As you can see from the above structure models, the questions of which structure to use is not an easy one. The most appropriate approach is a hybrid model that allows support management to choose a combination of structure models depending on the needs of the organization as well as the constituencies. Technical support structure is far from an exact science and for this reason the best approach is what makes sense to your support organization.

The trouble with organizing a thing is that pretty soon folks get to paying more attention to the organization than to what they're organized for.

—Laura Ingalls Wilder

---

[11] Joe Fleischer and Brendan Read, *The Complete Guide to Customer Support* (Gilroy, CA: CMP Books, 2002) pp 76-79. The authors describe the Divide and Channel approach as a way in which the support organization makes the best use of its resources by dividing the support personnel depending on the medium that the customer requests come into the support department. Specifically, they address the support via email which may come to one group of support people devoted only to that medium. Others may be devoted to other mediums of communications; hence, the name Divide and Channel approach.

■ ■ ■

CHAPTER 9

Process and Practice

Taking care of business in our daily jobs takes a lot of distinct actions, decisions, and interactions. We depend on the ability of our coworkers, managers, and even customers to follow a specific set of steps that progress a support incidence from start to finish. This sequential set of events that we do in technical support takes us from the unknown and, perhaps even obscure, into the light of a solved problem. This chapter deals with the formal life of the work, the process. Those things we do every day that make us functional support professionals. In the next few pages, you will learn about processes from both the theoretical and practical levels. This chapter assumes you are already familiar with the processes employed in your current support job and are, at least, somewhat proficient in those processes. The chapter also gets into some concepts that may be unfamiliar to you as we don't normally hear about them in our support organizations. However, these concepts are intended to incite you to think a bit more globally about the role of support processes and their impact. You will read about the definition and characteristics of a process, the discretionary process principle, and the reasons why we sometimes needs to change processes,

You will also read about what it means to practice something and the natural progression from a process into a practice. The notion that you can do something routinely and consistently is extremely powerful, because it provides anticipation and equivalence in the way we are expected to perform our duties in the support group. Practices are not something you can simply use now and then, but instead are the processes made into permanent behaviors. The group with the most adequate practices usually comes up on top and deserves the glory. In fact, if you analyze the nature of support work, all of our actions and decisions start with a formal or informal process and, eventually, through constant use become embedded into our habitual behaviors, hence practices.

Probably the most interesting concepts in this chapter are on incompetence and problem solving as a waste of time. After thinking through those two proposals, a lot of things that I have witnessed throughout my career suddenly made a lot of sense. The reality of very successful people turning ineffectual as soon as they ascend in the hierarchy of the support organization opened my eyes to a lot of examples and questions about why specific individuals become utter failures when they reach the proverbial top. We've all seen the big shot who seems to be completely out of place in a position and who appears to be doing the job right below his. That particular segment of the chapter left me with a sense of self-awareness that I had not felt in a long time. As a result of that passage, it is my sincere hope that you will become a much better-prepared support professional, both in the practice as well as the theory of support. After all, we don't exist in a bubble and all support work has to serve some business purpose.

As always, read this chapter with an open mind and a desire to accentuate the most fundamental aspect of our profession: the desire for knowledge.

Change is not a process for the impatient.

—Barbara Reinhold

What's a Process?

The word gets thrown around quite a bit in the business world. We all hear about the process for this and the process for that. Everything that is anything in the corporate world has to have a definite and well-documented process otherwise it's not taken seriously. Yet, the word is used for so many things and actions that a clear definition is not always perceived equally by the majority.

In Chapter 8, we learned about structure and how the structure comprises the formalized pattern shaping the support organization. The structure may have tiers, be flat, or follow a different type of model based on service, skills, and so on. However, the structure is just the skeleton of the organization. The structure is what gives the organization its shape. You can view the structure in an organizational chart, and immediately see who works under whom as well as the different levels at which each person rests in relation to one another. Nevertheless, the people in an organization's chart are not just there to fill in space; they have to do something. This is where processes come in.

Processes are what make the structure move, do work, communicate, and make decisions. By definition, a process is a systematic series of actions directed to some end.[1] However, those actions do not exist by themselves. Action requires something physical to do the action just as a verb requires a subject, otherwise it's incomplete. Processes bring life to the organization via action and movement of the parts with the intention to bring a result.[2] Everything we do in the support group is because of a process either formal or informal. We don't always think about our informal actions as a process, but whenever the actions are taken in an orderly fashion and are reproducible in a similar circumstance, than it is a process. In Chapter 8, I made the analogy of processes as the muscles that enable our bones to move. It is the same thing with organizations. A structure by itself is just a chart full of people with some orderly arrangement; however, processes make it come alive.

The actions we take in the course of supporting our customers, communicating within the organization, collaborating with our colleagues, handling the technology, learning, training, documenting, and researching for answers are some examples of processes that take place in our field. Processes exist whenever there is a systematic and orderly action within a group. Processes in technical support have the following characteristics:

- *Orderly:* the process has to provide a good level of order to the action. Actions, choices, and decisions in a process must be broken down to a level that is understood and do not conflict with any of the other parts of the process. Regardless of the length or complexity of the process, the actions must be simple enough that even the longest process can be easily followed by anyone intended

  to follow the process. Order in the process comes with proper development. If the process is properly analyzed and, at least, the major contingencies taken under consideration, then the process can be considered orderly. Order also comes in the ability for the process to take the person following the process from finish to end, regardless of what occurs within normal and expected possibilities.

---

[1] "process." Dictionary.*com Unabridged (v 1.1).* Random House, Inc. 12 May. 2009. `http://dictionary.reference.com/browse/process`

[2] Ned F. Kock, *Process Improvement and Organizational Learning* (Hershey, PA: Idea Group, 1999) p.17.

- *Reproducible*: a process must be capable of being applied to a similar situation over and over. A process must be a general set of steps, actions, provisions, and decisions that anyone can follow multiple times, regardless of the normal circumstances. It must yield similar results via the proper actions time and time again, even when the people taking action change. It is like a recipe for actions and results. As long as the steps are followed properly and as stated in the process, the results should be the same. It does not mean that the result is always identical, but comparable. Effective processes allow the organization the ability to continue its operations, even when the people doing the work change. It is a roadmap for getting something done over and over again.

- *Sequential*: a process must be sequential. This means that the steps come in order, and randomness of actions will only cause the end result to be unintended and wrong. The actions of the people in support have to follow steps that yield actions and reactions based on inputs and decisions. This has to happen in sequence until the process yields the result. Support has many processes dealing with taking issues, logging problems, documenting answers, and many other things that require processes to be in place.

- *Transparent*: the steps or actions as well as the decisions in a process must be transparent to everyone involved in the process. Keeping parts of the process a secret from the people who are supposed to carry out the process results in problems of expectation. Most support people who receive a process from management or their peers must know how the inputs or decisions that go into the process were created. Keeping vital steps in the process secret arouse suspicion and have the potential to make the process inefficient. Only through transparency will the process gain better acceptance from the people doing the process.

Our definition of process assumes there is a useful purpose and rationale behind the orderly action. In other words, a process should not exist only to make work or for the sake of activity. A process has to have a definite purpose and identifiable results. Also, the process has to provide some value to the people doing it and to the recipients of the action. In our case, the process has to have some value or benefit to the supporters and also to the end recipients of the process, such as our customers, managers, colleagues, or anyone else to whom the process is meant to provide a result.

There are many other aspects to processes that affect their effectiveness and efficiency. Properly preparing the people who will follow the process ensures some level of success, but more importantly is the collective acceptance of the process from the support group. This is not an easy thing to accomplish, especially with a new process. The process has to be given time to work and prove itself worthy of being executed. As with every other human endeavor, the support process has the best chance of success when the support professionals implement it with the best intentions and an optimistic approach.

The organizational architecture is really that a centipede walks on hundred legs and one or two don't count. So if I lose one or two legs, the process will go on, the organization will go on, the growth will go on.

—Mukesh Ambani

Discretionary Process Principle

When we talk about processes, we think of a generic term that describes the actions necessary to accomplish something. A process, in the context of our work, is the set of actions, decisions, and interactions that allow the structure in the technical support organization to accomplish work. The set of steps to answer customer calls, the way we escalate tickets, interact with others in the company, and even the specific way we find the solutions and deliver them are all part of some process that we use. Someone had to figure out how to do all the work we do and the way to go about doing it. Nevertheless, the granularity that a process goes into is inversely proportional to the possibilities of the unknown inputs that go into the process. The granularity necessary depends on the uniformity requirements of the output and the intellectual capacity required of the worker. For the lack of a better term and an already established theory, let's call this the "discretionary process principle."

The ideas came to me while researching for a quality of service training I was preparing along with three other colleagues. I noticed that some of the processes in technical support were very open to the discretion of the practitioner and wanted to know if it was possible to have a more rigid and exact process for the work we do.[3] After analyzing the possibilities and doing some reading, I came across the concept of process theory,[3] which states that to achieve the same decision or results time after time we must follow the exact same steps over and over. I thought this to be a very logical approach to reproducing success in technical support, except for a huge problem. Very few calls are identical, especially in a complex technology. How then do we account for being able to achieve the same results if we are not even sure we'll have the chance to reproduce the identical steps in every call?

As mentioned, when I was a teenager I worked nights in a production line making frozen foods, such as pizzas and hamburgers. The process we used was extremely strict. There was absolutely no room for any discrepancy. The cheese had to weigh exactly three ounces, the bread had to be of a specific size, and the final product had to have a very specific weight and mass. I realize now that the reason we were so stringent on the process is that the results had to be uniform. Additionally, the intellectual capacity required of the workers was very low. We were like robots that did the exact same thing for eight hours.

Compare the production line to support work and the differences are vast. Our work is almost entirely dependent on the intellectual capacity of the workers. We work with our mind in reasoning and troubleshooting, not to mention juggling customers with different demands and idiosyncrasies. We cannot follow a rigid process because so much depends on the problem, customer, and situation. By this statement I am not suggesting that we don't have specific processes to follow when doing support, such as what we can and cannot do, who to get help from, or even at what stage of the call we can escalate, rather I am referring to the level of granularity that we can put into a technical support process. For instance, in a production line, the process states exactly what the worker does, how, and for how long. In some manufacturing, they even employ ergonomic processes that dictate how the worker must move his body so as to avoid fatigue or injury and save time. Technical support is very different in that it is all up to the individual and his capacity to use experience, knowledge, skills, and intuition when looking for a solution. It would be very hard, if not impossible, to put a process around such a complex set of actions.

The discretionary process principle states that the granularity and rigidness of the process increases as the necessity for output uniformity increases. The more the output relies on the discretion of the worker, the more flexible the process should be. For example, suppose that today you have to work technical support issues dealing with a complex technology but tomorrow you have to fill in for the receptionist who is out sick. Today you will rely on a process that allows you to take the input from a customer in the way of problem description, things already done, symptoms, impacts, and any other possible information required from the customer. Then you have to take all this information, rely on

---

[3] Jon E. Roeckelein, *Dictionary of Theories, Laws and Concepts in Psychology* (Westport, CT: Greenwood Press, 1998) p 170.

what you know and your skills, then try to find the best way to solve the problem based on a systematic approach to problem solving. Writing a process with all possible combinations would be futile. The best you can do is a general process that leaves most of the decision making to you. On the other hand, tomorrow you will have to follow a strict process that dictates what to do with people calling in for sales, education, support, and customer service. It also dictates exactly what to do with telemarketers and what to do about requests for information. The process you will follow tomorrow leaves almost nothing to your discretion.

In terms of theory, how do we apply it to our work in the support ranks? The discretionary support principle helps you in understanding that, for technical support work, the process you create must leave a lot of the decision making to the people doing the support. If you ever receive a process that attempts to tell you exactly how to troubleshoot, decide what to try, and how to derive a solution then you will be leaving out a lot of what makes our work special and rewarding: the ability to shine by carving out our own niches of support.

For the person making the process decisions, it is paramount that a process tells people what steps to take when handling a technical support issue, but only to the extent that the process serves to keep the supporter from getting stuck, and to provide visibility into what everyone involved in the issue does. The process should allow for the support issues to have a proper route and flow, so that the supporter can move it along when he runs out of options. This may be in the way of transferring to the next tier or how to escalate the issue to management. The process should also serve to let all the parties involved know each other's responsibilities and actions. Just remember that any process in technical support that attempts to dictate specifically how to solve an issue beyond the generalities of the scientific method will only hinder the support staff's ability to think outside the box and come up with the next round of support breakthroughs.

> *When one has finished building one's house, one suddenly realizes that in the process one has learned something that one really needed to know in the worst way—before one began.*

> —Friedrich Nietzsche

The Reasons Behind Process Changes

Technical support is a fast-moving and ever-adapting field. We encounter changing technologies and different environments that seem to evolve constantly regardless of the industry. Either the technology changes or the way we approach the work changes, but one thing is almost certain, our processes change to accommodate the demands placed on us by the different constituencies of the support organization. If you work in technical support long enough, regardless of the industry, you will face changes in the processes, sometimes very often. The question is why do we have changes in processes? Why do we have to do things differently in what seems to be a reinvention of the wheel?

We face new processes when we have to change the way we do things and modify them in accordance to someone's idea of a better approach. The new changes are typically involuntary because they are often new mandates by management. This can be positive or negative to some members of the support group. However, the changes always make sense and are viewed as better to someone. The typical scenario goes like this: a support group is not working too well. The work does not get done in the most effective manner and its management is replaced. The new management takes over and studies the situation. After some observation and analysis, the new management determines the best approach and rolls it out. The group, who were accustomed to doing it differently, complains and moans about having to change. They may even sabotage the process, but go through some pains in accommodating the new way of doing things. It is also possible that things remain the same, but this would be a different situation. New management comes in typically for three reasons: to turnaround a business, to realign it, or simply to continue the success.[4] New processes are the most beneficial in the case of the turnaround, when the group is doing badly, and change is absolutely needed in order for the group to make a turn, stop the current way of working, and adopt a new one. A turnaround is very hard to do under the old management. That's why the new management takes over.

Multiple reasons dictate the need for a new set of processes. A new structure may also be necessary, but for this discussion we will assume the structure remains. The reasons for a change in processes include the following:

- *Counterproductive existing process*: if the actual support process takes more in the way of resources than the output it produces, then it needs change. We can see this in support groups that produce very few resolved issues and cost more to operate than the number of handled support issues merit. The support organization, just like every other unit in a company, has to abide by the financial requirements placed on it. Processes have a huge influence in determining the desired productivity of the support department.

- *Adhering to company policy*: the support group may also be doing things against company policy that requires realignment to existing policy to correct the situation. This scenario occurs frequently after an acquisition where the acquired company must change to comply with its new owner. Depending on how the acquiring company handles the assimilation, the management may remain or may be ousted so new management comes in to make the changes.

- *Changing demands*: the environment may change and the support group is required to change with it. This scenario occurs frequently in high technology industries where the factors change rapidly and the support has to adapt the processes to industry growth. For example, the automotive and energy industries are undergoing fundamental shifts in the way they operate that will require changes to the people who support those industries and that will augment processes

- *Labor effectiveness*: the typical support structure is tiered, consisting of different levels of technical expertise and experience, so the labor resources must be organized in such a way to derive the most benefit, or excess value, out of every resource. In addition to the structure of the support group, we must also align the way the group performs the support work to provide the maximum excess value out of the structure. For example, in a structure with multiple levels, each level must concentrate on doing the work to their maximum efficiency levels and then transfer the support issues to the next tier. This organization of labor requires processes to dictate how the issues transfer among the tiers.

- *Group uniformity*: sometimes everything is in tip-top shape. Suppose the structure is appropriate for the work, the processes appear to be designed as to ensure the most output, yet in the end the work is falling short of the expected results. One thing that existing structure and processes may be missing is the concept of checks and balances. Even in the best designed organizations, there is a need for people to check on others and make sure everyone pulls their own

---

[4] Michael Watkins, *The First 90 Days* (Massachusetts: Harvard Business School Publishing, 2003) p. 157–184

weight. In the case where individual elements, or even whole tiers, consistently fall short on their productivity because of lapses in the processes, a new way to ensure proper compliance must be implemented. This new idea of checks and balances comes in the way of new processes that ensure that specific things occur and provide consequences when those required actions do not take place. The process may involve management, the group only, or a combination both.

Things always change in the technical support profession. For some it is more frequent than for others, but change is always in the air to some extent. Understanding the reasons why a support group has to change their processes goes a long way in actually making that change possible. Changing things just for the sake of changing them is most likely a very remote exception as most new management changes occur for good reason, at least in the eyes of those making the decisions. The more you understand why the change is happening, the easier it will be to adapt.

Matrimony is a process by which a grocer acquired an account the florist had.

—Frances Rodman

The Support Practice: A Definition

Few groups function like clockwork. However, the ideal group is one that needs little management, little oversight, and produces optimal results without extra input in the way of external efforts from management or consultants. Imagine a technical support group that delivers on all the requirements set forth by the customer, the company, and meets, or even beats, the expectations of management. The group members work on their own, have few doubts or questions, and can keep going even when regionally detached from the larger organization. The group I am describing is the one that reaches the pinnacle of efficiency because of its well-defined and efficient way of processing support issues. Do such groups exist? They sure do.

A few years ago I was part of such a group. The small startup I worked for was headed by a genius in customer service. He had the company working like a well-oiled machine. Everyone knew what to do and how to do it. We all knew where to go to get answers, help, and no one questioned authority, mainly because we all had some of it and did not mind sharing. The processes were not even written down. We just followed a very consistent set of instructions that were given once by our CEO. Of course, it was an 18 person company so the CEO had his office next to the support group, which consisted of three people in the US and one in Israel.

In this company, there was no question that did not get answered in a matter of minutes. If there was a need to do something, we just did it and followed the exact same way of doing support every time. As most successful startups in the late 1990s, we were acquired three different times. Through each acquisition we remained the same small group working alone, detached from the bigger organization. Our CEO left, our manager left, and we were left pretty much to our own devices. Yet, even when we had no clear manager and were part of a much bigger company, we remained in our original office and continued to support our customers as if nothing had ever changed. Later we moved to one of the acquiring company's offices and we were lost in a sea of cubicles. Yet we still did the same support work without anyone overseeing us, and without any delay or hindrance. We followed the same practice that had been imparted to us by the ex-CEO in the small startup.

I have often asked myself exactly what made us so constant and successful in our work. I came to the realization that it was our very simple, but efficient way of doing the work. We simply answered the phone quickly, helped customers as much as possible, and closed as many cases as we could. It was so simple it was not even a process, but a practice. A practice is defined as a habitual or customary action, or way of doing something.[5] On the other hand, a process is a systematic series of actions directed to some end.[6] In our practice, we did not perform a systematic series of actions, but simply exercised a work habit. It made the group very successful even when it grew in size.

You don't often hear work practice as a buzz word or even as part of the formal corporate jargon. Yet a practice is what most successful processes become. In fact, practices are the foundation of a corporate culture. The esprit de corps of any successful organization is not in the processes, but in the practices. Practices are what remain when everything else is taken away. A group with solid practices can go on auto-pilot even when left without a CEO, a manager, or an organization. The group does what comes natural and the only thing that comes natural is habitual.

When the support group adopts processes and those become ingrained in the group's consciousness, they eventually become practices. In other words, there will no longer be a need to look at the process map or consult a support manual. People will know what to do, because the process becomes a habit. In effect, if you analyze your technical support skills, they may simply be habits you learned to apply over and over until they became second nature, hence the practice. Behaviors, the things that people do, are simply actions; they become a practice when they are done repeatedly. Eventually, they become an instinct. Have you ever noticed that when you meet a technical support colleague from another company and start exchanging ideas, you both think very much alike? The good, acceptable, and desirable support practices are universal. Having the correct practices will make you desirable anywhere you go. This is why it is so important that practices be adopted into your professional repertoire.

Developing the right support practices takes some time and comes in the following ways:

- *You follow a specific process repeatedly*: this is a good way to adopt a practice. You are given a process either by management or by your colleagues in the support group. You follow the process on a regular basis, until you no longer think about it as a new process, but as the status quo. Essentially, it becomes your habit then your practice.

- *You integrate into a group with the practices*: this is the easiest way to become accustomed to support practices. As long as the group you join already has good practices, the best way to adopt them is by watching and adopting the existing culture. The group serves as your support structure as they will let you know if you are doing it wrong, and hopefully coach you through the adoption of the practice.

- *You develop the practices on your own by trial and error*: this is the worst way to do it, because it takes a long time and costs considerably more in effort. In the computer industry, it took the original mainframe support people years to adopt the practices that made them very successful until today. The rest of the industry adopted many of the practices and benefited from their work.

Now that we know the true meaning of the work practice in our jargon, we should be aware of how we use it. It is not just something we do, but rather something we do as a habit. A process eventually becomes a practice, and practices eventually become a culture. This is why having well-defined, enforced processes is so important in developing a desirable corporate culture. Look at your current situation and see what you can identify as your support practices. Which are desirable and which are not? From here on, make sure that anything you adopt as a practice has the potential to add value to your career.

---

[5] "practice." *The American Heritage® Dictionary of the English Language, Fourth Edition*. Houghton Mifflin Company, 2004. 12 May. 2009. <Dictionary.com>
[6] "process." *Dictionary.com Unabridged (v 1.1)*. Random House, Inc. 12 May. 2009. <Dictionary.com>

Good ideas are not adopted automatically. They must be driven into practice with courageous patience.

—Hyman Rickover

Group Process Evolution

Making things better in their support group is one of those challenges that every support person should face continuously in their career. Improving the status quo and aiding the management team in continuously upgrading the processes is the best way for a group member to help the group keep up with the market, both in the support world and within the specific industry. The responsibility to make things better is not the monopoly of the manager, but everyone's duty to improve their situation by finding ways to gain more out of the same or less resources. This betterment of production is what sets the exceptional groups apart from the merely good ones.

In the mid-1990s Texas Instruments (TI) started to implement a very smart idea for increasing the productivity in both technical and intellectual output, even while inputs decreased. TI calls this approach Center of Excellence and consists of setting up a structure and process in which the members of the organization increase their skills level in order to drive the production in the different competitive areas.[7] The concept is quite interesting as it transforms the organization in a horizontal structure, with all the members responsible for their own development and that of the organization along with the ability to adapt and produce the output demanded by the market. It appears to have worked well for TI.

In the support world, we need something that allows us to do almost the same as the Center of Excellence, but with more emphasis on the support group and with minimal or no change to the structure. Since we already have structures in place, modifying them would be too time-consuming, not to mention difficult. What we need is a way to collectively improve the processes to allow us to move on a dime, respond faster and better to the demands placed on us by our constituencies, and to beat our competitors to the punch.

To improve our groups and productivity, we need to adopt a way in which all the members of the group are empowered to aid in the continuous progress of our way of working. What we need is to exercise the concept of group process evolution in which a group collectively enables its members to propose improvements to the existing processes with the only intention of exploiting opportunities and threats present in the environment. This idea rests on the concept that the people closest to the work are the ones most capable of exploiting the opportunities for process efficiency. However, improving processes requires much more than just the direct knowledge of the work; it also requires skills that have to do with process improvement. People must advance their skills in processes and efficiency before they can propose the changes necessary to drive efficiencies in the work. This sounds very theoretical, because it is. However, you can make some very real direct applications immediately.

In order to put the group process evolution to work, you must look at the things you do in a normal working day and identify the processes you and your colleagues follow:

- *Repetitive tasks that do not directly contribute to the output:* the repetition of tasks, such as using time and resources, to reproduce every customer environment when the reproduction is only to satisfy our curiosity or simply to abide by a long-standing practice. Other repetitive tasks may include something as trivial as printing customers' diagrams only to toss them after you are done with the support call.

---

[7] Steven W. Lyle and Robert A. Zawacki, "Centers of Excellence: Empowering People to Manage Change" *Information Systems Management* 1997, vol. 14, number 1, p.26–29.

- *Interactions among members that only serve protocol*: in the tiered support group some of the practices of obtaining second opinions and suggestions do not lead to any additional value to the issue; they may only exist to satisfy and understand protocol, but not a formal process or company policy. For example, if you work in a first-level support tier, you may employ the practice of letting the upper tier members know that you are about to give out a solution or explanation. However, there is no policy that dictates that you must do so, and it adds nothing to the end result.

- *Unnecessary approvals from constituents*: getting approvals from managers, upper tiers, or anyone else to perform tasks, such as giving out a specific document to a customer that does not merit this approval. The problem with chasing approvals that are merely for the sake of the approval itself is that it expends energy and does not help produce more output. Approvals need a pragmatic reason within a process; otherwise, they should be eliminated.

- *Documentation requirements that do not add value*: documenting every single action and interaction in relation to the support issue when the information does not add any value to the issue. Some groups take this unnecessary documentation to an extreme when they enter information that is irrelevant to the case and even counterproductive; they fill the notes with so much text that it becomes difficult to read the issue notes quickly to get to the technical details of the case.

- *Involving more than the people absolutely necessary to work an issue*: I have seen this phenomenon taken to the extreme. Some time ago, I called for support on my cable modem. The first tier person asked me a few questions and did not get anywhere. Then he remained on the line while the second tier attempted to troubleshoot the problem. When the second person did not get anywhere, he attempted to get someone in the third tier involved. It took nearly one hour just to get someone from the third tier on the phone with me. All along, I had the first and second tier guys also on the line. When I asked why they had to wait on the line with me they did not know what to answer. The third tier person solved the problem in just a few minutes by resetting something on his side, yet it took almost two hours for the entire call. Two guys held on the line with me for almost the entire time due to an informal process. This was truly a terrible use of resources.

The five preceding items are not exhaustive, but occur very often in the support group. Once you identify the informal process, you will need to find ways to cut down on the process waste and try to carry on the process without it. As you may know, we already have process improvement methodologies such as Kaizen,[8] Lean,[9] and Six Sigma[10] to name a few, but with much more research to what I just proposed. In fact, this idea of group process evolution is very close to Kaizen with the exception of the informality of process and the lack of standard operating procedures. If we were to give it a very layman term, it's like Kaizen on the cheap and at a more accelerated pace. However, the difference in our

---

[8] Kenneth W. Dailey, *The Kaizen Pocket Handbook* (DW Publishing, 2005) p 421. Kaizen is a Japanese philosophy of continuous small change and improvement while eliminating waste.
[9] Focuses in elimination of waste in a speedy manner. Attempts to achieve improvement in procedures.
[10] James R. Persse, *Process Improvement Essentials* (Sebastopol, CA: O'Reilly, 2006) pp 253-287. Six Sigma is a quality improvement method focused on the minimization of defects while improving processes. Much more complex than Kaizen and Lean.

concept of group process evolution is that it is done at the support-group level without any need for major structural change and does not focus on new product or service development, but a true organic improvement by members of a group. We can even call it a grassroots process improvement method that relies on the individuals to figure out a better way to use their efforts to produce more output from their support processes. Additionally, the processes should not be formal or part of the organizational policy. The group process evolution deals only with informal processes that in reality make up the majority of the work performed by the typical support group.

The main idea is to avoid wasting time and resources at the individual level, because it will have a direct impact on the productivity of the group. We don't have to change structure, modify any formal processes, and impact anyone or anything other than our own personal work in order to contribute to the collective production of closed support issues and customer satisfaction. Carrying out process improvement on our own will have a direct effect on our productivity, that of our group, and eventually our organization. Once your information process modifications show results, you can start sharing them with your colleagues and even management.

The older I get the more wisdom I find in the ancient rule of taking first things first. A process which often reduces the most complex human problem to a manageable proportion.

—Dwight D. Eisenhower

Process and Maturity

Have you ever been in a support organization where the processes seem overly complex or way too simple? Did you ever encounter a situation in which the process just did not seem to fit the requirements of the work? Was it perhaps the wrong process for your level of knowledge in either support or technology? The process and the way it's applied must fit the group and its maturity. As you read earlier in the chapter in the "What's a Process" topic, a process is a systematic series of actions directed to some end.[11] However, the series of actions as performed by any support group varies greatly depending on the maturity level of the group.

Maturity in a group refers to more than just the stage of the group's life cycle. The life cycle varies from the time the group is first formed by people with little or no experience in the profession to the fully mature group, which is at the pinnacle of its life, so its members are very well-versed in the discipline of support as well as the technology. The process rolled out to the group must take into consideration the life cycle of the group to a great extent, but also the maturity.

The maturity level of the group may be explained as simply the collective professional maturity of the individuals and how they use that maturity with each other. We can explain the group's maturity by how well they do the work, the level of independence they employ, and the level to which they can be left alone. It starts with the individual and spreads to the way they work communally.

The immature group may be explained by specific characteristics that hinder the group from thinking at a higher level. The immature supporters often complain excessively, display poor work habits, look out only for themselves, require a lot of guidance despite having been told previously, and simply demonstrate the need for more rigorous management. For this reason, the process that works well for the immature group is highly detailed and leaves little to their interpretation. The process must be implemented with little input taken from the group. It must be a proven process that has worked

---

[11] "process." Dictionary.*com Unabridged (v 1.1)*. Random House, Inc. 12 May. 2009. <Dictionary.com

elsewhere in a similar situation and with a similar maturity level, so it should also work for the immature group.

The way the process is rolled out is just as important as the actual content of the process. For the immature group, the process must be rigidly executed and enforced. The reason is that the group needs to learn the correct way of performing support tasks and must not be allowed to make their own version of the process. The benefit of this approach is that once the process is correctly implemented, the process will become a practice and increase the maturity level of the group.

The maturing group is one where the individuals are learning fast and adopting the proper support practices on the soft skills, group dynamics, and the technology. This group is at a stage where the members are eager to learn new ways of doing the work. The collective mentality of the group wants to do the right thing and develop even further to reach a better place in the support organization and the market. The group members are still working and learning, but are beyond the immature level and well on their way to achieving the mature stage. At this stage, the group serves customers well, carries their support load with little effort, and is still finding better ways to work together and cooperate with others outside of the group.

The process for the maturing group should allow them to make some of the collective decisions and use their individual discretion for some portions that will not be detrimental to the organization if mistakes are made. The ideal way to roll the process out is by first making the group aware of what is coming, and allow them the privilege to modify the process, without changing the input or the outcome. As long as the changes improve efficiency and allow the members to continue maturing, the maturing group should be allowed to help adapt the process to the environment, customer base, and technology in order to get the group to share the privilege of creating the process as well as the responsibility for making it work. With more time and experience, the maturing group should become a fully mature group.

The mature group is the summit that all groups should aspire to. The group at this level of maturity functions in auto-pilot and needs very little intervention from management. The group members know the work, organization, technology, and each other. The group itself, with minimal management support, should develop any new processes that are necessary for the group to do their job better. In this case of a non-support process rolled out to the entire support organization or company, the process should just be presented to the group, allow them to critique or question, and the mature group should be made responsible for following the new process on their own. Management should intervene only where there is actual need, as in the case of misinterpretation or abuse. The mature group is rare in emerging technologies, but prevalent in legacy ones.

Developing the appropriate processes for a technical support group comes much easier when the manager has some experience with working under the processes he is about to implement. However, a manager with no support experience, or no experience in the specific technology supported, can still be very successful at managing the group and implementing support process; it will just require more initiative to understand the work.

The process must match the maturity level so that it has a better chance of success. Any process can be forced on any support group, but it is more successful when it is done in accordance with the groups' maturity level.

Aristotle taught that the brain exists merely to cool the blood and is not involved in the process of thinking. This is true only of certain persons.

—Will Cuppy

Practice and Incompetence

Let us take a look at a hypothetical colleague whom we admire as an expert in a technology. She knows just about everything there is to know about the product she supports and can help any customer in any situation. She is simply a great supporter and definitely a very knowledgeable person. She works for a support organization in which a supporter can climb the support ladder and get all the way to the highest tier in role and in title. Like many other companies, hers is one where the supporter can escalate three, four, five, and even more titles. The job starts with the most basic of support troubleshooting, and goes to the highest level where the supporter is in charge of driving change, innovation, and can perhaps even propose to develop policy and strategy. This is a very real proposition for a support career in the right company. Among many others, this is only one of the ways that our profession is advancing; we are attaining titles that are more meaningful with added or expanded responsibilities, authority, and scope.

Let's assume that our colleague is the model Support Level 3 person. This title requires that she solves issues, one by one, and that she provides customer satisfaction. She does this extremely well and her management singled her out for the next title of Support Level Four. At the new title or job tier, she will be responsible for providing advice to management, carrying out educational tasks for the support group, and finding ways in which the group can further develop and attain its goals. In addition to those new responsibilities, she will also have to dedicate time to handling the issues of most impact to the highest number of customers possible. For this role, she will make more money, have more authority and freedom to choose her tasks, and set her own goals.

Once she has the new job title, she does not change her tasks and continues doing the same thing she has always done: providing great support. In other words, she continues to do the job of a Support Level Three, but while having the Support Level Four job. Soon her management grows dissatisfied and demands the appropriate output from the job. She grows dissatisfied and eventually leaves before being demoted or, worse, fired.

What happened to our colleague? Why couldn't she do the job? How did she get into this situation? In one word: incompetence.

Incompetence is the inability to perform because of lack of skill or behavior. In the case cited above, the ineptitude came directly from the practices that our colleague brought with her to the new job. The practices that made her a success as a Support Level Three now made her a failure as a Support Level Four. Of course, we are slightly exaggerating, but this professional failure happens all the time in many professions. This concept is neither new nor original to me, rather it is known in management literature as the Peter Principle.[12] This theory states that as a successful worker climbs up in hierarchy, the lack of adjustment to a new role by continuing the same practices that made that person successful in the first place will result in a complete failure in the new role. The authors state the lack of adjustment that results in incompetence can happen to anyone in the company at any level of the organization. Furthermore, they claim that every position or role will at some point be occupied by an incompetent person who did all the rights things to climb up the hierarchy and then did all the wrong things while there.

Applying this concept to support should be quite easy as we've all seen the very successful supporter be elevated to manager, only to fail miserably, and be sent back to his old job or perhaps even fired. It is not that the person is a bad worker or doesn't have the right working philosophy or attitude, but rather that the person reaching the incompetence level does not let go of old practices. In his mind, he still thinks that a promotion is doing the same thing, maybe just doing more of it.

I once had a manager who provided absolutely no value to the group, at least that we could see. He was just a go between his manager and us. He did not provide any work, advancement, and deferred all major decisions to his manager. He could have simply gone on vacation for a year and we would not

---

[12] Laurence J. Peter and Raymond Hull, *The Peter Principle: Why Things Always Go Wrong* (New York: HarperCollins, 2009) pp 9–23.

have missed him. He actually went on long leaves and we hardly even noticed he was gone. I tried to figure out why he did not do more to live up to his title. It wasn't the role, because it actually demanded a lot of decision making and innovation. It was not his manager, because he also demanded a lot out of the role. It was not even us, the group under him, because we demanded a lot of help, decisions, and guidance. Because of this manager's lack of decision making, those who worked under him, including me, had to handle the situations on our own and make our own decisions. The problem was this manager's practice of acting as a messenger between us and his manager. That was the extent of what we could see. It made him successful in his previous job, but became his demise in the new one. He was eventually made redundant.

As support professionals, we can prevent this from happening to us. It requires adjustment and some willingness to change our habitual behaviors. It also requires that we study and figure out what made others in the same role successful and then do the same thing. We must not let ourselves fall into the state of incompetence that plagues so many people in all walks of life and all professions. Incompetence can happen to anyone from the cashier manager at the local grocery store to the President of the United States. Someone pushed hard enough will eventually find the level at which he is no longer effective. What we need to do is figure out how to make that level as high as possible. You can do this in the following ways:

- *Study the role*: you must learn as much as possible about the new job and the people who are currently doing it. Specifically, you must identify the responsibilities and expectations of the new role.

- *Let go of your practices*: you are good at your current role; otherwise, you would not be getting the promotion. After all, no healthy organization will promote someone who cannot even do his or her current job well. You must stop doing the things that made you successful before and start executing the new practices that will make you successful in the new job.

- *Get in the new mind-set*: learn what impact the new support role has over the entire support organization or support group. Understand how it differs from the old job so that you can understand how your scope must change to meet the demands placed on you by the new role.

- *Identify the practices that make the new role successful*: you must find out what makes someone successful in the new role. The best way to do this is by speaking and observing someone who is already doing the job well. You only want to learn from the best. Figure out the consistent actions that makes that person successful. Those actions or behaviors are the practices. Do as the successful do and you should also reach the level of success.

- *Constantly renew your practices*: if your keep the practices up-to-date you will ensure that you do not fall into a routine that leads to incompetence. You must figure out from the best people in that job what makes them successful and how they are different. They must perform some habitual actions, practices that you can adjust to your situation and even improve upon.

Incompetence is not something that anyone plans on. It just happens when we face a position that demands skills that we do not immediately have. The biggest mistake we can make is thinking that we can simply keep doing the same things we did in the old job and that it will make us successful in the new one. Incompetence and practice go hand in hand. The trick is to adjust our practices so that they allow us to succeed in the new job, just as the old practices allowed us to succeed in the old one.

Man cannot live by incompetence alone.

—Charlotte Whitton

The Process Map: Friend or Foe?

The actions and decisions of support group members must follow some pattern of accepted behaviors and practices that the constituents rely upon and know well enough to anticipate the decisions and patterns of the individuals within the group. Customers who call the group for support should have some level of expectancy that must be met regardless of who handles the support request. This is not something hard to do or even too much to expect out of a group. After all, the customer must rely upon the uniformity of the service so that the customer may make decisions around it, such as when to call, why to call, and even if he will renew the service agreement. Customers are not the only ones. Entities within the company and within the support organization expect certain consistency across the members of the support group and within the specific support tiers. This is where the common processes prove their value.

Take for example, the case of the support organization that services many products, such as a manufacturer of electronics. When the customer, calls for support on his DVD Player and receives great service in a prompt manner with enough attention to satisfy his needs, he will come to expect the same service every time he calls that company. Suppose he calls again the next day for support on his television set, but this time the support person fumbles the call, manages to upset you, and has no distinguishable process to follow. Would you find something wrong with that electronics manufacturer? What if you call again for the television set and you get a different person who turns out to be just like the DVD Player support person? Would you be even more inclined to think there is something wrong with the way the support organization handles their internal processes?

In technical support, customer satisfaction, effectiveness, and efficiency of the work are all related to the way the internal processes are implemented, enforced, and evolved. The members of the support group must relate to the processes in the following four ways:

- *They must know the process*: everyone in the group has to know what they are supposed to do. If they don't know, their work will be a disaster, and each individual will develop their own way, causing inconsistency in their handling of the problem and the customer.

- *They must understand the relevance of the process to their success*: individuals must know how and why following the process will result in positive results and in their work being of adequate quality.

- *They must know how they fit in*: each support person must know the responsibilities, limits, and position in the flow of actions relating to the work. This knowledge will prevent the individual from doing too much or doing too little.

- *They must never be lost in it*: the individuals must know where they stand at all times and how to advance the work. A process should not allow anyone to be stuck in any one stage of the process.

This is where the process map comes in. The process map is the sequential, logical, or graphical diagram of all the actions, decisions, inputs, endings, and outputs, plus all the people involved and where they fit into the process. The process map or process diagram should be viewed as a tool to help

195

the group succeed. It should provide the immediate guidance that a support person needs to help him in moving a support request along to the eventual completion, referral, or transfer. The process map requires nothing more than a glance and some reading for the individual to know what happens next, who is responsible, and what to do to make the next step possible.

A support person who finds himself lost in the process is of no use to the customer or to the group. It is up to the people in charge of the work to make sure that no one ever wonders what should happen next. The supporters in the group must know the entire process in order for them to stay ahead of the situation and make the resolution or transfer as fast as possible, while still providing the best service possible to the customer.

Think back to early on in your support career, or perhaps you are there now, when you found yourself completely lost because you had no idea what to do next. This should never happen to anyone, especially not to anyone in the lower tiers of the support hierarchy. A support group is very complex in nature, and it's impossible to foresee all possible routes that a technical problem and demanding customer will take, but we can make provisions to ensure that exceptions are taken care of . As long as the supporter knows what to do next, he will have the confidence to go and do it. Most colleagues lose their confidence when presented with complete unknowns and, even worse, when they do not know how to proceed next. I have been there many times and I am sure that you have been there also. Unfortunately, this happens often and the best solution, next to a dedicated manager with all the answers, is a process map that clearly explains who, what, how, when, and where.

The process map is only as good as the process itself, so for this reason we must assume that the process illustrated on the process map is both effective and efficient. However, the process map is not a silver bullet. There are many outcomes, good and bad, that can happen when you are introduced to a process map. First, let's look at the possible negative consequences of a process map:

- You adopt it as the law.

- You never deviate from it.

- It is the only thing you follow.

- You think it's set in stone.

- You get discouraged because it kills your creativity.

- Management uses it to reprimand you.

In contrast, the following are the positive outcomes from having a process map:

- They provide transparency to your work.

- They reduce the effort you put into non-essential actions.

- They remove the conflict from the interactions.

- They serve as the common guidance for all in the group.

- They allow your group to discuss, question, and improve.

- They introduce you to the big picture and help you understand how your work fits in.

Determining whether a process map is a good thing or not depends a lot on how it is derived, presented, and implemented. I had good experiences and bad ones with process maps in both receiving and following, as well as creating and presenting them. The effective process map allows the television set support person to follow a similar set of actions as the DVD Player support person. One thing is certain, a process map has the potential to hinder a group, all but kill its ability to "think outside the box" but also to provide a deeper understanding of the works and how you and everyone else is involved in it.

> *I know that two and two make four—and should be glad to prove it too if I could— though I must say if by any sort of process I could convert two and two into five it would give me much greater pleasure.*

—Lord Byron

Problem Solving: A Waste of Time

Yes, you read right. Problem solving is a waste of time. I am not referring to the type of problem solving that we do as support people, but rather to the "fires" that we must often put out internally, because of a problem in the process and practice. We spend so much time dealing with internal problems that result from a bad practice, an inadequate process, or simply the improper rollout and execution of either. I am referring to the messes that arise when we have a process that creates more work or conflict for us, and eventually affects the recipient of our support, the customer.

Take this example from the early 1990s: John worked in a group that followed a process in which the customer had to send the support person helping him specific information via only a specific medium. This was in the days of floppy discs and very expensive bandwidth. The customers were required to send in the old 5 1/4 inch floppy discs, and the support department would not take anything different despite the presence of newer formats with higher capacities. As time went on, this process was putting customers in a situation where they had to keep an older set of hardware just to send support the files in the required format. The support people often had to explain to customers how to create the older discs and how to format and transfer the files. Management also had to take an earful from customers when the customers were frustrated with the format requirements. Lots of time was spent on the problems arising from this process.

The preceding example illustrates the discrepancy between fixing processes and dealing with the problems that result from a bad process. Instead of changing the process to be more accommodating and proficient for the customer, the support organization chose to deal with the problems that process created. The support group could have simply made an adjustment to the process and saved itself a lot of time and energy. The same type of challenge still faces technical support groups today. We try to fix the problems that result from an outdated or simply improper process, instead of just fixing the process, and removing the problems altogether. Practices are a bit harder to fix, because they are ingrained in the people and require constant conditioning for the practices to change. However, it can be done.

When the group faces too many occurrences of the same problem, the person in charge of the process must take a hard look at the specific actions or decisions that are causing it. It is not only necessary to change the process to eliminate the problem, but perhaps to redesign it so that the fixing of one problem does not result in another. For example, solving the problem that arises from transferring support issues to the upper tiers too soon should not be fixed by simply removing the ability to transfer issues. If that happens, then the lower tiers will be forced to handle issues long after they can continue to add value. The people in charge of the process must study the situation and find the best approach. It may be a process change or it may simply be the correct enforcement of the existing one.

When to change, fix, or eliminate a process is not an easy topic to decipher. The challenge comes in knowing what to improve and results in the highest value to the organization and the customer. Such a decision requires unbiased knowledge of the work and the current practices. The first thing that you must do is figure out if you need to simply modify the existing process to solve that specific problem or to redesign the entire thing to reengineer the work. That all depends on the depth and the grievance of the problem presented.

Take for instance the common problem of customers returning the product and demanding their money back that arises when the support people are required to do an initial diagnosis by asking a series of basic questions. You notice that customers often get upset and this often results in the customers wanting to look for other options that do not include your product. Would you stop asking the initial questions? Would you shorten the questions to be more concise? Would you ask the customer whether he wants the questions asked? Or, would you stop doing the support the current way and opt perhaps for training your group to be more knowledgeable in the product rather than just ask questions and then look the answers up in a manual in order to figure out the cause? Obviously, these are not easy questions and every option may be appropriate depending on the severity of the problem and the length that you want to go in order to fix it. Of course, this assumed that you are in charge, perhaps in a management or upper tier position with the authority to recommend or change the process.

Improving processes is not work for the weak. You are taking risks because if the problems are not fixed and the process change ends up with more problems than before, it is you who will be responsible. This is what separates the proactive and reactive actions on your part. Do you want to simply solve the problems as they arise and be reactive, or do you prefer to be proactive and change the process with the hope of avoiding such problems in the future? The answer is simply: it depends.

It all depends on whether the problems are significant enough to devote the effort and investment in a process change. It also depends on the impact that the change will have on the support group, and whether that will be more detrimental to the overall customer base than simply dealing with the problems as they come. It also depends on the group and whether they are prepared to undergo a change in the way they do the work. All these matters are rather complex and difficult to make a decision on. Whatever the decision, if it's the right one, it will save the organization money by way of improved efficiencies in the use of resources, and, hopefully, result in higher customer satisfaction.

When you confront a problem you begin to solve it.

—Rudy Giuliani

PART 4

■ ■ ■

Working with Customers

You are now in the part of technical support that deals directly with the interaction of support professionals and customers as well as the outlook of the technical support discipline. The topics in this last part will allow you to look at customers and the service we provide to them in a different light. The means we use to communicate and the efficiency of how we get our message across represents the culmination of all our efforts in support. The very reason we exist as a profession is to deliver value to our customers by way of technical answers. Our delivery of that value, today and in the future, is the subject of this part.

CHAPTER 10

■ ■ ■

Customer Service

Technical support consists of two main functional areas rolled into one discipline, technical/product expertise, and customer service. The technical portion is a variable that each support professional must have to adapt to, and possibly face multiple times in his career. Technology changes while only customer service remains a constant. The importance of the customer service is one that we often take for granted as we typically concentrate more on the technical side of support. However, customer service is the foundation to a successful career in technical support, and just about any other customer-facing profession.

The term customer service is one that has many meanings to many people. As practitioners of the support profession, we must understand this term and define it for our purpose, so that we can build theories, models, and practices around it, the humble beginnings that I will provide to you in this chapter.

In this chapter will you read about the different dimensions of customer service, such as the customer reality, the importance of behaviors, problematic interactions, coping strategies and a few others topics of importance to technical support. The approach I take is a compilation of ideas and concepts derived from practice that goes beyond the typical definition of customer service that mainly deals with pleasing customers by attitude, practices, and positive behaviors. I take a slightly different approach with the inception of value into the customer interaction and definition. It is only through value that we can justify the function of customer service and the very existence of a set of ideas in dealing with customers. Customer service is far more than just pleasing or agreeing with customers; it is giving them the type of worth that they can put a price tag on and lend their loyalty to in a crowded marketplace. Customers prefer those support organizations that can add value to their support interactions beyond what is simply promised on a support contract. The beauty of the concept is its simplicity and the huge returns that even minimal effort can have for the vendor.

In developing the succeeding topics, I studied many ideas and definitions from existing literature from inside and outside of customer service, but only found a few to be of any value and rational significance to our field. As mentioned, our career is a subject matter that does not have a huge body of literature. What exists does not follow a common topic, but I did find some strong research and used it as sources. Due to the lack of an expansive body of knowledge, I was forced to draw from the practical and extract the examples and experiences to formulate a group of topics that are theoretical enough to be further developed, critiqued, or refuted, but at the same time provide practical value that you can use in your support work to improve your own perception and practice of customer service.

I urge you take the time to think while you read and try to come up with your own ideas that can expand this field of ours. It is in all of you that the future of technical support rests. Make the best of it.

To give real service you must add something which cannot be bought or measured with money, and that is sincerity and integrity.

—Douglas Adams

Customer Service: A Dimensional Explanation

We all use, demand, swear by, and claim to have the best type of it. At a macro level, customer service is the "nous se qua" that market players provide and often makes the difference in an environment filled with commodity products and services. The concept of perfect competition[1] in economics assumes that all competitors are equally matched with undifferentiating goods and services. The concept of perfect competition also requires that no product or service vendor have any disproportionate market share. Of course, I am oversimplifying a fundamental theory of economics, yet this notion of homogeny in goods offered leaves little for the vendor to use as a leverage to gain an advantage over the competition. In effect, these commodity vendors cannot set, affect, or regulate price much less supply and demand in any way, so they must rely on something other than the things they sell to gain new customers. A good example of near perfect competition is the insurance industry. Just think of auto insurance companies and how uniform their policies are, regardless of the company. These companies must rely on something other than the actual product. They rely on something we know as customer service as their main differentiator, which comes in the form of faster response, better care, easier processing of claims, and many other things that we come to expect from the best insurance companies. Yet customer service is not one specific thing, but a conglomeration of "perks" that customers receive from the vendor. There is hardly one single metric that would make the difference between providing customer service and the opposite even without getting to the qualitative nature of branding it good or bad.

Can you think of a proper definition for the term "customer service"? Most likely, you can think of many examples, but not of a definition. Current literature dealing with the subject matter attempts to define customer service in different forms and contexts. John A. Woods defines it as "a relationship with people who are an essential part of everything you do."[2] Richard Gallagher defines it as "a science of how to tell people that you have just towed their car away."[3] Sterne defines it indirectly as the way that ever more demanding consumers continue to demand products and services progressively throughout the 20th century.[4] All very good definitions, but not entirely any that fit our purpose as technical support professionals. We need something a bit more general, but still appropriate for our field.

For the technical support discipline, customer service is the intangible benefit that vendors provide to their customer in order to support, facilitate, improve, and assist in the use of the product or service purchased by employing behaviors, practices, and approaches that deliver satisfaction to the recipient.

---

[1] Frank Machovec, *Perfect Competition and the Transformation of Economics* (New York: Routledge, 1995) pp 70–72.

[2] Ron Zemke and John A. Woods, *Best Practices in Customer Service* (New York: HRD Press, 1998) pp 3–4.

[3] Richard S. Gallagher, *Great Customer Connections* (New York: AMACOM, 2006) p 3. Gallagher is probably the only author that views customer service as a science that employs concepts from psychology. He provides a refreshing view of the field of customer service from both the practical as well as the theoretical approach.

[4] Jim Sterne, *Customer Service on the Internet* (New York: John Wiley & Sons, 1996) p 27.

Customer Service is inherently positive in nature. The opposite would be a disservice or bad service. The customer service that a consumer receives is the value over what they paid in terms of professional etiquette, which adds positive significance to the product or service. In effect, it is what is "thrown in" with the purchase in the form of qualitative added help, support, or attention that provides peace of mind to the customer and gives us an edge over the competition while also allowing us to constantly improve for our own sake. Customer service has many purposes from the ethical and legal responsibility to the market differentiation between similarly equipped and priced products and services. It also aids in the prevention of cognitive dissonance, also known as buyer's remorse.[5] The logic is that a consumer of a product or service will be less prone to experience remorse or second thoughts on the purchase if that consumer receives an extra benefit or value in the form of added service from the vendor. We can relate that to technical support in the form of a customer who recently purchased our technology and is on the brink of experiencing cognitive dissonance. If the customer contacts support and receives only the necessary assistance, the customer may be more likely to rethink his purchase decision than if he received extra assistance over what he expected and over what he thinks he paid for. Providing that extra value in the form of customer service does not cost the vendor any more or any less, but it is perceived by the consumer of that service as an added value and may even associate a monetary assessment to that service. This explains why consumers are willing to pay more for vendors with a reputation of better customer service.

Customer service is not about being extra nice, always smiling, or smothering the customer with niceties into liking us. Pretending or even genuinely being nice to a customer by itself has nothing to do with customer service. The term is much more global in nature and it has value at its core. In effect, customer service is a deliverable that customers demand in a competitive marketplace. Just think of your favorite restaurant, you probably like it for the food, but also for the higher level of customer service you receive. The optimal point for consumer preference is at the intersection of customer service and product quality. Moving away from that equilibrium point in either direction would result in sacrificing either customer service for quality or vice versa.

By this definition, customer service must be something that we, as the producers and providers of it, must not incur at any marginal cost. This refers to the added cost of producing one more unit of the whatever it is we are producing; in our case, resolved technical support issues. In short, it must be inherent in the quality of the supporters because it is intangible. Of course, just because something is not physical does not mean it has to be free or without an incurred cost. However, if we had to pay for providing customer service, then it would not be an added value, but rather a paid-for value. At the risk of sounding like a riddle, customer service is more than just "going the extra" mile," by spending extra time, giving him products for free or hours of service when the customer requires our support. Customer service does not try to "buy" the customer, but improve his experience. Customer service is a behavior that produces value for the customer in itself, but not something that must incur any additional cost.

We have established that customer service is an intangible benefit with no marginal cost to the vendor, but of potentially higher monetary value to the customer. So if it's free, then why don't all vendors provide it at its peak level? Customer service must be fomented and maximized in the optimal environment. Customer service is not the cause, but the result of a set of behaviors. The behaviors become practices, which in turn form the culture that every member of the support group abides by and becomes their standard. Customer service may not have an added monetary cost to the producer, but it has a cost in effort starting with each individual.

Customer service is not altruistic in nature. It carries very real benefits to the producer because it allows for the minimization of problematic and costly interactions with dissatisfied customers and

---

[5] Ernest Cadotte, Robert Woodruff and Roger Jenkins, "Expectations and Norms in Models of Consumer Satisfaction," *Journal of Marketing Research* 24, August 1987, p 305–308.

escalations. Imagine the amount of time, effort, resources, and money saved if we did not have to put up with angry customers who demand immediate action, conference calls, refunds, returns, and freebies. Additionally, the vendors that provide customer service develop a positive reputation, which draws more business so the benefits to the vendor are very real. The companies that succeed in providing customer service enjoy a better market position than the competition.

We just went through a definition of customer service as experienced and defined by the terms of technical support. This is a not necessarily a different approach, but an expanded and multidimensional definition to existing literature on the subject, because it explores the benefit in customer service to the consumer as well as the value and cost to the vendor.

> *Business is not just doing deals; business is having great products, doing great engineering, and providing tremendous service to customers. Finally, business is a cobweb of human relationships.*

—Ross Perot

Customer Reality

Customer service is an objective approach by the vendor to provide added benefits to the consumer of our technology. We strive to modify our behaviors in accordance to what our research shows as being valuable to the customer. We may develop that research and analysis internally or hire a consultant to help us. Whatever the source, we strive to shape our practices to the ideal view of customer service. It is objective because we rely on the facts in the pursuit of our business goals, such as market share, return on investment, industry dominance, and we attain our goals via customer satisfaction. The satisfaction of customers is not the end, but the means to a higher business reality. Additionally, we pursue the satisfaction of all our customers, not just some. However, our customers view customer service as subjective, that is, according to their biased view of the ideal quality of support and service we provide. Customers will not be as objective as we are because their reality is different than ours, and is not the same for every customer. Of course, I am using the terms objective and subjective loosely, because the topic of customer reality does not lend itself to absolute truths, at least not yet anyway. Customer service is still, much like technical support, a developing realm of business. Because we don't yet have a consistent definition and because customer experience is inconsistent in nature, we must assume that customer reality is a pluralistic approach to the vendor, because every customer will have a different reality.

Perception is at the core of customer reality. However, there are more variables shaping customer reality as it is a multidimensional concept that cannot be explained simply by perception. The famous maxim of "customer perception is reality" proves a bit limited and empty without understanding the nature of reality. Customer perception is simply how the customer views the situation, product, and environment. Fundamentally, it is their opinion of whatever is happening. What is somewhat disturbing for us in technical support is that two customers receiving the same level of customer service from our support will view the experience differently, and perhaps even disparately polarizing. In effect, we could provide the same answers, language, timing, and effort but two customers may use their own interpretation of customer service to rate us dissimilarly.

Customer reality forms in a customer via multiple variables that will inevitably differ by customer:

- *Perception*: Everyone thinks of this when defining customer reality. Perception refers to how the consumer analyzes and processes the service received.[6] This analysis allows the individual to form a picture of the world, and may be completely different than what the vendor attempts to convey. For example, a customer may view a courteous greeting from the support person as a canned or scripted greeting. Calling a person by their first name may evoke a different perception, such as disrespect or personalized service; it all depends on how the customer processes the interaction.

- *Expectation*: The level of support the customer expects from you has a huge impact on the reality that customer forms about the interaction. Suppose the customer expects to speak to an inexperienced person who will go through a canned script before transferring the case to a more knowledgeable colleague, and then the first person he speaks with turns out to be an expert in the technology who fixes the problem in a short period of time. That expectation will shape the reality until it is modified by us proving his expectation wrong. Of course, the opposite could also happen, and we could make his reality even worse by providing the customer less than what he was expecting to get from us.

- *Experience*: The customer's experience with other support people or even with other vendors will have a huge impact on his reality. Since all customers will have different experiences, their realities will also be different. If the customer service we provide is above what he has previously received, then his reality will be positively shaped. If we fall short based on his experiences, then the reality will be negatively changed.

- *Beliefs*: A customer's beliefs are a huge determinant of his reality. Beliefs consist of the very large number of mental or verbal statements such as "I believe..." that reflect a person's particular knowledge and assessment of something such as a product, technology, support process, value or brand.[7] A person's belief of what customer service means will inevitably have a huge impact on his reality by shaping expectations and interpretation of the service he receives from us. It is not our fault if those beliefs do not coincide with ours, or if we abide by his. Nevertheless, we will be judged by those beliefs. Beliefs are not limited to simply customer service. There are many things a person believes that will shape their interaction with us. I once had a customer demand to speak with someone else because of my accent. He believed that I would be unable to understand him or be understood by him. His belief that someone with a foreign accent is unable to provide customer service to the level of his acceptance shapes his reality.

- *Values*: These are a special type of belief. Values differ from other beliefs because they meet the following criteria: they are relatively few in number, they serve as a guide for culturally accepted behavior, they are enduring and difficult to change, not tied to a specific object or situation, and are widely accepted by members of a

---

[6] Ford, Wendy S. Zabava. "Communication Practices of Professional Service Providers: Predicting Customer Satisfaction and Loyalty." *Journal of Applied Communication Research* 31, no. 3 (August 2003): 189.

[7] Leon G. Schiffman and Leslie Lazar Kanuk, *Consumer Behavior* 5th Ed. (Englewood Cliffs, NJ: Prentice Hall, 1994) pp 409

society.[8] The presence, and lack, of values dictate to a great extent the reality of the customer and the effectiveness that our customer service has on him and his view of the situation. If a customer's value consists of handling technical issues without blaming the support person for the shortcomings of the product, then that customer would form a much different reality than someone who does not share that value. Another customer's value revolves around the value of treating others with respect. I took a support call from a customer who did not appear to like my answers, and immediately began to curse me and call me all kinds of names. His reality did not include the possibility of respecting support people and their expertise. I called his manager who immediately apologized and asked that I continue with someone else from their side. A few days later, the initial person called again and our call turned into another cursing fest. Once thing was sure, his values were enduring.

Customer reality can't be easily explained by simply citing perception as the only determinant of reality. There are a few other variables that go into reality and greatly determine the effectiveness that our customer service has on a customer. We cannot control customer reality; we can only adapt to it and make the best of the situation. The subject of customer attributes that determine reality are quite complex and fully understanding them rivals the complexity of demands placed on us by the technologies we support.

There may always be another reality to make fiction of the one we live in.

—Aaron Franks

The Customer's Iceberg

In his book, *Great Customer Connections*, Richard S. Gallagher makes the claim that customer service, as a study, utilizes psychology principles that allow us to understand interactions with customers from a more educated and fundamental angle.[9] Gallagher's thesis is quite credible, but he takes customer service from the approach of language and practical psychology to involve the reader into Gallagher's view of the meaning of customer service. The text sticks to the practical applications of customer service without dwelling on the fundamental theories of psychology.

One aspect of psychology that I would like to have seen in Gallagher's literature is the concept of psychoanalysis synthesized for customer service as viewed in technical support. The text did not claim or hint at using such an approach; nevertheless, it left me wanting to learn and decipher a bit more about the role that Freudian principles have on customer service. After all, customers have a predetermined idea of what customer service involves and a reality that greatly determines the level of satisfaction they will have with our level of customer service.

When you think of psychoanalysis, you may imagine a troubled patient lying on a leather couch with an old bearded man sitting next to him on an armchair taking notes on a small notepad, stroking his white beard while looking into space with his glasses tied around his neck with a string. I know that's the first image that comes to my mind. However, what if instead of a leather couch, the patient is our customer sitting in a cubicle on the other side of the phone sounding very troubled by a problem he is experiencing? The bearded man sitting on the chair next to him is you, and instead of writing on a note

---

[8] Ibid

[9] Richard S. Gallagher, *Great Customer Connections* (New York: AMACOM, 2006) pp 2–10.

pad, you may be typing on a computer while trying to figure out the problem by asking questions and looking up answers. In effect, this thing we call technical support is much like psychoanalysis. We troubleshoot the technical problem, but at the same time psychoanalyze the customer. Granted, not all customers who call us will be troubled by the problem, but the mere fact that they called us means that they have a need and perceive us to have the answer.

Sigmund Freud (1856–1939) developed the theory of psychoanalysis to explain human personality and as a way to develop therapy for his patients with psychological disorders. The beauty of Freud's approach is that he explained a very complex subject matter in such simple terms that anyone can understand the main idea behind the iceberg analogy. In essence, Freud stated that human personality is comprised of the conscious and the unconscious. The conscious is like the tip of an iceberg that peaks above the water while the unconscious is the huge mass that lies hidden and controls the conscious. What we see is the conscious, but the individual cannot fully control personality because it is subject to the hidden part of the iceberg. The bulk of the iceberg that lives underwater, the unconscious, is made up of impulses, wishes, and desires. The therapy portion of psychoanalysis focuses on bringing the unconscious above the surface in order to understand the entire "iceberg," or personality.

We can apply the theory of psychoanalysis to customer service in technical support. In order to fully provide that extra value to a customer's experience, it is necessary to take up the issue of the repressed experiences, which give rise to the impulses, wishes, and desires of the customer calling us for help. The way to decipher the underwater mass of the iceberg is to ask questions and get to what afflicts the customer as well as what the customer really wants and needs. Finding these three items is the essence of our use of the Freudian theory of psychoanalysis and forms the customer service portion of technical support. The following are how we accomplish this feat:

Find the Affliction

When a customer calls you for technical help, he has an affliction. His affliction may be dire or subtle, but it is an affliction. You want to find the affliction because it allows you to devise the best solution for the customer. For example, suppose a good customer calls you on Friday at 4:59 PM asking you to help him resolve a problem with the technology. He sounds stressed and is very insistent on getting the problem resolved quickly. You can figure out what the affliction is by looking at the following three things:

- *Situation*: What situation is the customer in that may be afflicting him? Is the affliction coming from the technical situation or from something outside the technical? It may be that the technical problem is causing a very real business detriment to the company. It may also be that he is scheduled to go on a weekend trip with his family and this problem is threatening his plans.

- *Conditions*: Are the conditions really conducive to the affliction? In other words, the customer may appear troubled by the technical problem, but are the conditions really conducive to the deterioration? The conditions refer to the set of circumstances around the technical problem. If the customer claims that the problem is keeping his company from achieving some business goal, and the conditions or circumstances of the problem do not warrant that severity, there may be something deeper to the perceived affliction to the customer.

- *Pressures*: Pressures to the customer from within his organization will certainly result in some level of affliction that affects the conscious, or what we see in our interaction with him. The challenge for us is in trying to find out what really is pressuring the customer without appearing too nosy.

Real Wants

What the customer says he wants may not be the truth that lies underwater. He may say he wants the problem fixed, but in reality he may just want a workaround to get the work done, or perhaps he just wants a confirmation that the technical problem is a defect. Getting to real wants only comes from hints that we pick up in the context of what the customer says or does. I once spoke with an irate customer who demanded he get his technical problem resolved because, according to him, my colleagues had just wasted his time. I spoke with him, listened to him, and came to realize that he didn't care for the problem as much as for someone to listen to his situation. The problem to him was secondary. My colleagues focused too much on the problem he described, the conscious, and ignored what he really wanted, the unconscious, which was for someone to listen to his situation and provide some reassurance that he was on the right path.

Real Needs

The customer knows, though unconsciously, what he really wants. However, what he really needs may not be apparent at all, even with some reflection on his part. As experts, that's where we come in. Assessing the customer's real needs, and providing those to him, is a prime example of customer service and the concept of the extra value we can add to the customer experience. What the customer really needs may be something completely different than what he is asking from us. It is up to us to use our expertise to figure out what will most help the customer and let him know. Those of us who work in technical support realize that sometimes the customer's demands on our product are simply a need for a feature or another product. The customer usually cannot make that determination on his own, so it takes an expert in both the technology and customer service to figure that out.

Customers who call us for help come with some baggage and most of it is hidden. This baggage consists of a contextual definition of a problem, hidden agendas, biases, political problems from their own organization and even a different jargon to refer to technical problems. It falls upon technical support to analyze the customer, and what he's saying, to figure out what afflicts him, what he wants, and what he needs. Applying the Freudian theory of psychoanalysis to understand the hidden characteristics of customers may be a long stretch for some of you, but we deal with people who will always be much more complex than any technology we support. It is only by borrowing from the great discoveries of others in different disciplines that we can enrich ours, at least until we start developing our own theories to make sense of our profession. Freud is not without his critics, but there is no doubt that his approach to human personality is of great value when we use it to make sense of our customer's afflictions, needs, and wants with the hope of advancing customer service in technical support.

> *It was his optimism that Freud bequeathed to America and it was the optimism of our youthfulness, our freedom from the sterner, sadder tradition of Europe which enabled us to seize his gift.*

> —Karl A. Menninger

All About the Behaviors

In the definition of customer service we've set for ourselves, the deliverable to the customer involves intangible benefits at a rate of more than what he contracted us for, but is not detrimental to us as vendors. We have yet to define what intangible benefits are and how we produce those benefits. We can provide customers actions in the form of improved assistance and other aid that the customer would not otherwise obtain from us. However, think about the actions at the core of customer service; we are not talking about mere gestures such as a bigger smile, a "Thank you," "Yes ma'am," or "I'm here to serve you." What these actions entail are a whole different way of thinking—the frame of mind that we can make a huge difference in the interaction we have with the customer. This requires us, as supporters, to change the very way we approach problems and customers. It means changing our behaviors in a way that this set of behaviors bring benefit to the customer and his work, so that he can walk away with more than what he expected, or even, more than what he needed.

The big question remains, how can we possibly change our behaviors alone? First, behaviors are the things we do consistently and without much thought. It is the instinct that drives our actions. Behaviors are ingrained and we do them consciously as a result of what we believe in our unconscious. Collective behaviors do not change as the result of reading a book, simply attending a training seminar, or an outing where we practice falling backwards on each other's arms. The technical support group must set the right environment for the behaviors to take place. In 1913, psychologist John B. Watson published a legendary article, which came to be the foundation for the school of psychology known as Behaviorism. In the article titled, "Psychology as the Behaviorist Views It," Watson simplified the study of psychology as the "study of behavior," in which he argues that behavior is measurable and observable and pinpoints the environment as its key determinant. Behaviorism dominated psychology until the 1960s and remains a part of modern psychology due to the research and literature of other Behaviorists.

The technical support organization must be the correct environment for the proper customer service behaviors to occur. Management and group members must enable the behaviors, reinforce them, and reward them in order for the entire organization to change. If the environment is not optimal for the behaviors that lead to customer service, then the desired behaviors will only appear sporadically and without uniformity across the group. It is like an open field that you want to turn into prime grazing pasture. If you do nothing with it, some good grass will grow here and there, but not uniformly cover the entire field. The unattended field will eventually have more weeds than grass, because it's easier for the weeds to take root and multiply, just like bad behaviors would be the norm if you left your support organization unattended. On the other hand, if you plow the land, sprig or seed it, fertilize it, irrigate it, and weed it, you will have a very productive grass field ideal for grazing cattle. As you can imagine, a support group with the correct customer service behaviors is not an accident, but formed by the right environment.

How can the support organization set the right environment that leads to appropriate customer service? The answer is not so simple, but the complexity can be broken down into several areas in order to make it easier to carry out. The first step is to know what type of environment you need to create. You have two sources of information for what behaviors need to be present in your organization and the environment to make those behaviors possible. They are the following

- *Ask your customers*: Customers usually know what they want even if they cannot always express it to us, what afflicts them, and what they need because only they know their situation. Customers across a specific subset of the industry will want specific things to make them happy. It all depends on the market segment you deal with. Customers are part of your environment and the part that most matters. To get the information about what customers would value the most from the support your organization provides, you will need to have a way to gather data after completed support calls, such as short survey, or even just a follow-up call from a manager asking what the customer would like to keep and change from the support he receives from your organization. The specific information you want to find out from customers is what set of behaviors they want to see more of and what behaviors they have found detrimental in their interactions with the support personnel.

- *Ask your best employees*: The "good grass that has grown amid the weeds" is the best way of providing customer service, because they are already doing it despite the environment. These are the people who time after time perform and provide the best experience, at least, for some customers. The best employees are those who produce the most, complain the least, and get the most customer kudos. They don't come in droves, so you will probably only have a handful. From these employees, you want to find out what they do and how they do it. This is where you will get the initial behaviors. Also, it is imperative that you ask what these employees see as a challenge to produce the best customer service possible. Once you find out the challenges, it will give you an idea of what to do away with or modify. Additionally, since these employees are already doing the right things, you will also need to find out what is currently working correctly in the environment that is conducive to these employees doing such a great job.

Once you know the behaviors and environment needs, you are ready to make the environment possible. The ideal environment that leads to customer service will have the following:

- *Structure*: The support staff has to be arranged in a way that the best people in terms of customer service enable others to act. In essence, the enablers are the customer service leaders that coach and foment the high necessity for customer service in others. The support organization must look up to the people with the best customer service practices and mimic them. The structure needs some proper titles and recognition to go along with adopting the customer service leaders as the people who will take the support organization into the next level to teach and transform their peers.

- *Process*: Now that we have the structure in place, the skeleton needs some muscle to enable the action. The process design must be one that provides some checks and balances, and does not restrict the ability for any individual to take the extra steps to add value to customer interactions. Rigid processes in technical support with no room for supporter discretion are detrimental to the behaviors that lead to customer service. As such, customer service flourishes where the support professional is comfortable and happy with his environment as well as with the knowledge that his efforts will not be reprimanded.

- *Policy*: The rules present in the support organization that wishes to make customer service a foundation for its business must have a way to promote people with the correct behaviors into positions of authority or seniority, and prevent people with the wrong behaviors from spreading them. The policies must also allow for the management team to prepare, promote, and acquire customer service trainings and events.

- *Reward system*: Despite our definition of customer service establishing that customer service is made up of actions, which must not have marginal costs to the support organization, it should still provide rewards and incentives to promote the correct efforts, examples, and initiatives from members of the support groups. It is via a proper reward system that the organization can encourage the technical support professional to strive to continue improving the behaviors that made him successful. Rewards should include both tangible and intangible rewards such as bonuses, gifts, and recognition.

When it comes to customer service it is all about the behaviors. The two best possible approaches are the following:

- Leave it up to each individual supporter to provide the customer service as he sees fit and leave the organization intact.

- Institutionalize the correct customer service in order to provide the ideal environment that leads to the correct behaviors.

In this section, we opted for the institutionalization of customer service, mainly because the Behaviorist school of psychology teaches us that behaviors are the results of an environment. As supporters, our actions toward customers are greatly influenced by the environment in which we work. Our support organization, its structure, processes, policy, and reward system create that environment.

No time is better spent than that spent in the service of your fellow man.

—Bryant H. McGill

The Open Mind Approach

According to our definition of customer service, the customer derives value from the way we approach the work and the extra finesse and value we add to the delivery of support. Yet one aspect of the work we do in our profession eludes this definition and the way we approach it. Because the added value that we bring to the customer lies in the intangible, it stands to reason that the value level will vary according to how much and to what extent we apply our customer service endeavor. The same customer may call the same supporter with the exact same question, receive the same answer, and still walk away with two different levels of customer service. If you've been in support long enough you understand that there are some calls that you simply are more "into" than others. You may answer the same question for different customers and each one may walk away with a different level of value and satisfaction. All other things being equal, such as the personality or demands and expectations of the customer, the differentiator is how you approach the situation and the problem.

I once supported a product in which there were a few situations that always occurred. This is not irregular as most technologies will have some technical aspects that will cause problems or doubts in customers, and in turn the support group receives plenty of calls for those questions. I noticed that I answered the same question over and over, possibly dozens of times a month. I created canned answers and emails that were ready to go whenever the question came up. I shared those with my colleagues. Nevertheless, I noticed that even while we all had the same question come up, and had the same documentation and instructions to send out or explain to a customer, the level of extra value in addition to the technical answers varied tremendously. I debated this theme for a few years, until I finally came to the realization while watching several individual colleagues answer many calls over time with a huge differences of extra value added to each call. In some calls, they added a lot of value and in some the value was absent because it was rather negative. I came to the conclusion that customer service, and the idea of adding value beyond what the customer expects and paid for, is all in the state of mind in which the support person approaches the customer and the problem.

The multiple approaches, as observed in dozens of the support colleagues, are not easy to categorize and put a label on. Because of the complexity of human behavior, the best way to describe them is by describing what the support colleague appears to be saying with his actions and approach to the customer. They are the following:

- *"I am trying to get through my day and you are preventing me from getting through it effortlessly."* Obviously, this colleague will try to do as little as he can to get through the day. This is the kind of person who can't wait until five o'clock to go home. Of course, just because someone leaves at the same time every day doesn't mean this is his prevalent behavioral approach toward the customer. If you find yourself in this frame of mind, you need to think about what possibilities exist to modify your approach. There is little you can do for the customer without changing your approach to the job.

- *"I am here to serve you but only as much as necessary."* The person exhibiting this approach does his job impeccably, performs well, and produces as expected. However, this support person does not add any more value to the customer than what is expected. The support organization comprised of this type of individual approach will never get past mediocrity. In a market environment with many competitors, the behavior of "no more than required" will have a harder time surpassing other players in the industry.

- *"I am your superior technically and I will make you feel like a moron."* This approach is prevalent in the high technology sector where the techie appears to have an inferiority complex. Those of us who were ridiculed in school or at home for being technology geeks find this type of approach very attractive as it provides a way to payback society for all the fun had at our expense. The only problem is that it makes the customer feel like they continuously have to put up with humiliation from someone who is supposed to serve him. The supporter who practices this approach is often considered too valuable technically, but in an increasingly demanding customer environment, the approach is detrimental to delivering the extra benefit required in customer service.

- "I love the technical work and dislike human interaction. Let me get to the technical problem and you can come along for the ride." The colleague with this approach is a true lover of technology. He finds any technical challenge fascinating and goes the extra mile to figure out problems and, at times, even gives more time and attention to a customer issue simply because he wants to know more. The human side of technical support means little to this colleague. In a support organization that practices multiple ways of customer communication, the supporter with this approach always prefers the one with the least personal touch, such as email or by going through another colleague. The reason this supporter does not provide customer service is not because he doesn't want to necessarily, but because he doesn't interact with the customer at a personal level to begin with. Customer service requires personal interaction, because the value comes in the form of intangible benefit, such as setting the customer in the right mood, adding some additional benefit to an explanation, or even providing undocumented suggestions to increase the probability of a customer succeeding in using the technology. The person with this love of technology to the detriment of the customer's needs may end up driving customer satisfaction down because the focus is technology, rather than the realization that it is the business that we must take care of, and not curiosity or the passion for technology.

- *"I am open to whatever the situation brings and I will deliver more value than what you are entitled to."* This is the correct approach to have when you seek to provide customer service. The supporter begins with the notion that everything is possible and seeks to add value, not simply deliver only what is necessary. The support professional with the open mind approach develops much further than anyone else because he has more changes to learn and experiment as well as simply deal with more customer interactions. The person with this approach is easily recognized, because in his mind he can do anything, so he actually does. The colleague with this approach is quite rare and it comes as a result of experience, personal realization, and simply an epiphany. I asked the few colleagues that I've met over the years with this approach, and they all told me they view their job in technical support as a much better option than the alternative. They also told me that their reason for striving to provide the best customer experience possible is because they truly care for what a customer thinks of them and of how their actions will impact the customer's business. The open mind approach also brings value to the support organization because they have in this person the equivalent of a Swiss Army Knife of the technical support world, because this person can do anything you ask him to. It may take him a bit, but he can do anything. If you want an example to compare to, just think of the colleague who, when asked to do something slightly different, he automatically spurts "I can't do that, I haven't been trained." The open-minded colleague doesn't whine about training or resources; he just finds a way and provides more value to the customer and the support organization than what he is paid for. This is why our definition of customer service includes the lack of added cost to the customer as well as the employer. However, don't think that you will always do this for free. Good people in technical support are hard to come by, and those exhibiting an open mind attitude are gold. Good support organizations who know how to recognize this approach will inevitably do everything possible to retain this type of support professional.

The approach to customers is only one of the dimensions of the supporter's mind-set when supporting their respective technologies. The other dimension is the approach to the technology and the company itself. However, this is most relevant to the concept of customer service, because it is here the customer directly receives the extra value and realizes the benefit of the open mind approach. The preceding concepts are theoretical in nature meaning that they are generalities, so individuals may exhibit more than, or even all of them, at different stages of their career. I know I did and many of my colleagues have also. However, as practitioners of customer service our approach is to achieve and promulgate the open mind approach.

I like the silent church before the service begins, better than any preaching.

—Ralph Waldo Emerson

Problematic Interactions and Coping Strategies

If you work in technical support long enough you will encounter difficult people, both customers and colleagues. Chances are that even if you have been in technical support for a short time, you will encounter such people. The problem is not so much that sooner or later you will have to deal with customers that will really annoy and anger you, but that when it happens you will be ready to cope with them. Allowing adverse customer interactions to affect you psychologically will have a huge detriment in how you are able to provide customer service to the other customers. Dealing with difficult customers gets easier with experience; nevertheless, if you have not yet mastered the art of letting things roll off your back, there are some simple, proven, and effective techniques that you can use to cope with these situations. The types of problematic interactions that may cause you emotional grief include the following:

- *Customer thinks you are not knowledgeable enough*: This one has probably happened to everyone in technical support. Eventually you will encounter a customer who knows a lot and is not shy about it. The altercation often occurs when the customer does not agree with you or when you do not keep up with him. Aside from the training needs you may have, putting your knowledge to the test and under doubt may make you feel inadequate and cause a bit of anxiety. This is especially problematic if you are new to support.

- *Customer thinks you are not the right person to help him*: Some customers simply have problems with sensitivity. Some do not like to deal with support people who are somehow different. I have seen customers who refuse to work with a colleague because they sound old, young, stutter, or some other reason that is beyond the colleague's control. On many occasions, I took calls from colleagues in which the customer refused to speak with a frontline support person. Somehow, the customer had the idea that only support people beyond the frontline tier could speak intelligently about the product. Of course, this was not the case and our frontline was quite capable.

- *Customer turns aggressive when you suggest a solution*: The typical customer who thinks he knows it all will try to ridicule, chastise, or even offend you when you suggest a solution that you know or at least strongly believe will solve the problem. The customer who has had dealings with other support groups from competitors or other vendors and knows how to play the system will often revert to this tactic, so that you accommodate his demands regardless of how wrong or impossible. Most of us can relate to the customer who threatens to take this up to our upper management if we do not give them what they want or approach the problem the way they demand, regardless of how irrational.

- *Customer sends in a complaint to your manager about you*: Some customer go so far as to not threaten, but actually send in a nasty email about you, file a formal complaint to your manager, or possibly contact your Chief Executive Officer. I had that happen once. I heard it from everyone and so did my manager. Luckily, by that time I was experienced enough in the profession that I knew I was right and no amount of complaining would turn a right answer into a wrong one. However, I can see how this could have caused anxiety and stress to a less-experienced colleague.

- *Customer curses at you or calls you names*: There is absolutely no room in a professional setting for name-calling, regardless of who the customer is. Nevertheless, it does happen and what is worse, it affects colleagues tremendously. For a colleague who does not know how to deal with cursing customers, the experience will sour their passion for support work. There is a strong possibility that the less-experienced colleague may stop wanting to take calls or handle issues for any customer once they sense that a customer may be the type that will revert to vulgarity.

- *Customer refuses to work with you based on accent, name, or location*: This is one of the most infuriating and unfair customer behaviors that you may encounter in your support career. The situation occurs when a customer refuses to work with you because of ethnic or regional reasons. Unfortunately, sometimes customers are within their rights to demand that you hand the case to someone else, mainly because they cannot understand you, because their company policy demands that they only speak with citizens of their country, or with support people located in their country due to security reasons. However, there are also very unfair situations in which the customer simply has a predetermined mind-set that he will not work with outsourced support centers or people with a strong foreign accent.

The previous examples all have the potential to cause emotional stress to colleagues who simply want to do their job to the best of their abilities. We cannot control what the irrational customer will do. However, we can certainly control how it will affect us. To counter the negative behavior from customers, we need to employ behavior and cognitive therapies that are used in the field of psychology for mental patients. We do not have to use them in a clinical fashion, mainly because we are not qualified, but simply use the concept to counter and eradicate the problems that these problematic customer interactions cause on our emotional well-being. In other words, we have to employ ways to prevent mean customers from getting to us and breaking our spirits. Specifically, we want to do this because one bad experience with a customer may cause us to sour the experience for many other customers who had nothing to do with the initial experience.

The coping strategies include the following theories which I have adapted to best fit the context of the technical support professional and the customer he services. I also came up with my own two based on observation, experience and results:

Rational-Emotive Therapy

Developed by clinical psychologist Albert Ellis in the 1950s, is based on Ellis's ABC theory.[10] The A is the event that initiates the situation, such as the customer sending a complaint to your manager. The B is our belief about the event, such as feeling that you are incapable of helping customers due to your lack of experience, strong accent, or some other negative belief about the event. The C is the resulting mental state that you perceive such as anger, frustration, stress, or depression. The theory is based on the premise that it is not A that causes C, but rather B that causes C. In simpler terms, it is not the event itself that causes our emotional detriment, but our belief about the event that causes the emotional detriment. Changing our beliefs about why customers do things will allow us to have different emotional consequences.

Systematic Desensitization Therapy

Developed by psychiatrist Joseph Wolpe, this technique consists of attaining deep muscle relaxation while confronting a graduating series of anxiety-producing situations, which may be real or imagined, until you can remain calm even while faced with the most feared situation.[11] The graduating series of situations refers to gradually increasing the intensity of the situation until you can attain a level that you feel confident and relaxed with the most irrational of customer interactions that used to cause you grief.

---

[10] Albert Ellis, *Overcoming Destructive Beliefs, Feelings and Behaviors* (Amherst, NY: Prometheus Books, 2001) pp 125—133.

[11] Joseph M. Wolpe, *Life Without Fear: Anxiety and Its Cure* (Oakland: New Harbinger, 1988) pp33—52

You would apply this technique by finding a safe place to relax and imagine the experiences that caused anxiety or even fear, get accustomed to the experience in your mind little by little, eventually not fear it, and are capable of remaining calm even when thinking about the feared situation. The ability to face the behaviors that you fear from customers is a challenge, and one that you can try to face alone first with this simple technique.

Cognitive Character Replacement

I developed this technique as a result of some adverse customer interactions that used to cause me and my colleagues stress. The technique consists in replacing the customer with an exaggerated character in order to make it easier to cope with the fastidious or difficult person on the other side of the phone. By mentally replacing the actual person with something that seems unreal, such as a cartoon, movie, or book character, the situation becomes a bit more bearable and keeps you from stressing out over something that is really not that important in the grand scheme of things. The character may also be some other customer whom you perceive as being more likeable or agreeable and, thus, easier to work with. This technique is really more of a flight mechanism that allows you to escape some level of reality and replace it with something more bearable.

Mindful Agreement Technique

I created this one once I realized that disagreeing with customers was a losing battle. The technique rests in the constant agreeing with the customer on any negative comment he has to say about non-technical matters and any criticism of the technology's features or shortcomings. When confronted with an overly critical customer who is more interested in bad-mouthing your product or your company, all you have to do is agree with everything he says to the point that you allow him to voice all his frustrations, real or imaginary, with the technology or your company. All you do is provide verbal cues in agreement such as "yes," "I see your point," "I would feel the same if I were you," or "I completely agree with you," to the point that he has nothing more to say. This technique works wonders as long as the customer does not attack you personally.

Sooner or later you will face unfair and irrational customers who will, at best, drive you nuts and, at worst, cause you emotional stress such as depression, anxiety, and angst. The trick is not to personalize the situation and learn to cope with it instead. The material presented above is by no means exhaustive and all-inclusive. There are many other things you can do and many other situations you will undoubtedly encounter in your technical support experience. Customer service becomes a harder proposition by the types of situations presented above; however, it is not impossible. The only limit is your patience.

> *Years go by and people are together, but there was an individual there for 26 years, or whatever, who was absolutely fine, coping without you.*

—Andrea Corr

Customer Service: The Hierarchical Approach

At this point, you may be wondering what customer service entails. We covered a few topics on the concept of providing added value to a customer interaction. This is our foundation for the definition of customer service. It may sound a bit theoretical, but that is because, just as in everything else, we have to start with some generalities and then apply them to real life. This brings us to the question of how to do this value added idea of customer service in the technical support arena. In addition, we have to define the added value inherent in customer service in a practical way so that we can apply immediately in the general course of our support duties.

Because our field consists of so many professionals across many industries and technologies, it would be quite difficult to cite specific norms that work for everyone. The notion of value added actions will inevitably vary in a software support setting as it does in a hardware support group as well as a legal or financial services support line. Therefore, we have to assume that all support people, regardless of the technology or industry, are after one goal, which is to provide customers with the following:

- At minimum, the level of support they are contractually entitled to

- At least the level of help offered by competitors

- Sufficient support to keep them as happy customers

- All the help necessary to allow them to use our technology successfully

- Genuine professional help without unnecessary niceties or protocols

- Honesty and integrity without putting ourselves at risk

If we start with the above six assumptions, then we can formulate a practical way to address the necessary actions for us to meet the assumptions and much more. The understanding is that the customer is after help to meet a business need, even if we do not agree with the definition of the business need. The focus for us is to make our approach practical, and still provide the customer with the additional benefit without it being a detriment to our company and us. The answer to this requirement is the hierarchical customer service approach.

The hierarchical approach to customer service consists of six steps to ensure proper customer service that meets all the requirements previously set by our definition and our constraints of no added cost to the support organization. We achieve this by doing the following in order from the first to the last without skipping any steps in the hierarchy:

Meet the Customer's Needs

When the customer contacts you for support, get to his real needs immediately and meet those needs. For a customer, a need is not necessarily a solution, but rather something to improve his situation, at least temporarily. Sometimes meeting a customer's need is simply the acceptance that you will work on his support request and will give it enough priority. Other times, the customer's need may be more tangible and may consist in addressing the problem to get the customer out of a bad situation. In the high-tech world, a need may be as serious as helping a customer return to a productive state or as mild as giving him a set of instructions, so that he can go and address the problem on his own. The dilemma with some support behaviors is that we try to address our needs first instead of the customer. This negative behavior may manifest in the form of placing burdens on the customer, such as filling out needless questionnaires or generating logs before attempting to help him.

Address the Customer's Requirements

Every customer who calls into support has some requirements, even if they are not apparent or practical. After all, no one calls into support just to salute us. The requirements are less important to support than the needs that came before. The requirements are those things the customer views as important and necessary to have. The discrepancy comes when support views those same requirements as unnecessary. The typical response could be to simply turn it down negatively, but this mannerism would most likely antagonize the customer. What we need is to make the customer a part of the equation and present our side to the customer from our angle, but without saying anything negative while addressing their requirements. I recently had a situation where a customer wanted to modify our product and to work with a competitor's product. This was a requirement for the customer. I explained to the customer my situation and what it would take for us to fulfill his requirement, which meant giving him a portion of our source code. In other words, I did not say anything negative. I simply addressed his requirement by explaining what it would take for us to fulfill it. He got the idea and backed off.

Accommodate the Customer's Requests

A request from a customer who calls technical support should not be a negative experience for the customer. Requests can either be met or unmet, but not turned down. The support person who provides customer service must accommodate requests from any customer. Of course, accommodating does not mean that the request will always be met. Accommodating refers to the act of accepting and fitting the request into your work day by giving it an honest try, whether it is up to you or up to someone else. The customer who immediately gets his request turned down will feel much more negative toward you than the customer who understands you accommodated his request, gave it a try, and were not able to fulfill the request, even if you would have done little else different. Of course, the idea here is to add value, but value has more forms to the customer than it has to us.

Respect the Customer's Wishes

Not all things are needs, requirements, or requests. Sometimes customers just wish they had something either from the product or from us. When dealing with a support request, customers will usually have a wish that can take the form of a specific way to address their problem to a preference on how they want to be contacted. After all, we deal with human beings, our customers, with peculiar preferences. We are not genies in a bottle so their wishes are not our commands, but when delivering customer service, we also don't want to pop their bubble by neglecting or denying their wishes. Going the extra mile is not as dire as it seems. No one will ask you to walk a mile; it is usually just a few inches that are asked of us. I read an issue once where a customer asked a colleague to please email him the instructions in an attached document, rather than as the body of an email. The colleague denied the request and simply said we had no such document. Amazingly, for that colleague a copy and paste seemed like a mile when it was hardly a few clicks. In the event of fastidious wishes, we should try to respect them as long as they are not going against any internal policies or external laws. The worse that can happen is we give it an honest try and if we fail, we sincerely apologize. Remember, respecting is not the same as fulfilling, and as long as we don't make promises we cannot keep and provide some extra value, we will be doing our part in providing customer service.

Consider the Customer's Suggestions

Any consumer engaged in the use or service of a piece of equipment of technology will form his own set of ideal situations and features that should be present in the product. When a customer comes up with such ideas, he will want to share them with you, the vendor, and support organization, in the form of suggestions and enhancement requests. From the customer perspective, these are honest attempts at improving the product. The fact the customer is going out of his way to provide suggestions to improve the product should be reciprocated with attentive consideration from us, the support professionals. Again, the fact that we consider the suggestions does not put us under any obligation other than just to consider the proposal or suggestion. The value to the customer is the feeling that his feature suggestion will be considered as well as the potential to have the desired feature eventually in the product. After some consideration, if the suggestion proves to be unlikely, or even difficult under the present or foreseeable circumstances, let the customer know nicely with a note of appreciation for his suggestion. Chances are he may submit another idea that may prove to be a nice addition to the product.

Reshape the Customer's Unrealistic Demands

Not all customer suggestions, requests, needs, wishes, or requirements will be considered, met, or addressed. The fact is that some customers will eventually make demands of you that you simply cannot meet or even contemplate. Examples of such demands are free product, extensions to a contract, help during odd hours, demand for work outside of support limits, and anything else that you could not possibly meet as demanded. A lot of it has to do with how it is asked of you. The particular tone of a demand is much different than a suggestion or request. A demand carries an imperative tone in which the customer commands or insists that we meet his request. When such imperatives are simply outside of what we can do or even consider, then they are unrealistic and must be reshaped. Reshaping does not automatically mean negating the possibility of the unrealistic demand, but carries a more diplomatic tone in which you state what you can do and not what you can't do. Reshaping the unrealistic demand means telling the customer what you can do and why you can do it. The aggressive customer will try to push you into a corner until you either agree to his unrealistic demand or get caught in a trap, lie, or contradiction. If you encounter such aggressive tactics, just stick to your reshaping of the demand and only state what you can do and nothing else.

The six hierarchical steps to customer service work for any type of support model and customer service goals. They never negate a customer anything and do not antagonize a customer in any way. The customer service hierarchy is a meaningful approach to handling customer interactions in a proactive manner that adapts the support person's conduct toward the customer depending on the customer's conduct in the situation. In effect, this hierarchy constitutes an adaptive approach to customer service. The trick is never to antagonize the customer or put him on the defensive by our conduct, because we have enough challenges with the technical side of support to add any more grievances with our behaviors. Following the hierarchy from one to six will allow you to put some order to your customer service style and prevent you from handling things too early or too late.

Customer service should not be a mystery to us. It should be a practical approach to helping our customers over what they expect and are entitled to. It doesn't mean that we have to shower them with unnecessary benefits, but that we provide added value where possible and without putting ourselves at risk.

Always render more and better service than is expected of you, no matter what your task may be.

—Og Mandino

The People Business

When we speak about technical support, the first thing that comes to mind to those of us in the field is a colleague sitting in a cubicle speaking with a customer in a very engaged conversation about a technical problem. We think of our jobs as a technical job with the primary subject matter being highly complex products, technologies, processes, or anything else intricate enough to need specialized technical people to answer support questions. That is the reality for most of us. However, looking at our profession a bit more closely, what we really do is deal with people; we receive calls from people, help people, and provide resolutions to people. In a way, we are really in the people business, but with a technical edge.

Looking at our technical support work as primarily one that deals with people allows us to expand the role we play in the professional and technical lives of those we help. It also makes our careers a bit more exciting and sociable, not to mention more successful. Developing the right approach to handling customers and people in general is a skill that few have and yet is very valuable in almost any profession, especially one that deals with customers such as ours.

If you look in your technical support organization and find the colleagues who are most productive and most successful in supporting customers, you will find a common denominator: a genuine passion for dealing with people. I am not basing this statement on any academic research, but on meeting hundreds of colleagues over the years in different companies, products, internal organizations, and groups. I have found that the people who do the best in technical support are not always the most technical or the ones who always have all the answers, but the ones who understand the importance of dealing with people and who truly have a passion for customer interactions.

Every time I meet an above-average colleague either in my group or another group, I always want to know what it is they do to be successful. Not one person yet has told me that they simply know too much or that they bury themselves in the technical aspects of the job. However, every highly successful support person told me that they enjoy speaking with customers, and that they tend to build friendly relationships with those they help. Of course, they are also great researchers, documenters, closers, and logisticians, but the main thing that always comes up is the topic of dealing with people. In my many conversations with successful coworkers, I found they all share the following characteristics when it comes to dealing with customers:

- *Clarity*: They don't talk down to people, nor do they make things sound complicated. These colleagues make themselves understood and are able to distill very complex concepts into a few sentences that anyone with some exposure to the technology can understand. The lesson here is that if you want to be an above average supporter, you must make every effort to speak in a way that your customers can understand and have no doubts about. We have all spoken with the geeky guy at a computer store who leaves us looking at the sky wondering what he just said. This line of work is about effective human interaction when people need us the most. This is not a time to impress anyone into thinking we are smarter or more knowledgeable.

- *Cordiality*: This is not the same thing as friendly. Friendliness is a very subjective term that may be misunderstood by cultures different than your own. I learned the hard way when I had to deal with customers from other continents who found my Texan friendliness a bit too imposing. Cordiality is more professional than simply being friendly. The dictionary defines cordiality as sincere affection and kindness.[12] Cordiality is somewhat like a diplomatic friendliness but not the kind

---

[12] "cordiality." Webster's Revised Unabridged Dictionary. MICRA, Inc. 29 May. 2009. <Dictionary.com http://dictionary.classic.reference.com/browse/cordiality>.

that would make people uncomfortable. The way these colleagues defined what they do can only be described as a very professional approach to being nice to people without resorting to slang, insolence, or crudeness. Customers deserve nice treatment without getting mushy or sentimental. The lack of cordiality is a turnoff that will make customers feel discounted.[13] Expressing cordiality to customers is one of the exemplary behaviors that successful support people have in common.

- *Respect*: We must respect our customers in trouble. When I say respect, I don't mean to simply call your customer "Mr. Doe" or "Mrs. Smith," but to have respect for the fact that he or she is calling you when in reality the customer would probably rather be doing something else. People who ask for help tend to be highly sensitive about how they are treated.[14] Think of the way you feel when you call technical support for any of the products you buy or have to deal with at work. You may feel like you are intruding on their time or like you are asking for a favor when asking for help. In fact, many customers who call into support are just happy to talk with you. In some organizations, customers are bounced around from department to department until they reach the right person. In regard to respect, all the successful colleagues always told me they never lose their respect for the customer, regardless of how irrational or demanding they are. In the case of enterprise or commercial technical support customers, they have a job to do just like we do. Treating them with respect and recognizing that they also have abilities, skills, and technical expertise is paramount to establishing a proper customer relationship with our customers.

The three characteristics above are found in the most successful support people, regardless of technology, product, level, or culture. In the thousands of customers I have supported all over the world, I have found that they all value clarity, cordiality, and respect.

I declare before you all that my whole life, whether it be long or short, shall be devoted to your service and the service of our great imperial family to which we all belong.

—Elizabeth II

Talk Is Not Cheap

As shared by customers, one of the most pressing issues with customer service is the constant repeating of situations, problems, definitions, and explanations to support people. The situation goes like this: A customer calls into the support line and a frontline person answers and immediately asks a barrage of generic questions. When the frontline person has exhausted his resources, he transfers the customer to the next tier who asks more questions, but along the same lines as the initial support colleague. The customer is forced to repeat the situation once more. The customer may be transferred to yet another support person, receive a preliminary answer, told to try it, and to call back if the problem persists.

---

[13] Paul R. Timm, Seven Powers Strategies for Building Customer Loyalty (New York: AMACOM, 2001) pp 31–33.
[14] Roseanna D'Ausilio, *Wake Up Your Call Center 4th Edition* (West Lafayette, IN: Ichor Business Books, 2005) pp 145.

When the answer doesn't work, the customer calls back and repeats the same information over again to a frontline person, then to someone in the next level, and so on until the problem gets resolved.

Naturally, most problems are resolved by support professionals in a timely fashion without overextended effort from customers. Nevertheless, the wasting of time in useless repeating of problems to support people is one of the most mentioned concerns of customers. The more complex the product or technology, the more occurrences there are of this problem.

The reason this problem is of high concern to customers is that any time wasted in repeating information equates to money. The old adage of "time is money" is not far from the truth. In our job, time is the equivalent to money spent by our companies. Our customers are very aware of this reality and this is why they demand resolutions with the least squander of time possible. Since our definition of customer service involves the concept of value delivery to the customer, the taking away of value in the form of time, and thus money, does not fit into our definition.

In understanding the problem, we need to find out why it happens in the first place. We need to analyze the causes and conditions in which the wasteful repetition of problems by the customer to support occurs. The following are the prevalent reasons why the customer has to repeat problems to the support organization.

Inexperience

The experience levels of the support people taking the calls is inversely related to the time a customer has to waste in explaining problems. The less experience the support colleague has in the technology, industry, or product, the more time the customer has to spend explaining problems and situations. Time is only one aspect of the waste. There are other ways that inexperience has a detrimental effect on customer service, such as asking for irrelevant information, generating needless data, such as log files, screenshots, and other proof that may not even be related to the cause of symptoms of the problem. A more experienced colleague can typically figure out causes and potential resolutions by simply listening to the problem description once. In fact, the big difference in troubleshooting between an experienced support person and the inexperienced one is that the experienced person bases new questions on previous customer responses, and only asks what is relevant, whereas the inexperienced colleagues asks what he knows and what he has been told to ask. The newer or inexperienced colleague does not yet know how to formulate coherent technical conversations with the customer, because he has not yet developed the technical maturity. I must also clarify one important caveat which is that experience does not necessarily have to come from only the technical aspects of the job, but also from the support aspects. In other words, the colleague with plenty of support experience is not greatly affected by the lack of specific product or technical knowledge. This is why support skills are just as important as technical skills in our profession. I have seen very good support professionals sound like an expert when answering a call for a product they know little about.

Buying Time

Another time waster for customers is the unprofessional topic of "buying time," which consists of the support person simply asking for things that will throw customers for a loop and are intended to entertain the customer for hours or even days, but are not intended to add any real value to the support problem or to the customer. This is a bad support practice that is prevalent in the support groups that are poorly managed and where support people do not have the resources necessary to do their job. I am not blaming this behavior only on the support people, but on the support culture that allows this behavior to happen. Supporters resort to this tactic of asking for needless information in order to prolong the resolution is because the colleagues do not have anywhere to go for help. This practice is prevalent in support groups in which the tiers are poorly setup and lower tiers are unable to transfer issues to the upper tiers. It also happens where the group lacks collaboration so support people are stuck with issues they cannot add value to. It is unfortunate that this happens, but it is always because of poor structure, processes, or management. This problem has no silver bullet and can only be wholly addressed by management. As an individual support person, you can alleviate this problem by setting up your own support structure by developing your own channels of internal support with other colleagues or people from other tiers or departments such as development, quality assurance, services, and marketing. However, until such practices are not widespread across the entire support organization, the problem will continue.

Inefficient Processes

The third major reason why a support organization asks for customer information repeatedly is because of flawed processes that do not exist for efficiency, but for bureaucratic reasons or simply to maintain the status quo. The type of process I am referring to exists predominantly in the public sector, such as state utility companies and other government agencies. I once had to renew my driver's license and never got it in the mail. I called multiple times and visited the driver's license office, but each time I had to repeat myself in detail and show all my relevant documentation. Finally, one of the ladies I spoke with said all the information about my case was documented in their system, making it apparent that the people I previously spoke with did not follow the proper process to look it up. The organization may have the right structure and experienced people, but without a process that adds efficiency to the individual effort, the support personnel will have to ask customers for the same information more than once. The processes I am referring to includes proper documentation throughout the life of the issue, warm transfers among colleagues with the adequate issue knowledge transfer, and collaboration practices that enable colleagues to share information and work together to resolve customer problems collectively.

The previous three causes are the ones responsible for the great majority of the problems with multiple collection of information by a support organization. I have heard other reasons, including lack of adequate systems, and problems with documentation of highly complex technologies that require every person touching the issue to hear the information from the customer again. These are very weak excuses for wasting customers' time in needless repetition.

As customer service professionals who deliver our value through technical answers, we must ensure that we deliver value as well as minimize or even eliminate the useless repetition of information from customers. Their time, as well as ours, is very valuable and ultimately equates to dollars for our respective employers.

The service we render others is the rent we pay for our room on earth.

—Wilfred Grenfell

CHAPTER 11

■ ■ ■

Communications

Supporting customers requires communication. There is no way around it. Effective communication in technical support is not a luxury, perk, or a pipedream—it is a basic requirement of the job. The better we communicate, the more people we help, and the better the quality of the support we provide. But, there are many sides to this topic.

In this chapter, covering communications in technical support, I included only those concepts that are not self-explanatory, evident, or too simple to merit your time reading them. The topics include how best to transfer information and understand this information from different angles and without making harsh assumptions.

The time and effort you put into learning to communicate effectively is one of the most beneficial investments you will ever make, as communication skills are useful in technical support as well as just about every field where you deal with colleagues, customers, and management.

This chapter explores some of the pressing topics in our field from the point of view of a supporter. . However, communications, unlike technical support, is a field with extensive literature and research, so there is no shortage of very good books and articles on the subject. With that said, what I did in this chapter is take the main challenges that deal specifically with communications in the support group and address them in a practical manner. In the next few pages, you will read the central role that communication has on technical support work. Yet, because communication is such as broad subject, this chapter includes specific and pressing areas of communication, such as periodic meetings, accents, and how to spin negative messages for the benefit of our support organization and the customer.

Communication changes rapidly within technology yet it is not how much technology we can pack in our daily work lives, but how we use technology to our advantage and for a clear business purpose. Support is even more sensitive to the use of technology in communications, because we deal with technology already, our customers use it, and we make a living out of supporting it.

I sincerely hope that while reading it you come up with your own ideas on how to better communicate with your constituents. This chapter is not an all-inclusive guide to support communications, but a spark that will hopefully light a fire in your desire for improvement. All you have to do is fuel the spark with your inspiration.

Ideas are like flowers; they bloom when you least expect them.

—Julio A. Sanchez

At the Core of Our Work

As technical support professionals, we do not sell a physical item and we do not really offer a tangible good. Rather, like plumbers, doctors, mechanics or attorneys, we offer a service. We are in the information business. More specifically, we are in the business of providing information in the form of answers to our customers—the end users who run into problems when using the products and technologies we support. Physical products are delivered, but information is communicated. Therefore, communication is at the core of our work. In technical support, communication is conveying information in the form of answers, processes, and knowledge and the acceptance and understanding of such information by the recipient. It is also about understanding such information using any medium necessary. By this definition, communication only exists when the conveyor and recipient transmit and understand each other; otherwise, it is not communication, but just a conveyance of information.

Suppose you ask your support colleague to call a customer before lunch, because the customer will have serious problems if he does not receive help. You check on the situation a couple of hours later and your colleagues ask in disbelief, "Oh, you wanted me to call the customer today?!" This is not communication because both you and your colleague understood something different from the conversation. Now, suppose your colleague replied with, "I know you wanted me to call before lunch, but I got tied up in something else so I'll call him in a few minutes." In this case, both people were under the same understanding. Whether the action took place or not, in terms of communication, what matters is that information is transmitted and understood. There is no communication without proper understanding. I realize this is not the vernacular use of the word, but communication really is a technical term that we must understand completely, before we set out on an excursion into its theories and practice.

I do not want to assume too much, but also do not intend to get into an explanation of message encoding and decoding, process, transactional theories and all the rest of the technical stuff that you would normally find in a communications textbook.[1] However, because of the nature of our work, communication is an imperative aspect of our profession. There are two major types of communication inside the support organization: organizational communication and personal communication. One occurs at the organizational level and the other between and among individuals. Organizational communication is obvious when you get the company newsletters and other communiqués. It is an important form of getting information across, and that is where we normally get the big picture information about the things happening with our support organization and company. However, I want to focus on the personal communication, because this is where we typically do most of our work. We communicate with colleagues, managers, third parties, and customers about our support work. The value you can provide and receive from each varies, but properly handling and understanding the communication with each will allow you to make the most for your benefit.

Communication for supporters is highly transactional and situational. We have to convey the right information to multiple constituencies and we have to ensure they correctly interpret and understand our message. The effectiveness of our solutions depends on our expertise in communicating those answers to our customers, colleagues, and even managers. However, it is not enough to just convey information. Our communication must also include multiple variables that affect the quality of our answers and information. The dialogue we have with each constituent varies to the intensity or level of the variable. If you have been dealing with customers for a while, you know that no two conversations are identical. With each customer you have to adjust the level of each of the following variables:

- *Tone*: This is simply the comportment, style, or demeanor of your speech. You may have a soft tone in which you sound pleasing to a customer, colleague, or

---

[1] Katherine Miller, Communication Theories: Perspectives, Processes and Concepts (New York: McGraw-Hill, 2005) pp 2–18.

manager. Your tone may also sound a bit unsympathetic, and possibly even harsh. A pleasing tone is something that some people have naturally and others have to develop. The tone in which you approach a customer has a lot to do with how you are perceived. I had colleagues who spoke first languages with more stringent accents, such as Russian, Hebrew, and Arabic that customers sometimes perceived to have a rude tone, despite the colleague having the best intentions; it was simply the accent that made them sound insensitive. Consequently, I also had colleagues with Spanish, French, and Italian accents and their tone seemed more sensitive to customers, regardless of their intentions. Aside from the foreign accents, the tone also has a lot to do with the personality of the individual. Tone due to personality is malleable and you can work on acquiring a more sensitive sounding one.

- *Diction*: According to the Random House online dictionary, diction "usually implies a high level of usage; it refers chiefly to the choice of words, their arrangement, and the force, accuracy, and distinction with which they are used."[2] Diction is really how well you use the language in which you speak. Next to accent, diction is the hardest aspect of a language to master for a non-native speaker. As someone who had to learn English as a kid, I know that diction is much easier to perfect when you have proper training and learn it at a young age. Nevertheless, some non-native English speakers develop perfect diction as adults, so diction is highly dependent on training, education, and practice. Supporting customers requires mastering diction in their language for the communication to reach its most effective level. Diction exists in the spoken word as well as writing.

- *Detail*: In technical support, we have to provide details in the answers we share. Detailed communication requires effort, because it does not come naturally to most people. This is not the same as when someone claims to be "detailed-oriented," but rather being able to articulate, or use diction in a way that conveys a high level of detail. The reason it does not come naturally to us is because we are accustomed to convey information quickly and easily. Getting a message across with a high level of detail requires abandoning the "quickly and easily" aspect of the communication that comes naturally to most of us. The importance in the concept of detail in a message marks the difference between giving an answer and giving an answer plus explaining why and how. To me, this used to seem superfluous, but as I acquired more experience I realize that providing a detailed message meant the elimination of many follow-up questions and increased time to resolution.

- *Timeliness*: The message may be the best in the world, but if it's late it is of less value than one that goes to a customer when the person with the problem needs it the most. For us, as purveyors of solutions, providing timely communication is as important as the solution itself. Customers pay for us to help them when they need it, not when we want to help them. Barriers to providing a timely solution are many, but providing a timely communication does not necessarily mean that you will communicate the answer. It is better to provide an update of what you are doing to find the solution and take a week to find the answer than to leave the customer in the dark for a week. Timeliness of customer contact is one of the most

---

[2] "diction." Dictionary.com Unabridged (v 1.1). Random House, Inc. 04 Jun. 2009. <Dictionary.com `http://dictionary.classic.reference.com/browse/diction`>.

pressing challenges to support organizations. The best timeliness communication approach regarding open support tickets is to maintain contact with the customer, even if you have little in the way of a solution than to tell him nothing and leave him wondering.

Communication represents one of the foundations of technical support. We are in the information business and the only thing you can do with information is communicate it, so that others can use it. How you communicate says a great deal in the quality of support you provide. Two people may have the exact same solution to the exact same problem, but how they communicate it to the customer makes all the difference in the world.

The strong man is the one who is able to intercept at will the communication between the senses and the mind.

—Napoleon Bonaparte

Colleague Communication: It's All About Us

Have you ever noticed how you get along great with some colleagues, but with others you really have to make an extra effort? Perhaps there are coworkers you simply can't get along with and anytime you try to communicate with them, it simply does not go well. Fellow support group members are as diverse as colors in a rainbow; they come in all varieties when it comes to personality types. If you are lucky enough to have something in common, other than work, with a colleague you can develop good rapport and communicate more effectively than with those you share nothing with. Yet even when there is nothing in common with a coworker, you can still establish good communication with the colleague and together become more effective in the work you share. Just like every other human relationship, you have to establish some commonality and since your relationship with the colleague is professional, you have to find things in common that pertain to the work. Sometimes that is all you have.

Establishing mutual rapport in your communication with a colleague with whom otherwise you have nothing else to share is not about topic, but about approach. We have all been brought up to believe that you can only communicate with someone when you share something in common, but that is not always the case. In fact, many of our support group situations are so unique that you may be dealing with colleagues in a completely different country, culture, time zone, and language. How then could you possibly find something in common without first establishing some level of effective communication? You do it by using specific techniques in the approach, not the content of the communication.

A few years ago, I worked in a large global support group and I had colleagues in almost all continents, except Antarctica and Africa. I was looking for a way to effectively communicate with my colleagues in Lebanon. I had previously worked for an Israeli company and thought I knew something about dealing with colleagues in that area of the world. I had a rude awakening when I realized Lebanese and Israelis are very different and the demeanor quite opposing. The only thing I could find in common to start with was the work. Culture, language, interests, and social background were quite different, and having never worked with colleagues in that country I was interested in building the relationship further. Initially, the only thing I found that allowed me to establish effective communication with the Lebanese colleagues was the approach in the work arena. Once I realized the technique worked well with the Middle Eastern colleagues, I tried it with the colleagues from Europe and Asia and it worked wonders. The following are the techniques in detail.

Talk in Terms of "Us"

You must be able to always put everything in terms of the collective, support group, or team using the pronoun "we" and "us." No one likes to be left out of a group, especially if they are in a different country, city, or region. When speaking with a colleague, never use "you," "us vs. you," or "me." In short, you always want to speak in terms that are common to you and the person you are communicating with, hence the emphasis on "us." With colleagues in a region, such as India, China, Eastern Europe, and Latin America, if you are in the home country for the company, it is imperative that you make your colleagues feel like they are part of the global group, and not just an outsourced entity. If you are the support professional in a geographic area that is not the one where the company headquarters resides, you must demand to be included in the group jargon and become part of the "us." The approach with the collective in mind must not be an empty gesture, but a genuine interest in what the colleagues do and how they do it. This is especially true if you are a senior support person trying to reach out to junior colleagues in other parts of the world, regardless of where you are. You may be senior colleagues in India, China, or Europe and the work approach works very well when you approach others as part of the group or team. For some western cultures that are more individualistic in nature, this collective approach may take some getting used to, but in the end the support group is a collective of individuals working to achieve a vision.

Be Genuine in Small Talk

In speaking with your coworkers, regardless of where they may be, small talk is a part of the daily rapport. It is customary to greet people and simply ask how each other are doing and regurgitate the "I'm good" automaton response, regardless of how we really are. If you are going to have small talk, make it meaningful. Small talk is how you learn about others, their daily lives, culture, values, problems, and challenges. Make small talk a way in which you can get others to know you first and then for you to know others. Those colleagues who know me and dealt with me over the years know that I am possibly the most curious person around. I like to know where people are and what goes on in their part of the world. Having colleagues in other countries is one of the greatest benefits in working for a global support organization. It provides a way to "tourist" a foreign way of life from the comfort of your cube. The beauty of small talk is that once you establish a common rapport at a personal level with a colleague, you don't feel him or her as being on the other side of the world, but as someone close to you that you can trust because you know him. In fact, the great thing about meaningful small talk is that sharing something other than just the facts about work with the other person allows both bonding and communicating at a personal level. After all, this is what camaraderie is all about. So, next time someone asks how you are doing, respond with something meaningful, such as "I've had a rough day. I ran over an armadillo this morning." or "I am hungry and can't wait to go have Vietnamese Ph'o for lunch." As you can imagine, those two responses can lead to some great small talk.

Speak a Common Language

The language of business and work are the same everywhere. I don't get the big deal some people make about culture and spoken language differences.[3] Yes, cultural differences exist and we must respect and

---

[3] Sonya Hamlin, *How To Talk So People Listen* (New York: HarperCollins, 2006) pp 40–45. The author talks about 'immigrants' as if they are people from other planets. I understand and realize that there are subtle differences but while at work the culture becomes one; not an ethnic or national culture but a business and work culture which is the same regardless of your background, national origin or even

be sensitive to our colleagues' backgrounds, yet in the technical support group we all have one thing in mind—servicing the customer and handling issues in the best way possible. It has been my observation that when we focus on the things we have in common rather than our differences we can achieve work support group harmony. When you speak the common language of business and support, then everything else becomes a nice addition to the communication. Having worked with many colleagues from other countries in the US and with colleagues based abroad, I can safely say that the common language of work is present everywhere. What I mean by this common baseline in communication is the presence of a common set of interests among all colleagues, regardless of where they are. For instance, we all want to do our jobs to the best of our ability. We all want to succeed in work and life. We all want to progress and have a fulfilling career. We know and understand the concept of being resources to our employers and hired to do a job. This does not mean that we are going to throw out all other cultural subtleties, but they are only an addition to, not a major cause of, our communication in the technical support group. Spoken language is another matter and a huge topic for discussion. However, it is only a tool to communicate, not the basis for communication. The basis for communication must be purpose and for our line of work, supporting customers and all its relevant topics is our purpose. The same goes for communicating with colleagues in the same spoken language and culture. The focus should always be the purpose of our work, and anything that does not revolve around the support of customers should be an addition to the communication but not the communication in itself. A Texan speaking with a New Yorker makes for an interesting soup of accents and mannerisms, just as a Mexican and a Spaniard or an Australian and a British, but in the end, the communication has to take place with the purpose as the only thing that we need to convey and understand.

It is all about us, the collective, when communicating with colleagues. The support group, regardless of other extraneous variables, is a functional conglomeration of individuals that are there to do a job based on a vision. The collective work-based approach allows you to establish a common level of rapport of your global and local colleagues, regardless of any subtleties that may exist.

The art of communication is the language of leadership.

–James Humes

Communication Challenges with Language Accent

Have you ever received a call from a national company, but the person who called you was in a different country? Are you working for a foreign company and have to deal with customers from the company's base global region? Have you ever been told that you are hard to understand or come across a customer who you simply cannot seem to figure out what he is saying? More and more, the topic of outsourcing has come to light in terms of customer satisfaction when it comes to the quality of communication. The typical complaint circles around the outsourced person having poor language skills that make it impossible for the customer to make their request or to receive the appropriate level of help. This does not only happen with support colleagues based in other countries; it also happens with colleagues based in the same country as the customer. The supporter may have a strong accent or a different way of interpreting the words and localisms that customers find frustrating, and eventually cite as an injury to their relationship with the support organization. The other situation arises when the customer is in a

---

geographic location. I realize this is a simplistic view of cultural situations but I view culture as something that enriches our work lives and not something that becomes a detriment to work. I was hoping the author would present the perspective of the non-native speaker but no such luck.

different country and we just cannot make out what he is saying. These are communication challenges that global companies face on a daily basis while even national companies with global customers have to deal with these sorts of support scenarios.

I wanted to find out more about this topic of communication barriers with colleagues for whom English is their second language and whom customers sometimes perceive as hard to understand and difficult to obtain proper service from. I spoke with several colleagues and found several very interesting perceptions on the topic. However, there is one specific situation that gives us the most grief. I include myself in this group since I have a Spanish accent, and have come across customers who claim the accent was a challenge. The most eloquent response to my inquiry came from a dear friend and colleague, Hongxu, a first generation Chinese American who put this topic in the most eloquent manner. He explained to me that a few native English speaking customers have higher expectations of non-native English speaking support people, simply because they have a discernible accent. It is typically the customer who has the predetermined idea that any problem in communication must be a direct result of the supporter's inability to either understand or explain himself fully in English. Of course, this may also happen in any other language, but English is the predominant language of business and technical support is no exception.

The higher expectation by some customers from non-native speaking support professionals add a huge level of frustration to the colleague who is simply trying to provide the best support possible. I had that happen to me a few times. I would receive a call and the customer immediately demanded to know where I was located physically. When I answered, "Texas" they asked to speak with someone else who spoke better English. Never mind that I was the expert who had to answer the question anyway, because the customer demanded to speak with someone they felt more comfortable with. We cannot control what customers think or feel about our accents, but what we can and should strive to do is provide the best technical support possible. If the customer feels more comfortable with a native speaker, and if we can accommodate it, we can try to provide one, or we can offer to communicate via some other way other than phone.

If the preceding situation ever happens to you, do not take it personally. Some people have preconceived notions of who they want to deal with. It is frustrating, but there are plenty of other customers who are simply interested in solving their problem, regardless of your accent. However, the best approach with this type of customer is to have a policy in place that allows the support to occur anyway, despite the customer's preconceptions, use a colleague as an interpreter, or simply hand the issue off to someone that can make the customer happy. We should not question the customer's judgment in the decision to not deal with us. It is not our place nor can we attempt to change anyone's preconceived ideas about who they want to deal with.

The second situation that comes up a lot is the one where the customer is not a native speaker of the language we use to provide the support. As customer-facing processionals, we typically deal with difficult to understand customers with lots of patience. Yet there are some situations in which we just can't keep on asking for the customer to repeat everything twice so that we may understand. In the case of the really hard to understand customer, we should opt for handing the issue off to a colleague that speaks the customer's first language or someone who can at least understand the accent better. The second option is to use another form of communication, such as chat or even email, as long as we can politely explain to the customer that it is more mutually beneficial to communicate more effectively by using a different medium.

I once had a very friendly customer from India. He was a contractor whom the end user hired to administer the firewall in their network. The firewall had a problem and I supported it. However, the problem was that I could only make out about one in three words the customer was saying. It took literally three or four times longer to speak with him than it would have taken had I understood the customer. He was able to understand me fine, but I could not figure out what he said. Since I did not feel polite asking for him to constantly repeat his sentences, I proposed that we try to chat and handle the issue via that medium. We tried it and it worked very effectively. We were able to solve the technical problems, and to this day that customer emails me and keeps in touch at a personal level, despite neither of us supporting that product anymore.

We have multiple medium of communication, so there is no need to prolong a technical support issue resolution simply because we cannot understand a customer. We can also try the same approach with the customer who cannot understand us. Simply offer to use some other medium and handle the issue any way you can. This will happen more and more, especially if you support a product or technology with a global presence.

There are a few challenges to customer communication as it relates to language accents. There are ways to deal with it, and ways to simply let those challenges go so as to concentrate on the next customer who will receive your help regardless of your accentuated speech.

Take advantage of every opportunity to practice your communication skills so that when important occasions arise, you will have the gift, the style, the sharpness, the clarity, and the emotions to affect other people.

—Jim Rohn

Get to the Point: Cutting the Useless Chatter

We work in a profession where time is of the essence. Our customers need answers fast and we need to get them even faster. In such an environment where time really is money, we cannot waste it by adopting useless protocol that only serves to elongate the resolution to a technical support case. Of course, all communication serves the purpose to get a message across. Useless chatter is simply not conducive to anything material, and may even be detrimental to the business.

The chatter I am referring to is anything that does not add either personal or business value to the communication. Specifically, anything that delays the transfer of information. I am not referring to small talk that serves the purpose of getting to know one another or of breaking the ice when there is time to spend doing so, such as while waiting for attendees to show up on a conference call. The protocol that I mean is the subtle, but time-consuming niceties. One prime example is the apparent need to greet on a chat conversation. While doing support, many times we come across a customer situation in which we have to get an answer fast. Just about any support organization has internal chat capabilities. In fact, we had them as early as the mid 1990s with the advent of ICQ and other internal forms of chat. However, there is typically an informal protocol where people have to first greet with a "Hi" or "Hello," and then wait for a similar reply before getting to the point. I realize that civility is necessary and etiquette is always the best practice, but when we need an answer in support, we typically need it immediately. Using up valuable time with useless niceties simply does not result in the most effective communication possible.

Getting to the point fast and in a concise manner gives more time for people to communicate over the problem at hand. This is the type of communication that goes very well with people you deal with on a regular basis, such as coworkers, managers, and even customers. People's time is valuable and the faster we get to the point, the more time they will have free to go and do other things.

The following are the main mediums of communication that we can improve by getting to the point first and then spending time on the details:

- *Instant messaging or chat*: As explained before, the medium is ideal for getting questions and answers or communicating news fast and without much chatter. It can also be used for personal conversations which are another matter altogether. However, when using instant messaging for business reasons, we need to get to the point fast. Typically an initial sentence with the question or problem should be sufficient. For example, "John, can you please tell me the threshold for X log file on a Y system?" or "Boss, I have a Dr Appt tomorrow, can I come in 2 hrs late?" Any of these two scenarios should suffice as an initial instant messaging transfer. Since this is a real-time form of communication, we can get a lot done by using it effectively and by cutting out the chatter.

- *Email:* This medium changed our work lives tremendously. It effectively replaced the old "memo" that had to be delivered physically across departments. In support terms, our attention span is not the greatest as we typically have many things going on at once. Customers calling, colleague collaboration, and issues piling up. We don't have the time to read long emails that do not get to the point in the first sentence or two. Whether writing an email to a single recipient or a group, we must respect their time and also realize that they have many others things to do than spent more than a few seconds reading an email. I don't want to sound preachy but this type of topic is not something that most people have a common set of practices for. Another bad practice is the generation of useless emails, especially to large groups. For instance, a colleague emails ten or more people a solution and one person replies with the word "thanks" and sends the reply to everyone on the initial email. Electronic messages are very cheap, but the accumulation of messages takes time to process and store, not to mention to open and delete. For this reason, we should treat email the same way we treat a paper letter. Choose your words well, but cut out the useless chatter, get to the point in a sentence or two, and don't make them longer than people can read in thirty seconds, unless it is something really important with details that can be referred to later, such as a list of colleagues and their phones numbers or some other non-explanatory message.

- *Conference calls:* Conference calls for a group are a great way to communicate in mass. Especially in global support organizations, the face-to-face meeting in a conference room is no longer possible, unless you travel or use video conferencing because both options carry some expense. For the most part, support people use telephone conference, which is rapidly becoming the virtual meeting room. The ideal and most effective telephone conference is one where there is some order to the meeting and where there is one person to moderate the meeting, thus keeping it from going in the wrong direction. Because people are less prone to shyness and more apt to having their opinions heard over the telephone, the presence of some guidelines ensures that the meeting goes well. One item of importance is limiting the meeting to the matter at hand. This responsibility usually falls on the organizer, or person, who wants the meeting in the first place. No one, unless it's a big boss in which case I don't recommend you make him look silly, should be allowed to rant on and on about useless chatter. Ideas should be conveyed once, repeated once again for clarification, and then discussed, but the useless repetition of the same idea over and over lends itself to an unproductive meeting. The ideal meeting is one where you have a defined agenda to discuss, come into the meeting, express the matter to be discussed, get feedback, come to a decision or fulfill the purpose of the meeting, and end it. With the advent of meeting scheduling tools, it is the norm to schedule conference calls for meeting purposes in thirty minutes or one hour chunks, but it does not mean that you have to go the whole hour in the event that you get the purpose of the meeting adjourned quicker. Cutting out useless chatter and matters not related to the topic help ensure that your meetings are effective.

- *Customer updates*: The customer side of communications is the most complex to master and the most sensitive, since customers can easily complain or ask for support from someone else when they sense that the current support person helping them is not delivering communication value. Considering all the possible situations in customer communication, it is nearly impossible. Therefore, the best we can do is abide by a few general principles. First, customers come to us for answers and useful information. Using useless chatter in issue updates, conversation, or email only adds agony to the customer. This is not to say that we shouldn't engage in small talk, but what it means is, that as customer-facing professionals, we need to keep in mind that the customer needs information, not irrelevant conversation. Second, the patience that customers have towards supporters is not infinite. You have to deliver value in your communications; otherwise, the customer will perceive the interaction as a waste of time. We can greatly cut down on the useless chatter by making sure we provide value in our communication, such as not answering a question with a question and providing relevant details when warranted. Suppose a customer asks how to do X process. The proper response is the inclusion of definite steps on doing X and not a question of why, how, and when he wants to do X. This may seem like common sense, but happens more regularly than necessary. Third, once the resolution, instructions, or answer gets to the customer, resolve the ticket or call with a definite action. Don't drag the support case out. If you allow it to drag on, the customer will think he has free rein to ask multiple questions and keep a permanent support issue open with you. This varies depending on company policy and your support/customer agreements, but for the most part the more issues you can open, process and close, the less useless chatter you will have to convey to a customer and receive from him.

Mastering the art of communication in the technical support environment should be a goal for everyone. This is how we do our work and provide the support to our customers. Both internal and external communication should be professional and concise without the presence of useless chatter. The less of it we use, the more time we will have to get our work done effectively.

The greatest problem in communication is the illusion that it has been accomplished.

—Daniel W. Davenport

Situational Communication

Call me old-fashion or antiquated, but I like to talk. I like to write also, but not as much as I like to discourse with colleagues and customers. In many ways, our profession via the use of technology is trying to get rid of the main form of communication we posses as human beings: language. Many of the technological innovations we gained in the 1990s revolved around doing as little talk as possible while still supporting customers. We started heavily using email, instant messaging, online chat, fax, online ticket updates, and forums. All are excellent forms of communication without a doubt and allow us to do more with less, but we are moving slowly toward technical support without the use of language. The call centers, where many support careers originated in the late 1970s, 80s, and 90s, and where there was nothing but phone conversations with customers, are slowly changing into call centers where chat, email, and forum support is becoming the dominant form of support communication. In many situations, customers now have to pay extra or get into a special support agreement just to speak with a real person. The practice stems from trying to do more with less and the technology adds a higher level of efficiency. I am not blind to technology, I've made a career out of supporting technology, but great technical support requires supporters and customers talking. There is no question that other forms of communication are much more convenient than a phone call, but at what expense?

Convenience has a price and it's not always money, at least not initially. Also, who does the convenience serve? For us in technical support, it is very convenient to sit back and just answer emails, other colleagues, forum questions, and online ticket updates. But, if you analyze the typical electronic only issue, many times it drags longer than if had you just conversed with the customer for a few minutes. There is a reason why humans evolved the use of language—it is highly efficient. Language conveys feeling, information, and most importantly, immediate response. Online chat and instant messaging approximate a phone conversation in that the information exchanges real time, but the added benefit of dialogue and voice inflection, tone, and diction are lost in the electronic conversation.

There are times when an email, a forum posting, and instant messaging are more opportune than a phone conversation, but many situations in technical support require the constant "try this and try that," and benefit much more from a conversation to get to a solution faster. There is no question that electronic communication added a lot of value to our work and allowed us to become more productive. The question becomes when and how to use the communication medium. Like many things in our profession, the answer is situational and depends greatly on the specifics of the problem at hand, the customer, and urgency placed on the support request. Let's start with the ideal way of using each communication medium and compare the pros and cons to verbal communication.

Email

Email is possibly the most widely used electronic form of communication in technical support today. I am sure you use email, so I won't bore you with descriptions and details because you already know them. Handling support via email is great when the expectations from the customer are not huge and support is done on a "best efforts" basis. Many of the consumer products, such as small appliances, applications, and business processes, like banking and account services, are done via email. If the customer doesn't pay for support and you are not required to make absolutely sure the question or problem reaches a satisfactory resolution, then email support is your best bet. The problem with email is that it takes time to write and read. Understanding email is not difficult, unless it enters into highly complex concepts and explanations. If the customer paid a considerable amount of money for the support, and has high expectations for the benefit support can provide, then email is not the best choice. Additionally, for very complex situations in which you need to do troubleshooting, email will just prolong the support case.

Online Chat

Online chat is the closest form of electronic communication to actually speaking with a customer. This is a great solution for support people who have to handle multiple customers simultaneously over not too complex products and processes. It is also great if you don't have to do a lot of troubleshooting with high impact problems. The beauty of it is that you can have prewritten answers or sets of instructions that you can just copy and paste into chat conversations. It allows one supporter to handle three, four, and even more simultaneous support cases. The customer doesn't know he is one of several that are receiving attention from the supporter. Therefore, chat should not adversely affect customer satisfaction from that perspective. The problem with chat is that when it comes to very complex situations where the customer needs the best attention and quick resolution, the value that a chat session can provide is not good enough. I am referring to situations in which a business-critical system, application, or appliance goes down and support is the only option, so a chat session will not suffice. Another situation is when the problem at hand is new and complex, and typing answers is not the best use of resources. You need something faster and only a phone call will suffice.

Online Forums

Online forums are a great way to provide suggestions and options to technical questions. Forums work best when the urgency for an answer is low. Additionally, forums have a huge benefit over other forms of communication in that multiple potential responders can view the posting and provide their input. Many support organizations offer support forums where customers with doubts, questions, and request for opinions can get the added benefit of receiving suggestions, quick answers, opinions, and links without much effort. Obviously, the expectation for information provided via a forum is less stringent than expectations from other one-to-one communication. The advantage for the support person is that forums do not require any specific person to answer, unless one has been assigned, and the answers can be more vague, inquisitive, and suggestive than a phone conversation. Forum answers also allow us to provide links and point customers to other sources, such as past support cases and documentation. Support done via forums is much less appropriate for operations critical technical support. If the customer has time to wait and to try suggestions via a forum, that is fine, but with operations critical support in the enterprise, a forum will just act as a secondary source. For the consumer market, forums are fine if the support is free, but customers who pay for support will probably not view forums as the best option. Forums also complement chat, email, and phone support and are great additions to the repertoire of any support organization.

Phone Support

Phone Support is the way of supporting customers most of us started with and is still the predominant form of technical support available across our profession. It allows for the immediate question and feedback, and for the quickest resolution to support problems. Phone support can be done from anywhere, just like the other forms of support communication, because all it requires is a phone, not a computer. With the advent of VoIP (Voice over IP) a support person can take calls from anywhere there is an internet connection and still be talking to a customer over the same phone support system available at the call center. The biggest advantage to a phone conversation is that it allows us the opportunity to do more than just answer questions real-time. It also allows us to persuade and use our personal skills, such as suggesting using a workaround more diplomatically, explaining in a lot of detail and emotion the resolution, and the closing of an issue. In short, phone support is still the best way to communicate with a customer, but there is one problem with it: it is expensive and time consuming. Support people are not cheap and handling only one customer at a time comes at a price. In a perfect world, every customer support interaction would be done over the phone, but it is very costly. Outsourcing has helped in the cost area, but sometimes at the expense of customer satisfaction. Whether the customer position in making a distinction over local or outsourced support is justified or not is a different story. Phone support is the best option for highly complex operations or business critical products and technologies. There is simply no substitute for a phone call to calm down customers and get their concerns addressed quickly, although remote assistance and system control is quickly making strides in the support arena.

As you can see, there is not a one-solution-fits-all approach when it comes to support communications with customers. The answer depends on the situation, customer expectation, costs and complexity of the product supported. One thing is certain though, misuse of the communication medium has the potential to result in terrible customer experience. Use technology wisely and keep in mind that support has yet to have a silver bullet.

Electric communication will never be a substitute for the face of someone who with their soul encourages another person to be brave and true.

—Charles Dickens

When All Else Fails

Any healthy technical support group should have a periodic meeting, reunion, or informal get-together where junior members of the group ask questions, clear doubts, and otherwise use the senior colleagues as sounding boards to get them on the right technical track to solve a support issue. It is a great practice and one that works in many support groups in all types of support organizations. The only difference is how big, small, formal, informal, and how often the meeting takes place.

There are three major reasons why support meetings occur. The first reason is we need regular meetings every week or every two weeks. No matter how good or experienced you are, there will always be two types of people: those who know more than you and those who can reason better than you. It is inevitable and not a reason for shame. Experience and creativity have huge effects on support expertise, and hardly anyone has a monopoly on both at the same time. Even if you are very experienced and don't need to ask anyone anything, meetings are still a good idea because you get to share what you know and help others in a more junior position.

The second reason why we need meetings is that support work is very individually-based. What I mean by this is that you support a customer by yourself. There is not a whole group of people, at least typically, that supports a customer issue. Support occurs by an individual on a per customer per issue basis. Therefore, we need to utilize all possible resources available to us, including colleagues. Colleagues helping colleagues should be done on an ongoing collaborative basis, but having a meeting allows the sharing of other non-issue related information, such as status of new products, big customer events, most pressing issues, and other related matters. The group meeting is where you learn about things that are occurring with your colleagues, especially if you don't work in the same office as the rest of the group, which is the case in a nationally or globally distributed support group.

In order for group meetings to be an effective medium for the distribution of information and knowledge, the group has to have a collaborative culture already. In other words, the successful team technical meeting is not the cause, but the result of collaboration. If your group is one in which senior people hoard knowledge or junior people don't like to ask, because they are afraid they will be ridiculed or, worse yet, denied any help, then you will have a huge challenge getting a team meeting to be anything more than a waste of time. There is only one salvation for such a predicament. Enter the support leader. As we discussed in Chapter 6, a support leader is someone who influences others to act by example, actions, initiative, or that special touch that can only be described as leadership.

But who can rise to the occasion and initiate an effort, such as a group meeting? The answer is simple: anyone in the group. Ideally, this should come from a need in the group, especially a need from the junior colleagues. A junior colleague can initiate the action and call a meeting, prepare an agenda, and act as a moderator. By the way, these meetings should not be a free-for-all event where everyone talks, answers, and argues. The group technical meeting should be an orderly process managed by a moderator who has a predetermined agenda, schedule, and who facilitates the dialogue. In addition, the moderator also puts a limit on who can speak and for how long. This is to cut down on the arguments, and the complainers, who just seem to go on forever with one mindset.

If the junior supporter does not initiate the action for a group technical meeting, then it should be the senior people who start it. Senior support people are not merely the ones who know more technical stuff, but also the ones who make things happens and can anticipate the needs of the group before anyone else. That is the reason why senior people get the title and, at least in theory, the big bucks. Incidentally, and without pointing any fingers, we should all be aware that if the junior people call for the technical meeting, it is because the senior colleagues are not doing their job. Otherwise, the junior colleagues would not have the need to call such a meeting. Additionally, if there is a need for such a meeting, and the junior and senior people do not initiate it, than management is at fault for not holding the senior people to higher standards. It is not my intention to stir any pots, but these are topics that most people think about privately but are not openly discussed. Also, you should know that when I refer to a colleague as a senior support person, I am referring to someone who formally holds a higher non-managerial position in the support hierarchy and whose job description calls for such initiative.

Let's assume someone initiated the technical meeting to get knowledge, information, and news across to the entire group and that the group is at least on its way to a collaborative group mind-set. The next thing is to make sure there is something to talk about. This is where most similar initiatives fail. The typical experience goes like this: someone comes up with the idea, the group gets all hyped up about it, the first few meetings take place, nothing worthwhile gets communicated, people lose interest, attendance dwindles, and finally the meetings are cancelled. If this sounds like your experience, don't be surprised. It happens a lot more than we'd like to admit. What are we to do? Call the whole thing off before it even starts? You should know that there are many support groups out there with very successful technical meetings on a weekly and bi-weekly basis. However, if all else fails, there is still one option: innovate.

You see, I can describe all of the above because I have lived it in multiple support groups. I also hear from colleagues in other support organizations and they tell me the same thing. It probably happened to you as well at least once. The effort of having a successful support meeting is a tough one and it takes more than just desire. It also takes skill. Anyway, back to the innovation part. When you step up and become the leader in the technical support group, you are expected, and even required at least in your own mind, to do things differently and to develop your own style. I don't have a general recipe other than just come up with an original idea that will make the meeting into something of an event in order to keep others interested and attending. I will tell you of two different things I've done and see if either of them will inspire you to develop your own.

A while back, I joined a global support group in a new technology with several enterprise software products that I had no expertise in. I came into a senior position but only in title. I was still a rookie in the technical aspects of it. The weekly meetings were a disaster and only had a handful of attendees. In fact, they had been cancelled at least once before. I really needed the knowledge and in speaking with the junior people, I found they also needed it, but did not like the way the current meetings were going. It was then that I put into practice the little I learned in a radio production class I took as an elective in college. I thought to myself, "What if I make the meeting into a radio show?" Of course, the challenges were obvious. I did not have a radio frequency, a studio, and it would have been pretty odd for colleagues to use a radio as a listening device. However, I came up with the next best thing, a conference call format in which I could inject sounds, music, and effects from the sound card on my computer. I basically just used the regular headset on the desk phone, but plugged it into my computer's sound card. It was amateurish, but it worked. As far as the content, I devised a one hour show in which I would invite someone of interest to the support group every week and interview them on a topic of high importance to all my support colleagues. I also had mini-trainings, news, issues, and other segments which lasted for no more than ten minutes each, so that the listeners would not be bored. In addition, I used virtual meeting technology to share slides, pictures, and links plus annotations and funny notes while the "show" was going on. I played music intro's, had sound effects, and prerecorded conversation for people who couldn't be interviewed at the time of the show. The production time was short, about an hour or so before show time. The resources were crude and simple, but they had a positive effect and were very different from the norm. People liked it and got value out of the meeting, and that was good enough for me.

On another occasion, I created a small one page newsletter on a weekly basis with short articles on topics from everything from tips and tricks to news and events happening of interest to the group. I also showcased individual colleagues and wrote about their background, activities, and whatever personal facts they cared to share with the rest of the group. This project was easy and did not take a lot of time to produce. The value from it was essential to both technical growth and in team building because every week the entire group learned about someone in the group at a level that they previously did not know because it had not been made public to the group. What made the newsletter so much fun was that I used a pseudonym, Señor BUG, and with a global group of over seventy colleagues, the intrigue and mystery of the whole thing just added to the value.

Communication is not a big deal when you are open to finding ways of making it work. The challenges to communication are not in technology or process, but rather in human disposition. Those who want to get information across and disseminate knowledge to other colleagues will find a way. If all else fails, find an innovative way of making it happen and you will, at the very minimum, get people to start talking.

To succeed, you will soon learn, as I did, the importance of a solid foundation in the basics of education—literacy, both verbal and numerical, and communication skills.

—Alan Greenspan

Spinning the No

Have you ever called into a customer-facing organization for a question, doubt, or problem only to be told that you are pretty much out of luck? Have you ever had to tell a customer that what he is asking for can't be done or that you cannot help him any further because his item is out of warranty, he misused it, or his support contract is up? Giving a customer bad news is a very uncomfortable thing to do. We do it all the time, but usually without viewing the situation from the customer's side. This is where communication is an art, in addition to being a systematic way of getting information across to someone who understands it.

No equates to rejection. No one likes to be rejected and customers are not the exception. Hearing the word "no" from someone who is supposed to support you and provide help is not what people expect to hear. No also makes an impact on people. Once they get one rejection, they will not ask anything again. We support customers and build relationships with the regular callers. However, even with the customers who only call us from time to time, it is rather difficult to reject their requests for help, support, or product features. I am sure you are wondering what we are supposed to tell customers when they ask for something that we cannot give them. The answer is very simple; you have to spin the no.

Before you go and think this is a trick to play on customers or some type of face-saving technique, I assure you that there is a way to derive value from spinning a no and it doesn't involve useless techniques at all as the literary world is full of them already.[4] This is also not about saying no in a polite

---

[4] Patti Breitman and Connie Hatch, *How to Say No Without Feeling Guilty* (New York: Broadway, 2001) pp 35–52. The authors make a point of using downright trickery for turning down work, requests and opportunities. This may work in other professions but I am afraid that support is not the profession where this type of advice will be successful.

way or trying to be nice to a customer by using a synonym for no. Life is too short and our support work too important for gimmicks.

Support is a profession that adds value and we as practitioners need to add value to the customers who call us for help. It sounds simple, but it is a very powerful guiding principle. If your intent is to add value to a customer query, then why would you ever say no? The fact is you wouldn't. I learned this the hard way early in my support career when I got a job at a small software reseller and for the first week on the job I got to sit with the person I was replacing and listen to her calls. She got a call from a customer and he asked if the product had a feature he needed. She said no. He then asked if she knew if it was going to be included in the future. She said no. Next, he asked if she knew of a workaround or second option to get the same functionality with that feature. She said no. Without losing his temper, he asked if she knew of any options or alternatives that could help him. She said no. In my mind, I thought she was being truthful and did not want to beat around the bush. I also thought she was being very professional by telling the customer what he wanted to do was impossible. Finally, he asked her if she thought that he should renew his support contract when every question he asked was answered with a 'no'. . To my amazement, she said no. It was on that last question that I realized the grave error we make when we say no to a customer. I was young and early in my support career, but I got the point that the customer made. We need to add value to our customer interactions, and that value involves spinning the no.

The trick is how to do it in a way that adds value and not simply to be diplomatic, nice or just to try and avoid a confrontation. Here's how you do it:

- *Tell the customer what you can do for him*: Chances are a customer asks a direct question because that is all he knows. For instance, when a customer wants to know if your product is capable of doing a specific function, and if you know for a fact that it doesn't do it, you have to anticipate and provide a way in which you can get him to do the same thing or similar functionality but with a different feature or with a workaround. Saying no is the easiest way, but certainly not the one that adds value. An example question from a customer would be, "Does product A do X feature?" Your answer should be "That functionality in Product A is handled in product B with Y feature and both Product A and Product B integrate." Of course, you have to know your stuff as this is not something you can fake. If you have to fake it, you are better off just saying no and not digging yourself in deeper. Another example is, "Will you support feature A in release X?" Your answer should be "Feature A is supported in release Y. I can show you how to upgrade to release Y so that you can take advantage of the feature." As you can see, the approach is not to say no, but to add value to the conversation and take the no as a possibility for adding your value to the situation.

- *Understand the situation and provide a better way*: The customer who calls support for a question does it because he needs something. There is a whole context that is often lost in the conversation. When we answer the phone, the customer gets to the point and asks his question, but by the time he got around to calling you, he probably spent many hours trying to find the solution on his own. It is also safe to think that even before that, the problem took a while to come up or the customer's operations functioned properly before it got to the point where the support call was necessary. This is the reason why you have to take time to understand the situation. As a support person for the product, you are the expert. If you do not know, no one will, at least in the eyes of the customer. Before just saying no, dig a little deeper and see if there is another way to go about getting the problem solved. An example would go like this: the customer calls and says, "Is there a way to generate report A using X data?" Your answer should go like this, "There may be, but I need to understand the situation better to see if there is a better way because perhaps we can generate report B using X data rather than report A and still get to the same functionality."

- *Give the customer some hope:* I don't mean false hope, but genuine hope that what he is asking for may be possible in the future. Any successful consumer product should be based on the needs, wants, and desires of customers. Whether it is functional or cosmetic, customers drive product innovation and it is up to us in support to do our part. Customers calling in regularly to ask for a feature which doesn't exist is a big red flag that the product needs to have that feature. Chances are that if you do not provide it, your competitors will. The opportunity for a product enhancement should replace the potential no in a support interaction. A support customer calls with the following question, "Does product A have feature X? I need such a feature to do work Y." If you know that such a feature doesn't exist, and there is no workaround or other way to give the customer the functionality, then you can say the following, "Feature X sounds like a great idea for product A and it is currently lacking that feature. However, I can present the idea on your behalf to the development group to consider it as a feature in a future release. Would it be okay for me to do that?" What do you think the customer would say? He has no choice but got more value out of it than just a no. Your product may also end up benefiting from the interaction.

As you probably guessed, spinning of no is not for the customer. Spinning of no is for you. You are the one that has to spin the no and you are the one that has to add the value. The customer is just the recipient of the value. There is no need for gimmicks or useless niceties. Support work involves adding value to customers while it is up to you to add the pride.

The two words "information" and "communication" are often used interchangeably, but they signify quite different things. Information is giving out; communication is getting through.

—Sydney J. Harris

CHAPTER 12

■ ■ ■

Perspectives

You made it to the last chapter; we both have. In this chapter, I will explain the things that seem the most probable to happen to technical support and the way we do the work. These are not predictions or simple wishful thinking. These are truly the changes that will impact the work in the future.

Throughout, you will encounter different topics that you may agree with while others you may completely be at odds with and see no possibility for. Whatever the case, these are my perspectives from observation and experience. One thing is certain, our profession will change and us along with it because we are in a field that does not remain stagnant. Technology holds promise for humanity and we wouldn't be humans without some form of technology. It also holds challenges and problems, which we should thankful for, because those challenges and problems provide us with a living. What the future will bring, no one knows exactly, but it promises to be an exciting one for technical support and whatever offshoots grow from it.

This last chapter is neither a conclusion nor a summary of the last eleven. Instead, it introduces you to different views about the most pressing issues facing technical support today, and those as we will meet as we move further into the new millennium, which look quite positive for those who make a living out of technology. The topics in this chapter include ideas about the future of technical support, the multifaceted view of the support professional, the preventive support model, a different way to look at training new support people, removing the customer from the support interaction, and how to go the extra mile when doing support work.

Again, although these are my perspectives I will not just give you opinions, disparaged ideas, or make wild predictions about what's to come. I will provide an insider's view, colleague to colleague, of what could bring us the brightest future. I am convinced that progress is in the air and that we will produce the next big thing in the professional world. When I look back to the early 1990s when I started in this line of work, I am amazed at how much our profession has progressed. The next decade will certainly bring much more of this progress. New advancements in the technical support world are coming and we will be making all this progress happen.

For now, go and make your mark. Take whatever things you agree with and leave the rest. If any of these pages you've just read inspire you to make even a miniscule change, I will have fulfilled my purpose.

> *The past is a source of knowledge, and the future is a source of hope. Love of the past implies faith in the future.*
>
> —Stephen Ambrose

What the Future Holds

The technical support profession has only been around since the late 1970s as a formal profession and with the name we currently know. It started out as a business necessity. Technology consumers needed a way to get their questions answered and problems solved. Initially, it was the developers, installers, and other administrative technical personnel that took care of the questions from the users of the technology. However, as more and more users originated questions, the need for a devoted supporter became apparent, so the technology vendors hired specialized individuals to do nothing but answer questions.

Technical support as a function originated much earlier than the 1970s as any technology from the wheel to the cotton gin needed technical questions answered. The only reason why a formal support position was not adopted earlier is due to the complexity of the product for a user to repair, and the business reasons for providing customers with the ease of getting the help they needed. In fact, early technical support professionals were known as mechanics, carpenters, machinists, and any other names given to the specialized individuals who serviced the technology products. Yet, it was not until the technology was made complex enough that it warranted a helpdesk that provided functional as well as breakdown help. Mechanical, electrical, and chemical technologies did not need a support person for functional questions; they only needed a support person for repairs and installations, otherwise the user could figure it out on their own. However, the repairs had to be done on-site and the support questions were simply known as service calls.

Our profession developed out of a business need, and unlike others we did not go through the experimentation, artistic, or philosophical phase. We went straight for demand to supply, but did not have the time to develop much else before the practice. Perhaps it's best since we did not have to go through any revolutions, movements, or anything of that sort. There was a need and we filled it, as simple as that.

Now that we have some nebulous idea of how the profession came about, the question is where is our profession going? Consumers will need technical support more and more to help them keep up with technology that keeps changing at a faster rate.[1] This is a fact of the industry. When technology increases in complexity, so does the learning curve to master the intricacies of the technology product. Remember the electronic watches of the late 1970s? They were quite simple and only required a battery and two buttons to change the time. That was all the complexity presented to the user. Over the years, electronic watches became as complex as mini-calculators, and now watches can even take your blood pressure while telling you the time in five different countries. Owner's Manuals to operate technology devices become bigger and bigger to the point that they won't even ship on paper and are only available for download in electronic format. For a user, it is much easier and makes more business sense to pay for a support contract than to spend a considerable amount of time reading the manual.

Technical support is here to stay and it will only grow in popularity and stature. However, the future is not entirely clear to most outsiders as even books that are supposed to foretell the future of technology jobs view technical support as nothing more than PC Support and Helpdesk Call Center jobs.[2] Those of us in the profession know firsthand the increasing complexity of our products and technologies, and the ever increasing demands on those supporting them. Our companies are putting out new products faster but more competition comes into the market every day. Opportunities in technology abound as the dotcom bust left many seeds of innovation and entrepreneurship that keep on blooming as we move farther into the twenty first century. Opportunity for growth is everywhere as almost any business, nonprofit, and government agency depends heavily on automation based mostly on technology that requires experts to support it.

---

[1] Eric Viardot, *Introduction to Information Based High Tech Services* (Boston: Artech House, 1999) Pp 172
[2] *Information Technology Jobs in America* (New York: Info Tech, 2007) pp 138

The support professional in the enterprise will not just be a PC Support or Helpdesk worker but a well-prepared, specialized expert who will need to master the technology, customer service, and the business aspects of the technology he supports. It will not be sufficient to simply be a technology geek with certifications galore anymore with only technical or functional knowledge. As technology becomes more embedded in business processes, the support professional will have to be an expert in the business of the customer to be able to understand how and why the technology is used by the customer. Demand for this type of professional looks very bright as the skills required to do this level of support will command more preparation, education, experience and, as supply and demand forces do their magic, a higher salary as well.

On the consumer side, the support professional with only technical knowledge will be on the decline. Consumer products such as computers, printers, cell phones, and anything else that you can buy at a computer or high tech store will continue to be mass produced and the manufacturers' profit margins shrink because of competition. Additionally, because of the need to make technology products more and more user friendly, the complexity presented to users of the gadgets of the future will be minimal. All you have to do is look at how simple computers, cell phones, and high tech appliances are to operate while providing an ever increasing number of features and functionality. According to Noel Bruton, the technical guru is on the decline and will have to develop other skills or move into the business side of the field to survive.[3] The supporter for consumer technology products will morph into something more development-like in the future as users require less knowledge to operate the products. The reason is that the complexity will be kept under the covers and the consumer user interface will become foolproof.

Just as the modern dentist started out as a barber doing tooth extractions in addition to shaving patrons,[4] so will the technologist turned supporter evolve into a more specialized professional with an array of technical, business, and service skills to solve customer problems with a direct impact on the operational side. We are slowly moving to that front on the enterprise or commercial side of the field. The consumer side will decline considerably. Just remember how often you used to call for support on your dot matrix printer and compare that to the support you require from your multifunction device. One thing is certain, as practitioners we will need to keep up and continue to improve our professional view of the world to succeed into the next decade.

The future hasn't happened yet and the past is gone. So I think the only moment we have is right here and now, and I try to make the best of those moments, the moments that I'm in.

—Annie Lennox

The Renaissance Professional

In the modern world of business, knowledge and innovation are more important as capital. The markets reward the best ideas and the companies with the most expertise. Only those technology players with the innovation and knowledge to make it work for consumers will survive in a future where the world effectively becomes smaller due to globalization. Companies that want to win in the next few decades will have to come up with the best solutions for the consumers both private and public to achieve efficiencies and help them win as well. Technology is here to stay and the more complex it becomes, the more support they will require. However, the support will look a bit different than it does today. In the

---

[3] Noel Bruton, *How To Manage the IT Helpdesk* (Oxford: Butterworth Heinemann, 2002) pp 288–289
[4] James Wynbrandt, *The Excruciating History of Dentistry* (New York: St Martin's Press: 1998) pp 27–38

next ten years or so, the supporter will also include functional knowledge about the business. It is happening to some extent today, but in the future support work will necessitate the inclusion of the functional expertise in the area the technology services. For instance, medical software will require the supporters to be very knowledgeable in the medical field, so that they can understand the user and the business situations under which the technology functions. Energy management software will require support professional who know a lot about the energy industry and the way that business functions. And so will be with any other technology's support groups. They will be made up of people with the technical expertise as well as the functional expertise on the business area of the customer base. Why will this be a requirement? Isn't technical expertise enough?

Current support consumers demand technical knowledge and customer service. As explained in chapter 10, customer service is value added during the support interaction. However, because of more competition and ever more demanding customers, the technology vendors of tomorrow will have to compete on something other than products and features; they will have to offer a better user experience, which includes better technical support. If you think about it, the typical technology consumer in charge of a technology product deals more with technical support than with anyone else from the vendor. Look at your own situation: As a support professional dealing with consumers every day, do you think that for any of your customers there is anyone from your company who deals more with them than you? Salespeople call on them on a regular basis but they typically don't deal with the actual user who calls you for support. Even in the consumer market, the person who calls you for support on their Blue Ray DVD player or the Anti-Virus software application probably spends more time with you than they did with the salesperson who sold them the product. In a near perfect market, how do vendors compete? They compete with service and technical support will be a bigger part of that service in the future.

Unlike today, where support people go into the field they support, initially the new supporters will do the opposite. Instead of using support as a stepping stone, they will use their field practical experience as a stepping stone to support. Sounds unfamiliar doesn't it? But why will supporters have to do this transition from being a user to being a supporter? Because the market will require it. In other words, employers or support organizations will prefer people with experience in the field sometimes overlooking actual support skills. This will be a short term error but one that will be corrected. Allow me to explain. One of the major problems with support groups today is that they are made up of support individuals who don't have experience in the field they are supporting. For instance, people who support X-Ray machines have probably never worked as an X-Ray technician or people who support accounting software are probably not accountants themselves. Currently, that is not such a big problem, or so we think. The challenges with people who don't have experience in the field they are supporting are that they take longer to train and do not fully understand the customer's situation. They often take longer to solve a problem than someone of comparable skills but with the field experience. However, the biggest reason why technology companies will be forced to look for people from the field to serve as support is because they can identify with customers more so than someone without the field experience. But there will be one problem, the shortage of field-experienced individuals.

Let's face it, good people don't grow on trees. It is very hard to find an exceptionally good support person, even among career supporters. If it's so hard now, there is no reason why it will be easier in the future. Some technology vendors will make the mistake of hiring people for their field expertise thinking they will be able to pick up support skills, but the result will be a very poor supporter with field experience. In fact, there is some of that going on now. In effect, what is going to happen is that the supporters of tomorrow will be going to work in the field as part of their training understanding the needs, challenges, and situations of the end users. Only this way will they be able to connect when they are dealing on a support issue. While this type of training will be more costly, it will yield much more benefit in return than the traditional classroom or on-the-job training many of us are accustomed to. In turn, this improvement in training will result in more productive supporters making the support organization smaller by having more experienced and productive workers.

The supporter of the near future will be a specialist in several areas. He will be a good troubleshooter, an experienced field person, and a customer service expert. The job will demand a higher level of understanding of the technology he supports. It will not be enough to simply learn the product well enough to answer questions; he will also have to understand and try to fix the use of the technology in business operations. For this to happen, many things will need to change, including the marketing and view of the support organization by technology companies. Nevertheless, one thing is certain, the future supporter will be a renaissance professional who can do several things well and excels at more than just the technology aspects of the job.

> *The cost of adding a feature isn't just the time it takes to code it. The cost also includes the addition of an obstacle to future expansion.... The trick is to pick the features that don't fight each other.*

—John Carmack

The Preventive Support Model

Up until now, the role of the technical support professional has been to solve problems when they arise and answer questions when asked. Enterprise and commercial customers enter into support contracts to make sure they get help when the need arises, and they are sure it will arise; otherwise, they wouldn't pay for support. However, the problem with the support role as it currently exists is that it's reactive in nature. It only helps shorten the downtime that customers go through when their technology product goes kaput. As technology becomes an integral part of business operations and decisions, the need for technology that stays up will be a necessity, not a luxury. Of course, as any supporter knows quite well, as soon as you start operating the technology product, it will break. Something will go wrong or some question may arise that was unforeseen. Even if nothing goes very wrong, the customer will find that he has a need for some feature that the product simply doesn't have and which the customer will claim is costing him millions, as the argument usually goes.

Up to now, customers settle for having their problems fixed in a reasonable time frame. Downtime costs them money and they make it known via escalations, complaints, and the typical threat to cancel or switch vendors. However, what we need is a new model for support. One that doesn't simply react to problems, but that actually foresees problems before they occur. We can call this model the preventive support model. It consists of the support person preventing problems, not before they happen, but before they cost the customer money in downtime, lost productivity, and delay in use. Yet, support alone cannot do preventive maintenance. It requires a radical shift in the product design, because it needs to have mechanisms that trigger alerts when the variables that are known to cause a problem are present. I am not necessarily referring to a set of intelligent features that automatically alert the vendor of problems. Such features already exist in many technologies. The preventive features need to foresee problems occurring that have the potential to impact productivity and operations. This is a value that development and engineering departments must add to the technology products.

In addition to having triggers that let us know about the upcoming problems that will adversely affect the customer, we need to have a way to repair the problem without having to involve a customer interaction. In other words, we need to get on the product remotely, fix the variables so that the problem doesn't manifest itself, check to make sure nothing got modified, and get out. Such a support service is beyond what most support organizations currently offer and has the potential to prevent many support issues. An analogy would be the preventive maintenance done on your vehicle. You do the oil and fluid changes, check the belts and compression, change spark plugs, and eventually the car will give you years of service all because you, in fact, performed preventive support, also known as preventive maintenance. Why do we do preventive maintenance on our cars? We do it because the opportunity cost of having our motor blow out is much greater than the preventive maintenance. Just imagine walking to work and the cost of a new motor, and you understand that a ritual oil change is imperative. The products we support should be no different. Some products currently have such feature, like mainframes and certain medical devices, but for the most part this is still a very specialized and pioneering area of technology.

Preventive support has several major implications on our current paradigm. The first one is the low need for customer interaction other than to explain what we did and why we did it. The preventive supporter will not have to be a master of the skills that the current supporter has to learn and use on a daily basis. There will not be a huge need to perform the typical soft skills and perhaps even to speak the same language as the customer. The preventive supporter will be mainly an outsourced or contracted individual who has a very definite job to do in order to prevent customer problems. The outsourced preventive supporter will work during the time that the customer is not working so the time zone differences will aid the effectiveness of the preventive support model.

The second change from the way we currently do support is in the need to be part of a group. The preventive supporter will be hired and trained to specifically service a select number of customers. The need to be part of a support group no longer will be part of the culture. The preventive supporter may never even work in an office, but rather work from home or telecommute. Many support people do that now in reactive support yet are still part of a support group. However, the preventive support model may not need a formal structure because it's all done before the problem even happens.

Probably the biggest difference between the way we support now and the preventive supporter is the need to troubleshoot problems. We do it because we get the problems after they occur. However, the preventive supporter doesn't need to troubleshoot because the product will be smart enough to know what the problem will be and how to fix it. The preventive supporter will have fewer troubleshooting skills and therefore be much easier to train and make productive. The skill so valued in the preventive supporter will be in knowing the customers' setups so well that he can take the preventive measures without affecting the system or causing any other problems.

One huge problem with the future of the preventive supporter model is that it leaves a lot of room for the preventive support to be replaced by technology, rather than a human being. In other words, the technology will eventually be perfected to a point that it can fix itself. Some vendors claim some form of the technology already, but it is far from perfected. The preventive support model will eventually be done by the technology itself. However, since it is technology nonetheless, it will still need someone to support it.

For ultimately, the only way to win wars, is to prevent them occurring in the first place.

—Owen Arthur

No More Training Down the Drain

How many times have you heard support people say they can't do something because they haven't been trained? How many times have you said such a phrase? It is true that people can't do something they don't know how to do. However, it is also true that training people is an investment that sometimes doesn't pay the dividends it should, yet it is necessary to train people to get the best results. Getting new technology employees ready to produce via on-the-job training is actually counterproductive in the short run and potentially even detrimental to the rest of the technical group.[5] Despite all the energy devoted to training and the growing industry that services the needs for educating technical people, the truth is that support organizations don't always get value out of their training dollars. People are sent to

---

[5] Frederick P. Brooks Jr. *The Mythical Man-Month* (New York: Addison-Wesley, 1995) pp 13–21

248

training seminars, courses and technical boot camps only to come back, work for a few months, and leave for better job offers. This is especially true for outsourced support personnel in areas of the world where there is a high demand for technology workers. It is not as bad as it used to be a few years back in the outsourcing boom of India and some other rising countries, such as Ireland, the Czech Republic, and New Zealand to name a few. However, the cycle of hiring, training, and losing workers cannot continue and still keep an outsource outfit cost effective. Something eventually has to give and the easiest thing to cut is the training, which is one of the biggest initial expenses when preparing a new person to support a product. How is the new supporter going to be ready to work if the support organization does not give him any training? The answer is simple: hire him already trained.

Here is the most likely solution. The potential supporter, whether he is a national employee or outsourced individual, needs to come into the support organization ready to work. He will be trained, just not by the support organization. He will be trained before applying for the job or after receiving the job offer, but will share in the risk of training. Here is how the plan will likely have the most success. The support recruiter will look for candidates with a high potential of success and with some previous support experience. The individual will be told exactly the training requirements and where to get the training. The actual education will be provided by a third party educational company who will be willing to finance the training for the newly hired employee. The new support employee will not be paid by the employer while the training is in effect, but will guarantee a job once the training is finished. Once the employee completes a specific period of time on the job, like a year or two, he will be reimbursed for the cost of the training. The employee will pay back the training entity and keep anything left over. This is a mutually beneficial arrangement for all parties involved. The employee gets the job and received reimbursement after he works and fulfills an agreed upon commitment time. He gets the benefit of being able to choose the best possible training without having to deal with the distractions of being in a new company. The training company sells their training and makes some money in the way of interest. The training fees may also be financed by a third-party financing company or bank that makes interest on the transaction. The support organization gets a fully trained individual ready to produce and with no upfront investment at risk. In order for this arrangement to work, the support industry has to adopt the practice starting with the very best support organizations and technology companies to work for.

Another possibility that could work well in the support field is the ability to provide the potential employee with all the training materials, train on his own time, and then hire him once he is ready to start producing. On face value it would seem like a huge burden on the potential employee because he has to invest time and effort into learning the technology before he even gets the job. However, if you have worked in multiple support organizations, undoubtedly you have come across at least one support job where the technology turned out to be very different than what you were led to believe during the job interview process. Imagine if you actually had a chance to try the technology before you decided to take the job. It might seem like a very odd idea, but it would revolutionize the hiring process and the ability for support professionals to get new jobs. Obviously, it would not work so well for the unemployed supporter, because his immediate needs wouldn't be met by learning first and then getting the job. However, there are ways around that problem as well. The support organization could find short-term loans that would allow the future employee to live on while doing the training. Once he finished and started working, he would repay the loan. This would work wonders for the supporters already employed, because it would give them the ability to try other technologies on their free time and if impressed, they could just change jobs. It would not hurt the current employer so much, because there was no initial investment in training and there would ideally be other new potential employees to fill the position. The support organization or technology company would also benefit greatly because there would be little to no upfront training costs associated with new support personnel. The organization could refresh the support employees often, but focus efforts on retaining those who hold the most potential to become the senior supporters in the technology. It would also diminish the work involved in prospecting and interviewing new employees who may turn out to be less than stellar. The only possible disadvantage to the support professional is the potential for support organizations to be more prone to laying off people due to the low costs of hiring new ones. However, it would also ensure that only the best support people are retained.

Training new support employees is a huge investment that is often lost when new employees leave quickly or simply don't work out and fail to live up to the expectations of the support organization. The ideal situation is one where everyone involved wins and has the least possible risk of losing time, effort, and money. Hiring people who are already familiar and trained in the technology and who come into the job ready to produce is the best option for the challenges that technology companies face when hiring new support personnel.

Luck is when preparation meets opportunity.

—Neil Peart

The Support Contractor

Wouldn't it be awesome if we could work from anywhere, work for whomever we want, and choose our own terms? Contractors do it all the time; the only problem is that there aren't many contracting opportunities for support people, at least not yet. The fact is that the very best support people usually want challenges, and the continuous support of the same product over a few years, or even months, may prove to be monotonous. The ideal situation would be for well-rounded support people to obtain short-term assignments from technology companies who simply need capable supporters to provide their service when there is a higher demand, and when the support organization lacks some specialized hard-to-find skills that a support contractor possesses. There are already contractors who provide customer support services, such as account management and complaint processing for banks, companies, and even support organizations, but that has not yet spread to support personnel on a large scale.

The benefits to the support contractor and to the technology company are mutual. For one, the technology company would not need to employ and internally train highly specialized support people, pay them regular salaries, and risk losing them to competing companies. I am not referring to the general support personnel for the support organization that always needs to have a fully staffed support group. What I am referring to is the need for the support organization to have the flexibility to add to its staff numbers in times of high need and to decrease them in times of lower demand, but without having to lay off people or have to pay salaries and not utilize supporters fully. Additionally, the support organization could pay only for the actual issues taken and resolved by the contractor, and would not need to invest in training and other staffing related costs, like benefits and taxes.

The support contractor would benefit by having the flexibility to work on his own terms. One of the most depressing topics for some supporters is working in an office or support center all day long. Some support employees have the option of telecommuting, but this is still not the norm. Being able to work only when you need to and to set your own location carries a lot of value for some. This is what contracting your supporting services can do for you. For the support work that must be done on-site, this model of contracting a supporter has added benefits in that the support organization would not need to keep a fleet of vehicles, pay for travel arrangement, and have to expense food and other personal necessities. The contractor will simply be paid a fee for his services and he would be responsible for all his own expenses. While this idea may be perfect for some colleagues; others need and require the security that comes in being employed by a support organization. There is absolutely nothing wrong with this and every supporter will have to choose the work option that is in his best interests.

The customer will benefit in several ways, but mainly in that the support contractor will cover the deficiencies of the regular support staff, which may be overworked or short on help because of the periodic and seasonal surges in demand for technical support. In other words, when calls and requests go up dramatically, the support organization may not be able to service all the customers in the most expeditious manner. The result is the detriment to the customer by having support tickets linger longer. By having support contractors, the customers' demands are always met regardless of how high the demand goes for the support services. The support organization simply contracts as many supporters as are needed.

The challenges to this idea include the training and mastering of the idiosyncrasies particular to the technology or industry. However, as mentioned at the beginning of this discussion, the support contractor would only be the type of supporter who is an exceptionally quick learner and who is adequately capable of training on his own time and learn by doing. It also means that there will be a readily available body of knowledge at the disposal of the contractor.

The other major challenge is the ability to master all the peculiarities of the technology and the technical support group already in place. Because the support group resides inside the company, the members already know how to navigate the organization to look for their own answers. The support contractor would not have that luxury, unless he is a previous member of the technical support group. In that scenario, the support organization would already be familiar grounds for the support contractor.

This model of support services should work in most technology areas that require professionals to answer questions and solve problems. However, it should work especially well in those areas where the technology is more generalized, such as known appliances, common machines, software operating systems, and industry norms that would allow a support contractor the ability to obtain the experience and training somewhere else other than the actual technology company. It would not work as well in areas of highly specialized products or closely held technologies for which experience is hard to obtain while outside the support organization.

The ideal candidate for the support contractor is the current supporter who has a need to add more flexibility to his work life and needs to be free of the requirements of the job; ideally, someone who retires early and needs to work part time and at his own pace. Stay-at-home parents and full-time students will also be candidates for support contractors. However, there is a possibility that under the right circumstances—financial and occupational—anyone with the need for more work and life balance would be a good candidate for this type of support work mode. It is all a matter of being able to do the work and deliver value to the customer who, in this case, would not be the end user but the actual technology company doing the contracting.

Just like other professions, technical support will benefit from the ability to provide some of its practitioners more work flexibility by using support contracting rather than the typical support job. It provides benefits to all parties involved including the customer, the technology company, and the support contractor. There will be challenges and the concept is not for everyone, but for those who decide to go this route, the benefits will be immense.

All sensible people are selfish, and nature is tugging at every contract to make the terms of it fair.

—Ralph Waldo Emerson

Opportunities in Global Labor Dynamics

The topic of outsourcing is a taboo in some circles and a blessing in others. Outsourcing helps some people and hurts others. Support professionals all around world in the more labor costly nations lost their jobs or job opportunities to other less costly countries. Whereas the workers would migrate to rich nations and meet the demand for lower cost labor in some industries such as agriculture, construction and manufacturing[6] the jobs are now being exported from those rich countries to lower costs workers in other parts of the world with the pursuit of taking advantage of the strengths in the labor pool.[7]

Let's get one thing straight. There is little we can do as support practitioners about the decisions of employers to shift strategies and move the jobs elsewhere. However, we can influence the way our value is perceived, whether you are the one losing the job or the one gaining the job. This is a fact of global economics. The owners of capital and the managers of that capital will do anything possible to get higher returns for their investments. This includes looking for ways to gain higher profits by reducing operational costs, such as the cost of labor.

There are competing labor forces at work in the area of outsourcing, and even insourcing for that matter, with vested interests in their point of view, yet the shift of labor from region to region has proven inevitable and is made easier by the nature of the work. Regardless of which side you are on, such as the displaced supporter or the outsourced supporter, there are bigger economic forces at work which will prevail as time goes on. Outsourcing, insourcing, inshore, offshore, contracting, and any other form of labor supply will eventually have to meet the ultimate goal of the support organization and that is to produce closed issues and satisfied customers at the lowest cost possible. It sounds simple, but it proves very complex given the experience with cost-cutting labor options.

The biggest challenge lies in balancing the need for the right skills and the equilibrium price for the labor at which point the profits from operations are maximized.[8] The dilemma in technical support outsourcing is the cost being in line with the skills. The outsourced workers in areas of labor cost must also meet the demands in skills from both the support organization doing the outsourcing and the customer consuming the support services. Both of these constituents have realized in many cases that lower labor costs have not delivered the skills promised. A lower-waged employee in a different area of the world may possess the technical skills, but not the soft skills to satisfy customers in ways other than the technical. Consequently, the outsourced work force becomes a major management effort if there is no significant presence of management to evolve them into alignment with the technology company's culture and policies. It is a tricky situation for a support manager to deal with people far away and get them to provide the same level of service as someone local. There are many cases where this promise pays off, but many where it fell short of the promised efficiencies.[9]

The other area of concern for outsourcing is performance and productivity. This goes in line with having all the skills necessary to effectively perform technical support, but it also requires the right mentality to produce. Outsourced colleagues sometimes view their foreign employer as an unlimited provider of resources and they buy into the idea of entitlement. When that mental shift happens, the productivity and performance drops and the benefits from the lower labor cost fail to materialize. Yet this problem has a solution, and it's not as drastic as the organized labor in the rich countries claim. They would rather do away with all outsourcing altogether, but that will never happen because the world has effectively become much more intertwined with societies and economies exchanging people, resources, and capital. The real opportunity lies in those who excel at supporting customers with the right skills and support cultures to take leadership roles in the outsourced organizations. It requires that the people who know the work, excel at the work, and advance the profession teach it to those who are still developing it. We must face the perceived problem by picking away at its opportunities and making it a way for us to succeed. This is what the global economy requires and where those visionaries who see the potential in a global field will advance to the next level of their careers.

[6] Roger Daniels, *Coming To America* (New York: HarperCollins, 2002) pp 388–418.
[7] Atul Vashistha and Avinash Vashistha, *The Offshore Nation* (New York: McGraw-Hill, 2006) pp 58–73.
[8] Bruce E Kaufman and Julie L Hotchkiss, *The Economics of Labor Markets* (Florence, KY: Harcourt, 2005) pp 228–229.
[9] Douglas Brown and Scott Wilson, *The Black Book of Outsourcing* (Hoboken, NJ: John Wiley & Sons, 2005) pp 233–237.

The progressive movement of labor across global regions will eventually involve everyone with potential and the skills and resources to take advantage of it. The model of the jobs going to the labor markets with low costs and gobs of employees will not prevail, because the demand for workers eventually fuels competition and the cost efficiencies disappear due to more companies chasing fewer employees. The labor demand results in the next innovation in labor dynamics utilizing not a region or country, but a specific decentralized supply of workers who can provide the labor necessary to support customers, regardless of where they reside. The cause of this shift in labor supply will be the maturing markets and the need for value from employees rather than mere numbers, as has been the case so far.

The future of technical support labor looks bright for the highly skilled supporter who sees the opportunity in the shifts of labor demand. Regardless of where the jobs go, anyone doing the work in the end will need training, expertise, management, consulting, suppliers, consumers, and all types of services that can be best provided by those who already know the work and who are entrepreneurial in spirit and practice. Outsourcing will cause discomforts in the technical support field just as it did in manufacturing, but the displaced workers will have to adapt and find their niche in the global arena as this is the only way to survive and succeed.

All men, if they work not as in the great taskmaster's eye, will work wrong, and work unhappily for themselves and for you.

—Thomas Carlyle

The Need for Uniformity

Support organizations need consistent quality in the people they hire to fill the support positions. Currently, it is somewhat of a gamble as to the quality of support individual you will get by just the interview process and the typical requirements for experience and exposure to the technologies required for the job. Even with people experienced in technical support, the quality of the work varies because of the places they came from. Support organizations vary in everything from policies to structure and culture. All these variables influence the work ethics and productivity levels of the support professional. Individuals' personal differences aside, this is to be expected because there is no clear set of principles to guide the profession.

Technical support needs uniformity and it will eventually get it. There are some standards in different industries which help technical support organizations, but there is not one standard set of knowledge and practices specifically for the support field. All we have to do is look at other similar professions, and we see that there is typically a body of knowledge that any new entrant has to learn and even master before he can enter the field. Doctors have medical school curriculum, lawyers have the codes and bar exams, CPA's have rigorous entry tests that ensure the highest quality of practitioners. Heck, even dishwashers have to pass a health inspector course before they can work in kitchens washing dishes. Technical support has nothing yet, not because we don't need it, but because the field is not yet mature enough to develop it.

The reason we need uniformity in preparation lies in the requirements necessary to do the work effectively. Specifically, the new support person must know about people. He must understand what motivates customers, what moves them, what makes them tick, and how to satisfy their technical needs. The new supporter must also know how to deal with technology in a systematic way; the theories and ideas behind problem solving. The third thing the new person going into support must know is about the technology in general. How systems work, the computing and mechanical theories, and anything else that arises in the area of specialization. All this knowledge would be a great foundation for any person going into the field and would help ensure success on the job, as well as value for the employer.

However, there is something of even more value to the profession, a body of highly trained professionals who could come up with the next breakthroughs for the advancement of the discipline. If you really think about it, this is how all major professions evolve. It's not by laymen who come into the profession with only the most basic education and learn everything on the job, but by learned individuals who think, do, and innovate.

What we really could use in the next few years is for forward-thinking, fully accredited, brick and mortar academic institution to put a bachelor's program together specifically for technical support. They can call it whatever they want to make it sound appealing, but it should be geared toward customer technical interactions and include subjects such as consumer behavior, systems analysis, technical analysis, psychology, and management, plus a wide range of electives from which the student can select specific areas of interest. Such a degree would at least ensure that the demand for labor receives a uniformly educated supply of practitioners ready to go to work and provide value. The professors teaching and counseling the students should have practice in the field and provide the industry with properly prepared individuals who can deliver the value promised.

I realize that there are a few entities that provide certifications, seminars, and trainings geared toward the technical support community of practitioners. However, what makes me a bit apprehensive about certifications is that they are not mandatory, may vary widely in the content, and do not do much for developing the intellect of the individuals. There is nothing wrong with certifications, but they have a very distinct place in a discipline, especially a new one. For instance, CPA's are certified, but they must also first possess formal education and a degree to go with it. In most states and countries, lawyers and doctors are also required to complete an academic degree. While I am not implying that our field is at that level yet, we have to start somewhere and a certification is not the place to start.

The benefit to the student who wishes to enter the support workforce is that he will have the fundamentals of the profession and he only has to acquire the practice. While that is easier said than done, it is not impossible and may soon be a necessity to ensure the best quality and development of the future support organization. Additionally, the degreed supporter will have the theoretical knowledge to go into any other role within the support organization, such as management, planning, organizer, training, sales, and all the way up the executive level. This is what preparation can do for the individual.

I realize that this is a radical approach to what we are accustomed to and most people don't think of going to a university and getting a degree in technical support, yet most of the people in technical support have college degrees. In fact, I have even had colleagues who came from being a college professor to technical support and a few others with master's degrees and even doctorates. So why devote years of school to go into a profession in which most of what you learned will not help you? I find myself in the same situation. Little of what I went to school for actually is of any use in my support career. I would have loved to have a degree that actually covered the work I do now, even if it was from a theoretical perspective.

The market for technical support is growing and with the advent of technologies at a rate which we simply have yet to see, the need for support people will only increase. Regardless of where the supporters live and work, they should have a common academic foundation that helps them be more productive to their support organizations and add value to the discipline. The only way we will accomplish such feat is with a Bachelor of Science in Customer Technical Interactions or any other name schools choose to give it with Master and Doctorate degrees to come later.

The first condition of education is being able to put someone to wholesome and meaningful work.

—John Ruskin

Going Customerless

Throughout the short history of our profession, the support models evolved and delivered more efficiencies with each phase. It started out as a strict call center where customer called in for answers. Now modern support organizations still handle customer calls, but also introduce the self-service model via the remote control tool, the wiki, forum, and chat plus a bunch more variances and combinations of each. As you read these pages, there is someone out there, perhaps you, with the next big idea to bring added value to the customer via your innovation. Naturally, the work of the supporter changes slightly with each innovation, but we have yet to experience a revolution, something so dramatic that it will change the work itself. We have experienced many advancements in process and technologies that have made our work more innovative, but our work has not changed dramatically—it has merely adopted the new innovations.

One possibility that could revolutionize the work the way it is currently done is the removal of the actual troubleshooting interaction with the customer. I know it sounds odd, but hear me out. In the whole support process, who do you think is the biggest provider of information as well as obstacles to getting an issue solved? Typically, it is the customer. We usually get issues from the customer, we ask him questions, have him try solutions, or ask him for permission to try it ourselves. He also tells us when the problem is resolved and when we can close the issue. Yet the customer interaction is usually what takes the most time, not in action but in the lack thereof. Let me explain: Usually the troubleshooting of the issue may take up to a few hours depending on the complexity and the knowledge and experience we have. Of course, most troubleshooting can be done within a few minutes. However, the bulk of the time the issue is open is because the customer does not get back to us or because he is not available to work on the technical case. The ideal situation would be for us to have the freedom to do the work without needing to deal with the customer. Still sounds odd, doesn't it? I know it works, because I have tried it with great success. Maybe after reading my example, it will make more sense.

A few years ago, I used to support an intrusion detection software application which had many complexities and the troubleshooting was typically very time-consuming. It wrote data to a MS SQL server and used other components for reporting. The core application had all kinds of features and policies. In any case, there were specific customers with whom I worked so much that I knew their systems better than them. I used remote control tools to connect and guide them through the resolution. However, it got to the point where I would ask them for the access and I would simply do the fixing on my own in a fraction of the time it took me to walk them through it. After the first few times, they realized how much more convenient it was to step out of the way and simply allow me to do the support without having them involved in the troubleshooting process. There were a few customers who simply sent me an email and asked me to connect at a specific time. I did work in less than ten or fifteen minutes that would have taken me at minimum thirty or so by involving them. With these customers I never even had to speak with them on the phone unless I wanted to explain specifically what I did or if they wanted to know what originally went wrong. The beauty of such a practice is that it accentuates customer service without having to involve the customer. In other words, the value the customers got out of it was much greater than anything I could have provided by walking them through the troubleshooting or support process.

I am quite certain there are many technical services and technology vendors doing this type of service currently and that have done so for years. However, those that do, act in more of a maintenance mode, such as hosted service providers or application service providers, and even some outsourced data centers. I have also seen it in hardware vendors and high-end manufacturing devices, such as robots and precision equipment where the support person can do everything remotely and without the aid of a customer serving as his eyes and hands. Yet this way of operation in support could benefit so many customers and support people that it could revolutionize our work and increase customer satisfaction. The perfect situation would be for the support offerings to be designed with this model from the beginning rather than have the supporter develop it individually as I did.

In order for support work to go into a customerless troubleshooting interaction, we would need for the technology and the product to facilitate such a support model. We would need the ability to remotely control the machine, software application, or system from our desks without any or minimal interaction from the customer. The product supported also must be designed in a way that such control can take place. The majority of software applications and computer and networking equipment are friendly to such control from afar, but other technologies such as non-computer devices and production system would have to include such capabilities. The next thing we would need is a way to undo changes with ease in case we get into a customer's system and screw it up with no way to revert back to original state. We also need support policies, contracts, and disclaimers between the customer and the support organization to allow this type of interaction.

The business of supporting our products must improve and continue to change, but we need a major innovation in the way we do the work. The most obvious is to cut out the middleman, the customer, from the troubleshooting process. If you stop and think, if we were left alone with the product and the problem we could resolve it much more quickly than if we had to explain or direct the customer to do everything the way most of us do it now. There are a few support organizations doing some of this now, but only time will tell if this way of doing support is adopted by the greater support and customer community.

If you work just for money, you'll never make it, but if you love what you're doing and you always put the customer first, success will be yours.

—Ray Kroc

The Extra Mile

While doing a small support project I looked into several support organizations to see what type of support they provided. Based on the published information and a few conversations into their support departments, mostly in the enterprise management software, security and mainframe field, I found that the typical support organization only does technical support and nothing else; pretty obvious if you think about it. In thinking about the role of the technical supporter, I asked myself why we would want to do anything other than just technical support. The more I pondered the question, I realized that we are the one that manages the relationship with the end user by way of supporting them with their support issues while they use our products. For most users and technology administrators, the bulk of their communication with us, the vendor, is by speaking with support. Simply stated, we have their attention and they listen to us. The typical support organization has yet to put this power to its maximum use. We have a captive audience with the customer more so than salespeople, account reps, and even product evangelists. Such a privilege, if understood properly, would be the envy of all these other players from the technology vendor's side. But where could support people provide value in addition to just the technical support? The answer is quite simple: anywhere where we need to interact and communicate with a customer. The following are some examples of where support people could provide value:

- *Sales leads*: Because we speak with customers all the time, we form relationships and mutual respect. Customers trust us to make the right decisions on their problems but also to provide advice on where they are deficient regarding their technical needs. The normal support interaction does not have any repercussion outside of the immediate problem, and sometimes huge opportunities are lost because all we do is support. Imagine if we could recommend, as a normal part of our job, additional technologies, services, or expansions to the technology and help generate more revenue to our companies. Many of us do that already and some support organizations have some lead generation already, but it is usually quite minimal. We could provide sales leads on training, documentation, product, and services. Chances are our companies are already doing lead generation through other means. Why not just try to expand the business we already do with the existing customer base through the support interaction, instead of depending on the sales department to be the only ones that do that? We could help and we could provide a lot of value in this area if we were just formally allowed to.

- *Contract renewal and maintenance*: How many times do we come across customers who just want to renew something—a license, a contract, or maintenance? Support usually has to refer them to some other department, especially in the commercial and enterprise markets. Consumer products are much better at this and the technical support departments can typically handle situations like this. The non-consumer support organizations could very well do a lot of the order taking by learning from the consumer support colleagues. You probably have come across customers who ask you flat out if they can just give you their credit card number so you can renew their contract or sell them an additional number of licenses or products. I know I have and it is disillusioning when we have to turn them over to some other department. Everyone has their job to do, but in the process of specializing everything, we forget that there are possibilities to provide customer service consequently additional value over just technical support.

- *Product demos*: If you work for a multiproduct company and support any number of them, chances are you are at least familiar with the functionality of those products that you don't support but are offered by your company. It would be great if during the course of a support call you realize that the customer could benefit from another one of your products and provide them either a small demonstration or trial. This idea may serve some technologies better than others, such as software and service rather than systems, devices and appliances. You can always let the customer know of the possibilities they have with another one of your products and how those additional technologies could help them solve a business problem or fulfill a current deficiency. I don't mean necessarily close the sale, but make it easy so that your sales department makes the same or perhaps just have someone else just take the order. Although if you think about it, there is no reason why you couldn't also take a customer's order, but that may be going too far for some support departments. I am amazed at how some support departments can do so much while others are just doing support. We've all called some support department and been amazed at all the things they can do such as process payments, handle returns, and even extend, cancel contracts, or renew them. Those support organizations realize that having the customer's attention in a support interaction makes it easier to do many other customer-oriented tasks by the same support person.

- *Provide extra services*: Have you ever come across situations where the customer needed some other service that you couldn't provide? Not because you didn't know how but because it's outside the scope of your duties? In every support organization, there are always situations in which the customer required more than they are entitled to. As much as we want to provide the extra help, it would simply take us into territory that would put us, as employees, at risk. Examples of such services are consulting, deployments, modifications, customizations, and even just plain expert advice. I had many such interactions, but one in particular where the customer wanted me to fly over to his office in New York and provide some additional service on the weekend. He offered to pay me, pay for all the expenses, and do whatever necessary to make it happen. He was asking for network design services which my support organization did not offer, but being an expert in the subject, it would have been quite easy for me to do. Of course, I did not take his offer. Not because I couldn't do it from a technical perspective, but because it did not feel ethical and I couldn't, in good conscience, moonlight outside of my job, especially with an existing customer. My job and loyalty to my company were more important than anything I could make on the side. I opted for giving him some general advice, but nothing more. However, these opportunities abound and we could be generating revenue for our departments, if we only could put our expertise to use whenever the need presents itself.

Technical support people know a lot and do a lot already. We could be doing more to help the bottom line, improve the support organization, and our technology companies overall by going the extra mile. The above examples are but a few as there are many opportunities where we could make a huge difference to provide more value to the customer and ourselves.

You can start right where you stand and apply the habit of going the extra mile by rendering more service and better service than you are now being paid for.

—Napoleon Hill

Where to Now?

If you read this book from start to finish, I salute you. If you just skipped to the end, I salute you as well, for I am about to tell you the reason I gladly took on this writing challenge and built up the courage throughout all the previous pages to tell you at the end. After you close this book for the last time, I want you to think of a way to go out and make a change to improve our profession. You see, the main reason I wrote all the previous pages is because this work we call technical support has given so much to me and I so little in return. I started out as a young man and now that I am much older, I look back at all that's happened throughout my adult life, the good and the bad, the sweet and the sour, and the only thing that's remained constant is my dear work. I got married, had kids, multiple degrees, medical maladies, job changes, successes and failures, but the work truly never changed.

I wanted to give something back and to share with you my ideas about as many aspects of support as possible. All the topics, concepts, thoughts, wishes, and frustrations you have read in these twelve chapters each came out of a support call. This was not an academic endeavor, a grandiose project, or something I was directed or told to go out and do. This was just a desire to spare the next generation of supporters all the problems I and many of you had to go through. I also wanted to share with you the sense that this is more than just a stepping stone job and that you can make, as I have, a nice career and have a decent life via the opportunities that a technical support job provides.

It is now your turn. I did my part and will continue to do what I can. But you have to do yours as well. There are many opportunities if you only keep an open mind. You can be the inventor of a new process, theory, or philosophy dealing with supporting technology customers. You may even come up with a variation of the profession and invent technology that fixes itself. Who knows, maybe you will be the next genius who gives us a new way to look at technology, work with it, and fix it. If you would rather keep it a bit simpler, you can start by coming up with an efficient practice in your own support group. If it is successful enough, you could publish it and share it with others. You could teach at your local college or through your company's education department. The opportunities abound, if you just look for them.

It's uncertain where the work will take us but one thing is certain, the future will be made by forward-looking individuals like you and others who you will inspire. We worked too hard and invested too much into the technical support field to just go sideways. Every issue you close, every person you teach, and every customer you satisfy brings us closer to that future where technical support will become a very formalized field with its own body of general knowledge, literature, and academic departments.

The horizon looks bright and the field wide open for anyone to make his mark. Men and women with the talent and the right ideas will find new and better ways to provide technology users with the answers they need. The test will come in the years ahead and in the challenges that come from outside of the field. The first economic downturn of the new millennium didn't faze us, and we kept going strong while other professions, unfortunately, suffered and even disappeared. We must remember that as long as there is technology, there will be questions on its use and problems arising from its misuse. This is our chance to change the world one technical issue at a time. Take the narrow path and do the unique, the special, and the innovative. It is quite lonely, but extremely gratifying. The support group and the technology organization are not going anywhere without individuals who can think and produce the next round of innovations.

As you read these last few lines, think of how you will be writing the last few lines in the future. You see, I am not different than you. I have been a newbie supporter, learned new technologies and products, with and without training if I may add, made thousands of customers happy and upset a few others as well. If I can do it, so can you. It is not a matter of having time, a high level of intelligence or prodigious inspiration; if you do support work, you have what it takes.

I feel like a voyager with teary eyes who is saying the last goodbyes from aboard a vessel that's moving away from the pier. I want you to know that I gave it my best effort all with the desire to inspire you to do the same. Only through individuals who take this sort of initiative can our beloved field flourish and mature as one of the most respected and admired professions.

I want you to know that I have the greatest admiration and respect for everyone who does technical support. All of you are the greatest and most hardworking people anyone will ever know. And to all of you, I say thank you and God bless.

When you do nothing, you feel overwhelmed and powerless. But when you get involved, you feel the sense of hope and accomplishment that comes from knowing you are working to make things better.

—Pauline R. Kezer

Index

■A

ABC theory, 215
absenteeism, incivility and, 84
accents
    beliefs and, 205, 214
    communication and, 226, 230
Access (Microsoft), 47
acquisition stage, of the technical support group
    development cycle, 87
acquisitions/mergers
    comforting a colleague and, 107
    self-sustaining groups and, 113
    support during, 74
    support group development cycle and, 87
action
    initiative and, 20
    leadership and, 119, 120, 133
    peer leadership and, 126
    pragmatic leaders and, 125
adaptability, 4
adding value, 255
    to the company, 6, 38, 59, 169
    even as you say 'no', 239
    through extra services provided, 256
    with every call, 16
    keeping an open mind and, 211–213
    to products, 39
    to technology usability, 39
adherence, relationship to manager and, 144
allocation of work, balancing the work load and,
    152
altruism, 98
analytic reasoning, troubleshooting skills and, 14
apathy, inventory for group analysis and, 90
assertiveness, leadership and, 122
assistance process, 156
automating repetitive tasks, 46
Avit, Steve, 32

■B

balancing work loads, 152
behavior
    of colleague, understanding, 108
    customer support and, 208
    high performance/high productivity and, 111–
      113
    identifying/managing, 151
    leadership and, 122
    organizational, 67, 71
behavioral research, 108
beliefs, customer reality and, 205
benefits
    using to your advantage, 169
    of belonging to a group, 73–75
business
    as a common language, 229
    its wider role in the future, 244
buyer's remorse, 203
"buying time," 221

■C

call monitoring, balancing the work load and, 152
capacity, to do the job, 7
career
    changing, value of technical support skills for,
      4
    flat support structure and, 179
    lifelong, technical support as, 5, 25
    making meaningful, 169
    moving around in dynamically, 5
    specializing and, 20
cases, 37
Center of Excellence (Texas Instruments), 189
certification, 253

challenges
    leadership style and, 132
    steps to resolving, 52
character replacement technique, 215
chat, 234, 235
    as alternative to spoken communication, 231
    as form of quick communication, 232
civility crises, 84
clarity, 219
cognitive character replacement technique, 215
cognitive therapies, 214
cohesiveness, inventory for group analysis and, 89
collaboration, 3, 35, 36, 84–86
    approachable experts and, 62
    inventory for group analysis and, 89
    vs. solo problem solving, 28
    technical support professionals and, 67–92
colleagues, 95–116
    behavior of, understanding, 108
    collaborating with, 3
    comforting, 106–108
    communicating with, 228–230
    dealing with when one becomes impossible,
        115–116
    electronic documentation and, 44
    high performance/high productivity and, 111–
        113
    as internal customers, 63, 110
    less-experienced, remaining approachable to
        as an expert, 62
    meetings and, 236
    peer leadership and, 126
    personal conflict and, 103–105
    self-sustaining, 113
    "untouchables" and, 110
comforting a colleague, 106–108
command groups, 68, 73
commitment, 9
    to customers, 3
    success and, 17
"communal group" value, inventory for group
    analysis and, 91, 152, 163
communication, 35, 225–240
    advantages of phone support and, 236
    chat/email as alternatives to speaking, 231
    with colleagues, 228–230
    with customers, 233
    forms of used in technical support, 234, 236
    getting to the point, 232–234
    group collaboration and, 77–79
    situational, 226, 234–236
    three models of, 77
    transactional, 226
    types of within the support organization, 226

company
    adding value to, 6, 38, 59, 169
    belief in, 3
    excess value provided to, 141
    helping achieve its priorities, 10
    policy changes and, 186
    resources within/outside of, 48
    support contracting and, 250
competence stage, of the technical support group
    development cycle, 88
competition, 202
competitiveness, groups and, 71
compliance with directives, relationship to
    manager and, 144
conference calls, 233
confidence
    leaders and, 128
    troubleshooting skills and, 14
conflict, 83
    colleagues and, 103–105
    personal/professional, 103
conjecture, 50–52
consideration, inventory for group analysis and,
    90
constructive criticism, 105
constructive input, 84–86
contacts (cases), 37
context, working as part of a group and, 73
Contingency Design Theory, 155
contingency structure model, 163
contract renewals, adding value and, 256
contracting, 249
contributor role, 143
controlling execution, as managerial function, 149
controlling expenses, through efficiencies, 11
Cooperative Supportive Analysis, 82
coping strategies, 213–216
cordiality, 220
cost controls, 11
coworkers. See colleagues
creativity
    meeting formats/communication and, 238
    solo problem solving and, 29
    troubleshooting skills and, 14
credibility, 12, 127
crises, 83
criticism, colleagues and, 105–106
cross-functional teams, 68
customer reality, 204–206
customer satisfaction
    adding value to, 39, 211–213
    outsourced support and, 236
    processes and, 195

customer service, 201–222
    achieving excellence for, 167
    colleagues and, 110
    components of, 216
    customer expectations and, 177
    future perspectives in, 245
    hierarchical approach to in six steps, 216–219
    keeping an open mind and, 211–213
    passion for, 32
    people business aspect of, 219
    psychoanalysis applied to, 206
    reshaping unrealistic demands for, 218
    Savvy Support model and, 162, 178
    service-oriented support structures and, 167,
        178
customers
    characteristics of supporters when dealing
        with, 219
    communicating with, 233
    customer reality and, 204–206
    customerless support and, 254
    emotional, 15
    preventive support and, 247
    problematic interactions and, 213–216
    saying 'no' while adding value, 238
    support contracting and, 250
    treating colleagues as, 63, 110
    using psychology with, 214
    value of technical support for, 4

D

the Davila Cycle, 152
Davila, Jose, 152
decision-making
    discretionary process principle and, 185
    leadership and, 133
    by managers, 157
    processes and, 58
decisional role, of support managers, 145
declines in quality, solidarity and, 100
dedication, 9
delegation, leadership and, 134
details, communication and, 227
determination, 32
development, 28
development cycle, of technical support groups,
    86–88
development engineering directors, 59, 60
diction, communication and, 227
disagreement, 85, 103–105
discipline, initiative and, 20
discretionary process principle, 183

Divide and Channel approach, 179
documenting what you learn, 44
"dysfunctional group" value, inventory for group
    analysis and, 91

E

economies of scale, 71
education, 158, 253. See also learning; training
efficiency, 46
    excellence and, 49
    practices and, 187
    processes and, 195
    upper-tier support colleagues and, 111
electronic files, 44
Ellis, Albert, 215
email, 234, 235
    as alternative to spoken communication,
        231
    getting to the point and, 232
emotions
    customers and, 15
    problematic interactions and, 213–216
empathy, 3, 90
employer. See company
end of life stage, of the technical support group
    development cycle, 88
entrepreneurial stage, of the technical support
    group development cycle, 87
environment, customer support and, 208
esprit de corps, 78, 187
esteem, need for fulfilled through work, 9
ethics, 12, 85
Event Driven Model, 78
excellence, striving for, 49, 53
excess value, 141
expansion stage, of the technical support group
    development cycle, 87
expectations
    communication challenges and, 231
    customer reality and, 205
    of customers, 177
    performance-driven support structure and,
        173
experience
    how inexperience contributes to wasting time,
        221
    of managers, 158
    shared during meetings, 236
    troubleshooting skills and, 14
experiences (past/previous), customer reality and,
    205

expert status, 5, 38
   "experts" and, 22
   remaining approachable and, 62
   respect and, 98
   responsibilities and, 28, 59
   sharing knowledge and, 102
   specializing and, 21
   "untouchables" and, 110
expertise, support structures and, 177
Experts-Exchange.com, 48

F

failure, colleagues and, 95
faxes, 234
field experience, 246
financial requirements, 80
financial security, fulfilled through work, 9
flat support structure, 176, 179
flexibility, 4, 131
formal groups, 70
forums, 234, 235
Freud, Sigmund, 206
friendships, 70
frontline managers, 156
future perspectives, 243–258
   field experience and, 246
   wider role of business and, 244

G

Gallagher, Richard S., 206
geographical flexibility, 4, 27
global labor, 251
goals
   behavior and, 109
   leadership and, 120
   vs. vision, 76
group dynamics. *See* collaboration
group process evolution, 188
groups, 67–92
   benefits of, 71–73
   crises and, 83
   group process evolution and, 188
   inventory for analyzing, 88–92
   maturity and, 132, 191
   preventive support and, 247
   relating to processes and, 195
   self-sustaining, 113
   success and, 95
   support contracting and, 250
   vs. teams, 68
   types of, 68

H

HDI (Helpdesk Institute), 26
"healthy group" value, inventory for group analysis and, 91
Helpdesk Institute (HDI), 26
Hierarchical Cross-Differential Openness, 82
honesty, leadership and, 128
hope, allowing for, 240
human needs, 9
hypotheses, 50

I

"idiosyncratic group" value, inventory for group analysis and, 91
impartiality of managers, 157
incivility, 84
incompetence, 192–194
independence, leadership and, 122
inference, 50–52
informal groups, 68, 69
information
   group communication and, 77–79
   improving use of, 55, 56
   sharing, 96, 101–102. *See also* teaching
   working as part of a group and, 74, 81
informational role, of support managers, 146
initiative, 19, 169
   groups and, 71
   leadership and, 126, 129
inspiration, leadership and, 120
instant messaging, 232, 234
integrity, leadership and, 128
interest, in the job, 7
interests, 70
internal customers, treating colleagues as, 63, 110
interpersonal role, of support managers, 146
intuition, 50–52
inventory, for group analysis, 88–92
involvement, groups and, 79–81
issues
   balancing the work load and, 152
   delivering value every time, 16
   high productivity and, 112
   tough issues and, 52
   tracking, 37

J

job description, excellence and, 49
job security, specializing and, 21

job titles
> evolving as the profession advances, 192
> tiers and, 170

■K

keeping an open mind, 211–213
keeping your job, 7–8
knowledge. *See* technical knowledge

■L

language, vs. other forms of communication, 234
lateral career moves, 6
leaders, vs. managers, 119, 120, 128
leadership, 119–136
> developing in others, 135–136
> followers and, 125, 133–135
> group/product maturity and, 132
> groups and, 73
> leader characteristics and, 128
> vs. leading, as managerial function, 148
> models of, 123–126, 131
> peer inspiration/initiative and, 126
> recognizing leaders and, 120
> skills for, developing, 129–131
leading, as managerial function, 148
learning. *See also* training
> constant learning and, 55
> documenting what you learn, 44
leaving work at the office, 15
legal requirements, 80
Level 2 support, 27
Level 3 support, 63
Linda Effect, 126
live chat, 177
lowering your guard, trust and, 96

■M

managers
> fallibility and, 157
> vs. leaders, 119, 120, 128
> role of, 145
> what makes a good one, 157
managing
> alleviating the need for supporters to resort to "buying time," 222
> contributor role of reports and, 143
> nature/four functions of, 147–149

support managers and, 145
support structure and, 155
technical support management job and, 6, 27
matrix organizations, 152
mechanical style of technical support, 30, 51
meetings
> reasons for, 236
> virtual meetings and, 233
mergers. *See* acquisitions/mergers
Microsoft
> Access, 47
> Outlook, 47, 58
mid-level managers, 156
mindful agreement technique, 216
Mooney, James, 164
motivation
> behavior and, 109
> groups and, 71, 72
> initiative and, 20
> recognition and, 153
> rewards and, 154
muscle relaxation, 215

■N

needs, groups and, 72

■O

objectivity, of managers, 157
the obvious, looking beyond, 53
online chat. *See* chat
online forums. *See* forums
onsite services, 6
open mind, keeping one, 211–213
openness, 81–83
opportunities, recognizing, 60
organizational behavior, 67, 71
organizational communication, 226
organizational culture, 101, 151
organizational structure, 67, 68
> multiple tiers and, 110
> vs. support structure, 155
organizing, as managerial function, 147
Outlook (Microsoft)
> calendar tool of, 58
> Contacts feature of, 47
outsourcing, 251

▓P

Parallel Communication Model/Non-Parallel
  Communication Model, 78
participative openness, 81
patents, 60
perception, customer reality and, 204
perfect competition, 202
performance, 111–113
    excess value and, 142
    focus on by managers, 157
    improving, 152
    outsourcing and, 252
    performance-driven support structure and,
      172, 179
    performing above average and, 45–47, 49
    rewards and, 154
    systems theory and, 149
personal communication, within the support
  organization, 226
personal conflict, colleagues and, 103–105
personal similarities, 70
perspective, 86
Peter Principle, 193
phone support, 236
physiological needs, fulfilled through work, 9
planning, as managerial function, 147
policies, customer service and, 210
political crises, 83
practices, 181, 187
    avoiding incompetence and, 192–194
    how to go about developing, 188
    vs. processes, 181, 187
pragmatic leaders, 125, 131
prepackaged solutions, 46
preventive support, 247
Principal-Agent relationship, 80
principles, 3
proactive support
    preventive support and, 247
    reactive/proactive tiered approach and, 170,
      179
    six-step hierarchical approach to customer
      service and, 216–219
problem-solving, 3
    sincerity and, 17
    solo-solving and, 28
    success and, 17
    tough issues, steps to resolving, 52
problem-solving teams, 68
process map, 195
process theory, 184

processes, 162–164, 181–198
    characteristics of, 182
    customer service and, 210
    eliminating waste and, 189
    formal/informal, 58
    group maturity level and, 191
    groups contributing to, 188
    improvement methodologies and, 190
    vs. practices, 181, 187
    process map for, 195
    productivity and, 49, 50
    reasons behind, 79
    reengineering, 57
    self-sustaining groups and, 114
    when inefficiencies in cause wasteful repetition,
      222
    when they're bad, 197
    why they change, 185
product demos, adding value and, 256
productivity, 8, 111–113
    group process evolution and, 190
    incivility and, 84
    outsourcing and, 252
    performance-driven support structure and,
      172
    relationship to manager and, 144
    working smarter and, 49
products
    adding value to, 39
    knowledge specialization and, 21
    lateral career move and, 6
    preventive support and, 247
    recommending, 11
profession, technical support as, 25–42
    contributing to, 59
    current status of, 26–27
    future prospects for, 27
    as multidisciplinary field, 35–37
professionalism, respect and, 97
psychology
    psychoanalysis, customer service and, 206
    using to deal with problematic customers, 214
publications, 37

▓Q

QA (Quality Assurance), 4, 27
quality of work, uniformity and, 252
Quality Assurance (QA) , 4, 27
quality declines, solidarity and, 100
Quality of Work Life philosophy, 168
queries, 37
queues, balancing the work load and, 152

■R

rational-emotive therapy, 215
reactive/proactive tiered approach, 170, 179
recognition, 153
reengineering processes, 57
reflective openness, 81
relationships
    cohesiveness and, 89
    group communication and, 78
remote control tools, 177
remote support, 247, 254
renaissance professionals, 245
repetition of problems by customers, avoiding, 221
repetitive tasks
    automating, 46
    eliminating, 47
reporting requirements, 79
reports, contributor role of, 143
'reproducible' processes, 182
resolutions, 33
resources, 14, 47–48
resources for further reading
    excellence, 49
    technical support, 13
respect
    colleagues and, 97–99
    for customers, 220
    need for fulfilled through work, 9
    recognition and, 154
revenue, how technical support helps generate, 10
rewards, 154, 210
Ritual Communication Model, 78
roles, 141–150, 193
    of reports, 143
    of support managers, 145
rudeness, 84

■S

safety (financial security) needs, fulfilled through work, 9
sales, 28
    leads for, 255
    pre- /post-sales support and, 4
    revenue generation by technical support, 10
satisfaction, rewards and, 154
Savvy Support model, 162, 167, 178
Scalar Principle, 164

scientific discipline, technical support as, 26, 40
scientific method, 41
scripts, scripting client actions and, 46
security, working as part of a group and, 74
self-actualization, 9
self-belief, leadership and, 122
self-directed teams, 69
servant leaders, 123, 125, 131
Service and Support Professional Association (SSPA), 26, 48
service. *See* customer service
service-oriented support structures, 167, 178
services, providing extra as added value, 256
servitude, leadership and, 122
sharing, peer leadership and, 127
sincerity, 12
    small talk and, 229
    success and, 17
situational communication, 226, 234–236
situational leaders, 131
skills, 4
    acquiring new, as dynamic career move, 6
    capacity to do the job and, 7
    developing, 55
    group process evolution and, 189
    leadership and, 129–131
    non-technical, 55
    organizing support structures by, vs. by technology, 165, 178
    outsourcing and, 251
small talk, being sincere about, 229
Smith, Adam,
    "invisible hand theory" and, 142
    pin assembly and, 162
social similarities, 70
socializing needs, fulfilled through work, 9
solidarity, colleagues and, 99–101
solutions, prepackaged, 46
specializing, 20
speculation, 50–52
SSPA (Service and Support Professional Association), 26, 48
stability stage, of the technical support group development cycle, 87
standardization, 80
standards, 252
strategies, for coping with customers, 213–216
stress, 15
structures, organizing by skill vs. by technology, 166
"struggling group" value, inventory for group analysis and, 91

success, 17–19
    characteristics that lead to, 219
    colleagues and, 95
    inventory for group analysis and, 88–92
    respect and, 99
    solidarity and, 100
suggestions, from customers, 218
support contingency support structure model, 163
support contracting, 249
support demand function, 33
support groups. *See* groups
support managers. *See* managers; managing
support roles, 141–150
support structures, 161–180
    adding meaning to the job and, 168, 178
    customer service and, 209
    flat structure and, 176, 179
    a hybrid structure and, 177
    organizing by product vs. by function, 165
    performance-driven, 172, 179
    processes and, 182
    reactive/proactive tiered approach and, 170, 179
    service-oriented structures and, 167, 178
    tiered structures and, 163
support systems, groups as, 72
supporters. *See* technical support professionals
the supporting manager culture, 156
sympathy, inventory for group analysis and, 90
synergy, 71
systematic desensitization therapy, 215
systems analysis, 35, 36
systems theory, 149

T

task groups, 68
task management, 4
tasks. *See* processes
teaching
    colleagues, 55, 101–102
    customers, 6, 36
    as part of multidisciplinary field, 35
    respect and, 99
team player attitude, 8
team support, 14, 95
teams, 68. *See also* groups
technical knowledge, 4
    peer leadership and, 127
    renewing/enhancing, 55
    sharing, 101–102
    "untouchables" and, 110
technical services, 4

technical style of technical support, 30, 51
technical support
    communication and, 225–240
    communication technologies for, 177
    companies specializing in, 39
    as emerging scientific discipline, 26, 40
    as an evolving profession, 168
technical support (*cont.*)
    future perspectives in, 243–258
    how the profession evolved, 244
    improving the profession, 149, 188, 257
    at intersection of technology and people, 5, 16, 27
    as liaison between customer and company, 4
    as link between development and marketing, 39
    making it more than just a job, 8–10, 168, 178
    as a people business, 219
    preventive support and, 247
    as profession, intricacies of, 25–42
    specializing and, 20
    success and, 17–19
    support demand function and, 33
    support structure and, 155
    support styles and, 30
    uniformity and, 252
    the value of it, 4
technical support professionals (supporters)
    achieving excellence as, 167
    characteristics of when dealing with customers, 219
    contracting and, 249
    coping strategies for, 213–216
    excess value provided to the company, 141
    field experience and, 246
    ideal, characteristics of, 3
    identifying/managing behaviors and, 151
    individual benefits and, 73–75
    leadership and. *See* leadership
    as part of a group, 67–92
    performing above average and, 45–47
    skills and. *See* skills
    strengths of, 25
    support group development cycle and, 86–88
    technical support group vs. technical support team and, 68
    when the helpers need help, 155
technical writing, 6
TechnicalSupportForum.com, 48
technology
    advancing/contributing to, 59
    organizing support structures by, vs. by skill, 165, 178